FABULOUS ORIENTS

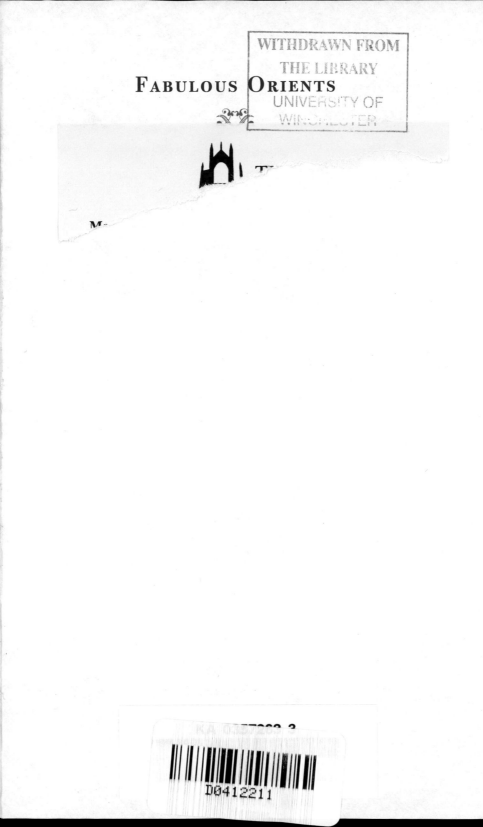

FABULOUS ORIENTS

Fictions of the East in England
1662–1785

Ros Ballaster

OXFORD
UNIVERSITY PRESS

OXFORD

UNIVERSITY PRESS

Great Clarendon Street, Oxford OX2 6DP

Oxford University Press is a department of the University of Oxford.
It furthers the University's objective of excellence in research, scholarship,
and education by publishing worldwide in

Oxford New York

Auckland Cape Town Dar es Salaam Hong Kong Karachi
Kuala Lumpur Madrid Melbourne Mexico City Nairobi
New Delhi Shanghai Taipei Toronto

With offices in

Argentina Austria Brazil Chile Czech Republic France Greece
Guatemala Hungary Italy Japan Poland Portugal Singapore
South Korea Switzerland Thailand Turkey Ukraine Vietnam

Oxford is a registered trade mark of Oxford University Press
in the UK and in certain other countries

Published in the United States
by Oxford University Press Inc., New York

© Ros Ballaster 2005

British Library Cataloguing in Publication Data

Data available

Library of Congress Cataloging in Publication Data

Ballaster, Rosalind.
Fabulous orients : fictions of the East in England, 1662–1785 / Ros Ballaster.
p. cm.
Includes bibliographical references (p.   ) and index.
ISBN 0-19-926733-2 (acid-free paper)
1. English literature—Asian influences. 2. English literature—18th century—
History and criticism. 3. English literature—Early modern, 1500-1700—History and criticism.
4. Middle East—In literature. 5. Orientalism in literature. 6. Exoticism in literature.
7. Orient—In literature. 8. Asia—In literature. I. Title.
PR129.A78B35 2005
820.9'3256—dc22

2005019964

Typeset by Newgen Imaging Systems (P) Ltd., Chennai, India
Printed in Great Britain
on acid-free paper by
Ashford Colour Press Ltd., Gosport, Hampshire

ISBN 978-0-19-926733-0 (Hbk.)   978-0-19-923429-5 (Pbk.)

1 3 5 7 9 10 8 6 4 2

'Sir, answered Scheherazade, I have a sister, who loves me tenderly, as I do her, and I could wish that she might be allowed to be all night in this chamber, that I might see her, and bid her adieu: Will you be pleased to allow me the comfort of giving her this last testimony of my friendship?'

For Cathy

Sister and fellow traveller

ACKNOWLEDGEMENTS

I could never have completed the research and writing for this book without the assistance of a Major Research Fellowship from the Leverhulme Trust from October 2000 to October 2003. Special thanks go to Sarah Wood, Lucinda Rumsey, and Paddy Bullard who replaced my teaching and administration with such impressive aplomb that I only feared I would disappoint on my return to these roles. The academic community at Mansfield College has proved a lifeline while I have been engaged in my solitary research pursuits, especially Michael Freeden and Michael Freeman. Undergraduates at Mansfield and graduate students at Oxford University both before and during the research project proved a constant stimulus and delight.

Many individual scholars and research institutions have been enormously generous and patient in response to queries. The staff in the Duke Humphreys Library at the Bodleian in Oxford (William Hodges, Russell Edwards, Jean-Pierre Mialan, and Alan Carter) were a source of humour and wisdom throughout. I found equally dogged determination to hunt down materials at the Indian Institute Library, Oriental Studies Library, and Chinese Studies Library at Oxford University.

Thanks to Alex Drace-Francis of the School of Slavonic and East European Studies, University College London and Paul Shore of Saint Louis University for references about Titus the Moldavian. And to John Gurney at the Oriental Institute, Oxford University, for locating a Persian source for me. Ron Nettler at the Oriental Institute Oxford for support throughout and careful reading of draft material. Sheffield archives and Isobel Grundy of the University of Alberta, Edmonton, on Lady Mary Wortley Montagu's reading. Monika Fludernik for discussions of representations of suttee. My dear friend, Lorna Hutson, invited me to speak early in the project at Berkeley

Acknowledgements

College, San Francisco. Linda Colley and Catherine Hall gave me an amicable grilling on my work on China at a London University graduate seminar on the global eighteenth century.

Many other forms of intellectual and personal support made this book possible. Janet Todd and Marilyn Butler have expressed their confidence in my research on too many funding applications to mention. Lucinda Rumsey and Lucy Newlyn read drafts and boosted confidence at vital moments. Jon Mee, Luisa Cale, Rajeswari Sunder Rajan, and Celia Kerslake all provided helpful references for and responses to my work. Rebecca Rees willingly shared animated conversations about the Turkish spy. Thanks to Laurence Williams for excellent graduate research assistance in preparing the paperback edition.

My debt to other scholars, who share research interests and have been unfailingly confident in this project, is more nebulous but equally profound. They include Felicity Nussbaum, Srinivas Aravamudan, Jim Watt, Joanna de Groot, David Porter, Gerald Maclean and Donna Landry, Mark Hutchings, Margaret Anne Doody, Marina Warner, and Ken Parker.

My children, Frances and Stuart, and my partner, Phil Harriss, have spent their own nights regaled by oriental tales. My own private djinns, their magic endures beyond the confines of any page.

CONTENTS

ix

Contents

LIST OF ILLUSTRATIONS

List of Illustrations

ABBREVIATIONS

ANE   The 'Grub Street' translation of Antoine Galland's *Arabian Nights Entertainments*, ed. Robert L. Mack (Oxford: Oxford University Press, 1995)

CLMWM   *The Complete Letters of Lady Mary Wortley Montagu*, ed. Robert Halsband, 3 vols. (Oxford: Clarendon Press, 1965–7)

PT   François Pétis de la Croix, *The Thousand and One Days: Persian Tales*, trans. by Ambrose Philips, 3 vols (1714–15)

1

NARRATIVE MOVES

Dinarzade, the second string

The unsung second daughter of the vizier must wake every morning before dawn in her makeshift bed at the foot of the magnificent raised alcove on which her newly married sister and the sultan sleep. Without fail, she must prompt her sister to continue a story. In so doing, she preserves Scheherazade's lovely neck for another day. And presumably hers too, since she, as the second daughter, might fall victim to the bow-string (the traditional weapon of execution in the 'eastern' court) if her sister were to fail in her dangerous narrative enterprise. Each successive morning, the sultan becomes so engrossed in his wife's fable that he puts off the threatened execution for another day.

The younger daughter is, we are told, 'a lady of very great merit, but the elder had courage, wit and penetration infinitely above her sex'.[1] Dinarzade is always 'behind' her older sister, always in her shadow, her accomplice, her supplement. A second daughter and a middle child, I worried there was nothing special about me. My mother reassured me with two stories. First, I was the only child that was

---

[1] *Arabian Nights' Entertainments*, ed. Robert L. Mack (Oxford: Oxford University Press, 1995), 19.

planned and, true to form, the only one to arrive on time. Second, I was born in the, to me, magical territory of India. My father's job in pharmaceutical sales took him to Bombay in the early 1960s and my mother embarked on a long sea voyage with one infant daughter to join him. From not very well-off middle-class backgrounds in Britain, they found themselves both more affluent and more leisured in India and decided to have a second child, delivered at Breach Candy Hospital on the expected date of arrival. These twin consolations, my timeliness and my purely accidental Indianness, gave me significance in my own eyes. Being 'on time' is, of course, the most significant element in the Indian vizier's second daughter's role in the Arabian Nights.[2]

But there are other consolations for the second girl. Even if there is no photograph that pictures you alone (baby, school, or family), even if every item of clothing you owned had first been worn by your sister, or was a miniature version of her 'larger' and first-purchased selection, you can take comfort in the fact that you will never have to do anything first. School, puberty, all other rites of passage, will never be as traumatic or shocking as they are for the oldest girl. You know about them through your older sister's stories before you live them yourself. Indeed, like Marianne, the second daughter of *Sense and Sensibility* (1811)—a novel itself written by a second daughter, Jane Austen—you enjoy the freedom of nonconformity precisely because you have been able to watch and learn from your older sibling's experience. And, like Marianne, you can fantasize your own primacy and primariness, rejecting the model of your sister's acquiescent and responsible behaviour.[3] Thus, Anthony Hamilton (1646–1720) presents his Dinarzade in a comic rewriting of the tales which he circulated in the first decades of the eighteenth century among the aristocratic French lady readers so eagerly consuming Antoine Galland's newly published volumes. Hamilton's Dinarzade speaks up directly against the

---

[2] Throughout, I use the unitalicized phrase 'Arabian Nights' to refer to the composite 'text' translated by numerous different scholars into European languages from Arabic sources since the early 18th c. to the present day. When the title appears in italics, I refer to specific translations or editions.

[3] Ros Ballaster, 'Introduction', in *Jane Austen: Sense and Sensibility*, Penguin Classics (London: Penguin, 2003).

despotic, paranoid, and self-obsessed Sultan Schahriar, using her tale to undermine the myth of his potency, which her sister's deferential stories seek to enhance.[4]

The story of Dinarzade is a familiar one to the feminist literary critic as well as the second daughter. In Britain, from the eighteenth century onwards, women turned to publishing fiction in increasing numbers.[5] Even larger numbers of works were written in the voices of women.[6] Today, women are the major purchasers and consumers of fictional texts. Yet, as we read as women, we are aware that the story only passes through us or around us, whistling past our ears in its passage to its 'true' addressee. We are not, despite appearances, its target. We 'listen in' to the story whose intended recipient is the powerful male, his presence eclipsing our own, his 'reading' completing a textual meaning otherwise left indeterminate and unresolved.

To be reminded of Dinarzade's position is to be reminded that the route taken by narrative meaning(s) is neither simple nor direct, no single flight path from the mouth of a speaker to the ear of a listener. The encounter between self and other, between feminine and masculine, between one culture and another, is, like the narrative transaction, often 'mediated' by a third term. The third term can deflect, redirect, even block, such passage. The collection of tales known to Britain in the early eighteenth century as *The Arabian Nights Entertainments* (1704–17) came to these islands from the 'East' via

---

[4] Anthony Hamilton was an Irish cavalier, now best known for his satirical writings in French about the court of Charles II. For further discussion of his pseudo-oriental tales, see Ch. 3.

[5] Cheryl Turner's statistical research into the publication of fiction by women reveals that this was 'not a simple, continuous growth' through the century, but rather there were two phases of development, one between 1696 and 1725 and another after 1740, with a severe decline between those two dates and an 'abrupt upward surge' during the 1790s (Cheryl Turner, *Living by the Pen: Women Writers in the Eighteenth Century* (London: Routledge, 1992), 38).

[6] James Raven's statistical bibliographical work concludes that only 14 per cent of new novel titles published between 1750 and 1769 can be identified as by women writers (James Raven, *British Fiction 1750–1770: A Chronological Check-List of Prose Fiction Printed in Britain and Ireland* (Newark and London: University of Delaware Press; Associated University Presses, 1987), 18). He notes a steady increase in the percentage of new novels by women from the 1780s onward and that in the last two years of that decade 'female authorship was being deliberately promoted' with women outstripping men (thirty-three to eight) and an 'unprecedented number' of title-pages bearing the attribution to 'a Lady' (James Raven et al., *The English Novel 1770–1829: A Bibliographical Survey of Prose Fiction Published in the British Isles* (Oxford: Oxford University Press, 2000), 48).

France; indeed, the French 'translator' and distinguished Orientalist Antoine Galland was one of the leading forgers of western European constructions of the 'East'. Stories are not simple freight; in their passage from East to West they are often radically altered to become hybrid commodities and the bearers of multiple new meanings. Thus, through their ostensible depiction of life in the eastern harem, the *Arabian Nights Entertainments* could, amongst other things, provide a window for English readers into the 'précieuse' culture of the eighteenth-century French salon.

The role of Dinarzade can be consciously reprised by heroines of the eighteenth-century novel. Emma Courtney, the passionate heroine of a 1796 novel by Mary Hays, describes the experience of being transported by the narratives of the Arabian Nights. Having been an enraptured listener and reader in her youth, this Dinarzade, like Hamilton's, usurps the place of the storyteller traditionally occupied by the older sister, to produce her own *Memoirs*. Emma is adopted as a child by her aunt to replace an infant girl who died at the age of four months; she is then a 'second' daughter, whose fate will, hopefully, differ from that of the first child for whom she now substitutes. She confides in her reader that at the age of 4 or 5:

When myself and my little cousins had wearied ourselves with play, their mother, to keep us quiet in an evening, while her husband wrote letters in an adjoining apartment, was accustomed to relate (for our entertainment) stories from the Arabian Nights, Turkish Tales, and other works of like marvellous import. She recited them circumstantially, and these I listened to with ever new delight: the more they excited vivid emotions, the more wonderful they were, the greater was my transport: they became my favourite amusement, and produced, in my young mind, a strong desire of learning to read the books which contained such enchanting stores of entertainment.[7]

Emma Courtney's account of her reading experience reproduces—as she does the lost child—a primary lost experience: the scenario of the oral tale told by a woman to household dependents while a powerful male may or may not be listening nearby (her uncle writes letters in an adjoining room). This experience was one nostalgically evoked in

[7] Mary Hays, *Memoirs of Emma Courtney*, ed. Eleanor Ty (Oxford: Oxford University Press, 1996), 14.

many eighteenth-century novels acknowledging the radical shift in the circumstances of producing and consuming fiction—from the shared public spaces of the marketplace, coffee-house, or living-room, to the private and solitary space of the boudoir. There is both a connection and a gulf between the figures of Dinarzade and Emma as consumers of fiction: both are voracious consumers of an 'entertainment' that enables multiple identifications with a variety of subject positions, yet Dinarzade is a representative of an oral tradition of politically charged storytelling, while Emma's narrative development is towards the introspective, self-critical, and apparently private 'memoir'. It is a long journey from the eastern magical tale to the formal realism of the English eighteenth-century novel, yet practitioners of the latter frequently conjure up the trace of the former in the act of narrating their own histories of becoming storytellers.

Like the childhoods of Dinarzade and Emma, mine was filled with stories and the Arabian Nights held a special kind of magic. Especially the magic of being able to imagine oneself into the role of multiple others: Aladdin, the idle son whose dearest wishes are fulfilled through a combination of luck and resourcefulness; the courageous princess Badoura who comes to command a kingdom by disguising herself as her husband; innocent Ali Baba saved from falling victim to the forty thieves by his clever serving-woman. Not only can the reader project into many roles, but the interpretation of the tales remains an exercise in openness and heterogeneity. If Scheherazade tells her fables with a purpose—many of them slowly shift her husband from his inflexible condemnation of all women by warning against the over-hasty performance of threats and the need to look twice at appearances—her sister is free to make of them what she will. We, Dinarzade's readers, are given no inkling as to *her* 'reading' of the fables.

This book looks at what western readers who imagined themselves into the role of Dinarzade—an observer from the sidelines of the dynamics of an eastern despotism—read into oriental tales, a form of narration that flourished from the late seventeenth to the late eighteenth century. It does so recognizing the expediency of such acts of imaginative identification. They enable a fruitful pose, especially for the British on the threshold of western empire in India, as dispassionate judge of fixed, indeed stagnating, power relations, emboldened to produce 'new' visions of the future of the 'East' precisely because of distance, disengagement, and comparative weakness. It does so, also, recognizing that identification with the position of a *female* narrator and/or reader is a recurrent feature of European fiction in the eighteenth century, especially in the burgeoning form of the novel.

The congruence of these two identifications—with the observer of the East and with the female narrator/consumer of fictions—suggests that we should approach with suspicion their claims to provide simple expressions of new and 'enlightened' understandings of liberty, and contemplate the possibility that they forged new models of subjectivity which could enable comparatively small and insignificant global territories to think of themselves as having wide-reaching influence and agency. Here I concur with the directions taken in recent studies of British encounters with distant lands and peoples by writers as various as Nigel Leask, Linda Colley, and Jonathan Lamb: directions that point to the fragility and insecurity of the 'self' who narrates such encounters, rather than confident imperial or colonial ambition.[8] However, weakness can be resourcefully turned into advantage and hybridity can provide a means not merely of survival but also of knowledge and power.

This book does not seek exhaustively to catalogue the many, various, and frequently conflicting attitudes of eighteenth-century western Europeans to contemporary Asian states. Rather, it makes a case that between the late seventeenth and late eighteenth centuries, the Orient came to acquire both a loose conceptual unity and internal difference through persistent representation of its spaces and peoples as consumed by and in fiction. That is, 'fiction' is presented, in a variety of texts, as the best way of 'knowing' the Orient and comprehending its legacy to the West, but also as the place of the Orient's undoing: the passage of its fiction from East to West a proleptic sign of a long transfer of power from one half of the globe to the other. In this

---

[8] Linda Colley, *Captives: Britain, Empire and the World, 1600–1850* (London: Jonathan Cape, 2002); Jonathan Lamb, *Preserving the Self in the South Seas, 1680–1840* (Chicago and London: University of Chicago Press, 2001); Nigel Leask, *Curiosity and the Aesthetics of Travel Writing, 1770–1840: 'from an Antique Land'* (Oxford: Oxford University Press, 2002).

respect my argument could be seen as a literary critical contribution to the recent work in economic history, which attempts to challenge that 'Eurocentric teleology that sees Europeans as the prime movers and everyone else responding to them'.[9] Literary historians could take their lead from economic historians by recognizing the opportunistic, sometimes piecemeal, but none the less discernible, advancement of Europe in the early modern period as the result of its interaction with the societies of Asia, Africa, and America, rather than a sign of its distance or difference from them.[10]

In the eighteenth century in England—until the development of more extensive material, intellectual, and political contact with the 'East' through its colonial relation to India—the term 'orient' is more often found embedded in the adjective 'oriental', which in turn features most often in the phrase 'oriental tale'. Eighteenth-century commentators view the 'fable' as the place not only where two spaces meet (western print culture renarrates the oral fables of the East) but also two temporalities: the ancient and the modern. Ancient oriental tales spoken critically in the context of an all-pervasive despotism recirculate in the context of debates over contractual monarchy and republicanism in Europe. But of all this, as Scheherazade would say, more later.

The state of narrative

The argument of this book is built on three propositions. First, narrative moves. Stories migrate from one culture to another, over vast distances sometimes, but their path is often difficult to trace and obscured by time. *Fabulous Orients* looks at the traffic of narrative between Orient and Occident in the 'long' eighteenth century. Narrative also 'moves' in the sense that it causes things and places to

[9] Kenneth Pomeranz and Steven Topik, *The World that Trade Created: Society, Culture, and the World Economy, 1400–the Present, Sources and Studies in World History* (Armonk, N Y, and London: M. E. Sharpe, 1999), p. xiv.

[10] See James M. Blaut, *The Colonizer's Model of the World: Geographical Diffusion and Eurocentric History* (New York and London: Guilford, 1993).

shift; a central argument of this book is that narrative is instrumental in constructing the very categories of Orient and Occident and marking the boundaries between the two. Eighteenth-century readers in the West came to draw their mental maps of oriental territories and distinctions between them from their experience of reading tales 'from' the Orient. The sequence of oriental tales moves over multiple oriental locales—especially the great empires of China, India, Turkey, and Persia—always categorizing, differentiating. It also 'moves' occidental states by drawing analogies between their history and those of the oriental cultures it ostensibly describes, suggesting that one can be mapped on the other.

Second, narrative moves its reader. Lovers of the oriental tale talk of being 'transported' into other worlds. They are also 'taken up' by the story, find their emotions stirred; they are prompted to sympathy or revulsion. Stories about shape-shifting and transmigration also 'move' their reader by fostering the experience of imaginary projection into the psyche and culture of an other.

Third, fiction makes distinct narrative moves—political, social, emotive—which serve to prompt desired responses in the reader. The sequence of oriental tales is often presented as a series of political moves or manoeuvres designed to produce some change in the behaviour or perspective of the addressee. Scheherazade paces her tales so that her husband, the Emperor Schahriar, will defer the sentence of death he has passed on her to hear each new conclusion. But she also tells tales that warn against too hasty execution of a sentence.

I return to each proposition in this chapter, using the Arabian Nights to illustrate the key arguments pursued in this book. Perhaps the only consistent feature of the Arabian Nights tales *is* their illustrativeness. Their twentieth-century Arabic editor, Muhsin Mahdi, presents them as a case study illustrating the perils of critical acts of ignorant totalization, which are undermined by evidence from histories of manuscript transmission, translation studies, and bibliographical research.[11] They can illustrate the principles of feminist

---

[11] Muhsin Mahdi, 'Introduction', *The Thousand and One Nights*, iii (Leiden: Brill, 1994).

criticism or Lacanian theories of subject-formation.[12] Mutually incompatible positions can be elaborated from the sequence: Robert Irwin uses them to illustrate the deep interrelatedness of western and eastern stories, myths, and traditions; others have seen them as evidence of the completely fabricated and fictitious nature of the West's construction of the Orient, as western European states rose to global pre-eminence.[13] Like their teller, Scheherazade, the Arabian Nights proves to be all things to all men; it can shift shape as swiftly as the genii and perii (fairies) that flit in and out of its narrative fabric.

One of the principal attractions of the tales for this reader is the illustrative interplay between temporal and spatial understandings of narrative agency: the way in which the oriental tale occupies both the past and the present, there and here. The Arabian Nights presents narrative as both a temporal and territorial 'occupation': it occupies time to deliver and consume (the *1001* Nights) but it also consumes the mind and transports the reader to 'other' spaces or the 'space' of the other (the *Arabian* Nights). Narrative's different 'movements' are not necessarily perfectly synchronized and harmonious, nor do they follow in a temporal sequence like the 'movements' in a musical piece. They can come into contradiction and competition. The stories told by Scheherazade may appear to be serving the third purpose of narrative as outlined above, that of effecting a change in the 'state' of the tales' addressee. She persuades Schahriar that his judgement of all women is too hasty by telling tales in which judgement is deferred in return for narrative pleasure. But the stories are most effective in terms of the second purpose, that of 'moving' their addressee into different spaces and times so as to 'transport' him away from his murderous intention. Scheherazade's narrative effect is accretive rather than morally or politically cohesive. In constant process, her narrative

[12] Eva Sallis, *Sheherazade through the Looking Glass: The Metamorphosis of the Thousand and One Nights*, Curzon Studies in Arabic and Middle-Eastern Literatures (Richmond, Surrey: Curzon, 1999); Daniel Beaumont, *Slave of Desire: Sex, Love and Death in the 1001 Nights* (London: Associated University Presses, 2002).

[13] Robert Irwin, *The Arabian Nights: A Companion* (London: Allen Lane, 1994). For the latter position, see Peter L. Caracciolo, *The Arabian Nights in English Literature: Studies in the Reception of the Thousand and One Nights into British Culture* (Basingstoke: Macmillan, 1988); Rana Kabbani, *Imperial Fictions: Europe's Myths of Orient*, rev. and expanded edn. (London: Pandora, 1994); and Dorothee Metlitzki, *The Matter of Araby in Medieval England* (New Haven: Yale University Press, 1977).

strives to maintain a state (keeping the narrator alive), while pursuing a necessary onward movement. Thus, her storytelling emerges as exemplary; narrative becomes a constant process of never-completed becoming, a becoming that fends off death. I address this idea of the 'state' generative of and induced by narrative through three different and recurring elements in Enlightenment representations of the Orient: the context of the physical space of the seraglio, the construction of the responsive or transformed reader, and the presence of concealed political intent in storytelling.

Geographical states

The vizier's daughter Scheherazade tells her stories in the space of the harem, or what seventeenth- and eighteenth-century commentators commonly called the 'seraglio' in an etymological slippage from the Turco-Persian word for 'palace' to the Italian word for enclosure: 'serrare'. We can understand the narrative significance of the seraglio in eighteenth-century European fiction when we recognize it as a dominant chronotope (or space–time metaphor) in the sense defined by Mikhail Bakhtin in his 1937–8 essay 'Forms of Time and of the Chronotope in the Novel'.[14] In the 'Concluding Remarks' (added in 1973), Bakhtin glosses chronotopes as 'the organizing centres for the fundamental narrative events of the novel. The chronotope is the place where the knots of narrative are tied and untied. It can be said without qualification that to them belongs the meaning that shapes narrative' (250). Bakhtin identifies a number of different chronotopes of the novel: the road in the picaresque, the salon or boudoir in Stendhal, the provincial town in Flaubert, the castle in the Gothic. These are metaphors—'almost, but not entirely' (84)—where 'Time becomes, in effect, palpable and visible, the chronotope makes narrative events concrete, makes them take on flesh, causes blood to flow in their veins' (250). Time and space get fused in the chronotope: 'Time, as it were, thickens, takes on flesh, becomes artistically visible; likewise, space becomes charged and responsive to the movements of time, plot and

[14] M. M. Bakhtin, 'Forms of Time and of the Chronotope in the Novel', in *The Dialogic Imagination: Four Essays*, ed. Michael Holquist, trans. Caryl Emerson and Michael Holquist, Slavic Series 1 (Austin: University of Texas Press, 1981), 84–258.

history' (53). The seraglio/harem is a 'metaphor' for the relation between narrative space and time that the text of the Arabian Nights (space)/1001 Nights (time) itself narrates. The generation of tales enables Scheherazade's continuing existence in a space where time 'stands still' or is immaterial since it is unchanging. In *The Sultan's Court* (1998) Alain Grosrichard traces the way in which occidental writers claim the superiority of western 'history' by marking its difference from the mythic space–time of oriental story as delivered in the seraglio:

In place of history—of which it can have no conception, and which it cannot beget—the Orient substitutes histories, fuelling the Western imagination. Its deep and silent night is peopled with countless dreams which are tireless variations on some major themes. But the Oriental tale, with its magic mirrors and talismans, its words and gestures with the power to transform men and things in an instant, its transportation through space without time, is nothing other than the rhetorical amplification of or free commentary on what the travellers record having seen in the Orient. The insubstantial shadows which move about in the seraglio are of the same stuff as the characters in the *Thousand and One Nights*, and their uncertain fate is the plaything of the same capricious divinities: the despotic Orient delights in *metamorphosis*—a simulacrum and negation of history—and under a perpetual alteration of forms, the identity and permanence of a structure, the repetitive dryness and rigid automaton of a machine, are affirmed.[15]

The Arabian Nights generates a sequence of stories whose forward progress is directed towards maintaining a continuous static state, Scheherazade's continuing survival. Spatial and temporal amplification and metamorphosis are an endless variation on a single theme, the condition of continued life which is defined solely by the capacity to tell a story.

The narrative generates geographical difference only to reinforce sameness and unchangingness. Stories from tenth-century India, Iran, and Persia are treated as evidence of the behaviour of Ottoman Turks, Safavid Persians, Gentile and Mughal Indians, and a number of minority religions or cultures of the early modern 'East'. Thus, Antoine Galland in his preface claims that not only are the *Arabian*

---

[15] Alain Grosrichard, *The Sultan's Court: European Fantasies of the East*, trans. Liz Heron (London: Verso, 1998), 79.

Nights Entertainments wonderful magical tales but:

They must also be pleasing, because of the Account they give of the Customs and Manners of the Eastern Nations, and of the Ceremonies of their Religion, as well *Pagan* as *Mahometan*, which are better describ'd here, than in any Author that has wrote of 'em, or in the Relations of Travellers. All the Eastern Nations, *Persians*, *Tartars*, and *Indians*, are here distinguish'd, and appear such as they are, from the Sovereign to the meanest Subject.[16]

The whole Orient is telescoped into the confined chronotope of the harem, indeed into the sultana's bedchamber. Metamorphosis and endless transformation become a means of keeping things unchanged. But looked at another way, change or movement is effected. The Arabian Nights allows the metamorphosis of the Orient into the Occident; Antoine Galland turns the seraglio into a French salon in which *précieuse* women orchestrate and regulate polite speech (at the expense of the folkloric elements more prominent in his various sources).[17] The sequence moves or transposes (transproses) one geographical state into another. Ruth Bernard Yeazell reminds us not to read Europe's 'obsession' with the harem in purely political terms but to recognize its narrative attractions; she comments that the motif of the 'harem' in European writing 'owed more to the lure of the unknown and the forbidden than to the desire for political conquest'.[18] The chronotope of the harem/seraglio, then, is one that often tells us more about the geography of European desire than the space it depicts.

Emotional states

The Arabian Nights may be a sequence generated on the pretext of the preservation of a single life, the life of the story, but it is also a sequence

[16] *Arabian Nights Entertainments: Consisting of One Thousand and One Stories, Told by the Sultaness of the Indies... Translated into French from the Arabian Mss, by M. Galland... And Now Done into English from the Last Paris Edition*, 8th edn. (London, 1736), n.p.

[17] For a striking contrast between the sexual and racial explicitness of Richard Burton's 19th-c. 'translation' and the preciosity of Galland's 18th-c. one, see Jennifer Thorn, 'The Work of Writing Race: Galland, Burton and the Arabian Nights', in Laura J. Rosenthal and Mita Choudhury (eds.), *Monstrous Dreams of Reason: Body, Self and Other in the Enlightenment* (London: Associated University Presses, 2002), 151–69.

[18] Ruth Bernard Yeazell, *Harems of the Mind: Passages of Western Art and Literature* (New Haven and London: Yale University Press, 2000), 8.

that looks very remote from the modern novel because of its complete lack of interest in what we now identify as the latter's defining characteristic, the construction of a fiction of interiority with its attendant concept of transformation and change in and within the person. Protagonists in the embedded and framed stories lack 'character' and are simply functions of the narrative structure.[19] Only Schahriar, the despotic sultan and surrogate 'reader', acquires some complexity because of the trauma prompted by the discovery of his favourite sultana's infidelity. Unlike Scheherazade, her sister, and the protagonists of the tales who tend to remain 'constant', he is driven by dark impulses, but is also open to correction and transformation. However, the sequence does illustrate narrative's capacity to engender a change in emotional 'state' through its larger and repetitive preoccupation with the representation of the ethical encounter between self and other that takes place in narrative. Adam Zachary Newton defines narrative ethics as implying 'simply narrative *as* ethics: the ethical consequences of narrating story and fictionalizing person, and the reciprocal claims binding teller, listener, witness, and reader in that process'.[20] Narrative is an exchange between self and other for Newton: 'narrative as relationship and human connectivity, as Saying over and above Said, or as Said called to account in Saying; narrative as claim, as risk, as responsibility, as gift, as price. Above all, as an ethics, narrative is performance or act' (7). Newton contrasts the *Arabian Nights Entertainments* with Samuel Taylor Coleridge's *Rime of the Ancient Mariner* thus:

In the *Arabian Nights' Entertainments*, narrative, through coercion, ultimately enables marriage; in Coleridge's poem, a similar process disables it. In one, the procreative capacity of narrative serves to model relations of friendship and conjugal love—teller, listener, and witness become bound to one another through the liberating force of story; in the other, storytelling

---

[19] Roland Barthes distinguishes between 'functions' and 'indices', the former complementary and consequential in the progress of a narrative, the latter 'a more or less diffuse concept which is nevertheless necessary to the meaning of the story'; psychological indices concern character and are more prominent in the psychological novel; folk tales are 'heavily functional'. (Roland Barthes, 'Introduction to the Structural Analysis of Narrative', in *Barthes: Selected Writings*, ed. Susan Sontag ([London]: Fontana, 1983), 251–95, 264, 265).

[20] Adam Zachary Newton, *Narrative Ethics* (Cambridge, Mass., and London: Harvard University Press, 1995), 11.

fastens on to its participants only to sever them from the world—driven out or emptied out, they remain forlornly yoked to one another only through involuntary and baleful narrative enchainment. (7)

This analysis may do no more than illustrate the difference between Enlightenment and Romantic models of narrative, the former leading to connection, the latter to separation and solipsism. But it also, if unwittingly, illustrates how often this distinction gets forged through the transformation in perceptions of spaces 'other' than those of western Europe.

We need to reconceive the formulation of the western novel during a century of imperial and colonial expansion to recognize that the movement is not exclusively inward—shoring up a sovereign self by contrast with the 'other' (the powers that had preceded the West across the globe, those of eastern territorial empire). The 'novelty' of western empire may have lain in its willingness to project outward, to imagine itself serially in the place of the 'other', especially the eastern other, not only through circulating fictions of transmigration (tales of shape-shifting by genii, perii, Hindu and Buddhist fictional protagonists), but also through the framing devices of oriental fictional sequences that dramatize reading as an experience of abandoning rather than reinforcing sovereignty; this is after all what happens to Schahriar, who 'forgets' his own condition(s) by immersing himself in story, the space of the other. This then is how narrative 'moves' the psyche, or transforms its readers' emotional states—less through patterns of identification and recognition of 'selfhood', than through pleasurable abandonment of the sense of self to an other in a space in which such activity is virtually free of risk.

Political states

If this proposition sounds naïve or idealistic it may be because it is built on a model of narrative derived from phenomenology which sidesteps the political dimension of the stories we tell. And, clearly, Scheherazade's narrative adventures are political. Their aim is a political one: to temper the despot's behaviour in order to make him better fulfil his role as absolute monarch. Moreover, Galland's early eighteenth-century translation is just one collection among many oriental tales that circulated in western Europe as critiques of despotism, designed to warn against growing absolutism in European states, especially France. The fable was defended as an oblique means of criticizing despotism by an oppressed people, voiced by the enslaved woman in the harem, or by the marginal brahman/sage/Sufi. If we take the political 'intent' of narrative into account, we can also see that it was in the interest of European states with aspirations to empire to present covetousness and expansion as a form of enlightened openness and pleasurable hybridity.

Slavoj Žižek provides a provocative account of what he terms 'perverse desubjectivization' which may prove a more productive means of mapping the psychic convolutions undergone by western Europeans in the encounter with oriental 'otherness'. According to Žižek, 'the subject avoids his constitutive splitting by positing himself directly as the instrument of the Other's Will'.[21] Desire is always the desire of the Other, a construct we posit in order to produce our 'self'. To clarify this account, Žižek gives examples of two different forms of perverse desubjectivization. First, that of the white western members of an anthropological expedition who are treated to a performance of wild dancing by the native inhabitants in the New Zealand jungle only to discover the steps have been reconstructed from the anthropologists' own accounts of what they expect to find/see there. Second, the man in Franz Kafka's *Trial* who only discovers when dying that the Door of the Law is the door intended only for him; he thinks himself an observer when in fact he is the addressee.

The 'fable' of the Orient in general (anthropologists/observers give accounts of the spectacle of an Orient that appears to be indifferent to their presence but is 'in reality' their own construct) tallies with the first and the narrative scenario of the Arabian Nights (Schahriar listens in on stories ostensibly told to Dinarzade, Scheherazade's sister, but he is their 'real' destination) with the second of Žižek's exemplary tales. Žižek concludes:

while we perceive ourselves as external bystanders stealing a furtive glance into some majestic mystery indifferent to us, we are blinded to the fact that the

---

[21] Slavoj Žižek, 'Hegelian Llanguage', in *For They Know Not What They Do: Enjoyment as a Political Factor* (London: Verso, 2002), p. xiv.

entire spectacle of Mystery is staged *with an eye to our gaze*; to attract and fascinate our gaze—here, the Other deceives us in so far as it induces us to believe that we were *not* chosen; here, it is the true addressee himself who mistakes his position for that of an accidental bystander.

What the two illusions have in common is that in both cases, the subject fails to notice how he himself *posits* the Other: by means of the very act of recognizing myself as the addressee of the ideological call, I (presup) posit the Other as the agency which confers meaning upon the contingency of the Real; by means of the very act of perceiving myself as the impotent, negligible, insignificant witness of the spectacle of the Other, I constitute its mysterious, transcendent character. (109)

Our route via Žižek allows a return to the so far silent but dominant figure of Edward Said in any discussion of the occidental encounter with oriental(ized) others. It also restores a political dimension to this account of the contribution of oriental narrative to the formulation of the 'enlightened' European subject.

This book expands on the elusive and allusive moments in Said's text where he complicates our understanding of the nature of Orientalist discourse, where he points to its fictionality, recognizes the tension between image/representation and narrative structure/emplotting/temporality. Said diagnoses a shift in the eighteenth century from Renaissance constructions of the Orient as barbaric 'other' (as a result of an expanding awareness of non-Islamic regions of the Orient and the popularity of paradigms of cosmopolitan history) to acts of 'selective identification with regions and cultures not one's own [which] wore down the obduracy of self and identity, which had been polarized into a community of embattled believers facing barbarian hordes'.[22] This projection of what Said also terms 'sympathetic imagination' (118) into spaces previously unoccupied by the European imagination—other bodies and cultures—is a striking feature of narrative fiction in the period and could be figured as an act of mental transmigration between Occident and Orient. Elsewhere, Said identifies the disruptive effect of narrative upon Orientalist writing, which prefers the forms of encyclopedia, dictionary, or monumental history: he concludes, then: 'Narrative, in short, introduces an opposing point

---

[22] Edward W. Said, *Orientalism* (London: Routledge & Kegan Paul, 1978), 120.

of view, perspective, to the unitary web of vision; it violates the serene Apollonian fictions asserted by vision' (240).

Said's comments complicate his customary apprehension of 'Orientalism' as a discursive process that transforms a changing history into a set of unchanging and repetitive images. The temporal consumption of narrative is, evidently, very different from the spatial consumption of an 'image'; the reader of the *Arabian Nights Entertainments* is aware of the shifting geographies and histories (personal as well as political) it narrates. Against the pressure towards a fixed and unified image of the East, the collection can open up difference, diversity, contradiction, and difficulty: a constantly shifting set of tropes of 'easternness' serving many different roles—social satire, attacks on priestcraft, critiques of absolutism and luxury, debates over female sexuality, explorations of the supernatural, the representation of subaltern experience. The temporal dimension of narrative introduces the potential for movement, process, acts of becoming and creation, as opposed to the spatial aspect of representation which apparently reflects, mirrors, or reproduces an already given relation. Scheherazade's tales can 'move' their recipient(s), transport them geographically, psychically, politically into new positions or conditions, or rather leave them in a state of permanent narrative becoming/ transformation. Such a state is remarkably close to the preferred method of representing European empire itself in this period: excessively mobile (because based on maritime success in the case of England particularly), accretive, and transformative rather than a set of already inscribed precepts imposed on an alien culture. That this is in itself a 'fable' developed as survival strategy should not leave us underestimating its material agency, just as in the case of Scheherazade herself.

Through analyses of fictional representations—prose and dramatic, travellers' accounts as well as lengthy sequences of tales—of the four oriental territories understood to be both powerful and ancient in origin (Persia, Turkey, China, and India), *Fabulous Orients* demonstrates the ways in which the East came to be understood as a (sometimes *the*) source of story, a territory of fable and narrative. The Orient is a place to be turned into story as well as a place where story originates and where story has political and material effect. In this pre-colonial or proto-colonial period in British history, the English encounter with the East was largely mediated not through government or commercial policy and documents, but rather through the consumption of material goods imported from the East, together with narratives about the East, both imaginary and ethnographic. Oriental narratives often claim to be a more 'moral' traffic than the acquisitive traffic in goods such as silks, indigo, muslin, spices, and jewels.

The period this book addresses falls between two significant dates in the history of the British acquisition of its first, most extensive and most profitable eastern outpost of empire, that of India. In 1662, as part of his marriage settlement with the Portuguese Catherine of Braganza, Charles II acquired Bombay. In 1785, Warren Hastings retired from his position as the first governor-general of India; the appointment of Cornwallis in his place saw a far more predatory and less hybrid form of government in relation to indigenous historical institutions. But the year previously on 15 January 1784, Hastings's intellectual ally, William Jones, had founded the Asiatick Society of Bengal, which was to continue the work of producing a more rigorous and academic relationship with oriental languages, religions, and history than the previous century had seen. Contact with the great eastern empires (with the exception of China which, after the failure of Lord George Macartney's 1793–4 embassy, becomes marginal to knowledge of the 'East' in Britain) is both wider and deeper than hitherto, but also has much more explicit political aims and interests. The piecemeal, sometimes random, contact of the eighteenth century acquires shape and direction. Enlightenment preoccupations with analogy, shared history, and sameness of self and culture, give way to an increasingly racialized sense of difference. Fictional representations of the East contribute to this shift in attitude with a turn, in the last two decades of the century, to the erotic and exotic fragment and oriental allegory, in place of the popular 'translation' of the sequence of oriental tales and the embedded moral fable.

The terms 'fable' and 'fabulous' recur in eighteenth-century representations of the East. Travellers refute the accounts of others as 'fabulous' and assert the veracity of their own work, while they take pleasure in rehearsing the cultural 'fables' of the eastern states they explore. The nature of the oriental tale is understood to be that of the 'fable': 'a feigned story intended to enforce some moral precept' as defined by Samuel Johnson in 1755. Not only are the major fabulists of the eighteenth century—Aesop, Bidpai/Pilpay, and Lokman— recognized as oriental, but collections of fables are also given more rather than less oriental 'context' or baggage in late seventeenth- and eighteenth-century translations. The tales of the Arabian Nights are presented as fables that restore moral order to Schahriar's state, personal as well as geographical. And historians of fiction identify the contribution of oriental cultures to the 'rise of the novel' through the fable.

Clara Reeve's feminocentric account of *The Progress of Romance* (1785) confirms the association of the eastern tale with female speakers, in that her two female commentators, Euphronia and Sophronia, champion its contribution to the novel—although they condemn it for being 'wild and extravagant to the highest degree'.[23] James Beattie, in his essay 'On Fable and Romance' written in 1780, inserts a section on the oriental fable after his account of classical, medieval, and Renaissance romance and before he reaches his celebration of the modern novel: 'the Oriental nations have long been famous for fabulous narrative. The indolence peculiar to the genial climates of Asia, and the luxurious life which the kings and other great men, of those countries, lead in their seraglios, have made them seek for this kind of amusement, and set a high value upon it'.[24] Both Reeve and Beattie see the oriental fable as inclined to the amoral, the fantastic, and the supernatural: tendencies that the realist fiction of the second half of the eighteenth century, they argue, has succeeded in curbing. Here too, then, oriental fiction is summoned as source and analogue only to be dismissed or overcome to make way for the 'adult' development of a Eurocentric form.

Fabulous Orients is structured according to territory rather than genre. I confine discussion in terms of space as well as time, in that I concentrate on fictional representations of the absolutist courts of

[23] Clara Reeve, *The Progress of Romance: And the History of Charoba, Queen of Aegypt*, Facsimile Text Society, ser. 1: Literature and Language, iv (New York: the Facsimile Text Society, 1930), 58.
[24] James Beattie, *Dissertations, Moral and Critical*, ed. Roger J. Robinson, *The Works of James Beattie* (London: Routledge/Thoemmes, 1996), 508–9.

those four oriental empires that were depicted by western European writings in French and English as both territorially and ideologically expansive. Fictional representations of these empires, and especially their courts, share certain common features: extensive territorial dominions, a history or prehistory of non-Islamic religion and culture (Zoroastrianism in Persia; Byzantine Christianity in Turkey; Hinduism and Buddhism in India; Confucianism, Taoism, and Buddhism in China), the enclosure of women, the employment of eunuchs, and the control of all circulation—of goods, people, money, property—by an absolute ruler. I exclude fictions and accounts relating to the North African satellites of the Ottomans (the regencies of Tunisia, Tripoli, and Algeria) and the independent Islamic 'empire' of Morocco, which were largely represented in English writing of the eighteenth century through the genre of the captivity narrative, rather than the 'fabulous' writings I concentrate on here.[25]

Although the regions I discuss are subject to considerable geographical confusion and intermingling in the narrative fictions that depict them, and much of that fiction is written originally in French and translated into English, there are crucial distinctions in their relationship to the two European cultures in this period. China is a trade partner for England and a missionary outpost for French Jesuits but never a potential colony for either state. Turkey is an increasingly less powerful competitor in Europe, at intervals a potential ally for Protestant England against Catholic France. England engages in wars, especially with the French, to make India its colony. These distinctions, and particularly the differences between Protestant and Catholic (and to a lesser extent, atheist and deist) readings of oriental empire, are illustrated at relevant points in what follows. However, the attraction of a 'fabulous' construction of the Orient often overrides national and geographical difference in Europe. Moreover, much French oriental writing, by anglophiles or *philosophes* such as Voltaire and Montesquieu, provides a means of satirizing French absolutism

---

[25] For discussion and examples of captivity writing see Colley, *Captives: Britain, Empire and the World, 1600–1850*, and Daniel J. Vitkus (ed.), *Piracy, Slavery, and Redemption: Barbary Captivity Narratives from Early Modern England* (New York and Chichester: Columbia University Press, 2001).

and influence for Protestant states proud of their native 'liberties' such as England and Holland.

The bulk of the book is made up of three sections exploring fictional texts published in England between 1662 and 1785 relating first to Persia and Turkey, second to China, and third to India. Each section opens with a renarration of an oriental story wherein a feminine character 'figures' western desire for the territory she represents: the courtesan queen of the Ottoman seraglio, Roxolana; the riddling Chinese princess, Tourandocte; and the illusory sati of India, Canzade. Each section explores the range of fabulous writings relating to each oriental territory in order to illustrate how certain narrative tropes can acquire hegemony in the representation of that space: the conflict between the male look and female speech, staged in the seraglio in the case of Turkey and Persia; the inauthenticity and/or dullness associated with China and its products such as porcelain; and the illusory dreams that are woven in the space of India, growing centre of the textile industry. Although my primary focus is on fictional tales or fables, travellers' accounts surface throughout the book and illustrate the mutual interdependence of fictional narrative and factual report. Travellers bring their knowledge of fictional models to bear in understanding the new cultures they encounter, while fictional writers weave travellers' tropes and evidence into their materials.

The next chapter, 'Shape-Shifting: Oriental Tales', uses the trope of transmigration, so popular in oriental tales, to describe the relationship established between Orient and Occident through the consumption of narratives of the East in eighteenth-century England. This chapter, necessarily cursorily, maps each of the major genres of oriental narrative so that readers of the book can orient themselves in the following discussions of the interaction between the representation of geographical spaces and generic traditions.

The passage of consciousness from body to body in a process of both penance and improvement (the 'oriental' doctrine of transmigration) can function as a metaphor for the passage of narrative from one cultural space to another. It is, moreover, and importantly, both a spatial and a temporal experience; the soul moves through time from one body to another, adapting to its new environment at each turn but also bearing the imprint of its previous 'life', if only in terms of the role (high or low status) it takes on in each new form. The act of reading narrative might also be figured as a kind of transmigration: the projection of the reader's 'spirit' into the place/space/time of an 'other' or many 'others', which requires a constant shifting of consciousness and perspective that transforms the reading self in the process.

These understandings of the encounter with the Orient through fiction as a form of transmigration were extremely visible and resonant to eighteenth-century western consumers and 'translators'/producers. The transmigration of oriental fiction to the West also contributed to the 'shaping' of the developing aesthetics of the period especially as applied to the emergent form of the novel; while often disavowing the supernaturalism and romance of the oriental tale, the topicality, seriality, and self-conscious fictionality of the 'new' novel all bear the traces of a past life in this 'other' textual body. 'Shape-shifting' demonstrates how widely the Orient was received and shaped in the West through the medium and techniques of narrative fiction, to the extent that the Orient could be perceived as a species of fiction itself: a hybrid and manufactured product of imaginative investments on the part of the West. The five genres under discussion which cover the spectrum of oriental narrative available to the eighteenth-century reader are: the framed sequence of eastern tales, the traveller's account, fictional letters of an eastern informant, the history of a state and/or life, and the heroic drama.

'Tales of the Seraglio: Turkey and Persia' argues that the oriental woman in narrative accounts figures not only the enclosing and constraining power of despotism but also resistance to it. In so doing, she represents an axis of temporality (the narrative time of storytelling and deferral of its conclusion, the keeping of her head quite literally) which counters the axis of space and looking associated with the oriental male. Her agency is that of the tongue and of time, his is that of the eye and of the masterful control of space. This chapter considers fictions relating to the Persian and Ottoman empires. It maps the gendered division of the labour of representation through a discussion of two tragic plays by Mary Pix and Delarivier Manley, oriental tales by Antoine Galland and his French and English imitators (not only the long sequence but also the burgeoning form of the short novella set in Turkish and/or Persian territories), and fictional letters in the voice of Turkish and Persian informants by Giovanni Paolo Marana and Charles Montesquieu.

' "Bearing Confucius' morals to Britannia's ears": China' charts the tendency to represent China as a space of inauthenticity, or fictionality, that emerged in the eighteenth century with the decline in the dominance and credibility of Jesuit missionary reports. However, this new preoccupation with the fragility and ephemerality of 'China' paradoxically allowed it to continue to play a robust and elastic role in the British cultural imagination. My analysis of fictional texts about China contributes to the increasing seriousness with which the cult of 'chinoiserie' is being treated by economic and cultural historians.[26] The four groups of fictional sources considered here are, first, oriental tales with a 'Chinese' setting by Thomas-Simon Gueullette, 'Hoamchi-Vam', Thomas Percy, and Horace Walpole; second, the group of tragic plays about Chinese 'orphans' written by figures as diverse as Voltaire and Elkanah Settle; third, the representation of China as an empire of 'Dulness' in poetry and fiction relating to Alexander Pope's *Dunciad*; and fourth, published letters written in the voice of the Chinese informant of which Oliver Goldsmith's *Citizen of the World* is the most impressive, if late, example.

' "Dreams of Men Awake": India' argues that fictions claiming to derive from and about India repeatedly trope India as a dream, but not always in the positive sense of a space to be possessed by the imagination. Equally, the dream can be a kind of consoling or duplicitous fiction. India generates illusions and illusionists; the fakirs and brahmans of ethnographic report are represented as master tricksters while Islam is, as in the case of Ottoman and Persian accounts, denounced as a gross imposture. I address three principal areas of fiction that relate to India: John Dryden's theatrical representation of the court of Aurangzeb; collections of oriental tales relating to India by Thomas-Simon Gueullette, James Ridley, and Alexander Dow; and 'translations' derived from the third-century Sanskrit collection of animal and

---

[26] Maxine Berg and Helen Clifford (eds.), *Consumers and Luxury: Consumer Culture in Europe, 1650–1850* (Manchester: Manchester University Press, 1999); Maxine Berg and Elizabeth Eger (eds.), *Luxury in the Eighteenth Century: Debates, Desires and Delectable Goods* (Basingstoke: Palgrave, 2003); David Porter, *Ideographia: The Chinese Cipher in Early Modern Europe* (Stanford, Calif.: Stanford University Press, 2001).

human fables, known to seventeenth-century Europe as the *Fables of Pilpay*.

A brief epilogue argues that the late eighteenth century ushered in a new aesthetics of difference in the place of the preceding century's tendency to attempt to understand the 'East' by means of analogy. Interest in the 'Orient' intensifies and becomes more sophisticated in this period, but fictional narrative is no longer the dominant vehicle of representation; the perception of oriental cultures is increasingly dictated by visual representations in both architecture and art, by antiquarianism and by a burgeoning ethnography. Readings of William Beckford's *Vathek* (1786), Byron's oriental poetry of the first two decades of the nineteenth century and *Don Juan*, and a short oriental tale by Maria Edgeworth of 1802, illustrate both the new stress on spatial and visual comprehension of the Orient and a newly ironic perspective on the observing 'western' eye.

2

SHAPE-SHIFTING: ORIENTAL TALES

Fadlallah and Zemroude: transmigratory desires

The impoverished Prince Fadlallah of Mousel[1] wins the hand in marriage of a lovely young virgin of Baghdad named Zemroude by pretending to be a mighty prince of Basra. She remains loyal to him on discovery of the cheat, and soon after he inherits the throne of Mousel. They live together in wealth and happiness until he becomes fascinated by a handsome and apparently unworldly young dervish (a Muslim friar). The dervish agrees to show the king the secret he learned from an old brahman of making his 'own Soul enter a Body, which is deprived of Life' (*PT* ii. 332). The king tests his new skill by migrating his soul into the body of a doe killed in hunting, only to find that the dervish has swiftly occupied his own abandoned body. The dervish proceeds to avail himself of the pleasures of the king's throne and bed, but the king now transfers his soul into the body of a nightingale which wins Zemroude's affections through its passionate song. When Zemroude's other favourite pet, a little dog, dies in labour,

---

[1] Mosul, a city in north-western Iraq.

the king reanimates its body, discarding that of the nightingale. The dervish usurper offers to console a grief-stricken Zemroude by reanimating the nightingale so that it can sing to her once more. As soon as the dervish has left the king's body, Fadlallah returns to his 'rightful' form, and strangles the nightingale. Zemroude, however, is devastated by the discovery of her unwitting infidelity and dies of grief, leaving Fadlallah to retire from his throne and live a life of solitude.

This fiction of 'transmigration' was told in François Pétis de la Croix's *Contes Persans* (1710–12) and can be found in English in the second of Ambrose Philips three volumes of translation in 1714–15.[2] It later migrated into a *Spectator* paper (no. 578, Monday, 9 August 1714),[3] in which Eustace Budgell uses the story to demonstrate John Locke's point that a person is defined by consciousness rather than a body or substance which may change over time. Transmigration is also transformation; the bitch that dies delivering her puppies in the *Persian Tales* (suggesting a more sinister anxiety about Zemroude's 'condition'—would a pregnancy resulting from union with the usurping dervish in the king's body be legitimate?) becomes in Budgell's summary simply a lapdog 'lying . . . in a Corner of the Room' (579).

Further transmigration occurred when the Italian playwright Carlo Gozzi took the story to the stage in the shape of his *Il Re Cervo* (1762). In this version, the heroine's virtue is proved by her ability to recognize her true love in his altered state. The story also has a parallel life in the fairy tale given by Charles Perrault in his *Contes de ma Mère l'Oye* of 1697 as 'Puss in Boots', suggesting the transmigratory interdependence of oriental and fairy tale in late seventeenth- and early eighteenth-century France.[4] Here, though, the story is not about the dangers of absolute princes falling prey to the influence of favourites.

---

[2] A rival translation of the *Contes Persans* appeared in 1714 translated by William King with the title *The Persian and Turkish Tales, Compleat*, 2 vols.

[3] Joseph Addison and Richard Steele, *The Spectator*, ed. Donald F. Bond (Oxford: Clarendon Press, 1965), iv. 575–9.

[4] It is unclear whether Pétis de la Croix's tales did have genuine oriental sources. It may be that he 'orientalizes' familiar, especially fairy, tales that were enjoying popular circulation in the decades preceding the Contes Persans. See Marina Warner's comment that 'the huge enthusiasm for literary fairy tales just preceded and then overlapped with the reading public's appetite for Oriental tales, inspired or adapted from the *Arabian Nights*' (Marina Warner, *From the Beast to the Blonde: On Fairy Tales and Their Tellers* (London: Chatto & Windus, 1994), 166).

In 'Puss in Boots', the dervish becomes the hero of the tale, an Aladdin—the idle son with small prospects—who makes his fortune and wins a princess with the aid of the magical powers of a trickster companion, the talking cat who persuades the wealthy ogre to demonstrate his shape-shifting powers and promptly gobbles him up when he takes the form of a mouse. This variant or possible source of the Fadlallah and Zemroude story makes clear the proximity between 'king' and 'dervish', both of whom gain access to Zemroude by inhabiting the identity of an other, whether prince of Basra or king of Mousel.

The shifts the tale undergoes are multiple. In Pétis de la Croix's version, the tale is told by Fadlallah to the young Prince Calaf who, as Fadlallah once was, is in exile from his court. Calaf will go on to mirror Fadlallah by winning, through his own adventurous intelligence, the love of an apparently unattainable woman, the Princess Tourandocte of China.[5] Both stories are delivered within the larger frame of a sequence of stories narrated by the nurse Sutlememé to the lovely princess of Persia, Farruknaz, who stubbornly refuses to contemplate marriage on the grounds that no man can match the fidelity and truth of a woman (and indeed Farruknaz is contemptuous in her judgement of Fadlallah, whom she considers to be lacking in the devotion shown by his wife since he survives her loss and even admits to living happily in his retirement).

The migrations of the story of Fadlallah and Zemroude trace a familiar, if partially fictional, trajectory for the oriental tale; it travels from Persia to France and thence to England. In its first incarnation—Pétis de la Croix's collection of tales full of supernatural event and oriental luxury—the tale suggests parallels between the Persian seraglio and the absolutist court of Louis XIV in France, both spaces of intrigue, duplicity, sexual and political plotting. One of its later incarnations is that of a paragraph in the pages of the English periodical press; the tale now serves to illustrate the new empiricism and politeness of eighteenth-century bourgeois English culture. What happens in this instance does not occur in the theory of transmigration; not only does the story change in shape—both the plot and the

---

[5] The story of Tourandocte was also used as the plot for a play by Gozzi entitled *Tourandotte* of the same year, 1762, as *The King Stag*.

genre are altered—but also in 'spirit', its message quite transformed from the source to 'a Story in some Measure applicable to this Piece of Philosophy' from Locke (iv. 576). Another reanimation routes the tale from French fiction to Italian stage in the shape of Gozzi's script, as one of a group of 'fiabe' ('fairy tale') plays that counter the trend for realistic comedy in eighteenth-century Italian drama.

Such migrations and transmigrations are not unusual in the eighteenth-century history of the oriental tale. Oriental fiction consists of 'shifting shapes' on the level of narrative content: Arabic djinns, lives of the Buddha, animals that become human and vice versa in Indian fable. It requires acts of transmigratory identification on the part of its European reader who projects him or herself into the place of the eastern interlocutor inscribed within oriental narrative. And on the level of meta-narrative, it is also a shape-shifter, undergoing powerful transformation when it migrates in diverse and numerous forms to a new continent in the eighteenth century, never wholly or entirely a fictional invention of the East by the West nor a colonizing or observing traveller maintaining its 'native' dress.[6]

Moreover, the theme of transmigration reminds us that in this period the encounter with the 'Orient' was enabling the discovery of and engagement with non-Islamic religious traditions (Hindu, Buddhist, and Taoist). Such traditions were given no more credence than Islam; all faiths other than Judaeo-Christian are characterized as fictional narratives rather than theological truths in western published writings of the period. But non-Islamic faiths, despite widespread ignorance about their nature until well into the late eighteenth century (when oriental scholars in India began to uncover more accurate information),[7] could present eastern cultures as something other than a monotheistic rival to the Christian West. Indeed, one strain in

---

[6] Oriental sources had been translated and considered in earlier periods, of course, especially in the Middle Ages as a consequence of the encounter with Islam through the Crusades, but never on the scale and in the variety seen in this period and, largely, initiated by Galland's voluminous translation. For earlier instances, see Dorothee Metlitzki, *The Matter of Araby in Medieval England*.

[7] On the late discovery in the late 18th c. of Buddhism's origins in India, as well as a more scholarly and sophisticated understanding of ancient languages and Buddhist philosophy through the activities of a number of East India Company men in India, see Charles Allen, *The Buddha and the Sahibs: the Men Who Discovered India's Lost Religion* (London: John Murray, 2002).

Fadlallah's tale concerns the problematic transmigration between 'idolatrous' religion and Islam: the Muslim friar, the dervish, has learnt the art of shape-shifting from a brahman and Fadlallah's penance after his wife's death involves a pilgrimage to Mecca. European commentators on Islam often complained that 'Mahometans' believed in the resurrection of the body on the day of judgement and that the pleasures of heaven as described by Muhammad[8] were physical and worldly rather than spiritual and transcendent, suggesting some proximity to the theory of reincarnation in Buddhism and Hinduism, since for the latter the intellect/consciousness must inhabit a material body. Of course, Fadlallah's story is an occidental representation of transmigration, one stripped of its philosophical and theological dimensions to become a secular fantasy about shape-shifting. Reincarnation for Buddhists, for instance, does not, except in the highest forms, entail memory of a past life or continuity of personality/ character. Eastern theories of transmigration were frequently conflated with Ovidian metamorphosis, as Budgell indicates when he puts an epigram from Ovid at the head of the paper.[9] In this respect, non-Islamic religions share the same fate as Islam in western representations; eastern theology and philosophy are ostentatiously dismissed or travestied as mere 'story' in order to deny epistemological credit.

Ovid derives his understanding of transmigration from the Greek philosopher Pythagoras who, it was commonly believed, learned the theory of metempsychosis from Indian philosophers while travelling in Egypt. This narrative tradition then can also be traced back to

---

[8] Throughout, I use the spelling 'Muhammad' to refer to the historical person, and 'Mahomet' and variant spellings to refer to the semi-fictional 'character' that features in writings of the period. The term 'Islam' is never used in early modern writings. Most common is 'Mahometanism' or 'Mahometism' and 'Mahometans'.

[9] Eque feris humana in corpora transit, | Inquo feras Noster'. John Dryden translates these lines from the fifteenth book of the *Metamorphosis* as 'Th'unbodied spirit flies— | And lodges, where it lights, in man or beast' ('Of the Pythagorean Philosophy' in *Fables Ancient and Modern* (1700), in *Poems, 1697–1700*, ed. Vinton A. Dearing, *The Works of John Dryden*, vii. (Berkeley and London: University of California Press, 2001), 240–2. Ovid's *Metamorphoses* were translated into English in 1567 by Arthur Golding and again in 1637 by George Sandys, the latter an important source for Dryden's translations in the *Fables*. On the circulation of Ovidian narratives in Europe from the early modern period and after, see Raphael Lyne, *Ovid's Changing Worlds: English Metamorphoses, 1567–1632* (Oxford: Oxford University Press, 2001); and Marina Warner, *Fantastic Metamorphoses, Other Worlds: Ways of Telling the Self*, Clarendon Lectures in English Literature, 2001 (Oxford: Oxford University Press, 2002).

'eastern' sources, although Pythagoras functions as a pretext rather than an important source in Ovid, his vision of an ever-changing universe presented as tedious and tendentious when described in the fifteenth book by contrast with the passion-driven transformations in the tales of the *Metamorphoses*. In the seventeenth and eighteenth centuries likewise, there appear to have been no converts in the West to the theory of transmigration, but considerable enthusiasm for its symbolic or narrative significance. Joseph Addison's essay on 'Transmigration' formed the preface to an early eighteenth-century translation of (entirely fictional) oriental tales by the French lawyer and Orientalist Thomas-Simon Gueullette, called *Chinese Tales* (1725). Addison argues that beliefs in transmigration are evidence of the credulousness and superstition prevalent in the East, concluding that 'they plainly discover a pernicious Design of the Devil, to confound the two Doctrines of the Immortality of the Soul, and of the Resurrection of the Body'.[10] However, elsewhere in his writings, Addison is one of the most active proponents of the use of oriental tales and sources as fables that demonstrate universal human truths: agents of narrative transmigration, indeed. Thus, *Spectator* no. 94 (Monday, 18 June 1711) cites a passage in the Qur'an where Muhammad is taken by Gabriel from his bed to see the seven heavens and hell to demonstrate the variable nature of our perception of time: no. 289 (Thursday, 31 January 1712) takes a story from John Chardin's account of his Persian travels about a dervish who tells a king that his palace is only an intermediate habitation to demonstrate the nature of mortality: no. 293 (Tuesday, 5 February 1712) again quotes Chardin, this time about how a pearl may develop from a drop of water, to prove that advancement is a result of fortune rather than our own actions: no. 535 (Thursday, 13 November 1712) takes a story from Galland's *Arabian Nights Entertainments*—about the idle dreamer who buys glasses with his patrimony but, when he stretches his legs during a daydream about his glittering future prospects, shatters them all—to prove that men of imagination overlook a nearby good in favour of a distant ambition. Addison, then, disavows the supernaturalism in

---

[10] Thomas-Simon Gueullette, *Chinese Tales: or, the Wonderful Adventures of the Mandarine Fum-Hoam* (London, 1725), i, p. xxi.

oriental narratives but asserts the usefulness of the fable, a form he repeatedly derives from the East, as a means of demonstrating empirical truth obliquely.

Over-privileging the Addisonian use of the oriental tale as a vehicle for abstract philosophical principle or general moral precept can, however, obscure the specificity with which different oriental territories are depicted in eighteenth-century writing. The claim of this book is that the forms of the oriental tale shift their shape under the government of different tropes, which evolve as means of representing the three regions that dominated the fictional representation of the Orient: the Persian/Ottoman empires, China, and India. As oriental forms 'inhabit' these different regions they acquire a new shape to accommodate the changing relation between each eastern culture and the Europe that 'represents' it. All the forms of oriental fiction are available as a resource in every region, but each genre undergoes transformation when it migrates from one locale to another. When we speak of the oriental tale we need to recognize both the force and specificity of those imaginative geographies that emerged as a means of representing oriental regions and the pressure of generic determinants in narrative not always specific to the culture represented.

Accounts of European writing about the Orient to date have rarely addressed the interaction between genre and geography. Literary historians such as Martha Pike Conant and Robert L. Mack have viewed the oriental tale as a genre in its own right, without addressing whether different geographical 'contexts' generate different 'shapes' in the tale told.[11] Historians such as Joan Pau Rubiés and Billie Melman look at ethnographic writing about the East and measure it against the geopolitical context of the moment it describes.[12] Bridget Orr's study suggests a fruitful method of enquiry through the exploration of a single genre, the English drama, and its representation of 'empire',

---

[11] Martha Pike Conant, *The Oriental tale in England in the Eighteenth Century*, Columbia University Studies in Comparative Literature (New York: Columbia University Press, 1908); and Robert L. Mack (ed.), *Oriental Tales* (Oxford: Oxford University Press, 1992).

[12] Joan Pau Rubiés, *Travel and Ethnology in the Renaissance: South India through European Eyes, 1250–1625*, Past and Present Publications (Cambridge: Cambridge University Press, 2000); Billie Melman, *Women's Orients: English Women and the Middle East, 1718–1918: Sexuality, Religion and Work* (Basingstoke: Macmillan, 1992).

European and oriental. Orr points out what she describes as the 'double-jointedness in the plays' effects, the process by which exotic differences are exploited at the same time as another culture offers a screen for the projection of local anxieties'.[13] These narratives of empire, she asserts, are not simply or solely allegories of national or local preoccupations; they are also shifting representations of the cultures—Spanish, Persian, Turkish, Indian, Chinese—they stage. The choice of a setting in Mughal India, Ottoman Turkey, or Manchu China, is not entirely arbitrary but motivated and works according to a set of tropes or concept metaphors associated with the region through other genres, especially travel-writing.

I provide a summary in this chapter of the principal forms of writing associated with oriental narrative and illustrate how they shift shape according to region. The summary also reveals that the western construct of the 'Orient' in the late seventeenth and early eighteenth centuries was shaped through the medium and techniques of narrative fiction, even in ostensibly non-fictional forms such as the traveller's account or the 'general history' of a state/people; thus, the 'Orient' could be defined as a species of fiction itself, a hybrid and manufactured product of imaginative investments on the part of the West.

The framed sequence

Oriental fiction is most often associated with the long sequence of tales more or less loosely held together by a 'frame narrative'. The narrative paradigm is, of course, the 'translation' from Arabic by the distinguished oriental scholar Antoine Galland in twelve compendious volumes published between 1704 and 1717 in France as *Mille et une Nuit*.[14] Each volume was published in anonymous translation in

---

[13] Bridget Orr, *Empire on the English Stage, 1660–1714* (Cambridge: Cambridge University Press, 2001), 11.

[14] Muhsin Mahdi in his introductory chapter to the Arabic text of *The Thousand and One Nights*, entitled 'Antoine Galland and the Nights', summarizes Galland's sources and the sequence of their translation and publication. He began in 1701 with a translation from a single manuscript containing 'Sindbad' which he obtained in Constantinople. However, the first volume did not contain 'Sindbad' and, up to vol. vii (1706), Galland was using

Britain hard on the heels of the French. By 1800 more than eighty collections in English had appeared in imitation of the *Arabian Nights Entertainments*. Galland's concoction provided the blueprint for imitators, but it is surprising how quickly the imitations of Galland's collection—which is drawn from various ethnic origins (Indian, Persian, and Arabic), and locates stories as far afield as China, Egypt, Mongolia, Arabia, Syria, Russia, and India—became known by the country of the frame narrative. Hence, François Pétis de la Croix's collection of 'contes' known in France as *Les Mille et un Jour* appeared under the title of *Persian Tales* in Ambrose Philips's English translation of 1714–15. His *Turkish Tales*, translated by William King and others, was first published in English in 1708.

Sequences of oriental tales share the common device of the 'frame' in which a lower order figure (the enslaved woman in the seraglio; or the sage, whether Brahman or imam; or the sultan's deputy, the vizier) uses narrative to instruct a ruler or potential ruler in the art of government, both of self and state. Framed sequences of tales with a Persian or Turkish frame incline to put the voice of the storyteller in the figure of a woman or a wily vizier. A collection of tales by the Comte de Caylus, translated into English in 1745 under the simple title *Oriental Tales*, is told by the gatekeeper's daughter, Moradbak, under instruction from an imprisoned and out-of-favour vizier, Aboumclck, to the despotic Persian ruler Hudjadge, in order to lull him to sleep each night. Pétis de la Croix's *Turkish Tales* are a storytelling battle between a vizier and a favourite wife, following an accusation of attempted rape by the latter against the sultan's heir; the sultana counters tales of unfaithful women who have endangered their husband's authority told by the vizier with her own tales of deceitful and disloyal sons and councillors.

three volumes of an Arabic manuscript purchased at Aleppo, dating from the 14th or 15th c. and assembled in Egypt—the earliest manuscript version of the Arabic *Alf Layla wa-Layla* that we have—and thereafter kept in Louis XIV's library. He inserted the Sindbad tales in his third volume and also incorporated tales from a separate unidentified Arabic manuscript volume of tales. Vol. viii was rushed out by his publishers probably without his involvement and contains two stories translated from a Turkish manuscript by fellow Orientalist, François Pétis de la Croix, and one story translated by Galland already in his publisher's hands. Vol. ix–xii were compiled by Galland from manuscripts obtained for him by a Syrian Maronite Christian from Aleppo and also told to him by the same man. He invented the conclusion (Mahdi, *The Thousand and One Nights*, iii. 11–49).

European 'translators' argue that the parabolic tale or 'fable' is an important instrument for an enslaved populace to criticize and correct an absolute ruler, harnessing the reports of travellers and historians about the absolutist nature of oriental rule in the service of structuring a disparate collection of tales. Thus, Joseph Harris in his faithful translation of the original French preface to a version of the Indian collection of fables, *The Fables of Pilpay* (1699, translated from Gilbert Gaulmin's 1698 *Les Fables de Pilpay*) asserts that:

> *one of the Reasons which oblig'd the Eastern People, to make use of Fables in their Instructions and Admonitions was, because the Eastern Monarchies being for the most part Despotic, their Subjects are no less restrain'd from Freedom of Speech; however being an Ingenious People they found out this way whereby they might be able, without exposing their Lives, to inform and advise their Princes who treat 'em as Slaves, and will not permit 'em the liberty of Speaking what they think.*[15]

Pilpay (or Bidpai), a Brahman hermit, tells the ancient Indian Emperor Dabschelim a series of framed tales, the majority animal fables but many also to do with priests and commoners and all concerned with the importance of recognizing enemies and making allies in government.

By contrast, tales 'translated' or invented from India or China incline to make their frame storyteller a figure of religious authority, a sage. Hence, Thomas-Simon Gueullette's *Chinese Tales* (translated in 1725) are told by a mandarin called Fum-Hoam ostensibly to prove the truth of transmigration theory to a Muslim princess of Georgia newly married to the emperor of China; his *Mogul Tales* (translated in 1736) are orchestrated by an imam named Cothrob who, it transpires, is Fum Hoam's son disenchanted with government and now taking the role of priest/adviser to the troubled king of Gujerat. James Ridley's 1764 *Tales of the Genii* are delivered by another imam, named Horam, to an English governor at Madras but were originally devised for the evil son of the Mughal Emperor Aurangzeb. Ridley concludes his collection by announcing the British Protestant inheritance of the

---

[15] Bidpai, *The Fables of Pilpay [Tr. By J. Harris from the Fr. Tr. Of G. Gaulmin and Dâwûd Sa'îd]*, trans. Joseph Harris (London: 1699), n.p. For a full discussion of the circulation of the fables of Bidpai in early modern Europe, see Ch. 5, section entitled 'The Indian fable: rational animals'.

government of India from Muslim rule. The split between secular and spiritual narrators is most apparent in Alexander Dow's intriguing collection, *Tales, Translated from the Persian of Inatulla of Delhi* (1768), an extremely loose translation of the *Bahâr-e dânes* by the seventeenth-century Persian officer, man of letters, and later Sufi, Inâyat-Allâh Kanbû. The majority of the tales are told by ministers at the court of 'Hindostan' to the young prince Jehandar, to dissuade him from his obsessive love for a Chinese princess by demonstrating the infidelity of women, but a short sequence of six tales at the close are given by a Brahman hermit to the prince to instruct him in moral restraint and the virtuous pursuit of love and glory. Dow, a soldier in the Bengal infantry under Robert Clive, here presents a critique of the sexual and moral corruption of Muslim rule in India and imagines an alliance between Christian governors and Hindu priests as a model for the new British authority in India.

The sequence of oriental tales in the eighteenth century could serve at least two purposes simultaneously: it could, like Ridley's collection, imagine the succession of a European Christian power to government in some eastern regions, particularly Britain in India; and it could explore the changing nature of government in the West. The female and prime-ministerial narrators of the Turkish and Persian sequences contest absolutism and voice the possibility of a civil, constitutional order and empire founded on peaceful trade and individual self-government.

The oriental tales derived from and set in China prove an exception, in that western states settled for trading relationships rather than aspired to government or engaged in protracted territorial conflict in the region. Perhaps as a consequence, the West tended to view Chinese absolutism as a form of gentle patriarchalism rather than violent despotism. Never imagined as a colonial or imperial possibility, characterized as a secular absolutist state of enormous longevity and security (if declining into a state of stagnant xenophobia), China becomes, paradoxically, the most fully transmigratory fictional space of the period. Sequences of Chinese tales such as Gueullette's, or d'Alenzon's *The Bonze* (1769), take the trope of transmigration as the frame narrative itself. Both narrate a series of fantastic reincarnations by a single figure which traverses the globe and the animal and human kingdoms. This literary 'chinoiserie' appears to have been made possible by the very inaccessibility and impermeability of China to Europe.

Travellers' tales

The accounts of European travellers—largely by missionaries, diplomats, and traders—were perhaps the most influential means of 'mapping' the different territories of the East for European consumers. From the circulation of manuscript copies of *The Book of Ser Marco Polo* in the late thirteenth century and the *Travels* of Sir John Mandeville in the mid-fourteenth century, through the appearance in print in the mid-fifteenth century of popular collections of travellers' tales—especially Richard Hakluyt's *Principall Navigations, Voiages, Traffiques and Discoveries* (1589) and Samuel Purchas's 'continuation' *Hakluytus Posthumous or Purchas his Pilgrimes* (1625)—European readers had been accustomed to a free combination of apparently accurate data and fictional or legendary narrative in the depiction of the globe, especially the far East.[16] Joan Pau Rubiés acutely observes, however, that the end of the seventeenth century saw a departure in travel-writing from the tradition inaugurated by Mandeville and Marco Polo of 'universal cosmography . . . guided by the desire to define the place of newly discovered religious diversity in a Christian frame-work' (351), to an increasingly secular rationalism identified with a 'curious' traveller claiming empirical rather than scriptural authority for the interpretation of cultural difference or similarity. We might note, also, that the publication of collections of oriental and pseudo-oriental writings and cultural dictionaries such as Barthélemy d'Herbelot's *Bibliothèque Orientale* (1697), itself translated from an Arabic source,[17] began to provide travellers with different narrative

---

[16] For some of these materials and an excellent introduction see Kenneth Parker (ed.), *Early Modern Tales of Orient: A Critical Anthology* (London: Routledge, 1999).

[17] The main source was Hajjī Khalīfa's bibliographical work *Kashf al-Zunūn*, along with a number of other manuscripts held in Paris's Royal Library and published texts in Arabic from the Netherlands and England (G. J. Toomer, *Eastern Wisedome and*

frameworks from the conventional models derived from Christian scripture, classical antiquity, and feudal romance. Even while they claimed empirical knowledge as their primary authority, travellers to the East begin to show an awareness of 'eastern story' as an aid to comprehension. Hence, Lady Mary Wortley Montagu concludes a description penned to her sister, Lady Mar, from Constantinople on 10 March 1718 of the splendour and wealth of the quarters of Hafise, favourite of Mustapha II, with the aside: 'This is but too like, says you, the Arabian tales; these embrodier'd Napkins, and a jewel as large as a Turkey's egg!—You forget, dear Sister, those very tales were writ by an Author of this Country and (excepting the Enchantments) are a real representation of the manners here' (10 March 1718, *CLMWM* i. 385).

Eastern 'story' is not only a source of scene or plot for travel writers, but also style. François Bernier, physician and sceptical philosopher in the tradition of Gassendi, spent fourteen years of his life between 1655 and 1668 exploring Asia, most of them in India. In 1668, just prior to his return, he writes to Claude-Emmanuel Chapelle from Persia that he plans to pursue his conviction that there is a rational intelligent divinity beyond matter when he resumes his studies in France. He does so in terms which demonstrate how his encounters with Sufism, with Brahman thought, and with the Persian language, have coloured his ideas: 'you must resolve for once to endure the Style of these Countries of *Asia*, the Air of which I have breathed so long.'[18]

Bernier's description was confined to India alone, but other travellers provided more comprehensive accounts, especially the French Huguenot jewel-trader Jean-Baptiste Tavernier and the curious French traveller Jean de Thévenot. Both traversed Persia, Turkey, and India and their published descriptions were swiftly translated into English on their appearance in the late seventeenth century, remaining popular throughout the eighteenth century. Tavernier's

---

Learning: The Study of Arabic in Seventeenth-Century England (Oxford: Clarendon Press, 1996), 35).

[18] François Bernier, *A Continuation of the Memoires of Monsieur Bernier, Concerning the Empire of the Great Mogol*, trans. Henry Oldenburg et al. (London, 1672), 21–2. Bernier's *The History of the Late Revolution of the Empire of the Great Mogul* was translated in 1671 by Henry Oldenburg, who produced the *Continuation of the Memoires* in 1672. All subsequent references are cited as *History or Continuation*.

preface announces: 'in my six Voyages, and by travelling different Roads, I had the leisure and opportunity to see all *Turky*, all *Persia*, and all *India*; particularly the famous Diamond Mines, where no *European* had been before me. Of these three great Empires therefore have I resolv'd to make an ample and exact Description.'[19] The claim to a true witness based on a long stay in the country described was the founding rhetorical gambit in the traveller's account. The preface to the English translation of the work, compiled from the daily memoir of Thévenot's travels, asserts:

The extraordinary Exactness of our Judicious Traveller, in observing the Minutest Particular of any thing that occurred to him abroad, may be dislik'd perhaps, by some who mind their pleasure more than their profit, in Reading the Relations of Travels, and had rather be shamm'd with some Romantick idle Tales, than instructed in real and substantial Truths.[20]

However, the claim to 'exactness', and 'ample and exact Description' is rarely reinforced by the use of a first-hand first-person narrative description of the individual traveller's experiences. The travels of Tavernier and Thévenot progress by tracing the routes they take through eastern regions, recording the nature of the roads and their perils for the European traveller. Each are punctuated by chapters that open out into generalized 'Politick and Historical Description', as Tavernier terms it, of classes and types of people, customs, manners, dress, geography, government, flora and fauna. Third-person accounts of 'Persians', 'Turks', 'Moguls', and 'Indians' serve to differentiate, hierarchize, and classify different eastern cultures. Thévenot, for example, shows a marked preference for Ottoman over Persian culture, complaining of Persian arrogance, aggression, and extravagance by contrast with the modesty and order he admires in Ottoman Turkey. Both view the 'Great Mogul' of India as the most wealthy and powerful of the eastern monarchs and both are interested in highlighting the contrast between 'Mahometan' and 'gentile' populations in India.

---

[19] Jean Baptiste Tavernier, *The Six Voyages of John Baptista Tavernier ... Through Turky into Persia and the East-Indies.*, trans. John Philips (London: 1677), n.p.

[20] Jean de Thévenot, *The Travels of Monsieur De Thevenot into the Levant*, trans. Archibald Lovell (London: 1687), n.p.

The rare occasions when travel writers slip into the first person prove to be the most interesting and illuminating moments in these compendious and much-travelled texts. Here, the 'transmigratory' nature of the encounter between cultures becomes more apparent and the traveller shifts from the role of 'witness' to that of judge and/or sympathetic jury. 'Selective identification' with different cultures becomes suddenly, sometimes surprisingly, visible. In the case of India, the representation of the practice of suttee (most often termed 'widow-burning' by European informants) among the Hindu population has a special status in western travel-writing; it is a requisite, often formulaic, element in any account. The author testifies that he has witnessed the event and expresses both his revulsion at the act and his sympathy with the female victim. Hence, Bernier in a letter of 1667 to his friend Jean Chapelain writes:

Concerning the Women that have actually burn'd themselves, I have so often been present at such dreadful spectacles, that at length I could endure no more to see it, and I retain still some horrour when I think on't . Yet I shall represent to you some of them, but pretend not to express to the life, with what courage and resolution these poor Women atchieved such a direful Tragedy; for there is nothing but the Eye it self that can exhibite a right *idea* thereof. (*Continuation*, 118)

The authenticity of the narrating self (the 'I') is confirmed by the testimony of the viewer (the 'eye'), even as the object described is presented as beyond expression. Again, it is narrative precedent that proves the means of 'comprehending' an act apparently beyond western representation. Bernier cites a parallel in Iphigenia's willing sacrifice for the sake of her father Agamemnon who seeks to pacify the Gods and secure a good wind to take his forces to Troy (128). The 'choice' of the sati can thus be 'explained' through the classical tradition of the national heroine.[21] Bernier's role is not only as witness,

---

[21] On European, especially British, attitudes to suttee from the 18th c. onward, see Monika Fludernik, 'Suttee Revisited: From the Iconography of Martyrdom to the Burkean Sublime', *New Literary History* 30 (1999): 411–37. I follow Monika Fludernik in using 'the Anglo-Indian term *suttee* to refer to the ceremony of immolation, and the term *sati* to denote the woman who thus sacrifices herself (or is coerced to do so)', 413. See also Rajeswari Sunder Rajan, *Real and Imagined Women: Gender, Culture, and Postcolonialism* (London: Routledge, 1993).

however. He gives a succession of stories concerning satis, and describes his attempts to dissuade the widow of a deceased friend from her determination, when those of her family and the Muslim authorities have failed. The positioning of the European male as a bridge between a 'gentile' native culture and a declining Muslim authority in India was to prove an attractive ideological strategy for ascendant European powers in India through the course of the century after the publication of Bernier's memoirs.

Travellers' accounts of China did not develop along the empirical and subjective lines that began to be explored by writers about Turkey such as Mary Wortley Montagu and India such as Bernier, perhaps because traders and ambassadors did not achieve the same cultural and territorial penetration as in other eastern empires. Access to the Chinese mainland and particularly Peking was debarred to traders who were confined to the coastal regions and, after 1760, to Canton. The accounts of China circulating in England and France in the eighteenth century were almost exclusively compiled from the 'lettres édifiantes' of Jesuit missionaries who from the mid-sixteenth century had established themselves through their mathematical and astronomical skills with successive Chinese emperors. Jesuit accounts were geared towards defending the viability of their mission in China by presenting the territory as a secular absolutist state, and Confucianism as an ethical system compatible with Christianity. Hence, Jesuits consistently represented Buddhism and Taoism as amalgams of idolatrous superstition perpetuated by itinerant and ignorant priests with no strong foothold in the country. They celebrated Confucianism, the ancientness of absolutist rule, and the deference to learning in China as signs of its receptiveness to their Catholic mission. The *Memoirs and Observations* of the Jesuit Louis Le Comte were translated from the French and published in 1697, taking the form of a series of letters to different correspondents in France. These letters detailed customs, manners, beliefs, and architecture in China but could easily be retitled for the second edition of 1739 as *A Compleat History of the Empire of China*, given that they were devoid of anecdote or first-person commentary.

The case of China, however, does share with other travel-writings the strong recurrence of a satirical vein. The traveller can deploy the eastern culture he describes as a means of criticizing European prejudices and practices. Le Comte can assert that when the government of Holland (Protestant rival to Catholic France) was described to the Chinese 'they looked upon a Republick to be a Monster with many Heads, formed by the ambition, headiness, and corrupt inclination of Men in times of publick disorder and confusion'.[22] The Protestant Whig Lady Mary Wortley Montagu consistently contrasts Muslim Turkey favourably with Catholic France and Spain, argues that Turkish subjects have more freedom under an absolutist ruler in thrall to his armies than English subjects would do under Tory exercise of constitutional monarchy, and revels in the freedom afforded her by the adoption of the veil in the streets of Istanbul by comparison with the constraint of society life for an aristocratic woman in England.

Fictional letters

Whereas the factual accounts of travellers—often in the form of letters and laced with fictional or semi-fictional narratives about the history and culture of eastern regions—were marked by impersonality and a claim to objective if empirical witness, fictional letters in the 'voice' of the eastern informant tended to the reverse. They were constructed to provide evidence of a kind of 'signature' derived from the stereotypes associated with the informant's culture. Whereas satire is a vein within European travel accounts it is the *raison d'être* of the fictional 'oriental' letter. Here too, however, eastern cultures are carefully differentiated and the informant voice put to different uses depending on the culture it 'ventriloquizes'. And here too, the genre of the eastern informant letter migrated to England via France in the shape of *L'Espion Turc* (1684–96) by the expatriate Italian journalist Giovanni Paolo Marana (translated 1687–94 from French and Italian by William Bradshaw) and Charles Montesquieu's *Lettres Persanes* (1721, translated in 1722 by John Ozell), both of which went into numerous editions and were widely imitated in eighteenth-century Britain. Marana's collection of letters was produced in the year after the Ottoman defeat at Vienna in

[22] Louis Le Comte, *A Compleat History of the Empire of China* (London, 1739), 243.

1683, which marked the beginning of the long retreat of the Ottomans in mainland western Europe. However, they were purportedly written between 1637 and 1682 when the 'spy' Mahmut, an educated Arabian and member of a minor 'Pythagorean' Turkish sect (hence, holding a belief in transmigration), lived concealed at Paris and reported on French manners, government, and policy to a variety of powerful correspondents in Turkey. Like Le Comte's letters, Mahmut's are carefully targeted to their recipients; he details the strength of European armies in letters to the General of the Janissaries, the behaviour of French women in letters to seraglio eunuchs, the state of the French king's coffers and his own to the chief treasurer and so forth. The preface to the reader asserts that:

By these [letters] may be known the Perspicacity of this Agent of the Turks; and by him the Prudence of those that command in that Nation, who chose (the better to penetrate into the Affairs of Christians) a Man, who could not be suspected by his Exterior; who was deform'd, but prudent and advised; and, for the better concealing him, destined his ordinary Abode in one of the greatest and most peopled Cities of Europe.[23]

As Ottoman powers declined through the course of the eighteenth century, the idea of the 'spy' lost its political and incendiary associations and became attached to the more general sense of the 'informant', an observer who by virtue of his (and it is always his) distance from the culture he occupies is able to provide a defamiliarized sense of its absurdity. Although the oriental tale continued through the century to be an important vehicle for overtly political satire through analogy and allegory (examples include satires on Robert Walpole such as Eliza Haywood's 'Chinese' novel of 1736, *The Adventures of Eovaai*, and George Lyttelton's Turkish tale *The Court Secret* of 1741), eastern letter fictions increasingly took the form of Montesquieu's more wide-ranging critique of social, religious, and cultural mores in Europe expressed in the voice of an oriental visitor. Montesquieu's representation of Persia, however, as Lisa Lowe has astutely pointed out, functions as both opposite and analogue to its near anagram, Paris. The Persian letter writer Rica contrasts Persian rule with

---

[23] Giovanni Paolo Marana, *The Eight Volumes of Letters Writ by a Turkish* Spy, trans. William Bradshaw, 6th edn. (London, 1707), n.p.

French and expresses some enthusiasm for French rationalism and law, the freedom of French women and the more representative nature of French government, but the account of the eventual collapse of his authority through the rebellion of the women in the harem he has left behind suggests an allegory with the 'absolutist' rule of Louis XIV, and the peasants' revolt following his death in 1715 under Philippe d'Orléan's regency.[24]

Letters in the voices of eastern informants continued to maintain this 'doubled' critique, both of oriental and of occidental cultures, in which what appears to be difference is often revealed to be (sometimes uncomfortable) proximity. It is perhaps unsurprising, then, that as the form evolved and relations between Europe and eastern territories shifted, especially with the emergence of British empire in India, the letter fiction moved eastwards. Whereas pseudo-Turkish and pseudo-Persian informant voices of the late seventeenth and early eighteenth centuries suggested a genuine conflict for authority between competing powers on European terrain and direct historical analogies between oriental and occidental rulers, by the mid-eighteenth century and onward, the informant voice from China was represented as insightful precisely because of a lack of cultural correspondence and shared geographical experience.

Jean Baptiste de Boyer's *Lettres Chinoises*, translated into English in 1741, announced the 'difference' in the voice of the Chinese informant:

here we have a new Scene; we see a Comparison drawn between the Manners of several European Nations and those of the Chinese; a People so singular in every thing, that it has given Occasion for abundance of new Reflections, which cannot fail to edify, as well as entertain. . . . To conclude, every body knows that CHINA *is a Country where the Sciences are carefully cultivated, and that the* Jesuits *have made it the* Theatre *of their* Missions, *which alone would furnish Materials sufficient for several Volumes.*[25]

Boyer, like Montesquieu, uses the eastern letter collection to produce a critical and libertine satire on Europe and to question the extent of its

[24] Lisa Lowe, *Critical Terrains: French and British Orientalisms* (Ithaca, NY, and London: Cornell University Press, 1991), 52–74.
[25] Jean Baptiste de Boyer, *Chinese Letters, Tr. [or Rather, Written] by the Marquis D'argens, and Now Done into English* (London, 1741), i, p. xx.

supposed 'Enlightenment'. Central to this project was the use of a non-Islamic culture which could push further the critique of monotheistic Christianity (to which Islam was more often paralleled than contrasted). The figure of the 'Chinese' informant in Boyer and Oliver Goldsmith, who based his *Citizen of the World* (1762) on information in Boyer, is contrasted with the 'barbaric' Turk or Moor. Lien Chi Altangi complains (Letter 33) that when he meets English company they fail to distinguish him from his spy forebears: 'They make no distinction between our elegant manners, and the voluptuous barbarities of our eastern neighbours. . . . To be born out of England, and yet have common sense! impossible! He must be some Englishman in disguise; his very visage has nothing of the true exotic barbarity.'[26] The highly educated Chinese scholar, already well informed about Europe through the information of Jesuit missionaries in China, becomes more than a vehicle for alienation effects in relation to European mores; he also serves as a figure for 'Enlightenment' itself, the epitome of reason. And he can also serve as a means of identifying the limits of Enlightenment reason and recognizing the continuing attractions of narrative romance, and instinctual passion. Ventriloquizing an 'eastern' informant provided European writers with the opportunity to celebrate as well as critique their native cultures. Charles Gildon's *The Post-Boy Rob'd of his Mail* (1706) includes a series of letters from an 'Asiatic' correspondent to an English knight that are opened by a bored club of young hell-raisers. The Asiatic, probably Chinese, correspondent falls in love with a Spanish nun named Euthalia, and finally elopes with her back to his homeland. He comments that 'What my own Native *Asia*, with all her Ease, and Luxury, cou'd ne'er effect, this bright Maid has done. The Bulwarks of *Philosophy*, with all the Pallizadoes of her Precepts, that us'd to guard me from the Follies and Knaveries of Mankind, are quite blown up, and all the strong, regular Fortifications, rais'd by repeated and judicious Observations are now dismantl'd'.[27]

---

[26] Oliver Goldsmith, *The Citizen of the World*, ed. Arthur Friedman, *Collected Works of Oliver Goldsmith* (Oxford: Clarendon Press, 1966), ii. 142.

[27] Charles Gildon, *The Post-Boy Rob'd of His Mail: Or, the Pacquet Broke Open, Letters. Both Vols. In One*, 2nd edn. (London, 1706), 242.

Goldsmith extends the form of the informant letter by weaving a love story into the satirical pattern. The distinction between the Far and Near East Lien Chi insists upon in Letter 33 becomes the basis of a fictional plot which sees Lien Chi's son, Hingpo, who has been exiled from China on suspicion of disloyalty to the emperor, save a beautiful woman named Zelis from Arab marauders only to lose her again to Russian bandits; he is restored to her when he comes to London and finds she has escaped to her native country and is in fact the English niece of his father's dearest English friend, known only as the 'man in black'. China and Britain, two centres of civility, enlightenment, and culture, find each other in the barbaric Near East. The civility, politeness, and romantic idealism of the Chinese is here proved to be closer to western European values than the near eastern cultures which had previously dominated the letter-fiction form.

Through these fictional inventions on the part of European writers we can trace the changing map of the Orient in the European imagination. Individual narratives themselves trace a movement towards proximity of Orient and Occident. They open with a series of startling alienations when the eastern informant physically experiences his difference from the West, expresses his shock at the total 'otherness' of the aesthetics and manners of European culture, and experiences his own 'otherness' in the curiosity and incomprehension he prompts in those he meets. Subsequent letters chart increasing habituation and acquaintance with Europe, and resolution is effected in recognizing the relativity of custom and the universality of human virtue.

Histories

Eighteenth-century 'histories' of the Orient encompassed accounts of both recent and ancient history, most often detailing the reigns of successive emperors or sultans in eastern states, and individual lives, especially the often retold life of Muhammad. As with the traveller's tale, the refutation of fictional sources was often a means of rehearsing them, whether in the case of Aaron Hill's conjectural account of the harem at Istanbul which he never entered, or Henri Boulainvillier's dismissal of the fictions generated by Christian authors to discredit Muhammad's claims as prophet.[28] The term 'generall historie' or 'description' was reserved to describe writing that narrated the story of a state or states, national or civic pasts; an influential example was Richard Knolles's 1603 *The Generall Historie of the Turkes* which Paul Rycaut extended to become in 1678 *The History of the Turkish Empire*, the historical companion to his 1668 account, *The Present State of the Ottoman Empire*. Jean-Baptiste Du Halde's composite account of China from Jesuit records was called *A Description of the Empire of China* when translated in 1738. The term 'history' or 'little history' (from the French *histoire*) was reserved for fictional tales concerning an individual and was commonly used in translation as a title for individual tales in the long sequence of oriental tales (such as 'The history of King Fadlallah'). An account of a genuine historical figure was more often signalled by a title such as Henri Boulainvilliers' *The Life of Mahomet* (1730).

Despite apparent differences in content, histories of Muhammad's life and histories of the Ottoman, Mughal, or Chinese empires did not differ much from each other in formal terms. The former tended to open with lengthy descriptions of Arabia in the period—its geography, customs, peoples—before proceeding to describe Muhammad's life as derived from reading in Arabic sources. This was a formula very similar to the one evident in accounts of the Mughal emperors in India, or the Ottomans in Turkey, which introduced the region and then proceeded to a series of summary accounts of individual rulers. Du Halde's 'Description' of China included 'Annals' of the Chinese emperors, a summary of the Confucian books, and a section that reproduced stories and a fourteenth-century play in translation for his readers. Fictional sources were thus set alongside historical and state documents to produce a compendious impression of the territory represented.

---

[28] Aaron Hill, *A Full and Just Account of the Present State of the Ottoman Empire in all its Branches: With the Government, and Policy, Religion, Customs, and Way of Living of the Turks, in General* (London, 1709); and Henri Comte de Boulainvilliers, *The Life of Mahomet*, trans. John Gagnier (London, 1731). The latter was translated from Boulainvilliers' 1730 *La Vie de Mahomet*.

Accounts of the lives of eastern emperors, and especially their more outrageous acts of sexual despotism, fit within a broader narrative frame which is the familiar account of the rise and decline of ambitions to universal monarchy. The collapse of oriental empire is most often blamed on degeneracy in the seraglio, in the shape of sexual excess, the influence of favourites (especially eunuchs), and a retreat from political to domestic concerns. Thus Paul Rycaut, English ambassador to Smyrna, concludes in his *Present State of the Ottoman Empire* (1668) that 'flattery and imoderate subjection hath doubtless been the cause of the decay of the *Turkish* discipline in the Time of Sultan *Ibrahim*, when Women governed, and now in this present age of Sultan Mahomet, whose Counsels are given chiefly by his Mother, Negroes, Eunuchs, and some handsome young Mosayp or Favourite'.[29]

However, oriental courts function alternately as both analogue and opposite. Hence, parallels can be made between the fates of particular rulers in Orient and Occident. Rycaut's *History of the Turkish Empire* (1678) gives an account of the insurrection against and eventual murder of Sultan Ibrahim in 1648 and concludes with an anecdote that suggests a parallel between the near contemporary fates of Charles I and the Turkish sultan:

In this manner Sultan *Ibrahim* ended his Days, which puts me in mind of the saying of a wiser and a better King than he, *That there is little distance between the Prisons and the Graves of Princes.* And this Example made a great Officer understand how King *Charles* the Glorious Martyr was put to Death. For he, I think it was the Great Vizier, falling into discourse with the Chief English Interpreter at *Constantinople*, not then calling to mind the Fate of Sultan *Ibrahim*; demanded, How, and when King *Charles* was put to Death? Sure, said he, Your King must have no Power, or your People must be more Rebellious and Mutinous than other Nations of the World, who durst commit an Act so horrid and vile as this. See, said he, How our Emperor is revered and observed; and how submissive and obedient half the World is to the Nod of our Great Monarch. To which the Interpreter replyed, that to recount unto him the History and Occasion of this prodigious fact, would be too long and

---

[29] Separately numbered in Richard Knolles and Paul Rycaut, *The Turkish History. With a Continuation, Whereunto Is Added the Present State of the Ottoman Empire, by Sir P. Rycaut*, 6th edn. (London, 1687), ii, bk. 1, ch. 3, p. 4.

tedious for him to hear: but that the time it happened, was some Months after the Death or Murder of Sultan *Ibrahim*; which was an *Item* sufficient to give him a perfect understanding of what he required.[30]

Although oriental histories represent expansionist and territorial empires (as opposed to the Dutch and English burgeoning naval and trading models) as destined to crumble under their own weight, this does not mean that they do not differentiate between them. By comparison with the characterization of Ottoman rulers as voluptuaries or tyrants, some admiration was evident for the Mughal emperors. Histories of India in the late seventeenth and eighteenth centuries traced the Mughal dynasty from Tamerlane to Aurangzeb, detailing in particular the accession of Aurangzeb in 1656 and the internecine conflicts with his brothers to seize the throne from Shah Jahan. These accounts claim to rival western traditions of heroism (epic) and romance. The Jesuit priest Father Catrou, who translated the manuscript memoirs of a Venetian doctor, Niccolo Manucci, into French in 1701, explains in his 'Author's Preface' that, although he only came across the work by accident, its tale of the Mughal emperors turned out to be one of heroic dynasty:

Who dreams of going in quest of Hero's as far off as the Indies, *while we have so many left in* Europe, *whose Memory moulders away for want of a Historian? How cou'd I possibly resolve on making in a distant Country all the necessary researches for tracing the Succession of the Emperors, who now Reign in* Indostan? *I was not Ignorant how small a Concern we in* Europe *have for Princes unknown, whose Interests are so little intermixt with our own. Our prejudices on this Head are no Secret.*[31]

China emerges with most credit from the exercise of comparison, largely because the Jesuit legacy viewed Confucianism as a secular morality, gave little credence to the popular authority of Buddhism, and hence argued that the Chinese invested their emperors with the role of divinities in the absence of rival conceptions of religious authority. In the case of China, despotic government does not

[30] Knolles and Rycaut, *Turkish History*, ii. 79.
[31] François Catrou, *The General History of the Mogol Empire, from Its Foundation by Tamerlane, to the Late Emperor Orangzeb. Extracted from the Memoirs of M. Manouchi, a Venetian, and Chief Physitian to Orangzeb for above Forty Years* (London, 1709), n.p.

necessarily imply abuse of power and inevitable revolt. Jean-Baptiste Du Halde summarizes: 'There is no Monarchy whose Government is more despotic than that of *China*. The Emperor is vested with absolute Authority, and to appearance is a kind of Divinity; The Respect that is paid him amounting to a sort of Adoration.'[32]

Central to the construction by the West of a discourse about 'oriental despotism' is the figure of 'Mahomet', who is cast as an early Arab paradigm for the Asiatic rulers; he is described by the majority of western 'biographers' as a low-born opportunist whose sway over his followers was maintained through a claim to divine inspiration and an aggressive military and expansionist policy which distracted from domestic disquiet, while he placed himself outside of his own law, and indulged his sensual desires to the full.[33] Islam is consistently presented in European writings, drawing on a tradition that dated back to the Crusades, as an extravagant fiction, an 'imposture'. Humphrey Prideaux concludes that 'a medley made up of *Judaism*, the several *Heresies* of the *Christians* then in the *East*, and the old *Pagan* Rites of the *Arabs*, with an Indulgence of all Sensual Delights, [Islam] did too well answer his Design in drawing men of all sorts to the embracing of it'.[34] Given the proximity of Islamic empire to seventeenth-century European states it was politically expedient to understand the nature of the faith, but ideologically necessary to discredit it. In an admonition appended to the English translation of André du Ryer's French translation of the Qur'an, the translator presents the text as an oriental narrative imported to England via France, full of fantastic incident that could only be given credence by the ignorant:

Good Reader, the great Arabian *Impostor now at last after a thousand years, is by way of* France *arrived in* England, & *his* Alcoran, *or gallimaufry of Errors, (a Brat as deformed as the Parent, and as full of heresies, as his scald head was of scurffe) hath learned to speak* English. *I suppose this piece is exposed by the Translator to the publick view, no otherwise then some Monster brought out of*

---

[32] Jean-Baptiste Du Halde, *A Description of the Empire of China and Chinese Tartary, Together with the Kingdoms of Korea, and Tibet*, trans. Emanuel Bowen (London, 1738), i. 241.

[33] See Grosrichard's chapter 'Mahomet beside Himself' in *The Sultan's Court*.

[34] Humphrey Prideaux, *The True Nature of Imposture Fully Displayed in the Life of Mahomet. With a Discourse Annexed, for the Vindication of Christianity from This Charge* (London, 1697), 13.

Africa, *for people to gaze, not to dote upon; and as the sight of a Monster or mishapen creature should induce the beholder to praise God, who hath not made him such; so should the reading of this* Alcoran *excite us both to bless Gods goodness towards us in this Land, who enjoy the glorious light of the Gospel, and behold the truth in the beauty of holiness; as also to admire Gods Judgments, who suffers so many Countreys to be blinded and inslaved with the mishapen issue of* Mahomets *brain, being brought forth by the help of no other Midwifry then of a* Jew *and a* Nestorian, *making use of a tame Pigeon (which he had taught to pick corn out of his Ears) in stead of the holy Ghost, and causing silly people to believe, that in his falling-sickness (to which he was much subject) he had conference with the Angel* Gabriel.[35]

Attempts were made in seventeenth- and eighteenth-century Europe to correct errors about Muhammad and Islam, but largely in order to protect the Christian case against it from countercharges of imposture, extravagant fictionalizing, and invention. Hence, Prideaux in his *The True Nature of Imposture* asserts that the 'whole of this *Imposture* was a thing of extraordinary Craft, carried on with all the Cunning and Caution imaginable' (48) and thus 'whatever Stories are told of this matter that are inconsistent with such a management, we may assure our selves are nothing else but Fables foolishly invented by some zealous *Christians* to blast the *Imposture*, which needed no such means for its Confutation' (49). Stories such as the pigeon trained to peck in Muhammad's ear with a piece of seed passed off as the means of conveying Allah's word to him or the bull who brings the Qur'an to him on its horns must therefore be rejected, not because they are a misrepresentation of a monotheistic and sophisticated religion to rival Christianity, but because they suggest a clumsiness and patent fictionalizing that would have been uncovered earlier and left Islam with a less powerful and convincing empire. Even the outstanding scholar and first professor of Arabic at Oxford University, Edward Pococke, who supervised his son's translation in 1671 from the Arabic of ibn Tufayl's story about the life of Hayy ibn Yaqzan, 'a text which was to prove one of the most influential oriental fictions in the shaping of seventeenth- and

[35] André Du Ryer, *The Alcoran of Mahomet, Translated out of Arabique into French; by the Sieur Du Ryer, Lord of Malezair, and Resident for the King of France, at Alexandria. And Newly Englished, for the Satisfaction of All That Desire to Look into the Turkish Vanities*, trans. Alexander Ross (London, 1649), n.p.

eighteenth-century philosophy and literature', could not give credence to Muhammad. Although Pococke refrained from the general tendency to denounce Islam as barbaric and ignorant, he concurred with the denunciation of Muhammad as a 'false prophet'.[36]

The numerous lives of Muhammad published in the late seventeenth century reveal their authors' sense of a pressing need for European Christians to understand the tenets and principles of a religion commonly understood to have risen to power as a punishment for Christian sectarianism. Indeed, as in the case of other oriental narratives, they have clear satirical and critical purposes, in particular with regard to the dangerous consequences perceived to stem from the popularity of deism in Christian Europe. Prideaux concludes that deists and atheists are driven by the same principle of sensual appetite as 'Mahometans' and argues that Muhammad was able to gain popular support thanks to the split and conflicted nature of the eastern Christian churches.

The rise of Arabic studies and partial defence of Islam in the seventeenth century have also been explained as contributions to Dutch and English Protestant critiques of Roman Catholicism. For most Protestants 'Islam was only a mask through which they denounced their arch enemy—the Church of Rome'.[37] The anonymous author of 'The Life and Actions of Mahomet' in *Four Treatises concerning the Mahometans* (1712) makes a parallel between Islamic and Roman Catholic credulity:

I nothing doubt but several things in my Account of *Mahomet* will appear fabulous to most of my Readers; and some perhaps will think that no Man in his Wits is capable to believe such extravagant Stories as are told of him: But I would have such Persons consider, that a great many Miracles related among us of antient Saints and Martyrs, would appear no less strange and ridiculous to the *Mahometans*, than those that are told of *Mahomet* seem to us; and that there are People of very good Sense and Understanding in all other

---

[36] Toomer, *Eastern Wisedome and Learning*, 224. On the interaction between *Hayy ibn Yaqzan* and John Locke's empirical theory, see G. A. Russell's essay, 'The Impact of the *Philosophus Autodidactus*: Pocockes, John Locke, and the Society of Friends' in G. A. Russell, *The 'Arabick' Interest of the Natural Philosophers in Seventeenth-Century England*, Brill's Studies in Intellectual History 47 (Leiden: Brill, 1994), 224–65.

[37] Ahmad Gunny, *Images of Islam in Eighteenth-Century Writings* (London: Grey Seal, 1996), 6.

things, who can swallow down all the Legends of the Church of *Rome*, how sensless and ridiculous soever they appear to every unprejudic'd Mind.[38]

The same pattern whereby an oriental source could serve as either analogue or opposite to the Occident can thus be traced in the voluminous literature about Muhammad of the period.

The recurrence of the terms 'impostor' and 'imposture' points, however, to the performative nature of the figure of Muhammad. Carrying the double meaning of 'deception' and 'to place in command' or 'to force', the 'imposition' of Islam on other cultures is understood to be both an act of force and an act of performance or counterfeiting. Muhammad's claim to restore Arab culture to its ancient monotheism and to undermine later idolatries and impostures is overridden in favour of presenting Muhammad as a performer who strings together elements from previous cultures—Arab, Christian, and Jewish—to produce a credible counterfeit of religion. Tropes of illegitimacy, hybridity, and bastardization are deployed in these representations which turn the Orient into a hybrid ventriloquism of ancient cultures (in the traditional contestation between oriental and classical empire). The western ventriloquism, indeed 'imposture', of Arabic sources about Muhammad is displaced into the figure himself, who is presented as a ragtag amalgam of half-digested prior truths. The proximity between narrative and dramatic fictions is invoked in the representation of Muhammad as 'impostor' in narrative prose, an association that dramatic depictions of Islamic figures through the eighteenth century were not slow to exploit.

Heroic drama

Unsurprisingly perhaps, Muhammad, along with other oriental rulers, transmigrated onto the European stage, most visibly in the eighteenth century in Voltaire's 1742 play *Mahomet*, adapted by James Miller and James Hoadly in 1744 as *Mahomet the Imposter* for the English stage.

---

[38] *Four Treatises Concerning the Doctrine, Discipline and Worship of the Mahometans* (London, 1712), 6–7.

Miller and Hoadly transport the term 'imposter' from other English and French sources into their title, reinforcing the sense of Muhammad as consummate performer, an actor of a role he has invented to convey his authority, religious and secular. The play is a heroic tragedy set in the eighth year of the hijrah when Muhammad re-entered Mecca and brought an end to paganism by destroying the idols of the Ka'bah. In the entirely fictional play, Mahomet lusts after Palmira, whom he abducted with her brother Zaphna from the family of the head of the Meccan senate, the pagan Alcanor (whose name is, of course, an anagram of the English rendering of the sacred book, Alcoran). Mahomet has raised both children in ignorance of their birth and relationship to each other, while Alcanor believes they were victims in the massacre by Mahomet's forces; Zaphna is tricked by Mahomet into committing the murder of Alcanor, as an act of holy vengeance, when the latter is at prayer. The play concludes with Zaphna poisoned and Palmira stabbed by her own hand, while Mahomet expresses pangs of remorse for his hypocrisy and chicanery.

Routing the arrival of the text in England through France involves transmigration; the English prologue claims that Voltaire's experiences in England prompted his libertarian critique of the established Roman Catholic Church in France. Thus, the play's attack on religious fanaticism can only be truly acknowledged in England where there is a moderate state religion and limited government:

> *TO point what Length's* Credulity *has run,*
> *What Counsels shaken, and what States undone;*
> *What hellish Fury wings th'*Enthusiast's *Rage,*
> *And makes the troubled Earth one Tragick Stage;*
> *What Blasphemies* Imposture *dares advance,*
> *And build what Terrors on weak Ignorance;*
> *How Fraud alone Rage to* Religion *binds,*
> *And makes a* Pandaemonium *of our Minds*;
> *Our* Gallick Bard, *fir'd with these glorious Views,*
> *First to this Crusade led the Tragick Muse;*
> *Her Power through* France *his charming Numbers bore,*
> *But* France *was deaf—for all her Priests were sore.*
>
> *On* English *Ground she makes a firmer Stand,*
> *And hopes to suffer by no hostile Hand.*

No Clergy here usurp the free-born Mind,
Ordain'd to teach, and not enslave Mankind;
Religion *here bids* Persecution *cease,*
Without, *all Order, and within, all Peace;*
Truth *guards her happy Pale with watchful Care,*
And Frauds, *tho'* Pious, *find no Entrance there.*

(n.p.)

From the reign of Elizabeth I onwards, Muhammad (along with
other Muslim figures) was conjured as a 'stage villain' of the most
extreme and monstrous type, even while the English pursued diplomatic and trade relations with a powerful and civilized Ottoman
culture.[39] As Nabil Matar notes, the English produced no anti-
Muslim national epic, unlike Spain (*El Cid, Don Quixote*), France
(*The Song of Roland*), Portugal (*The Lusiads*), and Italy (*Orlando
Furioso*), but 'the theater took up the cudgel against the Muslims and
appealed to a populace that felt threatened by, and confused at, the
appearance of the Muslim Other in their metropolis, in their har-
bors, and across their Mediterranean and Atlantic trading routes'.[40]
Matar concludes that, precisely because the English could not entertain colonial aspirations in relation to Islamic powers in the Renaissance period, they produced 'a discourse—without colonialism—that
was generated by superimposing the conquest of America on Islam'
(17). Hence, Islamic peoples were characterized in this period and
in this form as sodomites, barbarians, and infidels. Bridget Orr
confirms the sense that the heroic drama served as a surrogate 'epic'
for a people new to the experience of empire: 'The heroic drama,
generically invested with imperial authority, was the genre best
equipped to both display and criticize imperial power'.[41] Orr sees
models of empire—territorial and despotic in the case of oriental
states, maritime and commercial in the case of England, or despotic
and colonial in the case of Spain—tested and explored in English
heroic drama.

---

[39] For a discussion of England's commercial, diplomatic, and intellectual engagement
with the Ottomans in the period and the contrast with literary representations, see Nabil I.
Matar, *Islam in Britain, 1558–1685* (Cambridge: Cambridge University Press, 1998).
[40] Nabil I. Matar, *Turks, Moors, and Englishmen in the Age of Discovery* (New York:
Columbia University Press, 1999), 13.   [41] Orr, *Empire on the English Stage*, 38.

The heroic drama in England, like the other forms already discussed, deployed oriental models as both analogue and opposite. Hence, the only play to deal with Mughal history of the seventeenth and eighteenth centuries, John Dryden's 1676 *Aureng-Zebe*, suggested an analogy between Aurangzeb and Charles II. In doing so, it presented the Mughal emperor—contrary to known facts about his militant orthodox Sunni Muslim beliefs—as a gentle and tolerant pacifier by contrast with his fanatical brothers (a reference to the known Catholicism of Charles's brother, James, duke of York). William Hatchett's *The Chinese Orphan* of 1741 reworked a fourteenth-century Chinese play, *The Orphan of Zhao* (translated into French by a Jesuit priest and reproduced in the second volume of Du Halde's *Description*), about the heroic concealment of a young heir to the Chinese throne from the vengeful pursuit of a corrupt minister, as a satire on the corruption of Robert Walpole's prime-ministry. Narratives taken from oriental history and literature could serve as a means of critiquing absolutism and warning against its resurgence on English soil. English women Whig playwrights such as Mary Pix in her 1696 *Ibrahim* celebrated the 'liberty' of companionate monogamous marriage by contrast with the polygamy and enslavement of the seraglio. However, the Tory playwright Delarivier Manley in her *The Royal Mischief* (1695) reversed the equation, presenting a Persian minister as a version of Oliver Cromwell and satirizing Whig/Protestant figures as driven by hidden venal desires that led to the dangerous influence of lust-driven women (Homais, the 'Protector's' promiscuous wife in the play).

Where the heroic drama departs from other genres is that it rarely contemplates or explores non-Islamic oriental models and never represents eastern states and governments outside the framework of absolutism. When pagan or idolatrous religions feature in these plays, ⟩ they serve as analogues to Christianity in their relations with Islam. Hence, Alcanor, the pagan senator of *Mahomet the Imposter*, is a proto-Christian in his concern for human life, as an exchange with the Muslim general Mirvan indicates. Alcanor asserts:

> true Religion
> Is always mild, propitious and humane;
> Plays not the Tyrant, plants no Faith in Blood,
> Nor bears Destruction on her Chariot Wheels,

But stoops to polish, succour, and redress
And builds her Grandeur on the Publick Good.
MIR. Thou art turn'd Christian, sure! Some stragling Monk
Has taught thee these tame Lessons—
ALC. If the Christians
Hold Principles like these, which Reason dictates,
Which all our Notions of the Pow'rs divine
Declare the social Laws they meant for Man,
And all the Beauties and Delights of Nature
Bear witness to, the Christian's may be right.[42]

Numerous oriental tragedies depict a conflict between a virtuous, gentle Christian woman and either the lustful Muslim who pursues her or the eastern courtesan; perhaps the earliest and highly influential example is William Davenant's *The Siege of Rhodes* (first performed in 1656 and extensively revised in 1661). The power struggle between the chaste Christian, Ianthe, and the sexually knowing and wily sultana, Roxolana, is one that is re-enacted in countless Restoration and eighteenth-century oriental tragedies. Pure Christian virtue, if often destroyed by the aggression and violence of the Muslim culture it encounters, always wins the moral argument. So too does a gentle and civilized Chinese femininity when pitted against a militaristic and barbaric Tartar masculinity in Voltaire's Chinese play, *Orphelin de la Chine* (translated into English in 1656 a year after its first production in Paris). The contrast then is between types of culture pitted against each other, represented on stage through dramatic characters, rather than an unambiguous reproduction of the wars between Christianity and Islam that had taken place in European as well as Asian territories.

If the heroic drama is a genre governed by simple and dramatic oppositions, it is important to remember that its status as a form of oriental narrative *experienced in performance* can complicate the reception of such oppositions. As in the case of the 'life' of Muhammad, the performer is simultaneously self and other, carrying the symbolic freight of his or her role but also evidently in his or her own person a representative of the western culture that is creating an image of the East for itself. In other words, when an English

---

[42] François Marie Arouet de Voltaire, *Mahomet: Tragedie* ([s.l.]: [s.n.], 1742), 10.

actor takes the role of Aurangzeb or Mustapha or Muhammad, in his own person he indicates the permeability of a national culture, the possibility that appropriative traffic is never one way: the Orient inhabits him at the same time as he impersonates the Orient. Mita Choudhury's complex and stimulating discussion of Restoration and eighteenth-century theatre's 'interculturalism' prompts a rethinking of a simple claim that plays 'act out' proto-imperial desire on the part of the West. She summarizes her argument as follows:

The Restoration and eighteenth-century London theater's scattered and unsystematic (metaphoric, real, or fictionalized) forays into Other domains ... signal its psychic, intellectual, and material links with distant objectified entities positioned in or belonging to the old world (Italy), along the borders of the civilized realm (Turkey), or in the colonial domains (Surinam and India). In conclusion, I ruminate about the extent to which or if at all the interculturalist desire—sparked by a haphazard combination of peripheral awareness, deliberate confrontation, and chance encounter—transforms into an intercultural consciousness, however self-centered, that is capable of acknowledging the moral and philosophical burdens of empire.[43]

Choudhury's method is well illustrated in her reading of Dryden's *Aureng-Zebe* where she discusses the depiction of male actors in classical, and female actors in contemporary London, dress in a 1735 frontispiece to demonstrate that the play's visible and visual disfigurement of its oriental source, the true story of Aurangzeb, re-enacts symbolically for its audience the 'documentary evidence of lives lived and defeated, of dreams fulfilled and mangled' (144) in the history of Mughal India.

A passion for tales

Tales of the East shift their shape because of changing historical relations between occidental and oriental states and also as a result of

[43] Mita Choudhury, *Interculturalism and Resistance in the London Theater, 1660–1800: Identity, Performance, Empire*, Bucknell Studies in Eighteenth-Century Literature and Culture (Lewisburg, Pa., and London: Bucknell University Press; Associated University Presses, 2000), 22.

the changing demands made of narrative fiction. Whatever the 'shape' of the tale, however, the East is consistently characterized as the original home of narrative fiction and such fiction is always 'fabular'. It carries a veiled message for its consumers; it seeks to 'move' them in terms of their response, prompting some change, ethical, political, or emotional.

The discussion of the eastern tale in Clara Reeve's *Progress of Romance* (1785) concludes with a discussion about the passion for fiction in 'all the countries beyond the Levant' (61). The male anti-romance disputant, Hortensius, tells a story of a young traveller in Egypt whose sleep is disturbed and he is surprised to discover when his host offers him the Turkish method of calming his mind that it is not opium or some other drug, but rather the reading of a pleasant story by a servant. The young traveller observes 'that it was strange that writers of Travels should censure the Turks and Moors for their passion for hearing Tales and Stories, when at the same time if this inclination did not prevail among Christians, their books would not be read at all' (63). Voracious romance-reader Sophronia concludes that 'In short the passion for tales and stories is common to all times, and all countries, and varies only according to the customs and manners of different people; and those who most affect to despise them under one form, will receive and admire them in another' (64). Indeed, the 'form' of the eastern tale constantly resurfaces in the eighteenth-century European novel, frequently transubstantiated into new forms that ostensibly reject its supernaturalism and 'extravagance'. The realist occidental novel, like the western Enlightenment of which it was a part, was always already 'oriental'.

3

TALES OF THE SERAGLIO:
TURKEY AND PERSIA

Roxolana: the loquacious courtesan

Sultan Solyman is besotted with Roxolana 'by condition a Captive, but so graced with beauty and courtly behaviour, that in short time she became Mistress of his thoughts, and Commandress of him that all commanded'.[1] She bears him four handsome sons and a daughter, but she remains troubled at the 'extreme credit' of Mustapha, Solyman's eldest son by a Circassian bondwoman, and the only figure to stand 'in her light, imbarring her and hers . . . of the hope of the Empire' (512). She persuades Solyman to follow the usual practice of the Ottoman emperors with regard to their sons and dispatch Mustapha and his mother to govern a distant province (Caramania). But she 'rest[s] not so, but beg[ins] straitway to plot in her malicious head the utter destruction' of the hopeful young heir (512). A base-born bassa named Rustan, husband to her only daughter, whose penny-pinching in court finances has already earned him the dislike of Mustapha, is enlisted as her ally.

---

[1] Knolles and Rycaut, *Turkish History*, i. 512.

59

'To begin this intended Tragedy' (512), Roxolana adopts a new piousness, and plans to build 'an Abbey, with a Hospital and a Church' (512) to win credit for her soul. When she questions him, the Mufti admits that, since she is a bondwoman, such acts will only count towards the spiritual profit of her master/lover, at which news Roxolana fakes a profound melancholy. Seeking to alleviate her misery, Solyman is quick to free her from her slavery. The eunuch he sends to her chamber to command her presence in his bed is, however, received with coldness. Roxolana 'with her Eies cast up to Heaven, demurely answer[s]' (513) that what was before a duty is now a terrible sin and refers him to the Mufti as proof that this is not a mere feint. The Mufti supports her claim that a free woman cannot give herself to a lover without marriage and Solyman, 'more and more burning in his desires' (513), is forced to offer her marriage.

'This Woman of late a Slave, but now become the greatest Empress of the East, flowing in all worldly Felicity, attended upon with all the pleasures her Heart could desire' (513) does not, however, rest on her laurels, but sets about assuring the succession of her own sons. She 'labour[s] cunningly by little and little' (513) to plant suspicions of Mustapha in her husband's thoughts. Rustan supports her endeavours with his own letters to neighbouring governors warning them of Mustapha's disfavour with his father and unlikely succession. Roxolana 'cease[s] not with pleasing allurements and flatterie (wherein she [is] most excellent) to infect *Solyman*'s mind' (513), presenting letters from Rustan's informants that appear to support the claim that Mustapha is plotting against his father. Mustapha is strangled by mutes in front of his father for supposed conspiracy with the Persian king's daughter, an event which leads Roxolana's youngest son, the hunchback Tzhihanger, who is truly attached to his stepbrother, to die of grief. With her first son also dead of unexplained causes,[2] Roxolana supports the succession of her younger boy, Bajazet, while her husband prefers the older Selymus because he reminds him so forcibly of Roxolana herself. Roxolana reconciles Bajazet and Solyman in 1555 after the former attempts to

[2] Knolles gives no details. In fact, Mehmed died of smallpox, a year after Suleyman appointed him to govern Manisa in 1542.

lead a rebellion, but on her death two years later, Bajazet revives his ambitions. The Persians, to whom he flees for assistance, first imprison him and then deliver him to his father, who summarily orders his execution.

This summary of Richard Knolles's influential account of the career of Roxolana, first published in 1603 in his *The Generall Historie of the Turks* (and thereafter in the numerous continuations by Paul Rycaut and others of the late seventeenth and early eighteenth centuries), stages all the characteristics of the Ottoman court for his English reader in the single figure of an oriental courtesan-turned-queen: luxury, concealed female agency, slave government, cruelty, despotism, the will-to-power, religious hypocrisy, and imposture. Knolles's account concerns Hürrem ('joyful') Sultan (1504–58), the courtesan and first wife of Suleyman I (known as Suleyman the Magnificent who ruled 1520–66); her ascendancy in 1533 upon the death of Suleyman's mother ushered in 'the Sultanate of Women' for over a century.[3] Roxolana's (European) name indicates her Eastern European origins (she was probably from the then-Polish Ukraine and the name derives from a Polish term meaning 'Ruthenian maiden'); she is described as a white-skinned red-haired beauty who could accord with western European standards of beauty as well as prejudices about the sexual attractions of courtesans. Indeed, throughout the eighteenth century in English writing the name 'Roxana' served as a synonym for 'whore', thus equating the Ottoman seraglio with the European brothel. James Cawthorn's 'The Regulation of the Passions' (1771) associates the brothel-frequenter with the oriental despot, his senses sated but his soul never at peace:

> For ask the man whose appetites pursue
> Each loose Roxana of the stew,
> Who cannot eat till luxury refine
> His taste, and teach him how to dine;
> Who cannot drink till Spain's rich vintage flow,

[3] For a thoughtful account of the contradictory nature of Hürrem Sultan's position as favourite of the sultan and promoter of her sons' interests, as well as an important reassessment of the roles women played at the Ottoman court, see Leslie P. Peirce, *The Imperial Harem: Women and Sovereignty in the Ottoman Empire* (New York and Oxford: Oxford University Press, 1993), 58–90.

Mix'd with the coolness of December snow:
Ask him if all those extacies that move
The pulse of rapture, and the rage of love,
When wine, wit, woman, all their pow'rs employ,
And ev'ry sense is lost in ev'ry joy,
E'er fill'd his heart, and beam'd upon his breast
Content's full sunshine, with the calm of rest?[4]

The figure of Roxolana merges in the late seventeenth and early eighteenth centuries with many other 'Roxolanas' and 'Roxanes'—some historical, some purely fictional—in dramatic, poetic, and prose narrative. In France, a similar process can be traced from the production of Jean Racine's *Bajazet* in 1672, its plot drawing on the events of 1635 to 1638 in the Ottoman court. Here, Roxane, the favoured courtesan of Sultan Amurat (Murat IV ruled 1623–40), has been left to govern the seraglio in his absence at war, but is more interested in the sexual pursuit of the sultan's handsome brother, Bajazet. Bajazet's affections are engaged by the lovely and noble-born Ottoman princess, Atalide, but he is persuaded by the treacherous vizier, Acomat, to play Roxane along. When she discovers the cheat, enraged with jealousy, Roxane orders Bajazet's death before herself falling victim to the sultan's emissary, and the play concludes with the suicide of Atalide. Racine's sources were largely oral, acquired from French ambassadors to the near-contemporary Ottoman court, but he also notes that the account tallies with the bare facts given in Rycaut's continuation of Knolles in the *History of the Turkish Empire* (1678), which only mentions Amurat's murder of his brother without reference to the role of Roxane.[5]

By the early eighteenth century, as Katie Trumpener points out, the name Roxane denoted 'the literary character, an oriental queen who always, no matter what the plot in which she appeared, embodied

---

[4] James Cawthorn, *Poems* (London, 1771), 88–9.

[5] The Preface to the 1672 edition comments that 'M. le comte de Cécy était alors ambassadeur à Constantinople. Il fut instruit de toutes les particularités de la mort de Bajazet; et il y a quantité de personnes à la cour qui se souviennent de les lui avoir entendu conter lorsqu'il fut de retour en France. M. le chevalier de Nantouillet est du nombre de ces personnes, et c'est à lui que je suis redevable de cette histoire.' Racine refers to Philippe de Harlay, Comte de Cézy, ambassador to Constantinople between 1618 and 1639 and to his close friend François de Prat, chevalier de Nantouillet (Jean Racine, *Bajazet: Tragédie*, ed. Marie-Claude Canova-Green, Classiques Larousse (Paris: Larousse, 1993)).

ambition, sexuality, revenge, exoticism; in fact, in the eighteenth century she came to personify womanhood itself: mysterious, sensual, resentful'.[6]

A further namesake with similar associations of jealous and vengeful passion, but without an Ottoman context, was Roxane, captured from her Bactrian tribe and married by Alexander the Great in 327 BC during his conquest of Asia. On Alexander's death (323 BC), she had his second wife, Stateira, killed. Roxane gave birth at Babylon to a son whom the Macedonian generals accepted as joint king with Alexander's idiot half-brother. She was imprisoned by Cassander, who later took the title of king of Macedonia, and was then executed along with her son. In Nathaniel Lee's play *The Rival Queens* (1677) and in Gauthier de Costes de la Calprenède's long prose romance *Cassandra* (1652), the cunning and violent barbarian princess serves as a contrast to her virtuous and loving Persian rival, Statira. The contrast with a 'gentle' female alternative—whether Atalide in Racine's account or Mahidevran, Circassian mother of Mustapha in Knolles's—becomes formulaic in representations of Roxolana/Roxane. In stage tragedies, the figure is often a virtuous Christian gentlewoman, such as Ianthe in William Davenant's *The Siege of Rhodes* (first performed in 1656 and extensively revised in 1661) who rivals the oriental courtesan-queen in the despot's affections. However, Persia, the Ottomans' chief rival in empire and Islam (the Safavid dynasty in Persia promoted the minority Shi'ite faith by contrast with the Sunni orthodoxy of the Ottomans), also frequently provided such figures. A different example from Statira is the lovely Persian princess who is secret wife to the eponymous Mustapha in the 1739 close adaptation of Knolles for the English stage by David Mallet.

Persian Roxanes are not, however, inevitably icons of purity and moral virtue by contrast with their Turkish sisters. The most famous Roxane of the French eighteenth century is the favoured mistress of the Persian traveller, Usbek, in Montesquieu's *Lettres Persanes* (1721), whose chaste refusal of his favours for two months after marriage and even after possession conceals a spirit that longs for liberty. The novel

---

[6] Katie Trumpener, 'Rewriting Roxane: Orientalism and Intertextuality in Montesquieu's Lettres Persanes and Defoe's the Fortunate Mistress', *Stanford French Review* 11 (1987): 178.

concludes with the chief eunuch's report to his absent master of a revolution in the seraglio and the disclosure that Roxane's 'stern Virtue was all a cheat; it was only a Veil to her perfidiousness'.[7] Here too, then, the figure of Roxane deludes her despotic master through the adoption of the dramatic role of faithful mistress; her performance is underpinned by her mastery over language, the power of verbal persuasion, until the disclosure of her inauthenticity, a disclosure that rocks the very foundations of government.

The figure of Roxolana/Roxane consistently signifies the most troubling aspects of oriental empire to the western European imagination: sexual obsession, duplicity, violent revenge. Such aspects prove troubling precisely because, while they appear to indicate the gulf between East and West, they consistently emerge as 'hidden' threats to occidental civil society, lurking symptoms of the 'other within': 'As if, by learning to decipher the structures of an impossible power from the outside, Europeans were discovering that they had equipped themselves with the best key for interpreting their own present. An endoscopic fantasy, in a sense, one in which novels and drama would find an inexhaustible source.'[8] Roxolana/Roxane is a figure of class insurgency (a slave who becomes a queen), a figure of ostentatious luxury and a figure of boundless passion, whether in her ambition for political or sexual absolute power.

The perils of the expansionist self embodied in this orientalized figure finds its fullest expression in the period in Daniel Defoe's 1724 *The Fortunate Mistress*. This representation/redaction of the oriental courtesan figure points moreover to the 'performative' and 'inauthentic' nature of Roxana's imaginative authority. Roxana is always 'most' Roxana when she is an imitation of herself, when she performs an act of European mimicry of her historical 'source'. Thus, Defoe's French Huguenot heroine finds her most effective stage in England when she performs her oriental dance for Charles II, the English king most often associated with oriental sultanate because of his sexual promiscuity and love of luxurious display: a familiar satirical target for the novel's dissenting and Whig author. Roxana unites in her person

---

[7] Charles de Secondat Montesquieu, *Persian Letters*, trans. John Ozell (London, 1722), ii. 305.   [8] Grosrichard, *The Sultan's Court*, 24.

the twin sources of foreign luxury for English readers, France and
Turkey, and her dance, she informs us, is more successful than that of
her rivals, two 'authentic' Turkish ladies from Georgia and Armenia
who perform without jewellery, unmasked and bare-headed. Their
dancing pleases with its novelty 'yet there was something wild and
Bizarre in it, because they really acted to the Life the barbarous
Country whence they came; but as mine had the *French* Behaviour
under the *Mahometan* Dress, it was every way as new, and pleas'd
much better, indeed'.[9]

Like that of her namesake, Roxana's power lies more in her verbal
than her physical agency. It is in the seductive and manipulative use of
fiction and fable, especially in spinning fictional versions of her own
selfhood, that Roxana controls her reception and wins her, always
unstable but at least for the moment effective, power. Performing the
role of Rox(ol)ana links European women of the lowest and highest
classes in the period, but always suggests women's hidden capacity to
control through visual and verbal language the consuming look of
their audience. When the working-class woman, particularly the
prostitute or actress, adopts Turkish dress she does so to turn a profit
from male voyeurs; when the aristocratic woman, such as Lady Mary
Wortley Montagu, adopts Turkish dress she does so to express her
freedom from the constraints of western marriage and government.

Contrast Lady Mary Wortley Montagu's description of her Turkish
habit in a letter to her sister Lady Mar from Adrianople on 1 April 1717
with the description by a prostitute named Mary who tells her story in
the second part of the popular picaresque series entitled *The English
Rogue* by Francis Kirkman of 1668. The prostitute Mary adopts
Turkish dress to keep the attention of her young lover, a country
gentleman who is enamoured of the image of Roxolana he has enjoyed
in a performance of William Davenant's play *The Siege of Rhodes*:

I so ordered the matter, that I got a Taylor, and other persons who were used
to make habits for the Players, to make me a habit in all things like to that of
Roxolana; this being done, I acquainted my young Gentleman, and told him
that for his better satisfaction, he should see the famed *Princess* at our

---

[9] Daniel Defoe, *Roxana, the Fortunate Mistress*, ed. Jane Jack (London: New York:
Oxford University Press, 1964), 179.

quarters, where he might have more freedom then at any other place; he was herewith very well contented; he habiting himself in the richest garbs he had, and a Colation was provided to treat his expected Mistris; all things being thus fitted on his part, I put on the provided habit; and instead of the expected *Roxolana*, I entred the Room where he was, attending by two or three, who bore up my train, and had set my self out with so many Jewels, both good, and counterfeit; and was indeed in all things so like the *Roxolana* he had seen, that he doubted not but I was the very same, and was much surprised at the matter: and although my face was as lovely as hers, yet I had added somewhat thereto to appear more beautiful.[10]

Lady Mary has also obtained a tailor and she too stresses the luxury of the garb; the jewels she describes are, however, all genuine and she provides a minute account of materials used and their treatment. She calls particular attention to the 'modesty' of her clothing, as well as its comfort, strangeness, and value:

The first peice of my dresse is a pair of drawers, very full, that reach to my shoes, and conceal the legs more modestly than your Petticoats. They are of a thin rose colour damask brocaded with silver flowers, my shoes of white kid Leather embroider'd with Gold. Over this hangs my Smock of a fine white silk Gause edg'd with Embrodiery. This smock has wide sleeves hanging halfe way down the Arm and is clos'd at the Neck with a diamond button; but the shape and colour of the bosom is very well to be distinguish'd through it. The Antery is a wastcoat made close to the shape, of white and Gold Damask, with very long sleeves falling back and fring'd with deep Gold fringe, and should have Diamond or pearl Buttons. My Caftan of the same stuff with my Drawers, is a robe exactly fited to my shape and reaching to my feet, with very long strait falling sleeves. Over this is the Girdle of about 4 fingers broad, which all that can afford have entirely of Diamonds or other precious stones. Those that will not be at that expence have it of exquisite Embroidery on Satin, but it must be fasten'd before with a clasp of Di'monds. The Curdée is a loose Robe they throw off or put on according to the Weather, being of a rich Brocade (mine is green and Gold) either lined with Ermine or Sables; the sleeves reach very little below the Shoulders. The Headdress is compos'd of a Cap, call'd Talpock, which is in winter of fine velvet embrodier'd with pearls or Di'monds and in summer of a light shineing silver stuff. This is fix'd on one side of the head, hanging a little way down with a Gold Tassel and bound on

---

[10] Francis Kirkman, *The English Rogue: Continued in the Life of Meriton Latroon*, Pt. 2 (London, 1680), 321.

either with a circle of Di'monds (as I have seen several) or a rich embrodier'd Handkercheif. On the other side of the Head the Hair is laid flat and here the Ladys are at Liberty to show their fancys, some putting Flowers, others a plume of Heron's feathers and, in short, what they please, but the most general fashion is a large Bouquet of Jewels made like natural flowers; that is, the buds of Pearl, the roses of different colour'd Rubys, the Jess'mines of Di'monds, Jonquils of Topazes, etc., so well set and enamell'd 'tis hard to imagine anything of that kind so beautifull. (*CLMWM* i. 326-7) (see Fig. 1)

1. Portrait of Lady Mary Wortley Montagu in Turkish dress, attributed to Jean Baptiste Vanmour

The contrast between these two Marys is not between the natural and the artificial, authentic and assumed identity, but rather between different kinds of performance. The working-class Mary puts together a show that successfully passes in the dim evening light for an authentic imitation of an imitation (she is copying an English actress playing the part of a Turkish sultana). Lady Mary, by contrast, calls attention to a sophisticated performance of beauty and ornamentation, finishing on the image of jewels carved into the shape of flowers, thus making the connection between her own aristocratic status and the luxury indulged in by Ottoman women of an equivalent class.

Like Roxolana, the two Marys use language to spin images of themselves that control the responses of their audience. The figure of the oriental woman in European narrative is, above all else, associated with the practice of plotting, whether for positive or negative ends. Francis Bacon cites Roxolana as a 'cruel' example along with Livia and Isabella, of the threat to empire posed 'when the Wives have Plots for the Raising of their owne Children; Or else that they be Advoutresses [adulteresses]'.[11] Roxolana's specific act of plotting can be associated with the dilatory and 'feminine' power of romance as outlined by Patricia Parker—a withholding of narrative closure (her refusal of her lover's advances until he concedes to marriage) that resists the drive to closure inherent in 'masculine' narrative action, that of epic and empire.[12] Dilatoriness is, of course, Scheherazade's major narrative tool, suggesting that when she first makes an appearance in early eighteenth-century European fiction she may have been recognizable through the more familiar figure of oriental womanhood, Roxolana.

Another early eighteenth-century woman, of a quite different political persuasion and social class from either of the two Marys already discussed, explicitly used the figure of Roxolana to point to the political and marital advantages of female 'dilation' or resistance to closure, narrative and sexual. In the story of Charlot in Delarivier Manley's scandal fiction, *The New Atalantis* (1709), the unfortunate

[11] Francis Bacon, 'Of Empire', in *The Essayes or Counsels, Civill and Morall*, ed. Michael Kiernan, Oxford English Texts (Oxford: Clarendon Press, 1985), 61.
[12] Patricia Parker, 'Literary Fat Ladies and the Generation of the Text', in *Literary Fat Ladies: Rhetoric, Gender, Property* (London: Methuen, 1987), 8–35.

heroine is seduced and then neglected by her guardian, the duke. She is befriended by an older countess who 'advised her to bestow no more favours, till he paid her price; made her read the history of Roxelana who, by her wise address brought an imperious sultan, contrary to the established rules of the seraglio, to divide with her the royal throne'.[13] Charlot's resolution wavers and she is cast off in favour of the countess who wisely refuses the duke sexual gratification until after marriage.

The countess's act is that of the worldly older woman who understands where women's power, visual and verbal, lies. Her acts of narrative deferral can be paralleled with those of her author, Delarivier Manley, who delivers a sequence of erotic tales which serve as political parables (critiques of corrupt Whig politicians from an ardent Tory defender). The duke is a man of considerable political power and by marriage the countess secures herself political influence. As with their oriental analogues, Roxolana (and Scheherezade), the 'motive' behind the acts of erotic manipulation and deferral performed by literary character and author might ultimately be understood as a desire for political rather than sexual sway.

Knolles's version of Roxolana's story occupies a few pages in a handsome folio edition that summarizes the reign of each Ottoman sultan until the early seventeenth century. Roxolana is the only courtesan/queen to be given the privilege of a portrait engraving, albeit of smaller size than those rendered of the sultans themselves (see Fig. 2). A poem beneath it warns: 'To fairest lookes trust not too farre, nor yet to beautie brave: | For hatefull thoughts so finely maskt, their deadly poisons have'.[14] Roxolana's fair looks belie her cruel intentions. Knolles's narrative account, however, stresses her verbal duplicity rather than her physical looks as the main source of her (political) agency. And Roxolana is a signifier of the 'duplicity' at the heart of oriental narrative; it may not be what it appears to be. Parabolic, seductive, repetitive, the oriental tale has a 'hidden' agenda; it is a veiled form, like the women who are so often its tellers.

---

[13] Delarivier Manley, *New Atalantis*, ed. Rosalind Ballaster (London: Penguin, 1992), 41.
[14] Richard Knolles, *The Generall Historie of the Turkes* (London, 1603), 759.

2. Engraving of Hürrem Sultana (Roxolana), in Richard Knolles, *The Generall Historie of the Turkes* (1603), p. 759

Speaking likenesses: Turkey and Persia

In October 1716, Alexander Pope wrote to his close female friend, Lady Mary Wortley Montagu, with an unusual request. Lady Mary was in Istanbul, for which she had embarked in August 1716 with her husband, Edward Wortley, Ambassador Extraordinary to the Court of Turkey; his mission was to attempt to prevent Austria from becoming embroiled in the war between the Ottomans and the Venetian Republic. Wortley was recalled in the summer of 1717, his mission in tatters. Pope's thoughts were not on diplomacy and politics, however, despite the known fervent Whiggism of his addressee:

This is what I really wish from my Soul, tho it would ruin the best project I ever lay'd, that of obtaining, thro' your means, my fair Circassian slave. She, whom my Imagination had drawn more amiable than Angels, as beautiful as the Lady who was to chuse her by a resemblance to so divine a face; she, whom my hopes had already transported over so many Seas and Lands, & whom my eager wishes had already lodg'd in my arms & heart; She, I say, upon this condition, may remain under the Cedars of Asia; and weave a garland of Palmes for the brows of a Turkish Tyrant with those hands, which I had destined for the soft Offices or love, or at worst for transcribing amorous Madrigals![15]

In Autumn 1717 he renewed the request to bring over 'the fair Circassian we us'd to talk of', again asking Lady Mary to 'look oftener than you use to do, in your Glass, in order to chuse me one I may like' (441). On 1 September 1718, he returns to the issue, but this time openly equates the imaginary slave-concubine with Lady Mary herself. Pope plays with a number of European prejudices about Muslim women to express his desire for access to her feminine self: that Islam does not accord women souls, that seraglio women are both more 'simple' and more sexual than their European counterparts:

I prodigiously long for your Sonnets, your remarks, your oriental learning; but I long for nothing so much as your Oriental Self. You must of necessity be *advanced* so far *Back* into true nature and simplicity of manners, by these 3 years residence in the East, that I shall look upon you as so many years Younger than you was, so much nearer Innocence (that is, Truth) & Infancy (that is Openness.) I expect to see your Soul as much thinner dressed as your Body; and that you have left off, as unwieldy & cumbersome, a great many damn'd European Habits. Without offence to your Modesty be it spoken, I have a burning desire to see your Soul stark naked, for I am confident 'tis the prettiest kind of white Soul, in the universe—But I forget whom I am talking to, you may possibly by this time Believe according to the Prophet, that you have none. If so, show me That which comes next to a Soul; you may easily put it upon a poor ignorant Christian for a Soul, & please him as well with it: I mean your Heart: Mahomet I think allows you Hearts: which (together with

---

[15] Alexander Pope, *The Correspondence of Alexander Pope*, ed. George Wiley Sherburn (Oxford: Clarendon Press, 1956), i. 364.

fine eyes & other agreeable equivalents) are worth all the Souls on this side the world. (494)

If Lady Mary responded to Pope's repeated request, she did not choose to include any response in the preparation of her *Turkish Embassy Letters* for publication.[16]

The myth of the beautiful, sexually accomplished 'Circassian' slave-concubine was a powerful and popular one in European writing about Ottoman court culture, serving a similar purpose to the representation of the Kashmiri princess in fictional and travel writings about Mughal India. Pope's language is particularly telling. Under the veil of a claim to be interested in a platonic union of 'souls', he presents a seductive eroticized address to the witty poetry-writing European woman he admires, through invoking the 'figure' of an oriental woman who can mirror her because of her 'whiteness'. Circassian women were slaves taken from the North Caucasus (Georgian Russia) and the term 'Caucasian' has of course come to describe ethnic whiteness. Similarly, travel writers are quick to point out that the terms 'Mogul' (for the ruling dynasty derived from Tamerlane in India) and 'Sophi/Suffee' (for the ruling dynasty derived from the caliphate in Persia) are simply terms for 'white', serving to differentiate the aristocratic ruling classes from the ethnic natives of those regions.[17]

Pope's letters illustrate a number of consistent features of popular discourse about the Orient in eighteenth-century Europe: first, the representation of oriental cultures as absolutist and the Ottoman empire as the dominant paradigm of such absolutism (the 'Turkish tyrant'); second, the tendency to take the enclosure of women in the

---

[16] On 11 December 1761, in ill health and expecting her death, Lady Mary left the 2-vol. MS of her Turkish letters (along with a preface by Mary Astell and an anonymous prefatory poem) with the Revd Benjamin Sowden, a British Presbyterian Minister living in Rotterdam, inscribed with her 'will and design' that they should be 'dispos'd of as [Sowden] thinks proper' (Isobel Grundy, *Lady Mary Wortley Montagu: Comet of the Enlightenment* (Oxford: Oxford University Press, 1999), 612). They were published on 7 May 1763 by Becket and De Hondt as the *Letters of the Right Honourable Lady M——y W——y M——e, written during her travels in Europe, Asia, and Africa* and were an immediate hit, generating a piracy in the same year with five alleged extra letters.

[17] On the term 'Mogul' see Catrou, *General History*, 99, and on 'Sophi' see John Fryer, *A New Account of East India and Persia, Being Nine Years' Travels, 1672–1681*, ed. William Crooke, Works Issued by the Hakluyt Society; 2nd ser. 19–20, 39 (London: Printed for the Hakluyt Society, 1909), iii. 45.

harem as a signifier of that absolutism (the oriental 'slavery' of women is a marker of outdated territorial empire by contrast with the 'public' freedom of women in the West whose power to purchase commodities is both a sign and rationale for the emergent model of maritime trading empire in Europe); third, the insistent return to a metaphor of visual pleasure and power exercised by the male tyrant over the 'veiled' and 'hidden' body of the owned woman with which European men powerfully identified, even as they ostensibly repudiated its savagery and philosophical poverty.

Lady Mary's silence is, however, uncharacteristic both of her writing and also of an alternative tradition in oriental fiction (of which she must have been aware given her enthusiasm for the *Arabian Nights Entertainments*) which counters the power of the male look with the agency of female voice. The most influential and pervasive model of a feminized loquacity which could challenge a despotism associated with the sultan's eye was of course Scheherazade. Significantly, it is a moment of shocking epiphany of vision that prompts Schahriar's decision to execute each wife the morning after he has enjoyed her. His brother Schahzenan, king of Tartary, shows Schahriar his queen and her women consorting with a number of black slaves in a garden. Many of the tales Scheherazade tells to defer her fate (particularly those told at the start of the collection when the frame is still at the forefront of the reader's mind) are tales about the withholding of arbitrary and tyrannical punishment in exchange for further storytelling, so that narrative content parallels narrative frame. Scheherazade, we are told, 'had courage, wit and penetration infinitely above her sex; she had read abundance, and had such a prodigious memory that she never forgot any thing. She had successfully applied herself to philosophy, physic, history, and the liberal arts; and for verse, exceeded the best poets of her time' (*ANE* 10). On the model of Scheherazade, the oriental woman in narrative accounts (whether prose fiction, drama, or travel-writing), could figure not only the enclosing and constraining power of despotism but also resistance to it. Her verbal agency counters the despotic male's visual mastery, her temporal dilation his spatial authority.

The association of oriental despotism with visual agency has been persuasively made by Srinivas Aravamudan in his *Tropicopolitans*

(1999), where he concludes that 'the fictions of oriental despotism investigate the ethics of subject constitution in the face of a blinding— and therefore unpresentable—tyrannical power'.[18] Aravamudan martials his evidence from the accounts of travellers such as John Chardin of the practice among the Persian kings of ordering the blinding of rival heirs on their accession, and from literary texts such as William Beckford's description of Vathek's capacity to kill simply with a look, itself derived from Barthélemy d'Herbelot's account of the historical caliph in his compendious *Bibliothèque Orientale* (first published in 1697). The power of looking and of withholding the look is exclusively associated with the absolutist oriental ruler, himself inaccessible and rarely seen according to accounts by European witnesses in Turkey, India, and China. Numerous commentators remark that it is death to attempt to look on the ladies of the Ottoman or Persian harem.[19]

For European male informants this monopoly on the agency of the look has the effect of 'feminizing' their own narrative accounts of the 'seraglio' and especially the women's quarters. Even as they strive to represent the activity of describing the harem (the term itself means 'forbidden' or 'sacred') as an act of penetrative masculine colonization it emerges rather as an act of seductive and feminized loquacity. Thus, Aaron Hill claims in his *Full and Just Account of the ... Ottoman Empire* to have gained admission to the harem:

which for many Ages has been kept a secret to the searching Knowledge of our *European Travellers*, and shall *now* proceed to entertain him with a wonderfull, but pleasant and sincere account of new Discoveries, which *like the Golden Indian World*, lay long unenter'd, as appearing barr'd against our View with unsurmountable Impediments,) but gain'd at last, will spread

---

[18] Srinivas Aravamudan, *Tropicopolitans: Colonialism and Agency, 1688–1804*, Post-Contemporary Interventions (Durham, NC: Duke University Press, 1999), 192.

[19] Jean de Thévenot comments in the second book of his *Travels into the Levant* that the Persian sultan 'is extremely jealous of his Wives though he has a vast number of them, and his Jealousie is so extravagant ... that if a man had onely looked upon them, he would be put to death without remission' (Jean de Thévenot, *The Travels of Monsieur De Thevenot into the Levant*, pp. 2, 99). Jean Dumont comments of the women in the seraglio harem in Istanbul that ''tis a Capital Crime to look upon one of these Women' and tells the story of a man spotted by Sultan Amurath with a prospective glass looking at the Sultanesses walking in the garden, who was promptly hanged at his window as a punishment (Jean Dumont, *A New Voyage to the Levant*, 4th edn. (London, 1705), 167–8).

throughout our *Western Regions*, such surprizing Plenty of her valuable Product, as may more than recompence the patient stay of your expecting Curiosities. (147) (see Fig. 3)

While the act of 'discovery' of a barred or enclosed space—the women's quarters and by analogy the female body—is represented as an act of masculine conquest, the dissemination and circulation of the 'valuable Product' (the rare account of the interior of the inner quarters) comes closer to the verbal 'trading' of the oriental woman like Scheherazade, recirculating folk tales in the space of the boudoir.

This chapter considers fictions published in England relating to the Ottoman and Persian empires, and maps the gendered division of the labour of representation across the major vehicles for 'oriental' narrative of the period: first the tragic drama; second oriental tales (both the sequence on the model of the *Arabian Nights* but also the burgeoning form of the short novella in English which frequently moves into Turkish and/or Persian territories for its action); third the fictional 'spy' genre and the letter sequence imported from France in the shape of the *Letters Writ by a Turkish Spy* and the *Persian Letters;* and fourth the satirical tale which uses Turkish or Persian locales and characters to critique western states and values.

By contrast with China and India, Turkey and Persia (and especially Istanbul and Isfahan) were familiar territories. British encounters were largely, but not wholly, confined to the Ottoman empire and its North African satellites, whether through trade, slavery, piracy, or diplomacy. Up until the deliverance of Vienna from the Turks by the Germans and Poles in 1683, these regions dominated the British understanding of other non-Christian cultures. As Nabil Matar summarizes: '[b]etween Britons and Turks and Moors there was engagement and conflict, piracy and trade, sexual affairs and marriage—a whole scope of relationships and associations, some conducted within and some outside the law, some ambiguous and some unprecedented, some clandestine and some public.'[20] There were English traders in the Ottoman empire in the early sixteenth century and, in 1581 with the establishment of the Levant Company monopoly to trade in the lands of the Great Turk, they gained

---

[20] Matar, *Turks, Moors and Englishmen*, 41–2.

3. Map of the Ottoman seraglio, in Aaron Hill, *A Full and Just Account of the Present State of the Ottoman Empire* (1709), p. 116

imperial protection and dispensation. A succession of English ambassadors, salaries and expenses met by the Levant Company, lived in the Turkish capital from the appointment of William Harborne in November 1582.

Encounters with Persia were less extensive, for the British especially, although an embassy was maintained there from 1627. They took the form largely of missionary activity under the auspices of the French East India Company (Abbas I, who ruled from 1587 to 1629, was famously tolerant of Christians) and independent trading ventures such as those of Sir John Chardin, the French Huguenot jeweller, who was the primary source for most information about Persia in the later seventeenth century. His contemporary, the doctor John Fryer, provided an English description of Persia from his travels there in the 1670s, *A New Account of the East Indies and Persia*, in 1698. English knowledge of Persia was, in the main, mediated through France; Louis XIV's ministers negotiated a treaty signed at Isfahan in 1708 which temporarily alleviated the growing persecution of missionaries in Persia.

Scholarship in Middle Eastern languages, literatures, and theology, after the brief flowering of English scholarship under Edward Pococke in the 1670s, was also largely mediated to Britain through France. Barthélemy d'Herbelot (1625–95), Professor of Oriental Languages at the Collège de France from 1692, never travelled to the Orient but was responsible for the major source of oriental knowledge of the eighteenth century, the *Bibliothèque Orientale* of 1697 based on the bibliographical dictionary of an Ottoman historian, Hajjī Khalīfa (1608–57). D'Herbelot was in turn a major influence for the leading European scholars of Islam and the Middle East of the period: Antoine Galland (1646–1715), appointed Chair of Arabic at the Collège Royale in 1703, spent much of the 1670s and 1680s in Istanbul collecting manuscripts on the instructions of Colbert to add to the Bibliothèque du Rei; Adrien Reland (1676–1718), a Dutch professor of oriental languages at the University of Utrecht from 1701 to 1718, was a leading advocate of the Persian language and explicator of Shi'ite Islam (his tract 'Of the Mahometan Religion' published in England in 1712 was a key text in the Protestant rehabilitation of Islam as a means of attacking the Roman Church); Simon Ockley (1678–1720), the leading English scholar of the early eighteenth century in oriental language and history, was appointed to the Chair of Arabic at Cambridge University in 1711, and was the author of a history of the Saracens which detailed the lives and military successes of the first three Caliphs of Islam. Ahmad Gunny concludes: 'Galland made himself the champion of the Turks, Reland and D'Herbelot of the Persians, while Ockley . . . warmed to the Arabs.'[21] André Du Ryer, French Consul in Egypt, translated the Qur'an from Arabic into French as early as 1647 and in 1649 a translation from Du Ryer, albeit presented as a '*gallimaufry of errors*' (n.p.) and a piece of imposture, appeared in England. However, the work of scholars appears rarely to have been diffused to a wider popular audience; even those with an ostensible enthusiasm for oriental wisdom such as Joseph Addison, Samuel Johnson, or Oliver Goldsmith draw their cited sources from the compendious vernacular histories of informants like Paul Rycaut or from popular sequences such as those of Pétis de la Croix or Galland. Despite their academic and linguistic credentials, neither of the latter presented their translations as part of a wider philological, theological, or philosophical effort to comprehend the East; the translation of these texts by 'Grub Street' translators with no scholarly apparatus indicates that they were marketed and circulated primarily as narrative curiosities. The disjunction between linguistic and historical scholarship in oriental cultures and popular narrative representations (even when they were the product of the same person) held sway until late into the eighteenth century.

As Ahmad Gunny points out 'Interest in Turkey went hand in hand with interest in Persia' (9). This does not mean that European commentators did not differentiate between the two cultures: far from it. Persia provided a model of a powerful Islamic alternative to Turkey, and the contrast between Sunni and Shi'ite was exploited (if not always accurately) frequently to make parallels with the tensions between Catholic and Protestant in Europe. Most accounts inclined to represent Persian rulers as even more despotic than their Turkish counterparts. Persia appears almost invariably in the comparative mode. Its women are kept even closer, its punishments are

[21] Gunny, *Images of Islam*, 64.

even more severe (rivals to the throne are blinded, which disqualifies them from succession in Persia where they are 'only' imprisoned in Turkey), its monarchs are more luxurious and its court officers more idle. Jean de Thévenot, a Frenchman who found Persian culture inferior when he visited it after his travels in Ottoman territories, demonstrates this comparative tendency even in discussing differences of dress, concluding that 'The *Persian* Apparel seemed to be more gay than that of the *Turks*, but it is more clutterly and less commodious'.[22]

However, when Persia figures as the sole representative of Islamic despotism in European representations, rather than being deployed as a contrast with its rival the Ottoman empire, the same common themes emerge. Thus, the two great French fictions in the voice of Islamic informants, *L'Espion Turc* (1684–97) and the *Lettres Persanes* (1721) mirror each other closely, providing sceptical and enquiring observers nevertheless committed to the hierarchical and absolutist order of their native cultures. The *Lettres Persanes* contain an inset story that contrasts the ancient Zoroastrianism of Persia with the religion of the Islamic invader.[23] One of the two main Persian informants, Rica, meets a happily married Guebrian (Zoroastrian) couple on his travels and discovers that they are in fact brother and sister (he claims that incestuous marriage is licensed in their faith). The brother has persuaded his sister to elope from her unhappy imprisonment by marriage to a Turkish eunuch. This inset story enables Montesquieu to rehearse the distinctions between a republic (governed by ties of virtue and love) and despotic rule (governed by fear) which he was to clarify in his *De l'Esprit des Lois* of 1748. But it also points to the enduring interest in ancient Persia in seventeenth- and eighteenth-century England. In fact the period saw only one drama set in Persia with a contemporary or near-contemporary (hence Islamic) context, Delarivier Manley's *The Royal Mischief* (1696), by contrast with the many which concerned the first ancient dynasty of Persia established by Cyrus, and the history of the empire under Cambyses, Darius, and Alexander. Bridget Orr concludes that

---

[22] Thévenot, *Travels*, pt. 2, 93.
[23] Charles de Secondat Montesquieu, *Persian Letters*, trans. John Ozell, 3rd corr. edn. (London, 1736), Letter 65.

'The attraction of Persian history as a template for the dramatic exploration of the triumphs and vicissitudes of empire depended not just on its antiquity and the perceived continuity of the Empire into the present but also on its status as a primordial other to the West'.[24]

That 'otherness', however, was most consistently manifested in the contrast between the oriental and the occidental court, and especially in the process of imaginative projection into the space least accessible to the observing, usually masculine, eye, that of the 'harem'. Alain Grosrichard's 1979 work, *Structure du Sérail* (known in English as *The Sultan's Court*) retraces this 'imaginary' journey of the European traveller from Montesquieu's framing understanding of the nature of despotism, the representation of the sultan and the basis of his power, the encounters with the 'less-than-male' figures of the Turkish/Persian courts (mutes, dwarfs, eunuchs), to the construction of the harem as the place from which power originates and where power ends.[25] The 'harem' is also the space of narrative, the place in which and about which tales are told, if often the same repetitive tale of rebellion and defeat. Grosrichard reminds us that the European representation of the Orient presents the latter as a place without narrative progress, but given to infinite citation and repetition. The person of the ruler is unimportant to the 'structure' of despotism; one ineffectual ruler can be replaced with another since power is a mere circulating 'letter', while monarchical power relies for its continuance on the monarch's capacity to continue to promote the well-being of his people and agents. Hence, the 'despotic' tale is one of substitutable histories (like those of Scheherezade) which repetitively reiterate the same central 'plot'. Thus, Grosrichard concludes, the West prides itself on its 'history', a narrative of progress and advance, by drawing a contrast with oriental 'histories', endlessly circulating stories which only serve to confirm an unchanging state of subjection. In the space of the harem where time stands still while the inhabitants await the command or presence of the despot, stories are a key item of exchange, a form of power and a means of passing time if not ultimately transformative (79).

---

[24] Orr, *Empire on the English Stage*, 99.   [25] Grosrichard, *The Sultan's Court*, 169.

Tales of the Seraglio: Turkey and Persia

The major sequences of oriental tales 'translated' for a European market, Antoine Galland's *Arabian Nights Entertainments*, François Pétis de la Croix's *Persian Tales* and *Turkish Tales*, have frames that confirm this sense of change without necessary progress; they are sequences told to their addressee in order to persuade him or her to restore the 'status quo', to bring his or her aberrant behaviour back into line with the necessary structure of the royal court. The tales are especially directed towards the restoration of a possibility of reproductive succession. Schahriar must learn to accept women's unchastity and limit the damage it may cause through the use of the harem as it stands and abandon his bloody daily executions of new-made wives if he is to secure a succession; Farruknaz, the Persian princess of the *Persian Tales*, must accept that men can prove worthy spouses so that her dynastic marriage can be secured and the peaceful coexistence of her nation with its neighbours be restored; the sultan of the *Turkish Tales* must learn how to tell male truth from women's falsehood so that he can vindicate his son from the accusations of rape and treachery made by his favourite sultana and secure the 'succession' of his worthy male heir.

These examples alone demonstrate how swiftly the attempt to prove oriental 'otherness' to a European audience transforms into a process of analogy and parallel. The succession crises of Europe amongst the Stuart kings and queens of England, between rival claimants to the Spanish throne, and in the later years of the long absolutist reign of Louis XIV of France, are replayed and reworked within the framework of the oriental tale, figuring a potential despotism in the heart of Europe (through Ottoman incursion or the threatened collapse of monarchical government into despotism in European states).

Grosrichard returns us to the relationship between the eye and the voice when he uses Lacanian theories of the structure of desire to conclude that the despotic state figures for occidental monarchists a 'pure', if essentially corrupt, form of power: 'The gaze, the letter: here we have the two key terms, the two driving elements, of despotic power in the Orient' (56). The sultan's look and the mere communication of his name (to the vizier as his agent, or in the form of a missive carrying his name which can authorize an act of execution or

81

blinding on the part of its holder) are imagined as all that is required to command in the occidental depiction of the oriental state. While Grosrichard pays more attention than Edward Said to the dominance of fiction in the representation of the Orient in the West, he does not differentiate between the 'letter'—the name-of-the-father which characterizes the symbolic power of the despot (as opposed to the 'imaginary' force of the gaze)—and the 'tale' or 'fiction' or 'narrative', conveniently ignoring how often the latter is spoken in the voice of a woman, the tale-telling inhabitant of the seraglio. For Grosrichard, all inhabitants of the seraglio are simply 'signifiers' of the sultan's power, by contrast (mutes, dwarfs, and eunuchs are deformed men who serve to magnify his complete masculinity) or by possession (the women of the harem confirm his authority by his ownership of them): 'The blind, the mute, the dwarves, the buffoons, the eunuchs, the women and children, and so on, all stand negatively for the fragmented body of the despot. They are the living analysis of his Unity, the active affirmation that he alone has eyes and speech, the cosmological proof of his omnipotence and uniqueness' (128).

The only point at which Grosrichard recognizes the transgressive or disruptive potential of female voice in the representation of the seraglio is in his identification of a sense of the 'illusory' or 'fictional' nature of the sultan's power in the occidental critique of the excessive influence of women in the oriental court, especially the valide-sultan (the sultan's mother): 'he who, to all appearances, *has* the phallus, *is* the phallus for his mother' (167). The sultan's authority is then a pure 'fiction', at its heart a negative space or emptiness which is only filled by the phallic authority of the mother. However, while European commentators did, occasionally, recognize the influence of the 'valide' or sultan's mother in their accounts of Ottoman and Persian courts, they tended to lay more stress on the rhetorical and sexual influence of the sultan's favourite courtesan or wife. Hence, accounts of Roxolana focus on her illegitimate authority won through verbal and sexual fascination by contrast with the filial loyalty and martial bravery of Suleyman's son and heir, her rival 'stepson', Mustapha. There are, then, acts of hidden speech, especially the spinning of productive 'fictions', which are consistently put in the mouths of women in occidental 'reproductions' of the seraglio, that are counterweights to the power of the pure 'name' or 'letter' or despotic 'gaze' of the sultan. These acts of subaltern speech, whether from the mouths of women or subaltern figures that are feminized precisely through their use of fictional speech, are the focus of my analysis, not least because they suggest an alliance between occidental fiction-maker (dramatist, traveller, or novelist) and a feminine/feminized Orient.

The sections concerning China and India in this book attempt a comprehensive discussion of the fictional texts of the period set in these territories. My approach in the following discussion has necessarily to be more selective given the quantity of such material relating to Turkey and Persia. I have found it most productive to offer closer readings of representative or transformative texts for the representation of Middle Eastern cultures. Hence, for example, the discussion below of dramatic texts focuses on only two plays, both by women, which 'stage' the conflict between the look and the voice in ways that call particular attention to the gendered nature of acts of representation. Bridget Orr's magnificent *Empire on the English Stage 1668–1714* has provided a full and detailed account of the many English heroic plays which are set in territories under Ottoman, Persian, and Arab rule.

Loquacious women I: staging the Orient

Morena and Almyna: female wits

Accounts of the lives of Islamic rulers were regularly plundered as sources for the popular form of the oriental tragedy in late seventeenth- and early eighteenth-century culture. Extravagant productions, with stage directions for mutes, eunuchs, and sumptuous decor, were familiar to audiences of the period. Two female playwrights, one Whig and one Tory, used the staged conflict between a sultan consumed by lust of the eye and seraglio women with loquacious powers in order to make analogies or draw contrasts between the position of women in occidental and oriental cultures as well as in order to pursue party ideology. Mary Pix's *Ibrahim, the Thirteenth*

Emperor of the Turks (1696) drew on Rycaut's account of the voluptuous reign and violent death of Ibrahim, in fact the twelfth emperor of the Turks (ruled 1640–8).[26] Rycaut had made an analogy between Ibrahim's death at the hands of his janissaries and that of Charles I which occurred in the same year (see 'Histories' in Ch. 2 'Shape-Shifting'), but Pix is more likely to be making the parallel with Charles's second son, James II, a ruler who, like Ibrahim, had spent many years in exile and uncertainty during a brother's reign. James's public avowal of Catholicism made possible popular associations with the absolutism of the French Catholic and Ottoman Islamic courts. In the invented figure of Amurat, son of the Aga of the Janissaries, Pix celebrates the Protestant William of Orange who had peacefully deposed his father-in-law, James II, in 1688; Amurat is a military genius and monogamous lover in whose name the savage rebellion of the armed forces against a despotic king is martialled but who denounces its violence. Pix replays the Glorious Revolution as a tragic oriental drama, placing at its centre a passively loving westernized couple, Amurat and his beloved Morena, the Mufti's daughter (whose very name echoes that of her political analogue, William's wife and James's daughter, Mary, as well as that of her author, Mary Pix).

Delarivier Manley also implies an analogy between author and dramatic heroine in her *Almyna; or, the Arabian Vow* (1707), since the name Almyna is a near anagram of Manley. The despotic sultan Almanzor has, like Schahriar, sworn to kill each wife on the morning after his marriage as a result of discovering his queen's infidelity with a Moorish slave. When he hears about Almyna's education at her father's hands and her intellectual brilliance, he dismisses her as 'A Contradiction, to her very nature'.[27] Manley appears to be suggesting a symmetry between her own ambitions for political influence through witty writing and her heroine's verbal agency. Manley based her play on the life of Almanzor (Muhammad Ibn Abu'amir Al-mansur,

---

[26] Pix comments in the Preface: '*I read some years ago, at a Relations House in the Country, Sir Paul Ricauts Continuation of the Turkish History; I was pleas'd with the story and ventur'd to write upon it, but trusted too far to my Memory; for I never saw the Book afterwards till the Play was Printed, and then I found* Ibrahim *was the Twelfth Emperour*' (Mary Pix, *Ibrahim, the Thirteenth Emperour of the Turks* (London: 1696), n.p.).

[27] Delarivier Manley, *Almyna: Or, the Arabian Vow. A Tragedy* (London, 1707), 10.

the chief minister and virtual ruler of the Umayyad caliphate of Cordoba from AD 978 to 1002) 'with something of a hint of the *Arabian* Nights Entertainments' (Preface, n.p.).[28]

These analogical heroines have been educated in classical philosophy and literature, which allows them to identify with a long tradition of resistance to despotism on the part of women. Morena's father, the Mufti, tries to dissuade Ibrahim from his interest in meeting her with the claim that:

> . . . the Girl is most unfit
> For you to see, Bred up in Cells, and Grotto's:
> Tho' so near a Court, wholly unacquainted with its Glories.
> Heaven not Blessing me with a Male, I have try'd
> To mend the Sex; and she, instead of (coining looks)
> And learning little Arts to please, hath Read
> Philosophy, History, those rough Studies.
>
> (p. 19)

Almanzor's brother, Abdalla, who has previously courted Almyna's sister, Zoraida, but is now in love with Almyna herself, remarks:

> Well has she too, Employ'd her early Years,
> Join'd Art to Nature, and improv'd the Whole.

---

[28] The setting for Manley's play may appear to fall outside the geographical remit of this chapter, since it is neither in Turkey nor Persia. However, this chapter treats the *Arabian Nights Entertainments* as an important and influential document in the construction of images of Turkey and Persia. The work was received in Europe in the context of Ottoman dominance as an Islamic power. Mahdi notes that: 'For the eighteenth century, the *Nights* was the "Orient" and the Orient was the world of Muslims and Ottomans: no one was interested in defending Indian origins' (Mahdi, *Thousand and One Nights*, 4). Galland spent the majority of his time in the East in Istanbul where he polished his Ottoman Turkish, Persian, and Arabic. Many of the tales, like Manley's play, are set in the early years of Islam under the caliphate derived from Abu Bakr, Muhammad's father-in-law, the nominal ruling power in Islam from AD 632. Manley's play concerns the Umayyad caliphate which was established in Spain after its defeat in Damascus, Syria, in the 8th c. Harun ar-Rashid (AD 766?–809), the 8th-c. Abbasid caliph whose capital was in Baghdad, is the night-wandering, wise, and all-powerful sultan in many of the tales of the *Arabian Nights* ('Harun Ar-Rashid', Britannica Student Encyclopedia. 2003. Encyclopædia Britannica Online. 07 May, 2003 http://search.eb.com/ebi/article?eu = 296699). Manley's and the English translators' use of the term 'sultan' to refer to the caliphs suggests that the Arab caliphs were identified with the Ottoman dynasty in this period; the seraglios these fictional caliphs command are described on the model of the reports of the Ottoman palace at Istanbul and the Persian court at Isfahan by 17th-c. travellers such as Galland himself.

What ever *Greek* or *Roman* Eloquence,
Egyptian Learning, and Philosophy can teach;
She has, by Application, made her own.

(p. 10)[29]

Morena, after her rape by the sultan, cries

Look down ye *Roman* ladies
Whose tracks of Virtue I with care
Have followed . . .

(p. 38)

while Almyna refers her husband to examples of oriental and classical heroic virtue in women—Semiramis, Judith, Virginia, Lucretia,
Portia, Clelia, and Cleopatra—as part of her attempt to disprove his
claim, spuriously derived from Islamic law, that women have no souls.

Both playwrights make extensive use of the potential of the stage, a
medium structured on the twin axes of visual and verbal representation, to draw the contrast between the sultan's power to 'stage-manage'
the scene of his pleasure or revenge, and the loquacious seraglio
heroine's capacity to use language to temper, transform, or instigate a
challenge to despotism. Morena, as a Turkish Lucrece, describes herself as 'by wrongs a Fury grown' (p. 29); her rape is the cause of the
insurrection of the janissaries. Almyna uses her intelligence and wit as
well as her beauty to bring Almanzor to recognize the immortal souls
of women; he comments when he gives her permission to argue with
him 'Is it her Eyes, or Tongue, this Change has caus'd?' (p. 45).

Note that Almanzor questions whether he has been more swayed by
Almyna's beauty than her argument. The introduction of women
taking female parts with the restoration of Stuart monarchy in 1660
only confirmed the sense that the visual axis of the drama frequently
outweighed its verbal pleasures, especially in the case of the oriental
tragedy.[30] Moreover, the accretive and cyclical nature of female-voiced

---

[29] Manley was the well-educated (though not classically trained) daughter of a cavalier
soldier, Roger Manley, who had contributed to the continuation of Knolles's and Rycaut's
Turkish History, a biographical detail which adds to the evidence for a conscious analogy
between the heroine and her author.

[30] Elizabeth Howe argues that 'It is no coincidence that at the same time as love, pathos
and female characters were becoming more prominent in tragedy, actresses were proving
themselves in a variety of serious roles'. Elizabeth Howe, *The First English Actresses:
Women and Drama 1660–1700* (Cambridge: Cambridge University Press, 1992), 110.

oriental narrative can have no place in the verbal sparring of the seventeenth-century dramatic dialogue. Almyna—unlike her model Scheherazade and her author, Manley (better known as the author of scandal fictions than as a playwright in the years just prior to the play's performance)—uses philosophy and history rather than narrative to charm her suitor/husband. As Bridget Orr comments, '[i]nstead of the hapless heroine keeping herself alive through the endless provision of stories, she actively takes up the challenge of dissuading the Sultan from his barbarous views through logical and historical argument, not narrative prowess'.[31]

Pix contrasts Morena's virtuous Lucrece-like resistance and desire to keep 'private' with the pursuit of publicity and public influence by Ibrahim's mistress and procuress, Sheker Para. Ibrahim, according to Mustapha the Aga of the Janissaries, 'exposes' this his favourite courtesan 'to publick view, lets her converse | With Visier, Bashaws, or whom she pleases' (pp. 2–3). A contrast with Morena is immediately established in the Mufti's response:

> But that I have a Daughter,
> Whose early Vertue and sincere Obedience,
> Ties my soul to dote upon:
> I for my Countries sake wou'd Curse the Sex.

> (p. 3)

Morena has lived privately and confined, as Turkish women are expected to do, whereas Sheker Para lives publicly. However, Morena has been educated on masculine lines, whereas Sheker Para has gained the privileges of masculine court life through the exercise of feminine charms. Morena is increasingly pushed into the 'public eye'. Called before the Sultan, Morena dramatically seizes Ibrahim's 'naked Scimitar' and draws it through her hands, crying 'are these hands | Fit to clasp thee?' (p. 24). In the following act she is presented as an erotically charged icon of rapine. Her call to her maid voices her reluctance to be used for this theatrical form of public display:

> Lead me, my *Zaida*, to Darkness, solid,
> Thick, substantial Darkness, where

---

[31] Orr, *Empire on the English Stage*, 132.

> Not one Ray of the all-cheering Light
> May peep upon me . . .
>
> (p. 29)

Morena, then, conforms to the stereotype of the oriental woman who resists being exposed, revealed to the masculine gaze, but who, by virtue of her very concealment, remains fascinating. Sheker Para is the agent of the public display of other women, while she keeps secret or fails to disclose her own motives and desires. In her final encounter with Amurat she declares '"Twas I disclos'd the | Cloistered Maid, and forc'd her on the King' (p. 37). If Sheker Para displays women to the male gaze in order to secure her own political advancement, Morena attempts to evade the gaze of men, only to call upon women to look at her as evidence of the abuse of masculine power and the virtue of their own sex.

Morena's position is then close to that of the playwright herself, seeking the approving gaze of western women as protection from the intrusive gaze of their male counterparts. In the Prologue spoken by the actress Letitia Cross, the ladies in the boxes of the Drury Lane Theatre are called upon for protection:

> The Pit our Author dreads as too severe,
> The ablest Writers scarce find Mercy there;
> Her only hopes in yonder brightness lies,
> If we read praise in those Commanding Eyes:
> What rude Blustering Critique then will dare
> To find a fault, or contradict the Fair?
>
> (n.p.)

Virtuous political agency is an impossibility for women within the despotic absolutist structure that is the play's historical context; protection for Morena lies outside of the oriental 'frame' of the play, in a space controlled by the discriminating powers of women whose looks are taken account of: the western theatre.

Similarly, the virtuous political agency of Almyna derives from western rather than oriental sources. Rather than narrating the sequence of oriental stories that her model Scheherazade uses to counter and defer her husband's despotism, Almyna rehearses the secular and historical arguments in defence of women familiar from seventeenth-century pamphlet literature in England—such as Rachel Speght's *A Mouzell for Melastomus* (1617) and Ester Sowernam's *Ester hath Hang'd Haman* (1617)[32]—but strips them of their Christian theology. The epilogue spoken by Thomas Betterton calls on the female audience of the play to take pleasure in the submission of the oriental sultan to their authority as embodied by Almyna:

> *Of you, bright Nymphs, our Author humbly prays,*
> *You wou'd forget what the rough Sultan says.*
> *Convinc'd, at length, he does your Empire own,*
> *And at your feet, lays all his Errors down.*
> *If his performance, chance to please the Fair;*
> *Joys so refin'd, no youthful Breast can bear:*
> *No more by Fear, or Modesty, conceal'd,*
> *He then will stand your happy Slave, reveal'd.*

(n.p.)

As this quotation implies, Pix and Manley deploy the oriental setting to invoke the notion of an 'empire of wit' associated with western femininity and its regulatory powers of surveillance in public culture. The oriental setting serves as a 'veil' or 'cover' for the performance of a verbal agency which is ultimately returned to the Occident. Women's wit may remain confined and constrained in the stage play by the convention of displaying the woman's body; the actress taking the female part dazzles the audience and her male counterparts so that they are seduced by her physical presence at the expense of her witty speech. But the female playwright, whose script simultaneously voices her wit and conceals her identity/person, suffers no such constraint. Indeed, like the veiled and hidden woman of the seraglio she can exercise her influence and verbal agency without being seen.

This imaginative identification with oriental femininity brings the female playwrights close to the female travel writer Lady Mary

---

[32] See *Female Replies to Swetnam the Woman-Hater*, intro. Charles Butler (Bristol: Thommes Press, 1995). On these arguments and the ventriloquism of a female insurgent voice in this pamphlet tradition, see Diane Purkiss, 'Material Girls: The Seventeenth-Century Woman Debate', in Clare Brant and Diane Purkiss (eds.), *Women, Texts and Histories 1575–1760* (London: Routledge, 1992), 69–101.

Wortley Montagu, who celebrates the veil as a means of looking without being observed: 'I ramble every day, wrap'd up in my ferigé and asmak, about Constantinople and amuse myselfe with seeing all that is curious in it' (May 1718 from Pera to Countess of . . . [possibly Bristol], *CLMWM* i. 405). Like Lady Mary too, the female playwrights can manipulate and orchestrate the responses of a mixed audience to their staged representations of the Orient.

Just as the encounter with the Orient feminizes the western male by placing him in the position of hidden observer and seductive speaker, it provides access for the western female to the masculine position of generating models of subjectivity through the objectification of 'others' (often the oriental female). However, the simple opposition of loquacious woman and gazing male is also destabilized in oriental fictions, especially the drama, by the elusive and allusive figure of the 'eunuch' who surfaces as a sight/site of indeterminacy.

'Half-men': the eunuch

There are references to the presence of the figure of the eunuch on the English stage in both *Ibrahim* and *Almyna*. *Ibrahim* opens on the figure of the sinister 'Chief of the Eunuchs', Achmet, instructing his fellow eunuchs to prepare the virgins in the seraglio for the attendance of Ibrahim. We quickly learn that Achmet is Sheker Para's creature and spy; the part was also taken by a woman (Mrs Verbruggen). In the third act of *Ibrahim,* Mary Pix has Achmet introduce to the sultan music which he claims is 'Prepar'd by the Italian Masters' (p. 16) and which includes 'A Dialogue Song' written by Thomas D'Urfey 'Suppos'd to be between an Eunuch Boy and a Virgin' and written for 'Boyn' (Jemmy Bowen, the popular pre-pubescent boy singer of the 1690s) and 'Mrs Crosse' (Letitia Cross, famous for playing hoydens and an accomplished singer and dancer, then in her early twenties). The song was set by Daniel Purcell and was printed separately in the same year as the play. An unpleasant little piece, it involves the virgin rejecting the eunuch boy's advances because he lacks the wherewithal truly to please her. To her complaint 'thou art not made like other Boys', he responds by claiming the power of storytelling, song, and games (the entertainments of the harem):

> HE. *Why, I can Kiss, and I can Play,*
> *And tell a Thousand Pretty Tales;*
> *And I can Sing the livelong Day;*
> *If any other Talent fails.*
> SHE. *Boast not thy Musick, for I fear*
> *That Singing Gift has cost thee dear,*
> *Each warbling Linnet on the Tree*
> *Has far a Better Fate than thee,*
> *For thy Lifes happy pleasures prove,*
> *As they can Sing, so they can Love.*

(p. 17)

Manley's play repeats this 'double' invocation of the figure of the eunuch, as both seraglio plotter and castrated singer. Morat, chief of the eunuchs, is a character loyal to Almyna and her father who conspires with Almanzor's brother, Abdalla, to overthrow the sultan in order to save Almyna from execution, enlisting the assistance of Muca, king of Arabia. Morat and his eunuchs break into the apartment of the women with Abdalla at the close of the play only to discover that the sultan has cancelled her threatened execution and revealed it to be a mere trial of her courage. Here too, then, the eunuch chief is portrayed as loyal to the women in his care rather than his master for whom he acts as surrogate in policing the harem. In this instance, however, the part of the eunuch chief was taken by a male actor, Mr Corey. Delarivier Manley's second reference to a eunuch does not fall within the play but in its preface, where she complains about the unfortunate timing of the first performance of *Almyna* on Monday, 16 December 1706 at the Queen's theatre in 'the immediate Week before Christmas between Devotion and *Camilla* (the Eunuch having then never Sung but once)'. Her reference is to one of the earliest productions of an Italian opera on the English stage at Drury Lane, and to the possible performance there of a male part by the Italian castrato, Valentini (Valentino Urbano).[33] Valentini

---

[33] Milhous and Hume note that the apparent reference to Valentini performing at Drury Lane is surprising since he was not advertised there until 8 March 1707 where he took the part of Turnus in *Camilla* (Judith Milhous and Robert D. Hume, *The London Stage, 1660–1800* (Carbondale, Ill.: Southern Illinois University Press, 1996), 327). The

was not the first castrato to visit England; Baldassare Ferri and Siface had visited before and John Evelyn records hearing Siface sing at Samuel Pepys's home in 1687, but it was not until the first three decades of the eighteenth century that the popular craze for Italian opera and the castrato took off.[34]

Both playwrights then deploy the 'double' appearance of eunuch figures, one associated with the Islamic seraglio and the other with Italian churches and theatres (castrati were first introduced in Ferraro and Rome in the mid-sixteenth century as church singers since women could not sing in church). Interestingly, although the use of eunuchs by middle eastern and Chinese governments was known to pre-date Islam—indeed the Byzantine patriarchs of Constantinople prior to its seizure by the Ottomans were commonly eunuchs— eunuch figures only appear in oriental plays set in Muslim courts.[35] In both plays under discussion, the eunuch is a liminal figure, ambiguously placed in the gendered economy of the oriental seraglio. In the Ottoman court, eunuchs were quite literally liminal figures in that their primary role was as guards and preceptors, white eunuchs guarding the selected boys and young men who were being trained for government service in the second courtyard of the imperial palace,

first all-sung opera after the Italian manner to be performed in England was *Arsinoe* adapted by Motteux with music arranged by Clayton, Dieupart, and Haym; it opened on 16 January 1705 to great success. The arrival of the castrato Nicolini (Nicolo Grimaldi) in London was to usher in yet greater enthusiasm for the form and bilingual productions in which the hero sang in Italian and the heroine in English. On Italian opera in England, see Robert Ness, 'The Dunciad and Italian Opera in England', *Eighteenth-Century Studies* 20 (1986–7): 173–94; Thomas McGeary, ' "Warbling Eunuchs": Opera, Gender, and Sexuality on the London Stage, 1705-1742', *Restoration and Eighteenth-Century Theatre Research*, 2nd ser. 7, no. 1 (1992): 1–22; Xavier Cervantes, ' "Tuneful Monsters": The Castrati and the London Operatic Public 1667–1737', *Restoration and Eighteenth-Century Theatre Research*, 2nd ser. 13, no. 1 (1998): 1–24; Angus Heriot, *The Castrati in Opera* (London: Secker & Warburg, 1956).

[34] Siface (Giovanni Grosse) was sent by his employer, the Duke of Modena Francesco II, to entertain the latter's sister Mary, wife of James II, a detail which is illuminating in light of the veiled anti-Catholicism of Pix's play and its attack on James, whereby his oriental despotism can be associated with Italianate cruelty and the practice of castration of boys in both Ottoman and Italian territories.

[35] The few plays that concern China in the late 17th and 18th c.—Elkanah Settle's *Conquest of China* (1676), William Hatchett's *The Chinese Orphan* (1741), Voltaire's *Orphelin de la Chine* (1755), and Arthur Murphy's translation and rewriting of the former, the *Orphan of China* (1756)—do not include eunuch characters although informant accounts of China from the 17th c., largely from Jesuit priests, had detailed their centrality to the Ming and Manchu courts.

and the black eunuchs guarding the female harem.[36] Eunuchs were, like those they guarded, slaves and not Muslim born (white eunuchs were obtained from Circassian, Georgian, and Armenian boy slaves and black eunuchs from Sudan, Egypt, and Abyssinia). Pix's Achmet and Manley's Morat, played by a white female and male actor respectively, should have been but probably were not black parts, since they are the chief eunuchs for the women's quarters, a role taken in the Ottoman court by the immensely powerful Kizlar Agasi.[37]

Representations of the oriental eunuch on stage commonly concealed the racial difference that was key to the organization of eunuchs in the Ottoman court, although the informant sources on which they drew were explicit about the distinction. This may have been due to the tendency to collapse the role of the eunuch into the western traditions of the 'boy-player' on the Renaissance English stage (as indicated by the boy-singer in *Ibrahim*) and the white Italian castrato. In line with the most famous precedent of Shakespeare's *Othello*, black male figures on stage are cast as sexually potent, sometimes violent agents; the 'Moorish slave' with whom Abdalla has seen his wife in congress (derived from the frame story of the *Arabian Nights Entertainments*) is not countered by the figure of the black eunuch in dramatic representation.

Travel and informant accounts were contemptuous of eunuchs who oversaw the female harem in Islamic courts but not dismissive of their power and inclined to represent them not as co-conspirators with their charges but rather as surrogate 'eyes' for the sultan, given to constant surveillance and suspicion. John Fryer in his description of Persia comments that their masters 'confide in their Impotency to preside over the Female Senate, setting them as Spies over their Incontinency, and as faithful Keepers of their Vertue of Necessity'.[38] Jean de Thévenot tells us of the black eunuchs in the Grand

---

[36] Leslie Pierce summarizes: 'With the exception of the sultan, only those who were not considered to be fully adult males were routinely permitted in the inner worlds of the palace: in the male harem household, boys and young men, eunuchs, dwarves, and mutes; and in the female harem household, women and children' (Peirce, *The Imperial Harem*, 11).
[37] It is particularly unlikely that Mrs Verbruggen, who played Achmet, would have 'blacked up' since it was considered inappropriate for white female actors to do so on the English stage.   [38] Fryer, *New Account of East India and Persia*, iii. 125-6.

Seraglio that 'there is no Woman cunning enough to deceive those half men'.[39] Black eunuchs were chosen to guard the women's quarters, commentators explained, because African features are considered 'hard-favoured'[40] and inclined to prompt 'strong *Antipathy*'[41] among white women.

If popular representations of eunuchs in Islamic courts on stage tended to conceal a racial difference within the eunuchs' ranks and inclined to represent them as allies of white harem women rather than of their despot masters, these representations did share with travel and informant writers the tendency to portray the eunuchs' liminality in terms of a blurring of gender boundaries. Paul Rycaut, for instance, comments that the white eunuchs who train the young men are 'naturally cruel, whether it be out of envy to the Masculine Sex which is perfect and intire, or that they decline to the disposition of Women, which is many times more cruel and revengeful then that of men'.[42] He refers to marriages that took place between eunuchs and women in which they 'exercise Lusts of an unknown and prodigious nature'.[43] John Fryer describes Persian eunuchs as 'a Map of Villany' for they look 'as if they had stolen an Old Woman's Face, and a Puppit's Voice'.[44]

These kind of descriptions were to become commonplace in satirical attacks on the Italian castrato in early eighteenth-century England and here too the eunuch appears to have commanded a particularly strong response as a 'liminal' figure who could choose either to police the gateway between gender identities and nationhood or open it, letting in a dangerous flood of femininity, luxury, and absolutism with his presence on the English stage. John Dennis's 'Essay on the Operas' of 1706 makes explicit the link between the feminizing force of 'opera' embodied in the castrato and the threat to English 'empire', describing how when the opera is not written with 'force', 'the whole Man is dissolv'd in the Wantonness of effeminate Airs' and concluding that 'the Declension of Poetry should portend the Fall of

---

[39] Thévenot, *Travels*, i. 24.

[40] Rycaut, 'The Present State of the Ottoman Empire', in Knolles and Rycaut, *Turkish History*, ii, bk. 1, ch. 9, p. 17 (separately numbered).

[41] Hill, *Full and Just Account*, 160.

[42] Rycaut, 'The Present State of the Ottoman Empire', ch. 5, p. 13.

[43] Ibid., ch. 21, p. 74   [44] Fryet, *New Account of East India and Persia*, 126.

Empire'. He warns his reader to beware 'that while the *English* Arms are every where Victorious abroad, the *English* Arts may not be vanquish'd and oppress'd at home by the Invasion of Foreign Luxury'.[45]

Delariver Manley in her preface comments that the character of Almyna was 'drawn (tho' faintly) from that excellent Pen of Mr. Dennis, who, in his *Essay upon Opera's*, has given us a View of what Heroic Vertue ought to attempt' (n.p.). Dennis describes such virtue as when 'great Minds bravely contemn Death to further that Felicity' of being 'the Preserver of Nations' which makes 'a World happy!' (388). Almyna of course bravely confronts her execution (the sultan having promised that she will be the last of his conjugal victims) as a means of saving her ruler and her nation from the bitter civil wars and possible foreign invasion that may result from his tyranny. It may not be too fanciful to suggest that Manley is not only complimenting but contesting Dennis in claiming that the heroic actions of the seraglio woman, supported by the indeterminately sexed eunuch, is less a dangerous incentive to luxury and foreign rule than a means of correcting despotism and importing 'civilized' values derived from a classical and Christian Protestant West into those hotbeds of 'foreign' absolutism, Istanbul and Rome.

Loquacious women II: narrating the Orient

As we have seen, the eunuch in the oriental court was a fascinating and significant figure for dramatists, travellers, and historians. However, he played little or no part in the long prose framed sequences of the eighteenth century, which tended to present the ancient courts of the East in terms of a simple tension between the authority of the ruler and the ambitions or desires of his concubines, wives, daughters, or (often female) subjects. Nevertheless, despite their tendency to mythologize

[45] John Dennis, *The Critical Works of John Dennis*, ed. Edward Niles Hooker (Baltimore: Johns Hopkins University Press, 1939), 389, 90.

oriental culture and their reliance on sources dating back to the first ten centuries, such fictions were marketed and framed as representations of the 'genuine' contemporary East for their readers.

European travellers and historians in and of the East testify to the status of Galland's sequence as an informant source about the cultures they encounter. Hence, Lady Mary Wortley Montagu writes in a letter to her sister that the *Arabian Nights Entertainments* 'were writ by an Author of this Country and (excepting the Enchantments) are a real representation of the manners here' (*CLMWM* i. 385). Galland prepared his first translations from an Arabic manuscript produced in Syria in the Mamluke period (the mid-thirteenth to early sixteenth century), a fact that would not have been known to Lady Mary.[46] It is striking, however, that she should claim the collection as 'Turkish', unless the 'author of this country' to whom she is referring is Galland, who spent many years in Istanbul.

How was it that a collection of tales originally derived from ancient non-Islamic India and Persia could come to be seen as an authentic source of information, even more so than the contemporaneous accounts of European travellers, about eighteenth-century Turkish culture? Why was it that consumption of 'the East' came in the eighteenth century to be almost coterminous with the consumption of fabulous narrative? My discussion is concerned not with the history of the production of the 'Nights', but rather with its reception and representation in eighteenth-century western European culture. The answer to these questions, I argue, lies in the particular purposes that the sequence of tales from the seraglio served in constructing images about the East in the West, especially in the demand to turn the East into a consumable narrative, a story that could be given credit and

---

[46] Textual scholarship into the provenance of the tales took off in the late 19th c. when Zotenberg examined the twenty-two surviving Arabic manuscripts and identified the main manuscript source used by Galland. The earliest owner recorded in the marginal inscription dated from the late 15th c. For the complicated manuscript history of this work see ch. 2 of Robert Irwin, *The Arabian Nights: A Companion* and ch. 1 of Muhsin Mahdi, *Thousand and One Nights*. Irwin states in summary that scholars now agree the *Nights* as Galland received them were a composite work; the earliest tales derive from India and Persia; it was probably translated into Arabic in the early 8th c. and Arab stories, including those about Harun ar-Rashid, were added in Iraq in the 9th or 10th c. Independent sagas and story cycles were added in the 10th c. and from the 13th c. onwards stories were added in Syria or Egypt, many of which concerned sex, magic, or low life.

exercise its own forces of enchantment upon the imagination of western readers.

The slippage between claims to narrative pleasure, an effect of moral improvement, and ethnographical information is repeated at every point in European 'framing' of oriental tales. The introduction to the translation of a sequence of Persian and Turkish tales from the translations of the French Orientalist, François Pétis de la Croix, is one of the most striking illustrations:

> *The wise and more discerning Part of Mankind need not dread the Reflection of misemploying their Time, when they read these for mere Trifles, since the following Tales are equally useful and instructing, as they are agreeable and entertaining; every one of them recommending the Fidelity and Honour of a Lover, or the Constancy and Affection of a Husband: In short, the Geography is exactly observed, wherein the Scene of every Action is laid, whether in Tartary, Persia, or Egypt; and the Manners, Customs, and Habits of the different People of Asia, which sufficiently characterize them, are here handsomely set forth; the Morals of the Mussulmen are display'd, and we may from hence understand a great deal of their Religion; besides, the Translator from the Original hath added Abundance of his own curious Remarks.*[47]

Scheherazade and her sisters

Dinarzade sleeps at the foot of her sister's marital bed and remembers to wake early each morning and request the continuation of a tale. The stories of the *Arabian Nights Entertainments* are thus framed as an exchange between women which is observed by a listening man, who is in fact their intended recipient. It is a frame that is repeated, manipulated, and parodied in eighteenth-century fiction in western Europe. European writers were quick to see the ludicrousness and potential eroticism in the scenario from the involuntary loquacity of the vaginal lips of the Congese court ladies in Diderot's *Bijoux Indiscrets* (1748) to the sleep-inducing effects of the ramblings of a Dutch princess on 'the doctrines of grace, free-will, predestination, reprobation, justification, &c.' to the 'giant' (five foot and three inches)

---

[47] François Pétis de la Croix, *The Persian and Turkish Tales, compleat* (London, 1767), 5th edn., ii, n.p.

Emperor of Cucurucu in Horace Walpole's 'New Arabian Nights Entertainment' (1785).[48]

Almost as soon as Galland's 'translation' appeared, it was subject to parody: Anthony Hamilton, an English Jacobite living at Saint Germain with the English court, produced a series of manuscript tales that mocked the extravagance and lapses in realism evident in the fairy and oriental tales so popular in late seventeenth- and early eighteenth-century France, especially at Louis XIV's court. Hamilton's tales were written in French and widely circulated in that language, but only fragmentarily and poorly translated into English before the mid-nineteenth century.[49] As it often does, parody serves to highlight the features and structure of the genre. Hamilton gives new prominence to Dinarzade, who persuades her sister to let her be the teller of the thousand and first tale to the doltish husband from whom Scheherazade extracts a promise that he will repeal her sentence of death at the close of the tales if he interrupts Dinarzade before she has finished her story. Dinarzade builds her story around the sultan's dismissive response to her question about what his reaction would be if she could tell him what had happened at his secret council with his ministers; he 'pooh-poohs' her claim and she accordingly tells a story about a disguised prince, Tarare ('pooh-pooh'), who is tormented by the fact that listeners are compelled to repeat his assumed name whenever he reveals it.

Dinarzade's story, 'The History of the Thorn-flower', is an involved fiction which plays with all the conventions of the oriental tale, inverting each in turn. Thus, Tarare is enlisted to find a way of suppressing the killing power of the gaze of the Princess Luizanta.

---

[48] Horace Walpole, *Hieroglyphic Tales*, Augustan Reprint Society Publication 212/13 (Los Angeles: William Andrews Clark Memorial Library, 1982), 7.

[49] *Select Tales of Count Hamilton* (London, 1760) was published with a reference to the success of the author's romanced biography of his brother-in-law which included a scandalous chronicle of the court of Charles II, the *Memoirs of the Count de Grammont* (translated from the French original of 1713 into English in 1714); the selection excluded much of the frame material making many of the references in the tales themselves meaningless. The 'Advertisement to the Bookseller' claims that 'The translations of the Tales of the Persians, Arabians, and Turks, were read by all the ladies both at court and in the city. He rallied them upon their attachment to reading what afforded them so little instruction; but in a manner so as not to offend them. One day they defied him to write any thing in the taste of these works; the Count, whose genius was capable of any thing he undertook, let them see in a few days, that he knew how to trifle with the Muses' (n.p.).

The compulsive power of the name and the deathly effects of the look are, as Grosrichard identifies, the twin properties of despotic power, but Hamilton/Dinarzade gives them to Tarare and the princess he loves, leaving the sultan himself a weak and ineffectual figure.[50] The claim to political authority on the part of the princess and her suitor thus provides a coded warning to the listening ruler, as do the tales in the *Arabian Nights Entertainments*.

Tarare asks the witch Serena for assistance in his task and she undertakes to resolve the problem in exchange for four objects including a portrait of Luizanta and a thorn-flower. Tarare successfully paints the portrait by observing the sitter through pieces of tinted glass and, in the process, sitter and artist fall in love. The thorn-flower turns out to be Serena's daughter, who has been abducted by a wicked aunt and imprisoned in Kashmir. Tarare saves the thorn-flower in an exciting abduction and chase and is then torn between his new love for her and his prior commitment to Luizanta. Thorn-flower nearly pines to death on the return to court when Tarare's affections reverse again and he declares his intention to populate the palace with little Tarares. The sultan is finally at this point driven to interrupt with the outburst 'Oh! for the little Tarares . . . I have nothing to reply to that' (i. 226). He concedes the victory to Dinarzade and promises to remit her sister's sentence not least because she has diverted him so well for two years with the 'liveliness of her tales' (i. 227). However he remains angered that Dinarzade has gained access to knowledge in the councils, only to be mollified when she reveals that he is her informant, that is, in another reversal, the woman has 'overheard' exchanges between men. He orders Dinarzade to finish her story in one minute and three quarters which she promptly does by revealing that the magic parrot which has prevented the blinding effect of Luizanta's eyes is in fact Phenix, Tarare's handsome and princely brother under an enchantment. Luizanta chooses to marry the handsome brother leaving Tarare free to be united with his thorn-flower.

Later in the century, an admirer of Hamilton was to undertake a similar parody of the oriental tale, highlighting the difference between

---

[50] Anthony Hamilton was William Beckford's uncle and no doubt Beckford also had this tale in mind when he produced his own oriental parody of 1786 written in French with a character whose gaze can kill, *Vathek* (see Ch. 6).

the moral and instructive tale told by a sage to a prince and the 'contes' of intrigue and magic told by female informants and so beloved by female auditors. Here too the sequence is presented as a means of diverting women readers from the frivolous to the moral. Voltaire's *Zadig* (1748, originally published as *Memnon* in 1747) is dedicated to the fictional Sultana Sheraa and is a 'translation' of the work of an ancient sage: 'a Performance, that comprehends in it more Instruction than, 'tis possible, you may at first be aware of'.[51] The story is supposedly composed in the Chaldean language but translated into Arabic, for the amusement of the celebrated Sultan Ouloug-Beg:

It first appear'd in Public, when the *Arabian* and *Persian* Tales of One Thousand and One Nights, and One Thousand and One Days, were most in Vogue: OULOUG chose rather to entertain himself with the Adventures of *Zadig*. The Sultanas indeed were more fond of the former. How can you, said the judicious OULOUG, be so partial, as to prefer a Set of Tales, that are no ways interesting or instructive, to a Work, that has a Variety of Beauties to recommend it? Oh! replied the Sultanas, the less Sense there is in them, the more they are in Taste; and the less their Merit, the greater their Commendation. (A3r–v).

The philosophical tale of a virtuous young Zoroastrian from Babylon, who falls from prosperity into misfortune and is restored to fortune through the agency of Providence, plays on the fascination with mutilation in the sequence of oriental tales and the representation of the Orient in general (the two opening chapters are termed 'the Blind Eye' and 'the Nose'). Like Hamilton's tales, it aims to challenge the idea that morality can be conveyed through the ridiculous and the magical. Women's fickleness and attraction to physical perfection in men consistently blocks Zadig's progress and disappoints his high ideals of equality and mutual affection. Voltaire challenges one tradition, the sequence of Arabic tales told by women in which women challenge male despotism through storytelling, with another, the sequence of Indian tales told by a sage which teach the young male listener or protagonist self-government, the oriental equivalent of the 'mirror for princes'. In England, Samuel Johnson was to take a similar route in his philosophical oriental tale, *Rasselas* (1759).

[51] François Marie Arouet de Voltaire, *Zadig; or, the Book of Fate* (London, 1749).

Four sequences of oriental tales, all 'translated' by French scholars and in turn translated into English, represent the former tradition and its dominance in eighteenth-century fiction: Antoine Galland's *Mille et une Nuit* (1704–17, translated into English *c*.1706–1721),[52] François Pétis de la Croix's *Contes Turcs* (1707, translated into English 1708), and *Les Mille et un Jour* or *Contes Persans* (1710–12, translated into English in two different editions in 1714, one by Ambrose Philips and one by William King), and Claude-Philippe de Tubières, Comte de Caylus' *Contes Orientales* (translated into English 1745). European reception of the oriental tale was always framed in terms of a claim for its potential as a vehicle for morality, but consistently revealed an enthusiasm for, indeed compulsive addiction to, the pleasure of narrative for its own sake. Like Schahriar and the myopic despots who listen to so many of the sequences, readers find themselves 'blind' to the message and caught up in the pure pleasure of storytelling and its continuance. Indeed, the 'message' of the tale must necessarily remain veiled according to the logic of the sequence so that the auditor is insensibly led to mimic or imitate its 'truth'. Too visible an intention would lead to the end of storytelling and retribution, since the despot is, by definition, not open to criticism.

Of the four collections, the *Arabian Nights Entertainments* is the least coherent and the least susceptible to a single overarching interpretation. Whereas the frame stories remain in evidence throughout de la Croix's and Caylus's collections, Galland's frame soon recedes from view. Muhsin Mahdi observes that even the most careful and diligent reader of his edition of the fourteenth-century Arabic manuscript that formed the basis of Galland's 'translation' (but by no means the sum of the stories he included in the twelve French volumes) 'finds no connection between *all* the stories in it other than the brittle thread woven by Shahrazad who narrates them, her sister Dinarzad who requests them, King Shahriyar who listens to them'.[53]

---

[52] There are no copies of the first English volume extant, but Duncan Black MacDonald's research indicates that it was possibly available in English by 1706, two years after its Paris publication. See Duncan Black McDonald, 'A Bibliographical and Literary Study of the First Appearance of the Arabian Nights in Europe', *Library Quarterly* 2 (1932): 387–420; Sheila Shaw, 'Early English Editions of the Arabian Nights: Their Value to Eighteenth-Century Literary Scholarship', *Muslim World* 49 (1959): 232–8.
[53] Mahdi, *Thousand and One Nights*, iii. 140.

Critics who write about the Arabian Nights have nevertheless traced relations between stories and between the frame narrative and enframed stories; Eva Sallis comments that we find in the collection 'a preponderance of stories which one way or another resonate with the concerns of the frame narrative and, no matter how organically this came to be, we are presented with a kaleidoscope of impressions on conflict of power, the sexes, art, life and death'.[54] Sallis prefers to see that resonance as a repetition of the theme of storytelling's power to defer violence and heal psychic rupture (in the disturbed despot Schahriar). Likewise, Robert Irwin claims that 'In time, each story comes to resemble another story, and the reader begins to recognise patterns and permutations',[55] proposing that the Arabian Nights may best be read as a narrative about the use of narrative as survival strategy: 'knowledge of a story and the ability to tell it may assure the survival of an individual' (236). Muhsin Mahdi confirms this claim with respect to the opening stories told by Scheherazade ('The Fable of the Ass', 'The Ox and the Labourer', 'The History of the First Old Man and the Bitch', and 'The Story of the Second Old Man and the Two Black Dogs') which prove that 'stories can be used to ransom someone's life' (iii. 133). In each a figure of power is persuaded or decides to hear a story with the promise that, if it 'satisfies' (and this can include fulfilling a craving for the pleasure of story), the speaker will be excused a proposed punishment. And we encounter this same structure again in the inset stories to 'The Story of the Little Hunchback'. Here, a Christian merchant, a purveyor, a Jewish physician, and a tailor tell stories in order to have remitted the sentence of death passed by the caliph on the merchant for the supposed 'murder' of the little hunchback; their stories must prove to be more extraordinary than that of the 'death' of the hunchback, whose body each of the tellers has encountered and disposed of surreptitiously. The tailor's story concerns a garrulous barber who has told him about the misfortunes afflicting his six brothers; then the barber himself appears and restores the hunchback to life.

Thus the juridical sentence can be overtaken or overcome by the narrative sentence; indeed the latter conjures the presence of the

---

[54] Sallis, *Sheherazade through the Looking Glass*, 83.
[55] Irwin, *Arabian Nights*, 215.

healing barber himself. Story is a form of agency in the *Arabian Nights Entertainments*; it brings about metamorphosis, especially the most profound metamorphosis of all, from death to life. Of course, we can take the stories as simple parables about the role of fate in individual existence. Predestination is a central tenet of Sunni Islam and the stories of the *Arabian Nights Entertainments* frequently demonstrate that the attempt to avoid fate only leads to it. Thus, in 'The History of the Third Calender', prince Agib is shipwrecked on an island where he meets a boy who has been immured in an underground cave by his father to avert a prophecy that he will be killed within forty days by the Prince Agib; Agib befriends him but when reaching for a knife to pare a melon accidentally stabs him to death. Irwin concludes that fate stands for the storyteller and asserts that 'Fate is a thoroughly literary affair. Each man has his story, and it is written on him' (197). To some extent this is Scheherazade's role; as Mahdi notes, she tells of past events as a means of foretelling future events and happy endings, returning her monarch husband to the path of virtue in a parable of revealed religion correcting the errors of a transgressive heathen royalty (127 30). However, Scheherazade might also be seen as an active averter of an unjust decree, correcting her husband's claim to act as a surrogate 'fate' who exercises a false authority in the name of the divine. The stories by no means advocate quietism and submission to a prescripted destiny; characters such as Sindbad are praised for their enterprising and individualistic action.

Thus, the merchant hero and the seraglio heroine are linked through their strenuous attempts to turn narrative destiny into profit and credit, Sindbad in terms of material gain and Scheherazade in terms of symbolic capital. However, as so often in the oriental tale, the symbolic capital accrued by women's storytelling activity does not always attach to women in general; Scheherazade's tale-telling tends to prove her eccentricity rather than her exemplarity in relation to other women.

Take, for example, the narrative fortunes of another witty female favourite who exercises narrative authority: Zobeide, favoured wife of the Caliph Haroun Alraschid. We first encounter Zobeide as the mistress of an all-female household who directs the pleasures and storytelling activities of the three calenders (mendicant monks) and a porter who enter the home she shares with her sisters, Amine and Safie. The caliph, his vizier Giafer, and the chief of his eunuchs, Mesrour, stumble upon the festive household on one of their incognito late-night rambles through Baghdad, but all the men fall under sentence of death from the sisters when they break the promise they made not to enquire into the ladies' strange behaviour: the weeping women whip two bitches in the company's presence and Amine bears strange scars on her neck. Zobeide promises to remit the sentence if the men tell their own stories to the ladies, is satisfied with their performance, and releases them; the next morning the caliph summons the women to have them explain their conduct. Zobeide reveals that the bitches are her two full sisters; a fairy to which Zobeide had done a service has turned the sisters into dogs to punish them for throwing Zobeide and her betrothed into the sea in a fit of jealousy, an act that resulted in the latter's death. The fairy orders her to whip them without fail each night. Amine's scars have been inflicted by her jealous husband for exposing her face to another man. He is revealed to be the caliph's son Amin. The fairy is recalled and is persuaded to transform the dogs back into humans and heal Amine's scars at the behest of the caliph. The caliph marries Zobeide while the other three sisters marry the one-eyed calenders. At this stage then, Zobeide's role mirrors that of her narrator, Scheherazade; both are women who win the love of a powerful ruler through their beauty and wisdom. Their cryptic surfaces conceal secret knowledge and purpose.

A character called Zobeide appears briefly in 'The Story Told by the Sultan of Casgar's Purveyor', once more in the form of a sympathetic ameliorator of the restrictions on heterosexual romance in the confined space of the seraglio; she recognizes the secret love between a young nobleman and one of her ladies and permits them to marry. However, Zobeide's freedom of action and speech turns into despotism in 'The History of Ganem'. The son of a merchant observes some slaves secretly burying a chest, and retrieves from it the drugged body of a woman. He revives her and discovers she is Fetnah, rival for the caliph's affections, whom Zobeide has drugged and arranged to be buried alive. Fetnah lives secretly with Ganem, while Zobeide informs Haroun Alraschid that she has died in his absence. Ganem's family suffer severe persecutions when the caliph discovers Fetnah is alive and it is only after much suffering that Ganem's innocence is proved and Zobeide is cast off. The caliph marries Ganem's virtuous sister and the vizier his equally virtuous widowed mother. When Ganem returns to Baghdad he finds his relations thus exalted and can marry Fetnah.

It could be argued that the *Arabian Nights Entertainments* is simply a catch-all collection of stories and readers are not expected to associate the Zobeide of one story with the Zobeide of another. Certainly, stories are not delivered in chronological sequence and they derive from different parts of the East and relate to different historical moments. Thus, Zobeide reappears a few stories after that of Ganem in a humorous tale called 'The Sleeper Awakened'; here, the sultan's favourite Abon Hassan and his wife, Zobeide's ex-slave Nouz-ha-toul-aonadat, trick Zobeide and her husband into giving them gifts to support them in their supposed grief at the death of a spouse; when the cheat is discovered, Zobeide and Haroun Alraschid are entertained rather than offended. However, similar reversals, especially in the characters of women, happen within single stories: Badoura, princess of China, is married to her physical and spiritual 'twin' Prince Camaralzaran of Khaledan, heroically sets off in search of him in male disguise when they are separated, advances to the role of vizier at Ebene, and persuades Camaralzaran when he reappears to marry her 'wife', the princess, only to fall criminally in love with her stepson (by the princess and Camaralzaran) and then accuse him of attempted rape when he rejects her advances. Princess Haiatalnefous, her fellow wife, acts in the same way towards Badour's son. Their perfidy is not discovered until after the two young men have been reported to be executed, and Camaralzaran orders both women confined to prison for the rest of their days. The two sons, after many adventures which prove their virtue and their exemplary Muslim behaviour in their encounters with idolaters, are reunited with their father.

Such reversals in character are, of course, common to long narrative sequences. They are familiar to modern readers from soap opera; a character can transform over a long period of narrative time from hero to villain and vice versa. However, they are largely confined to the female characters of the *Arabian Nights Entertainments* and could also be seen to point to the ambivalence of the position of the loquacious politically active woman in the oriental tale. It is always possible that she may revert to 'type'. In his *Bijoux Indiscrets*, Denis Diderot has Mirzoza, the female favourite of the sultan of Congo, Mangogul, complain that imitations of the oriental tale such as Crébillon fils' *Le Sopha* (1742) simply invent 'new calumnies' against women. She rejects the sultan's 'compliment' when he excludes her from the general contempt for women he has acquired as a result of his magic ring which makes women's 'jewels' (genitals) reveal their true promiscuity; Mirzoza responds sharply: 'I do not . . . relish compliments which are addressed to me at the expence of my sex.'[56]

Silence is the only guarantor of female virtue in the *Arabian Nights Entertainments*; thus, in 'The Story of Beder, Prince of Persia', the prince's mother is acquired as a slave by his father but refuses to speak until she is pregnant, when she reveals her true identity as a princess of the sea and becomes the queen-consort to her newly monogamous husband. The Queen Gulnare acts to protect her son at various points in his story; he falls prey to the magical powers of two women, the princess of Samandal (sovereign of another watery kingdom), who is so offended when he declares his love that she turns him into a bird, and the queen of Labe, who turns him into an owl as she has done all the other men she has taken to her court as favourites. It is Gulnare, his mother, who transforms him back into human form from this last metamorphosis.

Why then does Scheherazade narrate stories that appear to threaten her own position, and, in equating female speech with incontinence, implicate her as storyteller in the potential unchastity of all women? The conclusion, which was invented by Galland and not found in his source, points to a way of understanding Scheherazade's risky strategy of inscribing ambivalence about female speech into her own:

The Sultan of the Indies could not but admire the prodigious memory of the sultaness his wife, who had entertained and diverted him so many nights, with such new and agreeable stories, that he believed her stock inexhaustible.

A thousand and one nights had passed away in these agreeable and innocent amusements; which contributed so much towards removing the

---

[56] Denis Diderot, *Les Bijoux Indiscrets* = : *Or, the Indiscreet Toys* (Tobago [London], 1749), ii. 5.

sultan's fatal prejudice against all women, and sweetening the violence of his temper, that he conceived a great esteem for the sultaness Scheherazade; and was convinced of her merit and great wisdom, and remembered with what courage she exposed herself voluntarily to be his wife, knowing the fatal destiny of the many sultanesses before her.

These considerations, and the many rare qualities he knew her to be mistress of, induced him at last to forgive her. I see, lovely Scheherazade, said he, that you can never be at a loss for these sorts of stories to divert me; therefore I renounce in your favour the cruel law I had imposed on myself; and I will have you to be looked upon as the deliverer of the many damsels I had resolved to have sacrificed to my unjust resentment.

The sultaness cast herself at his feet, and embraced them with the marks of a most lively and sincere acknowledgement. (*ANE* 892)

Both the motive behind and the nature of Schahriar's decision are confused here, suggesting that perhaps the one lesson learned from his consumption of so many tales is the agency of ambivalent statement. When we are told that he has chosen to 'forgive her' we must necessarily ask what crime it is that he forgives; the crime of all women, of unchastity, which has not in any case been proved against her, or the crime of speaking out in his presence, of daring to 'teach' an absolute ruler and question the absoluteness of his decisions?

Moreover, the reason for his reversal of intention (the decision to 'forgive') is not clear. He nowhere suggests that the stories themselves have proved the possibility of female virtue. It is the fact that they amuse and divert him—rather than return him to the obsessive jealousy that tormented him before they commenced—which has 'contributed so much towards removing the sultan's fatal prejudice against all women'. How can one woman telling many stories prove to the listener that all women are not unchaste? What they have proved is that their teller is clever, entertaining, and a fit, if not superior, intellectual companion.

Indeed, Scheherazade's greatest success as storyteller may be in her delivery of stories that have nothing to do with 'proving' or 'disproving' female virtue. Sindbad's voyages, for instance, like Robinson Crusoe's adventures, prove the resilience of the protagonist, while his fortune magically accrues without much positive action on his part. 'The Story of Cogia Hassan Alhabbal'—in which the rope-maker loses a vast fortune given to him by the rich Saadi but succeeds in turning an even larger profit from a simple bar of lead given by the poor Saad—demonstrates the same magical power of profit without intention. Scheherazade's stories similarly appear to succeed by their circulation alone; their producer need not husband or manage her resources particularly, but rather simply keep them in circulation and her symbolic capital magically grows.

This may be why the Arabian Nights remain the touchstone and paradigm of the oriental tale, the sequence ever burgeoning and expanding, but always retaining its magical power as sign of the East for its western readers.[57] The stories of the Arabian Nights, like the woman who tells them, transform the world around them by repetitive acts of simple accretion. It is not what they tell that matters so much as the stubborn vitality of their matter itself, which continues to survive and grow requiring only the assent to 'hear more' rather than complex acts of interpretation or organization on the part of their auditor(s). In this, the *Arabian Nights Entertainments* chimed with and indeed confirmed common prejudices about eastern cultures expressed in travel and historical accounts throughout the early modern period: that eastern nations can only imitate rather than originate genuine art, that eastern economies accrete wealth at the centre and fail to turn the circulation of wealth into genuine commerce and trade between nations. Above all, the East is understood as not only a place of fiction, but also as a fictional place, in so far as it only appropriates, transforms, and mimics (the 'imposture' of Mahomet, the imitation

[57] Jacques Cazotte, a French writer of fairy and pseudo-oriental tales, and Dom Chavis, a Syrian priest, produced the *Suite des Mille et une Nuit* as vols. 38–41 of the *Cabinet des Fées* (1788–91), in part a genuine translation of Arab tales drawn from the Paris Bibliothèque nationale MS Arabe 1723. They were translated into English by Robert Heron in 1792 as *The Arabian Tales, or a Continuation of the Arabian Nights*. Jonathan Scott, Warren Hastings's secretary in Persia, produced a new translation of Galland in 1811 and added a few stories from other sources. Edward William Lane's translation from the Arabic printed text of 1835 (known as the 'Bulaq' edition because printed in the Bulaqu suburb of Calcutta) published his translation in nine monthly parts over the years 1838–41, resulting in a 3-vol. bound version. John Payne produced a new translation from the Arabic text of 1839–42, ed. W. H. MacNaghten (the Calcutta II text), *The Book of the Thousand and One Nights* (9 vols. completed by 1884) and Richard Burton swiftly followed with his *A Plain and Literal Translation of the Arabian Nights' Entertainments* (1885–6) in 10 vols. from the Calcutta II text with stories from other printed texts and manuscripts.

of western designs in Chinese porcelain, despotism according to Montesquieu is in its essence a perversion of 'genuine' government).

As simulacrum, or copy without original, the East is also imagined as feminine and feminized, a weak and derivative copy of the male according to early modern theories of sex.[58] Here too, the *Arabian Nights Entertainments* both imitates and confirms the myth in its deployment of a female storyteller as framing device. However, the feminine imitator/mimic also generates copies in her image, not only in the shape of the male Orientalists who 'translate' her and find themselves 'translated' into the position of feminized imitator without a claim to originating genius, but also within the narratives themselves. The preoccupation of the *Arabian Nights Entertainments* with the representation of physical mutilation is apparent; stories are populated by the lame, the hunchbacked, and amputees, but especially the blind. This is partly due to the repetitive structure of threatened or partial punishment, usually rescinded when parties are reconciled. In the 'Story Told by the Sultan of Casgar's Purveyor', for instance, the purveyor tells of a young man whose thumb and big toes are severed in a punishment by his haughty wife for failing to wash his hands after eating a garlic sauce at their wedding ceremonies; the couple are reconciled but he continues to dislike garlic sauce. The removal of male protuberances is treated with some comedy, implying the inversion of sexual hierarchy in the marriage which turns the husband into a 'eunuch' (cut as a sign of his role as the servant of a woman). Often, indeed, the mutilation of men is the result of their transgressive actions with or against women, and not infrequently it is demanded by women.

However, the blinding of a man has a special symbolic and narrative significance in the *Arabian Nights Entertainments*, pointing to the power of narrative to transform its auditor into a copy of itself. The association of blinding with castration also suggests a link between the plays discussed earlier and the oriental prose tale; mutilated men and women can be co-conspirators, as well as enemies, in the context of

---

[58] See Thomas Laqueur, *Making Sex: Body and Gender from the Greeks to Freud* (Cambridge, Mass., and London: Harvard University Press, 1990). Laqueur argues from his reading in anatomical and medical literature that, until the late 18th c., 'the dominant discourse construed the male and female bodies as hierarchically, vertically, ordered versions of one sex', the male (10).

the seraglio. Six tales in the Galland translation involve the blinding of a man or blind men. In terms of the dominant theme of fate, blinding serves as a means of indicating men's failure to 'see' or 'foresee' their narrative destiny. In 'The Story of the Blind Man, Baba Abdalla' a covetous man slowly divests a generous dervish of all his wealth but ignores the dervish's injunction regarding a magic pomatum which, when applied to a single eye, allows the viewer to see where treasure lies beneath the earth, but if applied to both will bring on blindness. Convinced that 'more' is necessarily better (a logic that, given the nature of the *Arabian Nights Entertainments*, one might be forgiven for pursuing), Baba Abdalla applies it to both and is promptly blinded. 'The Story of the Barber's Third Brother' tells of the blind man Bacbac who confides to his blind companions where he has hidden his treasure unaware that a sighted highwayman has overheard him and joined the group in hopes of taking the money. The blind men realize there is a cheat among them and, when they appeal to a magistrate, he has the whole company whipped; the highwayman opens his eyes and announces that all the company are, like him, sighted and if whipped enough will admit their fraud. All are whipped and banished and the highwayman makes off with the unfortunate Bacbac's money. This story, told to prove that the barber's unfortunate brothers are all more loquacious than him, illustrates the helplessness of those who lack control either of the temporal or spatial dimensions. Bacbac's tongue is loose and he cannot see to identify his abuser. The voyages of Sindbad include the story of how Sindbad and his fellow sailors defeat a one-eyed flesh-eating monster by blinding him.

However, the three other stories that concern blinding are all found in the group relating to Zobeide and the three calenders and all point to a different use of the theme of blinding, to illustrate the contest between male scopophilia and female loquacity as axes of power in the seraglio/oriental tale. In all three cases, blinding in one eye is the result of a transgression; in their wanderings, the three princes each break a prohibition or a trust. The first fails to reveal to his uncle the where-abouts of his cousin and cousin's mistress and is forced to return to his own country where a usurper blinds him; he returns to his uncle and discovers that the mistress was in fact full sister to the young man and that the charred bodies of both have been discovered. He adopts the disguise of a calender to escape the further wrath of the usurper and flees to Baghdad. The second engages in a romance with a young woman held captive by a terrible genie and is turned into an ape as his punishment. He loses his eye in a conflict between the genie and a princess conversant with magic in the court where he has become the sultan's favourite pet thanks to his writing talents; the princess is so weakened by the battle with the genie that she dies and her inconsolable father requests him to leave. The third calender loses his eye in an inverted version of the bluebeard story. He encounters ten men blind in one eye and shut in a copper castle and, despite their warnings, determines to find out what happened to them. Disguised as a sheep, he is carried off by a roc (the huge bird of oriental myth) and taken to a castle where forty beautiful young ladies each spend a night in turn with him and then leave, prohibiting him from passing through a pair of golden doors in the castle. He of course opens the doors and rides a vast black horse back to the copper castle but is blinded by the swishing of its tail. He is called to Baghdad where he will meet with someone who will decide his destiny (presumably Zobeide).

The swish of a tale, then, blinds a man in one eye. This state of half-blindness stands metaphorically for the experience of the reader/ consumer of the tales, hovering between redemption and sin, suspended in his/her judgement by the story itself; the story suspends the judgement of both internal 'reader' (Schahriar) and external (the reader of Galland's *Nights*). Female storytelling repeatedly converts violence into fiction, while it includes violence within its fiction, opening the male auditor to the pleasure of deferred gratification and/ or punishment. Galland's translation repeats in the frame the narrative trajectory of the stories, capturing and converting male violence and action associated with the gaze into a pleasurable subjection to narrative deferral associated with the ear. Schahriar is 'captured' by Scheherazade's control of narrative and speech and sublimates his scopophilia to the new auditory pleasures she offers.[59]

The transformation of male gazer and female speaker is mutual, each testing out and performing each other's positions within narrative itself. This might also be understood to be the pleasure of the oriental

---

[59] See Sallis, *Sheherazade through the Looking Glass*, 103.

sequence for the occidental reader, as a game of fictional metamorphosis where s/he can test out a series of 'exotic' roles, male and female, safely distanced by being placed in a historically and geographically remote 'East', in order to adjust her/his own mental horizons. The contest, however, is an ambiguous one: does the reader transform 'stories' into a copy of his/her own condition, or is the reader transformed by story into a copy of the fictional 'teller', Scheherazade herself? In other words, does the process of 'translating' the Arabian Nights into European language, terms, and contexts 'orientalize' the West so that it comes to occupy the place of potential victim of a despotic eastern tendency (that of Scheherazade), rather than 'occidentalize' the East so that it is turned into a resource that can mirror the purblind desire of the auditor (the position of Schahriar)? Imitations and further 'translations' of the oriental sequence return repeatedly to the contest between the position of female speaker and male looker to replay this imaginary conflict between alternative 'powers' (male/female, East/West).

Suzanne Rodin Pucci offers a rather less sanguine version of this 'contest', pointing out that the sequence of oriental tales conjures up the image of the harem woman who 'speaks' her desire (Rodin Pucci's models are the female harem correspondents in Montesquieu's *Lettres Persanes* and the talking 'jewels' in Diderot's *Bijoux Indiscrets*) as a means of commodifying the East for the West, putting on display the speaking woman as synecdoche of the whole East. Thus:

Each new story, like the separate voyages of Sindbad and so many of the other merchants, like the multiple figures of the harem, adds to something that is in one sense already there: another individual, discrete entity both superfluous and endlessly replaceable.... '[F]ictions' of the harem provide a paradigm basic to the currency of exchange and to the commodification inherent in the eighteenth-century notion of the exotic. To cast the exotic Orient in the fictional 'parts', in the synecdoche, of the multiple harem woman is to represent the objects of the Other as commodity that Western man could and indeed did appropriate in the name of those delightful exchangeable and seemingly inexhaustible minimal differences.[60]

[60] Suzanne Rodin Pucci, 'The Discrete Charms of the Exotic: Fictions of the Harem in Eighteenth-Century France', in *Exoticism in the Enlightenment*, ed. G. S. Rousseau and Roy Porter (Manchester: Manchester University Press, 1990), 167–8.

Rodin Pucci is quick to associate the western reader with the role performed by the Sultan Schahriar and to see that role as an unchanging one of demand for new experience, new fodder (tales or wives) for his own despotic desire. But the 'performance' of the Orient is a more troubled and dynamic exchange than a simply confirmatory and celebratory production of a commodifying and imperial European identity, at least at this early stage of European trading empire. Like Scheherazade, the European seeks to 'trade' with the oriental ruler in the early eighteenth century, to barter for a survival that may turn a profit, rather than imagining the possibility of a sovereign gaze or displacement of the power of the sultan from East to West. Such imaginings do not attach themselves to the oriental sequence—except perhaps in those English sequences devoted to India in the second half of the eighteenth century (see Ch. 5 ' "Dreams of Men Awake": India')—until the early nineteenth century.

The sequences of oriental tales 'translated' by Pétis de la Croix and Caylus can be seen as part of the accretive matter of the Arabian Nights, a process which also sees transformation and shifts of emphasis in the structure and delivery of oriental narrative: in particular, both sequences strengthen the sometimes tenuous link between frame and tales found in Galland's sequence. The English preface to the 1708 translation of Pétis de la Croix's *Turkish Tales* insists *'they are not to be consider'd as a confus'd Heap of extraordinary Events jumbled together without any Design or Judgment, but the deliberate Work of one whose principal Aim was to render Virtue amiable, and Vice odious'* (n.p.). Like Galland, Pétis de la Croix and Caylus probably acquired their sources as a result of the remit of French oriental scholars to acquire manuscripts and transcriptions for the royal library; like him also, they took considerable licence in their acts of compilation and translation and produced profoundly hybrid texts.[61]

---

[61] Pétis de la Croix has an even closer association with Galland's *Nights*; his translations from a Turkish source were included in the eighth volume (1709) in the shape of 'the History of Prince Zeyn Alasnam' and 'The History of Codadad and his Brothers', tales he had intended for his *Thousand and One Days* (the first volume was published in 1710); Galland had provided only one tale for the eighth volume of the *Nights* ('Ganem') and was seeking new material for translation; the publisher compiled the volume to meet demand without the permission of either writer (Mahdi, *Thousand and One Nights*, 31).

Tales of the Seraglio: Turkey and Persia

Jean-François Pétis de la Croix (1653–1713) studied oriental languages from childhood as his father was 'secrétaire-interprête du Rois' for Ottoman Turkish and Arabic. At 16 he went to the Levant to further his study of Arabic and spent three and a half years in Aleppo before leaving for Isfahan, the capital of the Safavid Persian kingdom, in 1674. He spent two years here and a further four in Istanbul, acquiring ancient coins and oriental manuscripts for Colbert before returning to France in 1681.[62] Pétis de la Croix's *Turkish Tales* draws on a pre-Islamic Persian cycle known as the *Sindibadnama*, which survives only in a Syriac manuscript translated into Hebrew and thence into European languages as well as Arabic.[63] In the latter, seven viziers tell stories to a king to dissuade him from killing his son, Sindibad, on the insistence of his wicked wife (a figure who could easily invoke a parallel with the familiar story of the Ottoman courtesan-queen, Roxolana, who also turns her verbal energies towards affecting the murder of a stepson).[64] The English preface to the 1708 translation of the *Turkish Tales* insists that they are translated from a text in 'Mr. Petis *Library*' and thus not '*the bare Invention of some French-Man, designing to recommend his Fictions to the World under the Umbrage of a Foreign Title, but the Work of* Chec Zade, *Tutor to* Amurath *the* Second'.[65] Pétis de la Croix's *Mille et un Jours: Contes Persanes* is translated from a Persian sequence by a chronicler, lexicographer, and poet of the late Mughal period in India, Ânand Rām Mokles (1699–1750), entitled the *Hazar Yek Ruz*, itself a translation from an 'Indian', presumably Sanskrit, source.[66]

---

[62] Mahdi, *Thousand and One Nights*, 31. 189–90.

[63] Irwin, *Arabian Nights*, 75.

[64] In the 19th c., Burton was to reincorporate this frame and sequence back into the *Nights* with the title 'The Craft and Malice of Women'.

[65] François Pétis de la Croix, *Turkish Tales; Consisting of Several Adventures: With the History of the Sultaness of Persia, and the Visiers*, trans. William King and others (London, 1708), n.p. All subsequent references are to this edition unless otherwise stated. Murat II reigned 1421–51, acceding to the throne on the sudden death of his father when he was only 17 years old. He spent two years fighting with his four younger brothers for his right to rule and went on to be one of the greatest Ottoman sultans, founding Ottoman power in Europe and Asia. He was a patron of poetry and learning and especially promoted the history of the early Turkish tribes and Turkish antiquities.

[66] In 1754 *A new Translation of the Persian Tales from the Indian Comedies of Mocles* by Edward Button was published. Button, like Ambrose Philips before him, used Pétis de la Croix's French translation as his source.

114

Tales of the Seraglio: Turkey and Persia

The preface to the second volume of the first English translation by Ambrose Philips asserts that

We are indebted (says he) to the famous Dervis Moclés *for those Tales. The Persians rank him in the Number of their great Men. He was the Principal or Chief of the* Sons *of* Ispahan; *and he had Twelve Disciples, who wore long white woollen Robes. The Grandees and the People had a more than ordinary Veneration for him, because he was descended from* Mahomet; *and they feared him, because he passed for a profound Cabalist. The King* Schah-Soliman *had so great a Respect for him, that if he happened to meet him any where abroad, he would alight from his Horse, to go and kiss his Stirrup.*

Moclés, *when he was very young, undertook to translate some Indian* Comedies *into* Persian; *which have since been translated into all the Oriental Languages. There is at present a Copy of a Turkish Version of them, to be seen in the* King's Library, *under the Title of* Alfurage Badal-Schidda; *which signifies,* Joy after Affliction. *But the* Persian Translator, *to give his Work the Air of an Original, threw these* Comedies *into* Tales, *which he called* Herazyek-Rouz, *that is* A Thousand and One Days. *He entrusted the Sieur* Pétis *(the* French Translator*) with his Manuscript, and gave him Leave to copy it, having entered into a strict Friendship with him at* Ispahan, *in the Year* 1675. (*PT* ii, n.p.)

Pétis de la Croix's two collections present to the European reader the two different traditions in the sequence of oriental tales: a 'Turkish' collection which characterizes women as irredeemably vicious and a 'Persian' collection which characterizes them as improvable. The claim in the Preface to the 1708 *Turkish Tales* that '*these Tales are equally instructive, tho' not so insipid as those of* Pilpay, *and have all the Beauties, without the Extravagance of our own Tales of the Fairies*'[67] locates the collection ambivalently between the eastern tradition of stories delivered by a male sage or Brahman to a prospective or actual male ruler (see 'The Indian fable: rational animals', Ch. 5 ' "Dreams of Men Awake": India') and the harem or salon/fairy tale told to groups of women by women, often older 'gossips'. The former

---

[67] The 1714 *Persian and Turkish Tales, Compleat* rendered this phrase slightly differently: '*the Tales have all the Solidity of the Fables of* Pilpay, *without their Dryness; and all the Agreeableness of our Tales of the Fairies, without any of their Extravagance*' (*The Persian and Turkish Tales Compleat*, 1767, 5th edn., n.p.)

teaches self-government by imitation of the virtues extolled within story, the latter how to govern others without appearing to do so, through the agency of story. The *Turkish Tales* stages this conflict between male and female storytellers, seeking to influence a male ruler through the agency of narrative. The Persian emperor, Hafikin, has a lovely adult son and takes a new wife named Canzada on the death of the prince's mother. She falls violently in love with her stepson and takes advantage of his vow of silence to make advances to him. He rejects her with a slap that makes her mouth bleed and she presents herself to her husband claiming the prince assaulted her when she refused his sexual proposition. Each night, the Sultana and numerous different viziers alternately tell stories to Hafikin, the former attempting to demonstrate the dangers of trusting one's heir(s) and counsellors, the latter attempting to demonstrate the dangers of trusting women.

If Pétis de la Croix chose to provide a frame to the *Turkish Tales* that asserts the moral supremacy of the male sage as storyteller over the harem woman (the Persian stories are (re)told by the vizier Chec Zade to an Ottoman sultan to prove the superiority of the advice of viziers in general), he recognized that the female readers of his own translation might take offence. The translator falls back on the familiar invocation of the gap between the educated western female reader and the enclosed Turkish woman for whom too much physical restraint engenders a total lack of moral restraint:

the Turkish *Ladies, perhaps because they are lock'd up, and restrain'd from those Public Diversions, which serve to amuse the Women of other Nations, think of little else but how to open a way to their own Pleasures. To effect which, they without any Scruples make use of all their Artifices, which the Constitution of their Bodies, and idle manner of living, can suggest unto'em. No Necessity of confessing their Weakness to the Ministers of their Religion restrain'em, nor do they stand in Fear of any but a Temporal Punishment assign'd by the Laws of Adultery, or Care a Rush for the Menaces of* Mahomet, *and his* Alcoran. (n.p.)

The frame to Pétis de la Croix's other collection, the *Contes Persans*, is more firmly located in the tradition (eastern and western) of stories exchanged between women. The beauty of the Kashmiri princess Farruknaz causes all men who see her to fall in love but, when she dreams of a doe who assists a young stag to escape a snare only to be trapped in turn, she determines never to put her trust in a man and marry. Farruknaz's father agrees not to marry her off without her consent, and her old nurse, appropriately named Sutlememé, volunteers to deploy her storehouse of stories each morning as the princess bathes, 'the recital of which, at the same time that they divert the Princess, may wean her from the ill Opinion she has conceived of Men' (*PT* i. 6) The stories are told to the young princess, as the English Preface claims, '*to reduce a young Princess to Reason, who had conceived an unaccountable Aversion to Men, and would not be perswaded to marry*' (i, n.p.).

However, here too the idea of the tales as a kind of 'mirror for princes', in this case a series of instructions imparted to a recalcitrant princess about mutual self-government in courtship and marriage, suggests the (at least) double purpose of the oriental sequence: moral instruction and the pleasure of story itself. Ambrose Philips reinforces the importance of a female readership by dedicating the first two volumes of his translation to the countess of Godolphin and the last to the countess of Dorset. He exalts the former—daughter of John Churchill, duke of Marlborough and widow of Godolphin and hence one of the most powerful women of the Stuart court now in abeyance—as a model of filial and conjugal loyalty. Edward Button's 1754 new translation of Pétis de la Croix's *Persian Tales* claimed to be prepared for '*the BRITISH LADIES*' and was dedicated to the Princess Elizabeth, second daughter of the Dowager, Princess of Wales with the comment:

If, therefore, the following noble instances of friendship, constancy, bene-volence, filial duty, and conjugal affection, may be deemed worthy of YOUR HIGHNESS's immediate perusal; age will mature your parts, and lead you on to those spacious fields of learning, which afford more exercise, and superior delight. (p. vi)

In a double move, the condition of the western court lady is seen as the model to which the harem woman should aspire, the end point of her education and growth. However, harem tales are also understood to be appropriate reading matter for the developing western European girl, a good preparation for more taxing intellectual and moral material in adult life. Pétis de la Croix's two collections were published together in 1714 as *The Persian and the Turkish Tales, Compleat* with two letters from French correspondents describing the Eastern territories of Madagascar and Siam, reinforcing the classification of oriental tales as 'informant' as well as moral and entertaining sources in the period. In his preface to the new translation, William King asserts that '*In short, we may look upon these Tales, as the Relations of Travellers; that is to say, as a Work full of faithful Observations, and such as are worthy of the Curiosity of the Public*' (ii, n.p.)

Caylus also mingles the competing traditions of male and female storytellers in his later collection of oriental tales. Claude-Philippe de Tubières, Comte de Caylus (1692–1795) was the son of an army officer, educated by his mother, who himself joined the army before devoting himself after 1714 to the study of arts and sciences, especially the antiquities of Greece, Italy, the East, England, and Germany. He was also a practitioner of painting and engraving and writer of fairy tales and fictional pieces. His preface to the *Oriental Tales* claims they are taken from manuscript exercises carried out by French youths sent to Turkey to be trained as '*Droguemans, or Interpreters to the Ambassadors, the Consuls and the whole Nation*' and then deposited in the Bibliothèque Royale.[68] He signals the tradition in which they should be read with the comment that 'M. Petit *and* M. Galland *had no knowledge of the Manuscript from whence this Work is drawn, they being not deposited there when those Authors presented to the Public the* Arabian Nights Entertainments, *and the* Persian Tales' (i, p. i).

In the frame to Caylus's *Oriental Tales* an insomniac Persian despot named Hudjadge demands that the man who keeps the gates and the prison of his palace tell him stories to send him to sleep. The man, Fitead, reveals that he is both illiterate and forgetful; his 14-year-old daughter, Moradbak, persuades her father to let her present herself to the sultan. She is prompted to this action by the imprisoned sage Aboumelek whom Hudjadge confined fifteen years previously because he dared to reprove him for his cruelty and suggest that a guilty conscience was the cause of his sleeplessness. For three years,

---

[68] Anne Claude-Philippe de Tubières de Grimoard de Pestels de Levis Caylus, *Oriental Tales* (London, 1745), i, p. ii.

Aboumelek has talked with Moradbak through a little opening between their rooms and imparted narratives, all of which serve to instruct the king in the importance of temperate government, a laudable aim somewhat hindered by the fact that Moradbak is often successful and the sleepy king consistently loses or misses the narrative thread of the tales she tells (see Fig. 4).

The *Turkish Tales* and *Oriental Tales* present their readers with rulers/readers, like Schahriar, whose intention to embrace violent action is diverted by the use of stories. Both Hafikin in the *Turkish Tales* and Hudjadge in the *Oriental Tales* are identified as poor or inadequate 'readers', perhaps building on the equivocal treatment of Schahriar in Galland's conclusion. Stories, it appears, do not produce more astute readers so much as a dependency on narrative and on the narrator which is as 'blinding', if less politically disruptive, as the auditor's previous propensity to violence. Hence, Hafikin is alternately swayed one way and then another by his viziers and his wife, calling in his son for execution on numerous occasions and having his hand stayed by a further fable. Indeed, so obtuse a reader is Hafikin that he often fails to see the covert messages in the fables he is told and has to have them explained quite explicitly. At one point Canzada tells him of a dream in which she saw herself piecing together a diamond ball broken by the prince and returning it to her husband; she explains that the ball is his kingdom and she its saviour.

The message that Hafikin is too literal a reader for the fanciful, fabulous, and parabolic structure of the oriental tale to 'work' is reinforced when the sultana goes on to tell him 'The Fable of the Two Owls' (*Turkish Tales*, 174–8). A vizier 'not daring to tell the King his Master plainly what he thought of his Reign' (174) claims to be able to understand the language of birds and 'translates' for his sultan Mahmoud a conversation in which one owl (in oriental tale consistently used as a figure of parasitism and trickery) offers the other a dowry for his daughter of as many ruined villages as he likes (all the product of the luxurious sultan's depredations). Mahmoud promptly rebuilds the villages. The story is ostensibly told by Canzada as a means of directing the king to take heed from her dream, reminding him that narratives have veiled meanings which can prompt their auditor to 'right' actions. The sixth vizier then interrupts to counter with 'The

4. Engraving in Anne Claude-P. de Tubières de Grimoard de Pestels de
Levis, Comte de Caylus, *Oriental Tales* (1745), vol. i, p. 164

History of Santon Barsisa' in which the devil tempts an ascetic hermit
to rape and murder a sick princess who has been sent to him for a
cure. Like Canzada, the vizier has to spell out the meaning of the tale
arguing that Canzada *'resembles this Devil, or rather it is the Devil
himself which influences that Princess'* (186). Hafikin determines to
give his son another day's grace.

Interestingly, in both these stories the narrators chose to deliver
their message by adopting the role of their adversary: the queen

presenting her position in the narrative through the figure of a vizier and the vizier presenting the position of the silent prince through the figure of embattled female virtue. The complexity of narrative imposture, disguise, and performance is evidently quite beyond the sultan's understanding, however. Where Galland leaves the sultan Schahriar's interpretation of the tales unspoken (beyond the comment that he remained interested enough to let them continue), Pétis de la Croix follows each tale with a record of the king's wavering judgement. If Chec Zade '*contriv'd*' the tales '*on purpose to arm the young* Amurath *against Womankind, to whom he already perceiv'd the Prince too much addicted*' (Preface, n.p.), he also indicated the impossibility of this task by illustrating the inability of the despotic listener to turn the consumption of narrative into a morally improving exercise. Indeed, should the pupil Prince Murat listen as Hafikin does, all he will learn is to be dependent on the judgement of his counsellors/ministers, such as Chec Zade himself, since he will not be able to understand the 'true' meaning nor recognize 'false' reasoning without such guidance. As so often in the case of the oriental tale sequence, a simple model of the fable as a transparent conduit for the imparting of a moral truth or piece of political instruction is overtaken by a recognition of the power of narrative to sway emotion, identification, and response, attaching the reader to the pleasure of narrative itself. The scopophilic reader fails to see 'through' the tale and is caught up in the pleasure of looking 'at' it and the pursuit of more of the same kind of pleasure.

The same kind of disorder characterizes the responses of Hudjadge to Moradbak's tales, all of which are parables either about the bad end that results from the slide into arrogance, luxury, and despotism, or about the virtuous influence of women in monogamous union with powerful rulers or aspiring young men. Many also reflect Caylus's interest in antiquarianism and ancient oriental fable, rehearsing Islamic myths such as the seven sleepers who recognize one God in pagan times and escape persecution by sleeping through to awake after Islam has come to the East ('The History of Dakianos') and the story of the birth of Mahomet to Zesbet/Aminta and the marvellous prophetic adventures of her four husbands, the sage, the judge, the soldier, and the doctor of law. The stories often fall, quite literally, on deaf ears, however. Hudjadge comments that he lost interest in 'The

History of Dakianos' when the little dog (which accompanies the sleepers into their cave in their escape from Dakianos' tyrannous persecution) was introduced to the tale, and was almost asleep by the point that Jemlikah, one of the sleepers, first awoke.

By the close of 'The History of the Merchant of Bagdad', in which a heroic female slave, Meimoune, assists a young merchant to escape imprisonment by a sheikh who drinks the blood of young men, we are informed that

> *Moradbak* had no sooner ceased to speak, than the King, who began to be more touch'd with her Beauty and Merit than with her History, and who took still more Pleasure in seeing than in hearing her, told her, That he insensibly, and by degrees, felt a Calm diffused over his Mind; and it is to thy Histories, doubtless, added he obligingly, that I owe the Tranquillity I begin to enjoy. But this that thou has related to me has filled me with Indignation: I will never again suffer a Cheik in my Dominions; or at least if they are ever met in the Streets by Night, they shall be imprison'd for a Year. (ii. 116)

The Persian king proves himself a poor 'reader' on two counts (at least); first, he is more attracted by the teller's physical charms than her verbal skill and second he can only 'read' literal meanings from parabolic texts. Ignoring the covert message about the power of women to temper and correct male despotism embedded in the tale, he takes it quite literally as a warning against allowing sheikhs into his dominions, branding them 'Giaours' or Infidels.[69]

Hudjadge reveals a growing addiction to the pleasures of story. Moradbak's next tale is the 'History of the Basket' in which the sincere and pure love of a pair of young lovers and the brave action of the hero's cross-dressing sister succeeds in persuading a vengeful genie to revoke a cruel and despotic enchantment. Hudjadge responds with the remark that 'Pleasure is a still better Remedy for my Disorder than Sleep' (213). His literal-minded and limited interpretive capacities are demonstrated when he adds that the young prince was lucky to have such a sister, thus identifying with the role of the victimized prince

---

[69] Herbelot defines the word 'Scheik' as 'pas seulement en Arabe, Un Vieillard; mais encore, Un Prince, & un Docteur celebre, & Chef de quelque College, ou Communauté Religieuse' (Barthélemy d'Herbelot and Antoine Galland, *Bibliothèque Orientale Ou Dictionaire Universel Contenant Généralment Tout Ce Qui Regarde La Connoissance Des Peuples De L'orient* (Paris, 1697), 783).

without seeing the parallel between his own situation and the vengeful bad-tempered genie.

Moradbak is forced to resort to an unambiguous story in order to prompt Hudjadge into a decision to reinstate Aboumelek. She follows the story of the basket with 'The History of the Porter of Bagdad' in which a jeweller's son squanders his patrimony, becomes a porter, and proves his virtue and intrepidity to the extent that he is promoted to the role of vizier of the king of Persia. Hudjadge approves the king's choice and expresses his own desire for such a minister, making it possible for Moradbak to reveal that Hudjadge's disgraced vizier Aboumelek has been the source of the stories that have so entertained him. Aboumelek is restored to his post and the porter's daughter and the king of Persia are happily married leaving the king to sleep 'in quiet' thereafter (ii. 252).

By comparison with these two sequences—in which male readers prove unsophisticated and literal-minded, if appreciative, consumers of the sequence of oriental tales—the responses in the *Persian Tales* of the Princess Farruknaz to the tales told by her nurse are subtle and taxing. They require that Sutlememé raise the stakes with each tale (and there are many) to live up to her name and subtly prepare the ground for her auditor's conversion to a belief that there are men who do not betray the women they love. Farruknaz is a feminine version of Schahriar, persuaded by a terrible 'vision' (in her case her dream of the stag betraying the hind who saves him) to pursue a course of action that results in the serial death of her lovers (they run mad at the sight of her beauty so that she must always appear veiled, and they pine and die when she rejects their suit). However, unlike Schahriar, Farruknaz is both the one who looks and the one who is looked at. Her 'readers' are encouraged to conjure up a vision of her beauty, as her lovers/suitors do, when they are informed that the stories are told to her each morning when she and her women are bathing. The first volume of the English translation by Ambrose Philips appeared with an engraved frontispiece depicting a bathhouse and the attractive bodies of the harem ladies disposed in careless half-somnolence listening to Sutlememé's seductive tones (see Fig. 5). Indeed, even if Mary Wortley Montagu did not have this text in mind when she first wrote her own description of the beauties of naked

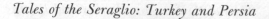

5. Frontispiece, François Pétis de la Croix, *The Thousand and One Days: Persian Tales*, translated by Ambrose Philips, vol. i (1714), p. 184

6. Daniel Chodowiecki, Frontispiece for Lady Mary Wortley Montagu, *Letters of the Right Honourable Lady M——W——y M——e* (Berlin, 1871)

ladies in a Turkish bathhouse at Sofia, it would have been a familiar text to her readers by the time her *Turkish Embassy Letters* appeared in 1763 (see Fig. 6).[70]

---

[70] Montagu's letter describing the women's baths in Sofia was written to a female correspondent (possibly Lady Rich) on 1 April 1717, several years after the first publication

Farruknaz listens critically to a series of tales in which devoted men undergo terrible trials for the women they love. Her attendant women are less critical than their mistress, admiring the virtues of the male heroes of the tales, where Farruknaz habitually finds something lacking in their behaviour. The king of China breaks his promise to the fairy queen of Cheheristany he has married, rebuking her for apparently murdering their children (in a reverse oriental version of the medieval tale of 'patient Griselda'), so that she is forced to abandon him for ten years in which he has to remain faithful to her if they are ever to reunite. Farruknaz comments that he is to blame not least because he was forewarned. She ironically deflates the general chorus of approval for the brave Prince Calaf who wins the cruel and bloody Princess Tourandocte by solving her riddles when she describes him as 'rather Vain than Amorous' (*PT* ii. 98). And she points out that Fadlallah 'instead of dying on the Spot with his dear *Zemroude* . . . could make a shift to live Fifty Years afterwards, to mourn for the loss of her' (*PT* ii. 99: see 'Fadlallah and Zemroude' in Ch. 2 'Shape-Shifting').

The *Persian Tales* concludes ambiguously with the conversion of the princess to an enthusiasm for marriage through the agency not of her nurse but rather the chief priest at the temple of Kesaya, a pagan sandalwood idol. Farruknaz solicits his prayers to aid her dying brother Farrukbrouz and he shows her pictures in which a haughty hind ignores the desperate stag in a snare. They make her weep and she reveals that she has had a dream in which she encountered and rejected Farrukschad, prince of Persia. Farruknaz returns to court prepared to marry and her father congratulates the priest with the comment:

We are obliged to you for the sudden Change that is wrought in the Heart of my Daughter. You are the Author of this Miracle. She hated Men, and you in

of the *Mille et un Jours*. Her library list from 1739 (Wharncliffe MS 135) shows that she owned a copy of *Les Mille et un Jours* (with thanks to Isobel Grundy and the Sheffield Library Archive for this information; see also *CLMWM* i, n. 1). She also owned a copy of the 1708 'Contes Turcs' by Pétis de la Croix (see *Lady Mary Wortley Montagu: Romance Writings*, ed. Isobel Grundy (Oxford: Clarendon Press, 1996), 17). The 'Embassy Letters' appeared in 1763 and a new translation of the *Persian Tales* by Edward Button had been published in 1754 with a Dublin edition in 1761, which might have made the association fresh in her readers' minds.

a Moment have triumphed over that Hatred. One Conference of yours had done more than all *Sutlumemé*'s Stories. Sir, replied the High Priest, I have done yet more. *Farruknaz* does not only not hate Men, she is even in Love with the Prince of *Persia*. (*PT* iii. 339)

Farruknaz is persuaded to join the priest and he leads her to an enchanted park where the witch Mehrefza holds a number of Asian princes under an enchantment which has converted them into stags and their mistresses into hinds. With the aid of Mehrefza's virtuous sister, Ghulnaze, the priest and Farruknaz succeed in breaking the enchantment and Farrukschad, prince of Persia, is revealed to be among them. We discover that the heathen priest is in fact a noble Persian courtier named Symorgue, friend to the prince of Gaznina whose son expired for love of Farruknaz. He marries Ghulnaze and comes to inherit the throne of Gaznina; Farruknaz and Farrukschad are happily married and succeed to the throne of Persia.

This conclusion locates the agent of metamorphosis in the figure of the sage/prince, rather than in the corrective powers of a female 'gossip'. This narrative trajectory came to be imitated in the English novel of the eighteenth century such as Mary Davys's *The Reform'd Coquet* (1724) in which a young suitor presents himself to the recalcitrant woman he loves in the guise of an old tutor/moralist, and Charlotte Lennox's *The Female Quixote* (1752) in which the romance-reading heroine is persuaded of the advantage of the sober virtues of the novel by a 'doctor', making it possible for her to accept the suit of her sensible cousin for marriage, a task in which her female guardians have failed.[71]

These four collections of oriental tales by Galland, Pétis de la Croix, and Caylus, especially in their depiction of the 'interpretive' strategies of their primary frame auditors, begin to suggest a critique of the power of story and an awareness of the shifting and unpredictable nature of the response to it. They build on the instability already apparent in the *Arabian Nights Entertainments* whereby the

[71] Mary Davys, *The Reform'd Coquet; or, Memoirs of Amoranda; Familiar Letters Betwixt a Gentleman and a Lady; and, the Accomplish'd Rake, or, Modern Fine Gentleman*, ed. Martha F. Bowden, Eighteenth-Century Novels by Women (Lexington, Ky: University Press of Kentucky, 1999); Charlotte Lennox, *The Female Quixote, or, the Adventures of Arabella*, ed. Margaret Dalziel (Oxford: Oxford University Press, 1989).

metamorphic power of narrative does not always follow the intentions of the storyteller. Unlike the 'genie', the storyteller cannot always harness enchantments to produce a desired end, but must rather rely on the inherently addictive and pleasurable qualities of narrative to keep him or her 'in credit' with the auditor.

The sequence of oriental tales provided its western European readers with a site for the exploration and testing of the dynamics of (gendered) reading. The positions of writer, narrator, and implied reader are played out in a variety of configurations which reveal simultaneously the transformative power of narrative and the uncertainty, often waywardness, of its effects. There is both an irony and symmetry in the fact that, as Daniel Beaumont points out, the medieval Arabic literature, from which these French translations derived, did not have a concept of 'fiction'. Written narrative precedents such as the Qur'an and the eighth-century *Life of the Prophet* and *The Raids*, concerning the life and military prowess of Muhammad and his followers, were treated as fact, while the narrative 'authenticity' of 'khabar' (a short piece of information recounted for someone else—the term literally means 'news') was confirmed through the 'isnâd' or chain, a series of names along which narrative passes from its original 'eyewitness' source: 'Thus, in its beginning, narrative literature in Arabic purports to confine itself to fact, to the recounting of real events by eyewitnesses, real people. . . . Within the literature proper, a generic space for fiction never really opened up. That which never happened is simply a lie'.[72] As a result, the length and fabricated nature of the Arabian Nights meant it was a marginalized work in medieval Arabic culture. This account has, of course, parallels with narratives about the 'rise' of the novel in seventeenth-century England: Lennard Davis identifies the novel as emerging from the discourse of 'news' (ballads, broadsheets, and other forms of 'news' records); the mutual dependence of periodical and novel is noticeable; and the struggle to make the novel a 'respectable' form has often been recounted.[73] The irony lies in the fact that a marginal Arabic form, denigrated for its failure as

---

[72] Beaumont, *Slave of Desire*, 27.

[73] On 'news' and the novel, see Lennard Davis, *Factual Fictions: The Origins of the English Novel* (New York: Columbia University Press, 1983); and Robert Mayer, *History and the Early English Novel: Matters of Fact from Bacon to Defoe*, Cambridge Studies in

truth currency, could become so dominant a model for the formation of claims to moral, historical, and sociological 'truth' through the medium of fiction in eighteenth-century western Europe.

Although the *Arabian Nights Entertainments*, the *Persian Tales*, and *Turkish Tales* circulated with equal success and influence in France and England, there are, however, discernible differences in the ways in which oriental fiction developed in the two cultures, not least in terms of the 'truth' function attached to such narratives. In her chapter 'Literary Estimates', Martha Pike Conant summarizes the differences between French and English uses of the oriental tale, pointing out that the French tradition is more fanciful and fantastic (coinciding as the earliest oriental tale sequences did with the flourishing of the fairy tale in France), the English tradition more moralizing. While the English use the oriental tale as a vehicle for satire, it tends to be in a more narrowly political sense, while the French deploy it for wider social and philosophical purpose. In the context of my own exploration of the gender dynamics played out within the use of the oriental tale in Europe, I identify two different trajectories taken by the figure of a loquacious feminized Orient at different moments in France and England. Even before Galland's translation appeared in France, the Orient is represented in long historical romances as a place of dangerous excess embodied in the figure of Roxolana/ Roxana; after Galland's translation appeared in England, a series of short prose fictions represent the Orient as a place of 'enlightened' values embodied in the figure of Scheherazade. In both these fictional 'traditions', European women are the major producers of the form; as we saw in the dramatic productions of Mary Pix and Delarivier Manley, then, European women ventriloquize the position of the loquacious harem woman as a means of figuring female political agency, whether dangerous or ameliorative, within their own culture.

Eighteenth-Century English Literature and Thought 33 (Cambridge: Cambridge University Press, 1997). On periodicals and the novel, see Robert Donald Mayo, *The English Novel in the Magazines, 1740–1815: With a Catalogue of 1375 Magazine Novels and Novelettes* (Evanston, Ill.: Northwestern University Press, 1962) and on the novel's transition from 'entertainment' machine to cultural status, see William B. Warner, *Licensing Entertainment: The Elevation of Novel Reading in Britain, 1684–1750* (London and Berkeley, Los Angeles: University of California Press, 1998).

These outbreaks of 'oriental fiction' produced by women coincide with periods in French and English history when claims that the 'civility' of a culture could be measured by the influence and respect accorded to women were particularly vocal and also when the influence of women in political life (the female Regency in seventeenth-century France and the Hanoverian queens in eighteenth-century England) was a matter of some concern. In apparent response, women writers address their own political and historical preoccupations through accounts of the Turkish and Persian Orient.

French Roxolanas: romancing oriental history

The French 'romances' of the late seventeenth century plundered the ancient and recent history of Turkey and Persia for narrative sources. In so doing, they invoked parallels rather than differences between Occident and Orient, using their materials to illustrate the 'universal' claim of the romance form in general: that all momentous political events in history are caused by romantic passion. This romancing of history necessarily foregrounds the role of women in state affairs, if only as spurs to military glory, dynastic change, romance adventuring.[74] The 'secret history' of the French romance purports to reveal a different 'truth' from the public or known history. Two of the best-known romances of Gauthier de Costes de la Calprenède and Madeleine de Scudéry, *Cassandre* (1642–5) and *Ibrahim* (1641) respectively, concern oriental history and draw a contrast between ambitious female plotters and their virtuous rivals for a hero's affections. Calprenède renarrates the story of Alexander the Great as a 'secret history' in which the cousins Roxana and Statira compete not only for Alexander's favour but also for the love of the disguised prince Oroondates, heir to the king of Scythia.[75] The main action concerns the attempts of Oroondates and Lysimachus to rescue the Persian

---

[74] For a fuller discussion of these aspects of the French romance, see ch. 2, 'Observing the Forms: Amatory Fiction and the Construction of the Female Reader', in Ros Ballaster, *Seductive Forms: Women's Amatory Fiction from 1684 to 1740* (Oxford: Clarendon Press, 1992).

[75] The English translation of *Cassandre* (1642–5) begun by George Digby in 1652 was completed by Sir Charles Cotterell in 1661. Madeleine de Scudéry's *Ibrahim* (1641) was translated into English by Henry Cogan in 1652.

princesses, Statira, widow of Alexander, and Parisatis, from the clut-
ches of Perdiccas, Roxana's co-conspirator. The report of Statira's
death at Roxana's hands (in 323 BC, on the death of Alexander, Roxane
did indeed have her Persian rival and the latter's son by Alexander
killed) which opens the narrative is, through a vast array of plots and
sub-plots, finally disproved so that the lovers can be united. Likewise,
Madeleine de Scudéry plays fast and loose with historical 'fact',
revealing the 'secret history' behind the death of Ibrahim Pasha, grand
vizier to Suleyman I, who was strangled when dining with the sultan in
March 1536; rumour had it at the instigation of Roxolana, the sultan's
queen-consort. His 'death' is retold as an elaborate ploy which enables
the Genoan-born hero, really named Justiniano, to return to his native
country with his mistress, Isabella: a plan connived at by the honourable Soliman despite his unrequited passion for Isabella.

Scudéry's Roxana and Roxelana are cast as types of the ambitious
sexually magnetic harem woman with a special hostility to the gentle/
gentile spirit of the 'occidentalized' rival: the Persian Statira or the
Christian Italian Isabella. They illustrate the dangerous sway that
harem women are thought to exercise over oriental rulers (Alexander
and Suleyman), an influence brought about through the combined
deployment of physical ornament and verbal dexterity. Thus, Roxana
is described in *Cassandra* as 'exceeding handsome, and very sump-
tuously apparelled' (pt. 1, bk. 2, p. 24); when her declaration of love is
snubbed by Oroondates she is given to a 'thousand malitious tricks,
and . . . as many little inventions' (pt. 1, bk. 4, p. 61) to attempt a
breach between Oroondates and Statira.[76] Scudéry's Roxelana is also
a plotter, who wins the emperor's attention through her beauty and
cunning deployment of dress; her father Bajazet presents her to
Soliman in the costume of her home island of 'Chio', a petticoat which
stops mid-calf and shows off the leg to advantage.[77] Scudéry rehearses
the familiar story of Roxelana's judicious use of language and presentation of a virtuous front to win political power, defeat her rivals,
and secure the prospect of becoming queen mother.

---

[76] Gauthier de Costes de La Calprenède, *Cassandra: The Fam'd Romance.*, trans.
George Digby and Charles Cotterell (London, 1676), pt. 1, bk. 2, p. 24; pt. 1, bk. 4, p. 61.
[77] Madeleine de Scudéry, *Ibrahim. Or the Illustrious Bassa*, trans. Henry Cogan
(London, 1652), 107.

However, the French romance is not unambiguous about its representation of the influence of women in political life, as befits a form popular in the late seventeenth-century female-dominated and orchestrated salons of France. The figure of the plotting Roxolana is usually countered by the presence of another female who stands for virtues explicitly associated with the Occident within the narrative: temperance, wifely devotion, the rational pursuit of virtue. If such women are associated with the Orient, it is not apparent that the Occident is imagined as the only 'source' where such behaviour is learnt. Soliman is naturally inclined to virtue and demonstrates great loyalty to his vizier and friend, but has to contend with the heat of his passion for Isabella.

While *Cassandra* and *Ibrahim* rewrite Persian and Turkish history as romance or court intrigues, they also claim to dispel misconceptions about these eastern cultures, their barbarity and their 'difference'. Scudéry spends much of her considerable verbiage on the vexed associations of the term 'seraglio', seeking to dispel the notion of the Ottoman palace as a form of state brothel. In her 'Preface' she comments that she has chosen to call Ibrahim's house a palace rather than a seraglio since '*this name of* Seraglio *would leave an* Idea *which was not seemly*' (n.p.). Ibrahim persuades his modest and virtuous mistress, Isabella, to stay in the old seraglio when he has to leave Constantinople to make war on Persia on the sultan's command:

At first that name of the *Serraglio* affrighted her, and her modesty could not suffer him to continue speaking without interrupting him; But after she had told him I know not how often that she could not resolve to go thither, she was constrained to alter her mind, *Ibrahim* having made it appear to her, that the old *Serraglio* was the only place of all the Orient, where the most vertues, and the fewest vices were. As indeed, it was not inhabited by any but the Mother, Aunt, Daughters, and Sisters of the Emperor, who never have any commerce with the *Sultana*'s of the other *Seraglio*, unless it be with the *Sultana* Queen, which lives in the *Grand Signiors* lodging. (91)

Scudéry converts the old seraglio into a place of refinement and leisure where the ladies learn needlework and music under the instruction of Jewish women, walk in the gardens and receive occasional visits from the sultan, looking out from their windows at public festivals but otherwise living retired, a kind of secular convent which would appeal to her salon readership.

In the early eighteenth century Madeleine-Angélique Poisson de Gomez was to return to the idea of turning oriental history into prose romance and 'secret history' with her *Anecdotes ou histoire de la maison ottomane* (1724, not translated into English), and *Anecdotes Persanes* (1727, translated as *Persian Anecdotes* in 1730). The year 1735 saw the translation of another work, *The Life of Osman the Great*, into English. The *Persian Anecdotes* tell the story of the lifelong friendship between the king of Persia, Ishmael, and Tor, prince and later king of Ormus: a friendship nearly undermined by the machinations of Tor's ambitious wife and cousin whom de Gomez calls Milla. This is a romance version of the rise to power of the founder of the Safavid dynasty, Isma'il I, in the first decade of the sixteenth century and establishment of Shi'ism as the state religion of Persia/Iran. Ishmael's military success and expansion of his territories is put down to the loyalty and ability of the friend with whom he has been reared, the prince of Ormus. The latter returns to his home country at the request of his cousin Noradin; Tor's luxurious brother, Zaisadin, is titular ruler while his eunuch tutor Atar rules in practice. Tor falls deeply and immediately in love with Noradin's sister, Milla, and she returns his feelings but conceals them out of pride since she is determined to marry a crowned head of state. After years of separation and Milla's agreement to marry Zaisadin, Noradin, with his sister's connivance, engineers the death of both Atar and Zaisadin; the noble Tor, innocent of their crimes, returns to take the throne. He is reunited with Milla of whom de Gomez comments: 'the ambitious *Milla* saw her Triumph perfect, and only study'd how to render it solid and durable, by taking Advantage of the Charms wherewith Nature had adorn'd her, to increase every Hour a Passion, which was to make her Sovereign Arbiter of the King and Kingdom.'[78] Milla proves a true Roxolana, keeping her husband in thrall to her charms: 'To see her, love her, and adore her, became his most important Cares; and this artful Princess knew so well how to take Advantage of the Power of her Eyes, that of a King, she made him her Slave' (300).

---

[78] Madeleine Angélique Poisson de Gomez, *The Persian Anecdotes: Or, Secret Memoirs of the Court of Persia*, trans. Paul Chamberlen (London, 1730), 299.

Milla accompanies her husband to Isfahan when he returns to aid his friend in wars against the Turks, and while the two friends are away on campaigns, she conspires with Sunni insurgents and court malcontents to see Ishmael murdered in order to advance her husband's empire. She wins both the Etmadoulet, or prime minister, and the Sadre Cassa, or chief of spiritual affairs, to her side as well as two noblemen called Evanglycha and Abouakamcha, both young relatives of the previous king of Persia, Alumut, whom Ishmael had beheaded with his own hand. De Gomez comments on her extraordinary powers of alliance-building and plotting:

> what was most singular, was, that this artful Princess had the Address to unite so many opposite Things, and form so great a Party against a Hero, in the middle of his Empire; and that being a Foreigner, and in an Age, wherein her Equals apply themselves wholly to Pleasure, she had projected a Conspiracy of such Importance, without being disturb'd with the least Fear, or Remorse. (372)

The novel concludes when the two noblemen, who have joined Ishmael's camp with the intention of killing him, are seized with remorse and admiration and reveal the plot. Tor returns to confront his wife, who takes her own life with a dagger. In this novel, de Gomez offers no alternative to Milla in the shape of a virtuous, marriageable woman, although her mother Artaxa is represented as an intelligent, wily, and virtuous diplomat at the court of Ormus. De Gomez chooses rather to suggest that the rivalry is between Ishmael and Milla for the attention, loyalty, and love of the passionate lover and military genius, Tor. A similar competition is suggested in *Ibrahim* between Roxelana and Ibrahim for influence over the Ottoman sultan. 'Romancing' history entails the transformation of political bonds into personal and passionate ones, including those of ruler and prime vizier or ally.

It is in the representation of the figure of the oriental ruler that the attempt to 'romance' the East by turning its history into a sign of universal human behaviour comes under the most strain. The rulers of oriental empire described in such fictionalized accounts veer inconsistently between conforming to the stereotype of the 'romance hero'—gentle, subservient, patriotic, and brave—and that of the oriental despot—lust-driven, self-interested, despotic, and cruel.

Their loyalty to their friends—Alexander to Oroondates, Soliman to Ibrahim/Justiniano, Ishmael to Tor—may be unwavering, but it also indicates their dependence on the superior military and political aptitude of such friends, undermining their claims to absoluteness, singularity, the oneness and autonomy of the despot in whose name the prime vizier acts. The individuality of these named friends and allies suggests the universal nature of homosocial bonds commonly represented in the French romance, but undermines the commonly held understanding of oriental despotism as entailing the submersion of all identity in the 'law' of the absolute ruler, whereby the vizier simply acts as surrogate for the despot's power.

The acuteness of this split between the claim to universality and the characterization of the specific nature of the 'despot' is apparent in de Gomez's representation of Ishmael. When Ishmael has obtained the throne of Persia with Tor's assistance he is extraordinarily cruel in asserting his government, killing all the descendents of his pre-decessor, ripping open the wombs of pregnant women of the previous royal house, and executing many more for sexual incontinence, including his own mother who is beheaded in the marketplace. De Gomez realizes the difficulty of celebrating Ishmael as a hero of romance given this aspect of his history: 'no sooner did *Ishmael* see himself Master of this large and fine Capital of the Empire, but this Prince, who was reckon'd so wise, so prudent, and generous, became cruel, barbarous, and inhuman, even neglecting the Advice of the Man who was most dear to him; that is, the Prince of *Ormus*, who indeavourd to inspire him with more compassionate Sentiments, but nothing could restrain him' (82). Other oriental rulers demonstrate similarly split personalities in such fiction: Soliman, driven by jeal-ousy and lust, passes an order to execute Ibrahim which he only revokes at the last minute. Alexander is charmed by Oroondates but has no scruples in demanding Statira for himself. Even the virtuous Tor is so blinded by his passion for Milla that he neglects his duties as a monarch allowing her brother Noradin to commit monstrous acts in the name of securing the throne of Ormus. Romance idealism cannot cover over or conceal Orientalist expectations about despotism and empire. Oriental 'history' undermines the universalist claims of oriental 'romance'.

English Scheherazades: domesticating the oriental tale

In England, oriental narratives provided significant opportunities for the exploration of Enlightenment models of transformation and progress, especially for women writers who used the form to argue for rational equilibrium, and a balance of power, both sexual and political. The readings of three such narratives below draw attention to the representation of female agency, particularly verbal agency, as a significant force in the establishment of a progressive and dynamic modern state which triumphs over the stasis and control associated with the oriental despot. In Penelope Aubin's *The Strange Adventures of the Count de Vinevil and his Family* (1721), Eliza Haywood's *Philidore and Placentia* (1727), and Frances Sheridan's *The History of Nourjahad* (1765), rational equilibrium, both personal and political, is brought about often through the agency of women—European if the tale stages an encounter between East and West but oriental if the narrative involves only eastern protagonists. These women succeed in curbing excessive desire (for power over persons, economic or political supremacy) on the part of the 'oriental(ized)' man.

Eliza Haywood's 1727 novella entitled *Philidore and Placentia, or L'Amour Trop Delicat* addresses the difficulty of securing a political mean, through the representation of an oscillation between closure and deferral in a romantic plot that traverses Occident and Orient. The 'delicate' love of Philidore and Placentia results in repeated deferral of their eventual union. Placentia is wealthy as a result of the mysterious absence of her only brother. Philidore, of good birth but unable to match her resources, loves her from afar and enters her service in disguise as someone who 'appeared of the Egyptian breed'.[79] Placentia insensibly finds herself falling in love with this servant, Jacobin, a passion which is confirmed when he saves her from abduction. Convinced he is in fact of good birth, she tries to persuade him to acknowledge himself, but he departs knowing that their fortunes are not equally matched. Philidore's ship is seized by pirates two days from the coast of Persia and he is set ashore on a desert coast. He saves a beautiful young man from an onslaught by three

---

[79] William Harlin McBurney et al. (eds.), *Four before Richardson: Selected English Novels, 1720–1727* (Lincoln, Nebr.: University of Nebraska Press, 1963), 159.

unknown men and bandages the young man's wounds with his turban. His new acquaintance is 'in everything habited like a Persian, though his speech as well as his words declaring he was a Christian made him not doubt but that he had been bred in England' (189). While the young man is being nursed back to health it is discovered that he has been recently castrated. This prompts an inset 'History of the Christian Eunuch' told by the eunuch to Philidore.

Taken by Persian privateers and sold at market at Liperda to the Bashaw, the young man became a great favourite of his master. He falls in love, however, with the bashaw's favourite wife, Arithea, and bribes a eunuch to admit him in a mute's disguise to the seraglio. Here, he sits and paints Arithea while she bathes in an artificial pond. All thoughts of liberty fade as he feeds his obsession. When his master finds out, he is cruelly beaten, but nevertheless agrees to an assignation that Arithea makes with him. At the point of coitus, the bashaw bursts in and has him castrated as a punishment. 'Thus wretched,' he comments, 'thus become the scorn of both sexes and incapable of being owned by either, there was now nothing to wish for but death' (23). All desire gone, he willingly and drudgingly continues a slave for six years until Arithea encourages him in a note to flee. Philidore has saved him from death at the hands of the bashaw's men.

On the eunuch's recovery, the friends part company and Philidore departs to join his uncle in Isfahan, Persia, inheriting the latter's vast fortune on his death a year later. He heads for home to propose to Placentia but is blown off course. Moored at Baravat in the Turkish dominions, he hears of the courage of a beautiful woman being sold at slave auction by an Algerian corsair. She tries to kill herself rather than leave with her purchaser, a merchant. Philidore sends a messenger to relieve her who returns with Placentia and the lovers are joyfully reunited. Placentia now delivers her own first-person narration, disclosing that her brother has returned and, with her wealth diminished accordingly, she embarked in search of Philidore in Persia. On the ship she became the victim of unwanted attentions by the captain, her rape only prevented by the seizure of the ship by the Turks on the Algerine corsair. Her suicide attempt was prompted by threats from the captain, purchased by the same master, to complete the rape and father slave-children with her. Philidore conducts Placentia to

England, but now she refuses to marry him because he is richer than her. This crisis is resolved when her returned brother, Bellamont, is discovered to be one and the same person as the Christian eunuch. Unable to father children, Bellamont gives her one-third of his estate and, now absolutely equal, the lovers are finally married.

Haywood's novella counterpoints obsessive lust with discriminating love in the contrast between Philidore's and Bellamont's behaviour in their respective love affairs. Both embrace 'slavery' as a means of access to the women they love, but Bellamont seeks his own gratification and his punishment not only codes the oriental cruelty of his master but also the nature of his feelings for Arithea. However, Haywood's sympathies with a Tory critique of Whig concepts of 'liberty' (the careful balance of prerogative between parties) are evident in the critique the novel makes of a too nice and discriminating sense of sexual equality. The eponymous lovers share 'L'amour *trop* delicat'; they seem to be trapped in an indefinite deferral. Power should not be absolute, but absolute equality seems unattainable, and indeed is only provided by an evident and artificial coincidence in the discovery of the identity of the long-lost brother. Haywood experiments with the idea that gender reversal—whereby Philidore learns to adopt the position of women, deferring and repressing desire in order to secure a relation of equality, and Bellamont's potential as patriarchal and reproductive head of the family is literally cut short—makes possible a union of equality. Philidore proves his virtue to his more wealthy suitor, Placentia, who can 'raise' him through marriage to a relationship of equality necessary to secure her family's lineage.

Jennifer Thorn, in discussing the motif of castration in three exotic tales by Haywood, summarizes its function thus:

castration not only protects women from conception; it also is imagined as freeing men to emotionality and loyalty. The intergender sympathy thus imaginatively facilitated by castration relies equally upon the tales' exoticism. 'Away' is where castration happens and where it can even be imagined as utopian, enabling male interiority and male-female equality.[80]

[80] Jennifer Thorn, ' "A Race of Angels": Castration and Exoticism in Three Exotic Tales by Eliza Haywood', in Kirsten T. Saxton and Rebecca P. Bocchicchio, *The Passionate Fictions of Eliza Haywood* (Lexington, Ky: University of Kentucky Press, 2000), 170.

The progress of the narrative towards the assertion of an equality brought about through the assimilation of the male protagonists into values associated with European femininity (stoic suffering, resistance to seduction and violence) is mirrored by the passing of narrative control into the hands of a woman. The novel progresses from a third-person 'ungendered' narration, to an inset narration in male voice (Bellamont's 'History of the Christian Eunuch'), to conclude with the first-person narration of Placentia.

Only the ninth (and very short) chapter of Penelope Aubin's *The Strange Adventures of the Count de Vinevil and his Family* (1721) is told in female voice: the inset history of Violetta, a Venetian lady abducted and raped by a Turkish bashaw named Osmin. However, Aubin's 'Preface to the Reader' defends the use of narrative fiction as a vehicle for virtue, and although she ostensibly makes the case for the agency of divine providence in the narrative, it is the agency of virtuous women on which her paragraph closes:

> the few that honor virtue and wish well to our nation ought to study to reclaim our giddy youth; and since reprehensions fail, try to win them to virtue, by methods where delight and instruction may go together. With this design I present this book to the public, in which you will find a story where Divine Providence manifests itself in every transaction, where virtue is tried with misfortunes, and rewarded with blessings. In fine, where men behave themselves like Christians, and women are really virtuous, and such as we ought to imitate.[81]

Aubin's involved novel sets Christian heroes and heroines (priests and women) against violent lustful Turks and, to a lesser extent, European male ambition. The Count de Vinevil takes his beautiful daughter, Ardelisa, and young male ward, Longueville, to the Ottoman capital with him in search of a better life, since in Picardy he finds 'his estate impoverished by continuous taxations, and himself neglected by his sovereign and no ways advanced' (115). The cost of this venture is dear: he is murdered, his daughter is forced to flee in male disguise and she is separated for ten years (and many adventures) from the husband, Longueville, she has hastily married in the hopes that this might avert

---

[81] Paula R. Backscheider and John J. Richetti (eds.), *Popular Fiction by Women, 1660–1730: An Anthology* (Oxford: Clarendon Press, 1996), 114.

the unwanted attentions of a powerful Turkish lover, Mahomet. Ardelisa, we are informed, is more than a model of innocence: she has 'all the Softness of a Woman, with the Constancy and Courage of a Hero' (12).

As in Haywood's tale, Aubin's charts the continued deferral of romantic closure, impeded by a violent and dangerous oriental landscape as well as people. But that deferral also enables the production of a new relationship of equality, largely through the transformation of the hero who learns to 'suffer' as women commonly do. On the death of Ardelisa's father, Longueville returns to France and immures himself in a monastery to await news of Ardelisa's death or recovery. Ardelisa meanwhile traverses the Orient obtaining assistance from Christian priests living in hiding, escaping another potential rape and imprisonment in a seraglio (along the way liberating a fellow European woman, Violetta) by dint of a fire set by her servant, setting up a Crusoe-like community on a small island in the Aegean. Here too, then, gender reversal is made possible by the unusual circumstance of an oriental locale, resulting in the formation of domestic relations of equality rather than hierarchy (with which the novel opened).

By contrast with the two early eighteenth-century tales, Frances Sheridan concerns herself with an exclusively oriental scene and eastern protagonists. However, this story is no less concerned with sexual and political relations in Europe. Here too, despotic and tyrannical modes of masculinity associated with the Orient are displaced by models of 'reformed' masculinity and heroic femininity. *The History of Nourjahad* (1765) aligns with Haywood's tale in its promotion of what Jennifer Thorn describes as 'homosocial passion and heterosocial commonality for Europeans'.[82] Sheridan conceived her fiction in the tradition of the 'speculum principis', a text addressed to a king-in-waiting. Her biographer, Alicia Le Fanu, says that the tale was meant to be 'the first of a series of instructive moral fictions which the author was to have obtained permission to dedicate to His present Most Gracious Majesty, then the young

---

[82] Thorn, ' "A Race of Angels" ', 178.

Prince of Wales'.[83] This context of the female storyteller addressing a powerful prince, along with the use of the eastern tale set in Persia, recalls Scheherezade's role. The newly crowned 22-year-old sultan of Persia, Shemzeddin, whom we meet at the opening of the tale, is uncertain whether his closest friend, Nourjahad, has the necessary qualities to assume the role of his chief adviser. Shemzeddin asks Nourjahad to tell him his dearest wish and when Nourjahad says he wants inexhaustible wealth and immortality, Shemzeddin is angered. That night, Nourjahad is visited by a golden-haired youth, his 'guardian genius', who allows him to choose between this wish and being restored to the sultan's favour. Nourjahad selects the wish and is given access to a room full of treasure which he secretes in a cave in his own home.

He proceeds to indulge in a life of pleasure, immersing himself in 'a tide of luxurious enjoyments' which make him 'lazy and effeminate'.[84] He falls passionately in love with one of his wives, Mandana, and secures the loyal services of one Hasem to act as his steward. However, Nourjahad falls prey to the punishment threatened by his 'genius': that he will experience bouts of sleep lasting long periods if he succumbs to evil. After a banquet in which he has assumed 'the pomp of an Eastern monarch' (136) and drunk to excess, he sleeps for four years and twenty days, waking to be told that Mandana is dead and has left a young son fathered by him. His attempts to console himself through dissipation result in a mock-ceremony where he presents himself as Mahomet and his favoured mistress as Cadiga (Mahomet's favourite wife). Again he falls asleep, this time for forty years and eleven months. He wakes to find his seraglio full of aged hags and his son fled after trying to obtain his father's wealth. Now he 'grew peevish, morose, tyrannical; cruelty took possession of his breast; he abused his women and beat his slaves, and seemed to enjoy no satisfaction but that of tormenting others' (162). When Cadiga chastises him, he stabs her in the side. Once again he falls into a sleep,

---

[83] Alicia Le Fanu, *Memoirs of the Life and Writings of Mrs Frances Sheridan* (London, 1824), 226.

[84] Frances Sheridan, 'The History of Nourjahad', in Robert Mack (ed.), *Oriental Tales* (Oxford: Oxford University Press, 1992), 115–96, 131.

this time of twenty years' length and wakes to find his only attendant is Cozro, brother to Cadiga, who has been charged by the latter with watching over him. Cozro's advice leads to Nourjahad's repentance and he now decides to use his wealth benevolently, but thereby breaks an order from Shemzeddin's newly ascended son, Shemerzad, that no one can do business in the city for twenty days in honour of his dead father. Cozro, who has been acting as Nourjahad's emissary, is imprisoned with him and executed. Nourjahad is called before the sultan where he willingly embraces his punishment of death. The execution is averted, however, by the disclosure that he has been the victim of a trick orchestrated by Shemzeddin. It has been only four-teen months since the visit from his genie. The latter is revealed to be Mandana in disguise, a Persian lady who had fallen in love with Nourjahad unbeknownst to him and sought Shemzeddin's assistance in winning him. Cadiga is not in reality dead and Shemzeddin had adopted the role of Cozro to bring him to virtue. Shemzeddin con-cludes the tale with the moral:

Let this dream of existence then be a lesson to thee for the future, never to suppose that riches can ensure happiness, that the gratification of our passions can satisfy the human heart; or that the immortal part of our nature, will suffer us to taste unmixed felicity, in a world which was never meant for our final place of abode. (194)

Nourjahad is united with Mandana and becomes the sultan's first minister, a role he conducts virtuously so 'that his name was famous throughout the Eastern world' (194).

In Frances Sheridan's hands, the eastern tale metamorphoses into a conduct fiction. Rational virtue replaces superstition, magic, and Faustian ambition, largely through the agency of female and feminized characters: Mandana, Cadiga, Shemzeddin/Cozro. As Robert Mack notes, the heart of the story is a homosocial (if not explicitly homoerotic) relation between the two male friends ('Introduction', p. xxxii), but it is Nourjahad who behaves as the tyrannous despot and his friend the sultan who exercises the wiles of fiction to 'correct' his craving for personal absolutism. Sheridan efficiently marries two traditions of fiction associated with female voice and the regulation of transgressive subjectivity: domestic fiction and the oriental tale. From this hybrid form emerges a parable about the formation of modern Enlightenment subjectivity, self-regulating, subservient only to moral rather than arbitrary authority, and, as Nancy Armstrong has persuasively argued, characterized as female.[85] Mandana—cross-dressed beautiful boy, eastern genie, chief mistress of the seraglio, but also virtuous wife—represents this hybridity most powerfully in the novel. Here too, then, the oriental tale is captured by an Anglicized version of revolution as domestic reform led by virtuous mothers, wives, and feminized companionship. Central to the agency of fiction in the stories is the communal activity of feminine or feminized protagonists; Scheherezade requires her sister Dinarzade to act as cover in addressing Schahriar with her tales. Shemzeddin enlists the help of Mandana, 'Cadiga', and his vizier.

These English fictions argue for ameliorative reform in line with enlightened ideals of civil humanism, a new model of personhood which, according to J. G. A. Pocock privileges 'commerce, leisure and cultivation' over the older model of civic humanism's stress on property and politics.[86] The cultivation of the private man as significant in the maintenance of public political order newly stresses the responsibilities of women as educators of children in the home and supportive wives, if it cannot conceive of them as political agents in their own right.

French and English writers deploy oriental settings and history as fables that address their own preoccupations about national identity and gendered agency. In so doing, they simultaneously open and close the gap between eastern and western cultures; for one culture to act as analogous to another there must be a perceived difference between the two, just as the individual tale which illustrates the message will necessarily be more than the message. In other words, there can be no exact correspondence if meaning is to come into

---

[85] Armstrong asserts that 'middle-class authority rested in large part upon the authority that novels attributed to women and in this way designated as specifically female' (Nancy Armstrong, *Desire and Domestic Fiction: A Political History of the Novel* (New York and Oxford: Oxford University Press, 1987), 4).

[86] J. G. A. Pocock, *Virtue, Commerce, and History: Essays on Political Thought and History, Chiefly in the Eighteenth Century*, Ideas in Context (Cambridge: Cambridge University Press, 1985), 49.

being. Difference is necessary to the generation of meaning, on the level of the narrative or discursive sentence as well as the individual speech act or grammatical sentence. In the French oriental romance, difference is at first denied with the claim that human behaviour is universally the same, but it is gradually reasserted as the narrative progresses. The specific characteristics of oriental despotism, derived from the genres of oriental history and political philosophy, emerge and begin to establish differences between occidental and oriental behaviours. In the English fictions, by contrast, exoticism and difference is stressed from the outset and, as the narrative progresses, rationalism and European values are uncovered behind the façade of difference.

The Turkish and Persian fictions we have so far surveyed have foregrounded the function of female voice, both within individual tales and in their delivery. The loquacious woman is both tenor and vehicle in these tales. However, an equally strong tradition of the eighteenth century centred the oriental male as both character and narrator. The dominant form that voiced the gender dynamic of eighteenth-century representations of the near East—a loquacious femininity challenges the despotic gaze of the oriental male—was the fictional epistolary account of the 'observing' or 'speculating' oriental male, who appears in the West as either spy or 'curious' traveller. The same gendered economy underpins writings that ventriloquize the role of the *male* speaker of Turkish/Persian extraction. As his ruler does, he tends to privilege the power of the look over that of voice, and this paradoxical 'blindness' leads to epistemological and psychic instability. The remainder of the chapter turns to the figure of the speculating and speculative oriental male in eighteenth-century fiction from France and England. I identify two strains in such writing, both linked by a much more overt tendency to satirical and partisan political intent than that found intermittently in the oriental tale, French romance, or female-authored English short fiction: the epistolary account of Europe in the voice of a Turkish or Persian 'informant' and the political satire or allegory that retells recent French or English political history through the vehicle of the ostensible narration of oriental history or scandal.

Speculative men I: spies and correspondents

One of the most familiar 'oriental' voices for readers in eighteenth-century prose was that of the male 'reverse' or pseudo-traveller, a fictional correspondent who travels from East to West and writes of his experiences (see Fig. 7). The *Letters Writ by a Turkish Spy* extended to 600 letters over eight volumes and covered the period

7. Frontispiece, Giovanni Paolo Marana, *Letters Writ by a Turkish Spy*, translated by William Bradshaw, vol. i, 6th edn. (1694)

1637 to 1682 in France from the last years of the Regency of Anne of Austria and Cardinal Richelieu through the long reign of Louis XIV under the influence of Cardinal Mazarin and, after 1661, without a first minister. The first volume in English translation of 1687 was compiled from four slim parts published in French in Paris (and the last in Amsterdam) under the title 'L'Espion Turc' between 1684 and 1686 by a Genoese author named Giovanni Paolo Marana (1642–93). The second English volume appeared with the first volume in 1691 and was claimed to be translated from an Italian edition of the work brought to England by a Mr Saltmarsh; this same edition was claimed to be the basis for the remaining six volumes. This English translation was the source of the first French version of the last seven volumes which appeared in Cologne in 1696. Marana's authorship of the first volume is undisputed and it seems likely that, although the remaining volumes were first published in English, this was to avoid the French censor, and that Marana was also their author.[87] Daniel Defoe was attracted to the deist rationalist sympathies of the purported spy; his *Continuation of Letters Written by a Turkish Spy at Paris* (1718) extended the narrator's account from 1687 to the year 1693. Unsurprisingly, given Defoe's known sympathies, the *Continuation* voiced a far more explicit support of dissenting, especially Huguenot, religion (see Fig. 8).[88]

Charles Montesquieu's *Lettres Persanes* (1721) addressed a later period in French history, Philippe d'Orléans's troubled Regency after the death of Louis XIV in 1715, through the eyes of two Persian travellers, fleeing political persecution in their homeland; the year after the letters' appearance in France they were translated by

---

[87] The consistency of style, and tone, across the eight volumes has led commentators to conclude that they probably did have one author and the most likely candidate remains Marana, but Robert Midgeley (who is known to have obtained the copyright to the work before the end of 1693) and William Bradshaw, his operative, have both been put forward as contenders for the authorship of the later volumes. For discussion about authorship see Arthur J. Weitzman's 'Introduction' to his edited selection, *Letters Writ by a Turkish Spy* (London: Routledge & Kegan Paul, 1970); Bolton Corney, 'On the Authorship of the Turkish Spy', *Gentlemen's Magazine* NS 14 (1840): 465–9; William Harlin McBurney, 'The Authorship of the Turkish Spy', *PMLA* 72 (1957): 915–35; Joseph Tucker, 'On the Authorship of the Turkish Spy: An État Présent', *Papers of the Bibliographical Society of America* 52 (1958): 34–57.

[88] Daniel Defoe, *A Continuation of Letters Written by a Turkish Spy at Paris.* (London, 1718).

8. Frontispiece, Daniel Defoe, *A Continuation of Letters Written by a Turkish Spy at Paris* (1718)

Ozell into English. Both the *Letters writ by a Turkish Spy* and the *Lettres Persanes*, the former an important influence on the latter, went into numerous editions through the eighteenth century, and spawned many imitations.[89] They inaugurated the fashion for

[89] The Ozell translation of the *Persian Letters* was in its sixth English edition by 1773 and the complete eight-volume *Turkish Spy* had gone into six editions by 1740. The last printing of the eight volumes of the letters of the Turkish spy came in 1801, but Montesquieu's collection has seen translation and new publication to the present day.

pseudo-travels written in the voice of a 'foreign', often oriental, informant.

These 'informant' voices are striking not so much because they express the confidence, expansionism, and authority of oriental 'empire' in the late seventeenth and eighteenth centuries, but rather because they draw European readers into the fictionalized psyches of fearful, paranoid, and subjugated 'representatives' of the subjects of such empire. We learn that the Turkish spy Mahmut is Arabian in origin and raised in Sunni Islam, spent four years in captivity by Christians in Sicily, where he learnt Greek and Latin and acquired a taste for ancient history, before arriving in the seraglio at Istanbul from whence he has been sent by Sultan Amurath (Murat IV) as a spy to report on western European affairs from Paris. The experience is not a happy one and the authority of the spy's 'gaze' is consistently undermined by his terror of discovery; any moment he may cease to be the one who looks and become the one who is looked at and exposed. Mahmut repeatedly requests that he be allowed to return to the Ottoman 'Porte' or to his native Arabia to take up a contemplative life, a different kind of 'speculation' from the one in which he is employed. Mahmut is an advocate of Cartesian rationalism, as well as a member of an Islamic sect with a belief in transmigration, and he is a great 'speculator' on the larger mysteries of life, revealing a sense of confinement that his remit from his employers is limited to peering into the secrets of political cabinets.

Usbek, main correspondent in the *Persian Letters* is, like Mahmut, a troubled soul who experiences his 'travels' as exile, although his purpose in coming to France is not espionage, but rather necessitated by political jealousies at the Persian court, from which he retired pretending a desire to pursue his interest in science at his country retreat. However, his discovery of a further plot has obliged him to live abroad, under the pretext of a now genuine interest in discovering more about western knowledge of science.[90]

---

[90] Montesquieu, *Persian Letters*, trans. John Ozell, 3rd edn. corr. (London, 1736), Letter 9, 21–2. All subsequent references are to this edition.

The conceit in both works is the idea of a 'reverse' gaze. The eastern spy/traveller puts the West on display to his correspondents 'back home'. The accounts are a reverse mirror of the representation of oriental empire by European writers. Mahmut complains that, because Christians deny oriental languages to their children and educate them in European and classical tongues, they encourage belief in the 'Monstrous Fictions of the Ancient Poets' and 'the Lying Tales and *Legends* of their own Priests'.[91] Christian and classical culture is for him the world of fiction and imposture, Islam that of truth, a reversal of western Christian denunciations of Islam as imposture. Mahmut criticizes Christians for allowing internal divisions in the Church, especially between Protestant and Catholic sects, which make them weak and vulnerable to attack from powers such as the Ottoman, reversing the western Christian representation of Islam as split between Sunni and Shi'ite at the expense of total Islamic empire. Usbek and Rica identify 'differences' in European cultures only to reveal their tendency to decline into similarity with oriental ones. Thus, monarchical government in the West is 'limited' by laws but these are designed only to maximize the ways in which kings can violate justice: 'The unlimited Power of our Sublime Sultans, which has no Rule but it self, does not produce more Monsters, than this base Art which strives to make Justice bend, tho' inflexible' (*Persian Letters*, ii. 64, Letter 94). Rica describes western governments as secretly driven by women, mirroring how western travellers and historians had described eastern states as being: 'We complain in *Persia*, that the Kingdom is govern'd by two or three Women: It is much worse in *France*, where Women in general bear Rule, and take the whole Authority to themselves, not only by Wholesale but even retail' (ii. 110–11, Letter 107). Montesquieu thus implies that French absolutism can be interpreted as only a more extreme variant of eastern despotism, rather than its opposite.

---

[91] Giovanni Paolo Marana, *The Eight Volumes of Letters Writ by a Turkish Spy at Paris.*, trans. William Bradshaw, 8 vols. (London, 1707), vi. 3.177, Letter 14. This is the 6th ed. of the full 8 vol. and 18th of the first. All subsequent references are to this edition by volume, book, page, and letter.

The idea of the 'reverse' gaze is complicated by two factors in both works: first, the tendency for the reverse gaze itself to experience reversal and, second, the slippage between fictional correspondent and his literary creator. As a result the letter sequence departs from the expectation of a secure and authoritative critique by a detached observer into an exploration of disturbed and dislocated psyches.

The reversal of the reverse gaze occurs in both collections of letters on the narrow canvas of the individual and the wider canvas of rival cultures. The letters do not concern themselves with occidental culture alone but include extensive comment on the oriental 'home' cultures of Turkey and Persia. Mahmut does not confine his speculations to Paris, but, in obedience to an instruction from the sultan, writes candidly to officers at the Ottoman Porte about affairs in the capital, reminding them of their duties and criticizing any shortcomings. Montesquieu expands the *Turkish Spy*'s epistolary technique of a single correspondent by giving letters from correspondents in Persia (and especially the women and eunuchs in Usbek's seraglio). So, these correspondents also 'open up' oriental spaces to the gaze of European readers who, like Schahriar, 'listen in' on their texts. The 'Prefatory Advertisement' to the 1736 'corrected' edition of the *Persian Letters* claims that the work:

> opened to us a Scene of Action, which all the Curiosity of our most famous Travellers cou'd never pierce into us, and given us so natural an Idea of the Manners of the Seraglio, the Thoughts and Passions of a number of Women confined for the Pleasures of a single Man, and the Notions and Cast of Mind of the Eunuchs, whose whole Lives are spent in guarding and watching them, that one wou'd almost believe the Letters to be Genuine. (i, n.p.)

On an individual level, the spy or informant finds that he becomes the object of the gaze of others, an object of curiosity in his own right. Rica writes to Ibben at Smyrna in Letter 28:

> When I arrived here, I was stared at as if I had drop'd from Heaven: old and young, Men, Women and Children, all must have a sight of me: if I went abroad, every Body got to their Windows; if I walk'd in the *Tuilleries*, immediately a Circle was form'd round me; the Women made a Rainbow about me, varied with a thousand Colours (i. 95).

Pictures of him are produced and he records: 'I saw my self multiplied in every Shop, upon every Chimney' (96). Curiosity abates when he abandons his Persian dress and the attention only reignites if someone mentions his nationality in public. When Mahmut is recognized by his old Sicilian master at Notre Dame, he realizes he has been too sanguine about his anonymity, his 'unseen-ness':

One would think it an easie Matter, for a Stranger to conceal himself in so vast and Populous a City as is *Paris*. Especially, one who makes so mean and contemptible a Figure, as does the supposed *Titus* of *Moldavia*. I little thought, that the *Lowness* of my *Stature*, and the *Deformity* of my *Body*, would have attracted any Curious Eyes, but, that my very *Habit*, would have prevented me from all Suspicion, and, that I might have pass'd an Age Houses and Streets of *Paris*. (ii. 3. 221, Letter 18)

The curious gaze of the traveller, the intentful gaze of the spy, or the authoritative gaze of the oriental despot, are undermined by the possibility that the tables can be turned, anonymity or authority lost, in the gaze that looks back and discovers a 'truth'—political weakness, physical failure, the hidden identity of the spy—that puts the power of looking at risk.

Second, both sets of letters suggest a correspondence between the fictional narrators and their 'real' hidden inventors. Mahmut is, like his creator Marana (whose patron was an ambassador to the French court), an admirer of France and its monarchy. Marana's profession of journalism was not far removed from the kind of spying his fictional creation undertakes: the transmission of cultural, social, and political information to a home culture and the maintenance of information networks with fellow correspondents across a region. The involvement of another journalist, Daniel Defoe, in establishing a country-wide spy network for Robert Harley in early eighteenth-century Britain suggests connections between the two professions. Indeed, in a letter to Harley, probably written July–August 1704, which suggests posting spies in France, he recalls:

a Book in Eight Volumes Published in London about 7 or 8 yeares Ago Call'd Letters writ by a Turkish Spye—. The books I Take as They Are, a Meer Romance, but the Morall is Good, a Settl'd Person of Sence and Penetration, of Dexterity and Courage, to Reside Constantly in Paris,

Tho' As tis a Dangerous Post he had a Larger Allowance than Ordinary,
Might by one happy Turn Earn all the Money and the Charge be well
bestow'd.[92]

Marana's roundabout means of publication (from Italian to English
to French for the last seven volumes), and his shadowy presence
behind the work, also identify him with Mahmut, who is constantly
shifting his copies of letters from one hiding place to another or
inventing 'dummy' letters in another language in order to put those
whom he thinks may suspect him off the scent.[93] The story of the
'translator's' acquisition of the letters suggests parallels with Mahmut
also, one who passes himself off as a translator or linguist in order to
conceal political intent; Mahmut has spent his many years in Paris
passing as 'Titus the Moldavian', a translator and instructor in oriental
and classical languages. Moldavia, although nominally independent,
was a state in which educated Christians lived in the style of their
previous colonizers, the Ottomans, and hence Mahmut's 'Turkish'
habits would have some explanation through adopting the cover of
this identity.[94] The translator of Mahmut's mysterious letters claims
to be an Italian visiting Paris in 1682 who 'discover'd, by meer

---

[92] *The Letters of Daniel Defoe*, ed. George Harris Healey (Oxford: Clarendon Press,
1955), 38. Paula Backscheider says that by midsummer 1704, Daniel Defoe was employed
as a spy by Robert Harley, Prime Minister and earl of Oxford, developing a spy network
on the model of that of the Whigs in the 1680s to which he would have been privy: 'With
Harley's acquiescence, he traveled, took note of opinions, reported objections and
reservations about the ministry's actions, infiltrated groups, identified influential men and
faction leaders, and wrote pamphlets and essays designed to reassure and win over the
suspicious or uncommitted' (Paula R. Backscheider, *Daniel Defoe: His Life* (Baltimore
and London: Johns Hopkins University Press, 1989), 160).

[93] In vol. iv, bk. 2, Letter 6 and Letter 7, he is given a scare when Eliachim, a
sympathetic Jew privy to his real identity who keeps his letters for him so that they cannot
be found with him in his chamber, tells him that his negro slave has absconded with a box
of letters. It transpires that the African does not know Arabic and hoped the box contained
jewels, burying it when he could not gain access to its secrets. The box is not found and
Mahmut determines to keep the remaining box and future letters with him. In vol. v, bk. 2,
Letter 19, dating from the year 1645, he reports that officers came to his chamber when he
was suspected of being of the Prince of Condé's party and when they find his box of letters
he claims they are a correspondence in Hebrew between a merchant of his acquaintance
and his brethren. He bribes the officers to leave and then has to give the letters to Eliachim
to conceal and receive some 'forgeries' written in Hebrew by the latter to put in their
place. The officers return three days later and a priest who knows Hebrew confirms the
nature of the letters before a judge.

[94] My thanks to Professor Peter Shore who suggested this explanation to me of
Mahmut's 'Moldavian' disguise.

Chance, in a Corner of his Chamber, a great Heap of Papers; which seem'd more spoil'd by Dust than Time' (i. A4). His landlord says they were left by a Moldavian who lodged with him for eighteen years from the year 1664 and departed suddenly leaving 'Manuscripts, that no Body understood'; report suggests he died having been thrown into a river (i. A4). The Italian sets about improving his Arabic so that he can translate the papers.

Montesquieu's preface to his work asserts that the French 'translator' of the letters will cease to write should his identity be discovered. The French 'translator' asserts that the letters were shown to him by their Persian authors who lodged with him and discussed their experiences with him. He admits, however, that he seized some that they would not have shown him and he shows no qualms about putting these on display. Like the Persian correspondents, the French translator presents himself as an enquiring mind who wants to share what he has discovered about a 'foreign' culture with his native countrymen. But, the assertion that he will fall silent should his identity be disclosed indicates a hidden political insurgency in the work; should it be known who wrote the work its political 'intention' would become apparent, stripped of the 'veil' of parable or cryptic style associated with 'Asiatic' speech itself. Of course, there was a not-so-hidden political agenda behind the work which was no doubt apparent to Montesquieu's readers whether they recognized the work as his or not: the rationalist critique of established institutions and the advocacy of the separation of executive, legislative, and judicial power in the state as a necessary means of preventing the growth of despotism in Europe. This was a position Montesquieu was to develop with greater clarity in his *De l'Esprit des Lois* of 1748 (translated as *The Spirit of Laws* by Thomas Nugent in 1750).

Despite their similarities, the *Letters writ by a Turkish Spy* and the *Persian Letters* warrant separate discussion, not least because of the very different political analyses that underpin their representations of French monarchy. But also because each delivers different insights into the gendered dynamics of looking and speech which not only dominated representations of the Turkish/Persian East but also contributed to the evolution of prose fiction in European, and especially British, culture.

The 'office of the eye': 'The Turkish Spy'

Samuel Johnson accompanies his gloss to the noun 'spy' in his 1755 dictionary with the comment:

It is observed by a German, that *spy* has been in all ages a word by which the eye, or office of the eye, has been expressed; thus the *Arimaspians* of old, fabled to have but one eye, were so called from *ari*, which, among the nations of *Caucasus*, still signifies *one*, and *spi*, which has been received from the old Asiatick languages for an *eye, sight* or one that *sees*.[95]

The etymology of the term 'Spy' is given as 'Asiatick', and the association would have been familiar because of the popularity of the *Letters Writ by a Turkish Spy* through the eighteenth century.

Mahmut's letters show a self-conscious awareness of the etymology of his 'office' with the 'eye'. They are peppered with references to sight: literal (one of Mahmut's friends and allies at the Porte is blinded as a punishment and Mahmut falls prey in old age to disorders of his own sight), and metaphorical (spying as a form of sight, the spy's activities entail disclosure of what he sees and his avoidance of being seen). The axis of sight is paralleled with that of the tongue and language; rigid control must be exercised over both if they are not to put the user in peril. Letters go astray, get stolen, are misinterpreted by their readers. Too great a mastery of an oriental language may expose Mahmut to suspicion; knowledge of it on the part of others may make it possible for them to decipher his letters. Outspokenness on the part of his fellow spies exposes Mahmut to possible discovery. When he gets no response to a letter to a spy named Carcoa in Vienna, Mahmut speculates that he may have revealed his correspondents' identities prior to being murdered: 'When I sit in my Chamber, and hear any discoursing in the House, I imagine 'tis about me; when I go along the Streets, if any Man fasten his Eyes on me, he arrests me with Fear and Apprehension' (ii. 1.2, Letter 1). The fact that a Frenchman recognizes him from the Ottoman seraglio is enough to result in Mahmut's arrest and detention in the Bastille for a period.

---

[95] Samuel Johnson, *A Dictionary of the English Language on Cd-Rom the First and Fourth Editions*, ed. Anne McDermott (Cambridge [England] and New York: Cambridge University Press, 1996).

As he ages, Mahmut's sight begins to fail him and he is prone to visions that make him vulnerable and liable to exposure. Mahmut comments on the restrictive self-surveillance that is his daily life:

'Tis not for a Man in my Station, to be open and talkative; but to distinguish Persons and Seasons; to understand the due Stops and Advances of my Tongue; sometimes to say Much in a Little, at other Times to say Little or Nothing at all; but ever so to speak, as not to lay my self naked to the Hearers; yet to seem a very frank, open-hearted Man, in what I discourse of.

I would not have thee conclude from what I have said, that *Mahmut* uses any Reserve to the *Ministers* of the *Divan*, who are *Mines* of *Science* and *Wisdom*, and can easily discern the Heart through the most artificial Veil of Words. But it is absolutely necessary for me, to use Dissimulation in this *Court*; seeming many times ignorant of what I already know, that I may not be thought to know more than they would have me. I was never yet so indiscreet, as to publish any Secret that was committed to my Charge; whereby I have gained great Confidence, with Men who delight to unbosome their Intelligence. They esteem me a Man of Integrity and fit to be trusted. Thus am I made privy to many Intriegues of the *Grandees*, and a Repository of the *Court*-News: Whilst they Whisper in *Mahmut*'s Ear what is Transacted in the Royal Bed Chambers, and private Apartments (to Vizier Azem, iii. 1. 42–3, Letter 12)

The impossible paradox of Mahmut's position is made apparent at repeated intervals. The truth-value of his statements in his letters to the Porte is premised on the effectiveness of the deceit, disguise, and dissimulation he practises in Paris. His correspondents must conceive of him as both honest and dishonest at once.

The question of Mahmut's 'credit' with his reader is always visible in the letters. The reader of all eight volumes 'sees' the measure and limit of his dissimulative use of prose, his capacity for fiction, where individual correspondents cannot. Thus in 1648, with the violent deposition of Sultan Ibrahim, Mahmut writes to the Mufti approving his revolt against the sultan following the rape of the Mufti's daughter (iii. 3, Letter 19), but only two letters later we find him commenting to his intimate friend and fellow Arabian, Dgnet Oglou:

I am Astonish'd and Vex't to hear, That the *Mufti* should be concern'd in so *Black* a *Tragedy*. How shall we have the Confidence hereafter to Reproach the *Christians*, with their frequent *Treasons* and *Murd'ring* of their *Kings*;

since it will be easie for them to retort that the *Supreme Patriarch* of our *Law*, has enter'd into the *Secret* of *Rebels*, Conspir'd the *Death* of his *Sovereign*, and caus'd him to be *Depos'd* and *Strangled*? (iii. 3. 286, Letter 21)

Mahmut tailors his writing persona to his correspondents and we only ever see his half of the correspondence. Thus to the Aga of the Janissaries, who has an interest in (military) history, he tells stories of national heroines in the West such as Joan of Arc and Queen Christina of Sweden. With his brother Pestelihali, who has travelled in Asia, he discusses India, Brahmanical religion and the nature of travel-writing. To Nathan Ben Saddi, a Jewish spy for the Turks in Vienna, he sends instructions on how to remain concealed and long tracts of argument about the falsity of Jewish law in an attempt to encourage his conversion to Islam. To the Kaimacham (the Grand Vizier's deputy and governor of the city) he sends political and state news and complains about those who conspire in the city to blacken his credit with the authorities. With Cara Hali, a physician, he discusses his mental and physical health and expresses spiritual doubts. He sends admiring letters to Mohammed, the hermit of Mount Uriel in Arabia, that voice his aspiration to share the reclusive life, where he could express his love for animals and espouse vegetarianism. The only letters in the voice of his assumed identity of 'Titus the Moldavian' are to a Christian recluse named William Vospel of Austria, whom he condemns for retreating from public affairs. To the Mufti he expresses spiritual doubts, asks for guidance on points of doctrine, and whether he will be forgiven for breaking Islamic dietary and ritual laws in order to maintain his disguise in Europe. To Hamet Reis Effendi he sends accounts of the different states of Europe, their government, manners, customs, and religion.

Part of the popularity of *The Turkish Spy* in Europe may have lain in the compendious, encyclopedic nature of the volumes which provide a form of popular European history for its readers, interspersed with some Cartesian meditation and held together by a conceit of a life led in disguise, which is largely uneventful and can be swiftly summarized. In the course of the eight volumes which take Mahmut from the age of 28 when he first arrives in Paris to his early seventies his cover is nearly blown when he encounters his old Christian slave master at Notre Dame, he renews his acquaintance and passion for the lovely Greek lady Daria, is imprisoned in the Bastille, loses a box of letters, is reunited with his mother and cousin Isouf in Paris, is suspected of being of the prince of Condé's party and has his apartments searched, is attacked on the street and kills his attacker to discover later that the assailant was Daria's husband driven by jealousy, falls prey to the treachery of his cousin Solyman, who joins with his enemies at the seraglio in Constantinople to try and discredit him, grieves over the death of his mother just a day after her wedding to his Jewish ally in Paris, and closes the sequence in fear of his life with the discovery of the probable murder of Nathan ben Saddi, his fellow spy in Vienna. At several intervals, his hopes are raised of a likely recall from a posting which has brought him nothing but misery, but they all come to nothing. His spying activities are in the main general rather than particular, although he does for several years employ the services of a dwarf named Osmin who can hide under tables and sneak into chambers to read private papers.

Despite his ability to fictionalize himself, Mahmut does emerge as a distinct consciousness; indeed, his condition as 'spy' is not infrequently opened out to stand as a metaphor for the condition of the enlightened subject in general, his mind ostensibly 'free' to wander over any subject but also prone to superstition, anxiety, and self-doubt. He writes to his fellow spy, Nathan Ben Saddi at Vienna, just after he has been released from the Bastille with the comment that even prior to this experience 'I look'd on my self, but as a Prisoner at large; owing the Freedom I had to walk about, only to the Carelessness of the *State*, and the Favour of *Destiny*' (iii. 1.2, Letter 1). Mahmut's Cartesian rationalism and his enthusiasm for learning, his speculations, do not generate happiness but rather ill health and continual self-doubt. He writes to the physician Cara Hali:

As *Nature* has fram'd my Body Infirm and Weak, subject to a thousand Maladies; so is my Mind also harrass'd with Distempers which have no Number. But above all, I labour under a kind of *Intellectual Fever*, a perpetual Thirst of Knowledge, which all the Books and Converse in the World cannot satisfy. There is no End of my Doubts and Scruples. Every Thing appears to me as Ambiguous, as the *Answers* of the *Delphick Oracle*. Nay, I am a perfect Riddle to my self. (v. 2.60, Letter 1)

Here too, the critique of the gaze of the oriental male, apparently mastering but in fact frustrated because it cannot 'know' everything, extends to the critique of the Enlightenment ideal of the rational self; the impossible desire for total knowledge results in obscurity, confusion, and interpretive chaos.

Mahmut's enthusiasm for travel literature, for ancient history and antiquarianism, and his pursuit of the skill of watch-making in his spare time (following Muhammad's precept that all Muslims should undertake some manual labour each day to avoid them falling into vice in their leisure hours as he explains in ii. 3, Letter 21), all feed into the presentation of his existential difficulties as spy, and especially his preoccupation with the determining power of time. Mahmut expresses an orthodox belief in predestination but also toys at different points with the idea of transmigration, the pursuit of intellectual perfection through strenuous contemplation, and a full-blown scepticism verging on atheism or polytheism.

Mahmut presents his position as one of ostensible freedom and actual constraint. For instance, he contrasts the role of the spy with that of the traveller/merchant; where he is 'perpetually shut up and imprisoned as I am' (vi. 3.192, Letter 21), his cousin Isouf, who is a merchant in Astrakhan, has the freedom to roam the earth. The spy's 'eye' is constrained to look purposively where the traveller's is free to wander curiously. Earlier in the same volume he writes to Zedi Alamanzi, a merchant of Venice and a convert to Islam who has sent him an account of his early travels through Europe, Asia, and Africa, commenting that travel 'is the only Way to learn true and complete Wisdom' (vi. 2.105, Letter 15) and that 'there is an infinite Pleasure in seeing the Variety of Objects, which every where expose themselves to a Traveller's Eye' (106).

However, in one respect the spy claims superiority over the traveller, which is that his purposive mission ensures that he does not succumb to the temptations of hybridity. The traveller's 'openness' and 'freedom' inclines him to lose his identity in the new ones he encounters. Mahmut advises his ever-dissatisfied cousin Solyman to visit Isouf at Astrakhan: 'But beware of the *Infirmity* of most *Travellers*, who, *Chameleon*-like, change their Humour and Manners as the Regions vary *through* which they pass. Mere Mimicks, Buffons, and Apes, who place their Excellency in imitating every *Thing* they see, or meet with' (vi. 2. 138, Letter 1). Rather than imitating those he meets, Mahmut adopts a false identity in order to measure foreign values against those of his native culture and find them wanting. The spy is thus anything but a traveller. He stays in one place and must always retain a sense of his native culture's authority and superiority. The traveller wanders across the globe and must be open to the new and curious. Mahmut's script is 'predestined' in that his letters are in a sense already written; they must report on the shortcomings and weaknesses of western cultures if they are to satisfy those to whom they are destined. Where they report western strength and power it must be in order to enable the East to seize an advantage or find a means of overcoming. Of course, Mahmut's view of the traveller's objective curious and unconstrained gaze is an idealized one and the irony of the letters may be that they imply a certain symmetry between travel-writing and spying in that both ultimately cannot escape the determinants of the culture from which the 'agent' originates.

Nevertheless, Mahmut is unconventional in relation to Islam in many respects: he challenges the injunction against alcohol and admits to becoming a connoisseur of wine; he explores the possibility of rebirth and questions whether it is indeed blasphemy to consider Christ to be God made flesh. But he is 'conventional' (according to western European lights) in his understanding of the place of women. To Useph Bassa, he complains:

the Stupidity of the *Nazarenes* provokes my Pen, who allow their Women all the uncontroulable Freedom and Opportunities that commonly give Birth to the most irregular Amours, and yet believe' em Innocent. They are perfect Idolaters of that Sex; not having learned, with the illuminated *Mussulmans*, that Women are of a Creation inferiour to that of Men, have Souls of a lower Stamp, and consequently more prone to Vice; and that they shall never have the Honour to be admitted into our *Paradise*. (iii. 1.57, Letter 16)

Elsewhere, he is more generous to women, admitting his own susceptibility to beauty and intelligence and arguing that it is wrong to deny women a liberal education as it tends to encourage modesty and obedience rather than rebellion (ii. 1, Letter 12). Yet, Mahmut's self-presentation often implies an analogy between his position as spy and that of the veiled women of Islam. To his brother Pestelihali, he writes 'Thou art he, to whom I can unmask. With others I converse (like our Women in *Turkey*) under a Veil' (v. 1.25, Letter 7). For Mahmut's Italian creator, the etymological slippage between the Italian 'serrare' (to imprison) and the Turko-Persian word 'seray' (palace/seraglio) would have been particularly visible, and Mahmut describes his condition as one of 'prison' and 'imprisonment' repeatedly.

His imprisonment in an office/role which determines the nature of his speech also suggests analogies with veiled women. He consistently represents dissimulation as a feminine characteristic displayed by women and eunuchs and asserts his preference for honesty and openness. 'There is something so satisfactory in Truth, and an honest blunt Carriage', he writes to the chief of the black eunuchs (who has written advising him to be more circumspect in what he says in his letters), 'as far surpasses the little Pleasures of Artifice and Dissimulation. And I shou'd be weary of my Life, were I forc'd to preserve it by such Effeminate Tricks' (v. 2.87, Letter 9). However, if Mahmut claims an open manliness in his dealings with the Porte, it is evident that he preserves his life in Paris through precisely such effeminate tricks and acts of artifice and dissimulation. By analogy, then, his experience of imprisonment in the service of spying is similar to that of the harem woman, her survival dependent on her skills of verbal entertainment.

Galland's 'translation' of the *Arabian Nights Entertainments* may have owed more to this French precursor than superficial comparison first suggests. If less overtly than the sequences of oriental tales that followed on its heels, the *Turkish Spy* also stages a contest between despotic power maintained through the agency of the look and subaltern speech maintained through the spinning of ongoing narrative entertainment. Mahmut's survival is dependent on his narrative 'credit' with his masters in Turkey and his ability to conceal his secret purpose in France. Indeed, Mahmut reveals a powerful identification with western and eastern women, especially those who use disguise and cross-dressing. He returns often to the cross-dressing figure of Queen Christina of Sweden whom he admires for her learning, and equates her with Semiramis, queen of Assyria, who dressed as her son in order to rule in his infancy. He tells the story of Joan of Arc to the

Aga of the Janissaries as an example of a national heroine. Mahmut suggests a parallel between these women who adopt male disguise in order to serve their nation and authority and his own 'passing' activity of living as a Christian in Paris in order to gain information for the Porte.

In the concluding letters of the eighth volume the analogy between the spy at the French court and the female or feminized/eunuch inhabitant of the harem becomes even more explicit. Mahmut receives dispatches from the disappeared Nathan Ben Saddi not written in his hand or style and suspects that there is a plot against him in the Ottoman palace. A messenger he sends to Vienna returns with news that Nathan disappeared eight weeks previously and that the dead body of a man found in the Danube has been so facially disfigured that he cannot be recognized. Again, the evidence of neither the verbal nor the visual text can be trusted and now Mahmut panics. His final letter is to his close friend Dgnet Oglou asking him to spy on Mahmut's behalf: 'I have not One Friend in the *Serrail*, whom I dare trust with such a Secret: Thou art my only Refuge at a Juncture which requires Fidelity, Prudence, and a dextrous Conduct in diving and searching into a certain Mystery, which, for ought I know, may concern my Life' (viii. 6.279, Letter 18). Dgnet is asked to listen to whispers at court 'and observe the Language of those who discourse with their Fingers Ends' (279), the signing mutes with special responsibility for discharging executions and punishments. Like a good spy, Dgnet must also act the mute: 'Feign to know something more than thou dost, so that thou may'st really learn what I would have thee know' (280). By the conclusion of the letters, Mahmut has turned the tables and appointed his own spy at the Turkish court, but it is an act of paranoia and fear, rather than one of authority and expansionism. The despotic authority of the oriental male embodied in the gaze is revealed to be itself a disguise or fiction propped up by a chain of verbal and narrative dissemination and dissimulation.

If Marana's text aspires to the status of existential parable, it does so through suggesting that the fiction of authority is simultaneously maintained and undermined by a web of language, the circulation of stories that give or withhold 'credit' to those that speak them and those they 'represent'. This narrative agency is always imperilled, always vulnerable, but always necessary to survival. The sheer volume of the letters in the *Turkish Spy*, like the accretive weight of tales ascribed to Scheherazade, are a witness to the survival tactics of their speakers. When Mahmut falls silent, however, it suggests the failure of his own plots to resist the counterplots spun against him, but it leaves open the possibility of a simple 'recall' and liberation from the enslavement of his occupation, the 'office of the eye'.

'The difficult art of ruling': 'Persian Letters'

The chief black eunuch of Usbek's harem writes to inform him that in Usbek's absence his harem is declining into chaos. The eunuch rehearses his own history of enslavement in Africa at the age of 15, his subsequent castration, and training under a chief eunuch to command a harem of some twenty wives and concubines:

'Twas under this great Master that I learnt the difficult Art of Ruling, and formed my self to the Maxims of an inflexible Government: I studied the Hearts of Women under his Tuition: he taught me to make advantage of their Weaknesses, and not to be shaken by their haughty Airs. He often took Delight in seeing me exercise them, and drive them to the utmost Verge of Obedience; he then brought them back again by Degrees, and made me seem for a time to give way my self. (i. 207, Letter 62)

Montesquieu's *Lettres Persanes* drew on the *Turkish Spy* for its narrative device of fictional letters by oriental informants, but it also transformed its source by presenting a plurality of voices, all 'Persian' but writing from and to the East, about both West and East. This apparent plurality of voice does not, however, detract from the central preoccupation of the text with the nature of government in all its forms: political, sexual, and social. Different aspects of government are explored in the eunuch's training in governing the harem, the struggles of the master Usbek to maintain his authority in his physical absence from the harem, and the espousal by Usbek's young companion Rica of the pleasures of more relaxed rules of social governance in the West. Usbek and Rica voice a critique of oriental despotism and the failure of western monarchy to differentiate sufficiently from it. A fantasy of utopia surfaces in the shape of the Guebre (Parsee) 'republic' described by Rica. The monitory account of the history of the Troglodytes rendered by Usbek warns, however, that republics inevitably decline into monarchy as they expand. Finally, various letters from Usbek's harem 'wives' express resistance to the control of eunuchs, and describe the women's failures of self-governance with respect to their sexual desires. Written and published after the immense success of Galland's sequence, the *Lettres Persanes* could exploit the analogy between sexual and political 'government' so apparent in the former collection. Usbek can be seen as a reverse figure of Schahriar; where Schahriar responds to the discovery of the incontinence of a favoured wife with despotism, only to learn temperance, self-government, and deferral of authority through the course of the tales told him by Scheherazade, Usbek learns to admire temperance, self-government, and deferral of authority in his encounters with western cultures, only to revert to despotism and violence with the discovery of the incontinence rife in his harem.

Montesquieu splits the central role of narrating 'traveller' between two figures, Usbek, the powerful and educated elder statesman who struggles to keep his eye on his affairs in his Persian harem, and Rica, the young, single, and curious cosmopolitan who becomes increasingly 'westernized'. Montesquieu also apportions them different roles as informant writers, associating Usbek with acts of visual authority and Rica with acts of verbal dexterity. Usbek writes to his friend Rhedi saying:

Tho' I have no important Affair upon my hands, yet am I continually employ'd. I pass my Life away in Observation: I every Evening commit to Writing my Remarks on what I have seen, and on what I have heard in the Day-time: every thing engages me, every thing surprises me: I am like a Child whose tender Organs receive strong Impressions from the least Objects. (i. 142–3, Letter 42)

He comments that Rica's 'lively Wit and natural Gaiety, which makes him court all Company, and be equally courted by all' has made them popular in social gatherings despite their 'outlandish air' (143).

Where Usbek looks and records, Rica speaks and performs. The contrast is maintained in their different responses to the issue of female liberty: Rica is given a long letter where he explores the contrast between European and 'Asiatick' ideas on the subject, and concludes that women should be given education to test whether they can indeed compete with men: 'try them in their Talents, which Education has not enervated, and you will see whether they are weaker than us' (i. 118, Letter 36). Rica's sympathy with the cause of female 'liberty' is implied when he writes to Usbek and renarrates to him a story he translated from Persian at the request of a court lady who expressed her curiosity about the 'seraglio' and the condition of women in Persia particularly (ii. 215–32, Letter 138). This act of narration associates Rica with Scheherazade. It is a tale told to a woman and overheard by a male despot (Usbek) as a warning about the dangers of tyr-annous government, i.e. that it will generate insurgency. It is also instructive for its French female listener in that it corrects her pre-judice that women under Islam are invariably ignorant and passive (Scheherazade's tales make a similar point for Dinarzade, of course: that women can resist and reform despotism through intelligent use of limited speech).

The 'Persian tale' Rica tells is itself also framed; it is told by a clever woman called Zulema, who is very learned in the Qur'an, to the other women in the seraglio as proof that the Islamic myth of a male-only paradise was invented by men to keep women in submission; women will enjoy, she argues, their own separate paradise equivalent to that offered to men, but in their case it will be a seraglio of men available for their pleasure and guarded by eunuchs. Her tale comes from an Arab source and concerns a jealous husband, Ibrahim, who executes one of his twelve wives, Anaïs, when she complains of his tyrannical treatment. Anaïs enters a paradise where she has her own seraglio of beautiful young men, but she does not forget her fellow sufferers on earth, sending one of her genii lovers to pass himself off as Ibrahim. The celestial Ibrahim gives the wives their freedom, dismissing the eunuchs, opening his house, and forbidding his wives to wear veils. When the real Ibrahim returns three years later he finds that his substitute has spent his entire fortune and fathered thirty-six children that he now has to support.

While Rica flourishes in Parisian company, enjoying the intellectual games he plays with French women and the pursuit of philosophical paradox in argument, Usbek, the primary instigator of their travels, declines (like Mahmut before him) into a sea of paranoia and anxiety about his declining hold on affairs at home:

I live here in a barbarous Climate, present to every thing that makes me uneasy, absent from every thing that may make me happy: a Heaviness seizes me; I am sadly dejected; I sink beneath the Pressure: methinks I am going to be Annihilated; nor do I scarce feel my self to be alive, but only at such times when a dismal Fit of Jealousy begins to kindle it self, and breed in my Soul Fears, Suspicions, Hatreds and Repinings. (ii. 269, Letter 150)

He wishes to give up his exile and return, but Rica 'opposes all my Resolutions: he frames a thousand Pretences: he seems to have forgot his Country, or rather he seems to have forgot his Friend; so uncon-cern'd is he at my Uneasiness' (269–70).

The threat of annihilation of self is, for Usbek, the result of his sense of a decline in his political authority, an authority that is only maintained by his seeing and being seen in his seraglio. The appointment of surrogate 'eyes' in the shape of eunuchs ultimately proves unsatisfactory. When the chief eunuch dies and another eunuch, Solim, reveals that every one of his wives except Roxana has been incontinent, Usbek responds, telling him, 'I have written to my Wives, to obey thee implicitly: in the Confusion of so many Crimes they shall fall down at the least Glance of thy Eye' (ii. 267, Letter 148). However, a few letters later, Solim reveals that he found Roxana in the arms of a young man: 'her stern Virtue was all a Cheat; it was only a Veil to her Perfidiousness' (ii. 274, Letter 152). Despotic authority cannot be maintained through the single instrument of the letter (and Usbek's letter instructing his chief eunuch to be severe on his wives was lost when the Armenians carrying it were robbed); it requires also the agency/authority of the eye. Grosrichard points out how the collapse of authority in Usbek's seraglio is explicitly paralleled with the decline in authority in France with a Regency taking the place of Louis XIV's absolute presence: 'In place of the firm but gentle absolute power formerly exercised by the gaze of an ever-present master, adored by the women, respected by the others, there is the mute, blind violence of the letter'. [96]

---

[96] Grosrichard, *The Sultan's Court*, 29.

By contrast with Rica's skills in verbal contest and the regulation of response to narrative, Usbek is associated with the government of the 'eye'; the fact that he is physically absent from the harem is the cause of the collapse of government there. As the first eunuch writes:

What can we do with that Fantom of Authority which we have, for it is impossible to communicate the whole? We but faintly represent one half of thy self: we can shew them [the women] nothing but an odious Severity. Thou minglest Fear with Hope; more absolute when thou caressest, than when thou threatenest. (ii. 71–2, Letter 96).

Usbek fails to translate the lesson he has learnt in his travels—that the 'Right of Conquest is no Right at all. A Society can never be founded upon any thing but the free Consent of all the Members' (ii. 68, Letter 95)—to the context of the 'society' he governs, the 'seraglio'. In other words, he fails to see the parallel between political and sexual 'government' which is the organizing principle of the satire in the work he inhabits.

Usbek's lack of insight into the workings of his own harem is particularly striking given that the work makes it clear that for men the only 'pleasure' to be had in the harem is political. In the 'private' space of the harem, men experience only the pleasures of political authority. The chief eunuch calls himself 'a little Emperor in the Seraglio' (ii. 26, Letter 9) and takes this as compensation for his loss of sexual capacity/ pleasure as a result of his castration. Usbek comments that 'Plurality of Wives delivers us from their Dominion and moderates the Violence of our Desires' (i. 181, Letter 54). The passion men fall prey to is jealousy, and political jealousy at that, in the shape of their fears of less-than-total ownership of women's bodies. However, the women in the harem are represented as experiencing powerful passions beyond those of political authority, although they take pleasure in the latter too. Thus, Zelis comments that 'In the very Prison where thou hast confined me, I am more free than thou: redouble thy Cautions to have me watched, I shall yet enjoy thy Inquietudes: and thy Suspicions, thy Jealousy, and thy Uneasiness are so many Proofs of thy Dependance' (i. 200, Letter 62). However, a woman like Fatme writes in terms which chime with the passionate invective of the popular *Lettres Portugaises* complaining that her lover's absence leaves her in a state of shattering suspension of desire: "'tis impossible to live in this Condition. The Fire burns in my Veins. Why can't I express to thee what I feel so sensibly!'(i. 18, Letter 7).[97] And at another point, Zelis expresses her contempt for her maid, Zelida, who plans to marry a eunuch, commenting that she can get no pleasure from him except that of his jealousy and will 'be always on the Verge of Pleasure, and never taste it!' (i. 168, Letter 52).

The novel concludes on a letter from Roxana to Usbek, written as the poison she has taken works through her body. The letter is a passionate denunciation of his tyrannous reign which reveals that love cannot be expected to be the product of despotic possession and confinement:

> How couldst thou think me so credulous, as to fancy my self sent into the World for no other Purpose than to adore thy Caprices? that at the same time thou allowd'st thy self all manner of Liberties, thou hadst a Right to confine all my Desires? No: I liv'd indeed in Servitude, but still I was free: I reformed thy Laws by those of Nature, and my Mind still kept it self independent. (ii. 275, Letter 153).

Roxana reveals that her apparent modesty has been dissimulation, a means of concealing her hatred for her oppressor. But she also asserts her own mental freedom in a speech that was to echo through much eighteenth-century fiction through to Samuel Richardson's *Clarissa* (1747–8). Sexual possession is not equivalent to ownership of the person, she insists. Indeed, the women of the harem can claim more 'freedom' in their passions than the despotic master in that they can experience sexual love rather than being confined to the frisson that accompanies the exercise of political authority to which uninhibited possession of women has dwindled the despot's emotional range.

Here, Montesquieu, like Marana before him, performs the double move whereby he at once associates the 'freedom' of women with the 'freedoms' of Enlightenment thought—the free 'speculation' beyond mere political contingency and the 'opening out' of the mind beyond

---

[97] On the *Lettres Portugaises* of 1669 (translated from the French by Roger l'Estrange as *Five Love-letters from a Nun to a Cavalier* in 1678), see ch. 3 of Linda S. Kaufmann, *Discourses of Desire: Gender, Genre and Epistolary Fictions* (Ithaca, NY, and London: Cornell University Press, 1986).

immediate horizons and limits—but simultaneously excludes women from the full rationalism which is the route to that freedom. Women, the despot, and the spy are all in their different ways 'enslaved' to passions that they cannot overcome, whether sexual love, sexual jealousy, or paranoid fear. These fears ultimately destroy and inhibit their power to move beyond the solitary and inward-looking psyche into wider social connection.

The gap between West and East can never be fully breached in the reverse traveller's text; it is imagined but ultimately the individual retreats from the possibility. If the texts narrate and dramatize these failures of imaginative expansion in the characters who speak within them, they imply that the responsibility for its achievement should lie with the reader, not through resistance to the passions, but rather imaginative sympathy with them.

Alain Grosrichard highlights the attempt in the *Lettres Persanes* to turn philosophical argument into narrative pleasure:

interest in oriental fiction and the feelings it arouses overflow in some way into the social and political analysis, colouring the latter with passionate overtones. As if, by exciting terror and pity for characters in the novel, Montesquieu had wished to find a means of provoking anxiety about the threat to a vain and unthinking epoch.[98]

We can take Grosrichard's insight a step further. Montesquieu is also exploring narrative techniques which encourage those acts of imaginative transmigration in his readers that allow them to move beyond the immediate political allegory of the tale to project themselves into the place of the other. This is, of course, Usbek's failure; he cannot imagine the mental landscape of the women in his seraglio except in terms of the stereotypes of submission and modesty oriental despotism expects. The novel asks its readers to put themselves in the place of the 'other' through acts of imaginative sympathy, as a means of crossing the mental divide between East and West.

One of Usbek's wives refers to her experience of being transported across a river enclosed in a box so that no man may catch a glimpse of her (i. 140–1, Letter 45). Zashi describes how the black eunuch refuses to liberate the wives even when a storm threatened to sink the boat,

---

[98] Grosrichard, *The Sultan's Court*, 27.

ignoring the pleas of women, servants, and eunuchs alike. The eunuch's response might serve as a metaphor for the mental enclosure of the traveller Usbek in the novel, who even as he traverses great distances refuses to 'open' his mind so far as to question his own practices of government, although he is capable of criticizing both eastern and western systems in general.

The *Letters Writ by the Turkish Spy* and the *Persian Letters* both generated close sequels or imitations by accomplished writers of English faction: Daniel Defoe's *Continuation of the Letters Writ by a Turkish Spy* (1718) and George Lyttelton's *Letters from a Persian in England, to his Friend in Ispahan* (1735). These texts illustrate the tendency on the part of English writers to deploy the oriental tale for overtly partisan purposes, shifting towards more transparent allegory and party advocacy and departing from the broader philosophical implications of their source works. Thus, Defoe's text does not bother to maintain the same set of correspondents, with the exception of Pestelihali's reprobate son, and uses the voice of Mahmut as a vehicle for anti-Catholic satire. Mahmut characterizes Catholics in similar terms to the Christian attack on oriental idolatry, describing priests as 'Belly-Gods' who 'wallow in Sensuality, Gluttony, and Wine' (Bk. 1, p. 54, Letter 12) and expressing a strong preference for Lutheran sects within Christianity (Bk. 1, Letter 4). Defoe provides no further personal information about Mahmut and concentrates on political and dynastic European history, as well as religious controversy, between 1687 and 1693.

George Lyttelton, Patriot and member of Cobham's Cubs, imitates Montesquieu in order to castigate 'party' divisions between Whig and Tory in the 1730s and to critique aristocratic affectation, especially amongst women. All the eighty-two letters are written from Selim to Mirza, two newly invented characters not found in the *Lettres Persanes*, although Selim claims in the opening letter that Usbek's account is what has prompted his visit: 'I shall', he asserts 'apply myself principally to study *the English Government*, so different from that of *Persia*, and of which *Usbec* has conceiv'd at a Distance so great an Idea.'[99] Here too, Lyttelton presents little of the psychological

[99] George Lyttelton, *Letters from a Persian in England, to His Friend at Ispahan* (London, 1735), 20, Letter 1.

depth found in Montesquieu's novel and the political satire is overt; he continues Montesquieu's history of the Troglodytes to demonstrate how attempts to limit monarchy and separate powers result in factionalism and conflict. The complex analogous relation between sexual and state politics disappears. Selim provides satirical comment on the social and sexual mores of England, but the only reference to his own sexual arrangements is a thin and unmotivated echo of Usbek: Selim promises to protect the wife of an Aleppo merchant named Zelis and, when he has restored her to her husband, finds his desire for her newly kindled. There is no suggestion, however, that his sexual desire should be read as a comment on political loyalties in Hanoverian England. Selim is solemn and critical, but demonstrates neither the wit and play of Rica nor the psychological depth and ambiguity of Usbek.

As its overt satirical uses demonstrate, the form of the 'reverse' letter might best be seen not as a critique of oriental power so much as a critique of the 'Enlightened' travel letter itself; while it ostensibly 'opens up' new territories, it always finds itself meditating on its own native condition. The mind can be imprisoned when it appears to be most free. The ostensible process of differentiating East from West in these epistolary sequences serves only to bring the two closer together. Difference becomes analogy, and one culture becomes simply a variant of the other. In other words, these letter sequences, whether intentionally or not, appear to demonstrate to the reader that meditation upon the other is inevitably only a form of speculation about the self.

For eighteenth-century English readers the 'self' under scrutiny is only tangentially (and usually in translation) the affective, emotional, desiring self; it is more often the political community. The English oriental tale is more often a plot-driven series of intrigues that demonstrate the monstrous nature of political corruption, than an investigation into the turbulent and contradictory nature of human identity to which both Marana's and Montesquieu's works aspired. If less congenial to our modern understanding of the role and pleasures of fiction, this aspect of eighteenth-century prose narrative should not be underestimated; it was immensely popular and a vehicle for the expression of questing and critical perspectives on Stuart and

Hanoverian politics. The affective tradition of epistolary writing has come to dominate histories of the 'rise' of the English novel at the expense of the numerous and equally influential political satires and scandal chronicles written in the same genre; the continuing popularity and critical attention given to Montesquieu's novel over Marana's is perhaps a measure of this critical trajectory. Aesthetically it provides a more unified and consistent study of the psyche, where Marana's text ranges from encyclopedia of philosophy to popular national histories and accounts of leading political figures.

Speculative men II: court secrets

The reigns of Charles II and George II in England both saw the publication of oriental scandal narratives concerning the monarchs' sexual and political weaknesses, calling attention to Charles's vulnerability to the influence of women and George's to the influence of statesmen, especially Robert Walpole. The analogy with the Ottoman dynasty proved a particularly fruitful one for English writers seeking to score points against a rival court faction: the covert pursuit of absolutism, effeminacy, and decadence in a court, the decline of empire as a result of luxury, were trends that could be located in Turkish contexts to suggest the imperilled nature of English limited monarchy. Moreover, the Sunni and Shi'ite split in Islam provided a useful analogue between Catholic and Protestant controversy, not least because the territorial distinction between the two (Turkey versus Persia) could provide support for the complaint that English Protestantism was threatened by French Catholicism. Finally, the erotic fascination of the harem could be exploited for titillation and scandal with regard to sexual indiscretions in the English court or to suggest by analogy the political corruption of England's statesmen (their self-interested pursuit of sexual gratification an indication of their greed and self-interest as politicians). These scandal novels offer a sequence of sexual intrigues, sometimes semi-pornographic, assembling the usual cast of eunuchs, corrupt priests, lascivious sultans, and ambitious harem concubines.

Tales of the Seraglio: Turkey and Persia

Two scandal novels concerning Charles II's amorous dalliances appeared in the 1680s, *Hattige: or the Amours of the King of Tamaran. A Novel* (1680, a translation of *Hattigé* by Sébastien Brémond) and *The Amours of the Sultana of Barbary. A Novel* (1689). Brémond dedicated his work to Henry Jermyn, duke of St Albans and reputed lover of the widowed Henrietta Maria, mother to Charles II. The novel appears to be a satire concerning Barbara Palmer née Villiers, countess of Castlemaine, chief mistress of Charles II from 1659 until she was supplanted by Louise de Kéroualle, duchess of Portsmouth, in the 1670s. The novel tells the story of Hattige's dominance over the king, her rivalry with his chief aga, Osman, and the latter's attempts to expose her affair with a gardener's nephew, Rajep, to the king. The novel includes some comedy of intrigue in which the king disguises himself as a Bedouin woman in a black veil and stations himself outside Hattige's door to intercept her lover; the king has fallen asleep at his post by the time Rajep arrives and the latter, catching a glimpse of an only partially hidden sword under the Bedouin cloak, retires, leaving Hattige's maid to usher in the king in his place, taking him for Rajep in disguise. Although Hattige's tender and seductive ways always succeed in pacifying the king, he turns his attentions to another woman, Roukia, attracted by a glimpse of her buttocks as from his terrace he watches her relieve herself in the garden. When the king discovers the passion of Roukia's gardener husband for Hattige, he engineers a swap, but Hattige makes pretence of a pilgrimage to Mecca to escape her new lover and finds herself a prisoner on a Maltese ship. Gourdan, an old corsair, tries to hide his lovely prize from the worthy Knight of Malta, who commands the ship, but the latter hears her story from her slave-woman, Razy, and liberates her from Gourdan's attentions by accompanying her to Tunis where he honourably leaves her despite his attraction to her.

The bawdy comedy of *Hattige* is given a more solemn treatment in *The Amours of the Sultana of Barbary*, an anonymous *roman à clef*, which presents Charles II as Acmat (the Ottoman Emperor Ahmet I, 1603–17) and his brother James duke of York as Mustapha (Mustafa I, 1617–18, 1622–3). The sultana of the title corresponds to Louise de Kéroualle, who came to England with Charles II's sister, Henrietta Maria duchesse d'Orléans in May 1670 as part of the secret mission to broker the Treaty of Dover between Charles and Louis XIV. When Henrietta Maria died suddenly in June, Charles placed Louise de Kéroualle as a lady-in-waiting with Catherine of Braganza, his queen, and their sexual liaison began in October 1671. Charles conferred the title of duchess of Portsmouth on her in 1673 (Acmat gives Indamora the title of Sultana of Barbary in the novel) and a generous income the following year. She proved to be one of the few mistresses whose interference in his political affairs he tolerated. She was vilified in the furore following the disclosure of a supposed Popish plot in 1678 and was widely suspected of being a French agent for Catholicism and absolutism. The novel rehearses these suspicions, going so far as to show the Christian slave, Indamora (the Portsmouth character), deciding to poison Acmat in order to be free to return to the embraces of her former, German, lover Agostos.

Indamora replaces Homira (Castlemaine) in Acmat's affections and Homira conspires with Mustapha's mistress, Zayda (Anne Hyde), while the latter's father, Mahomet the Grand Vizier (Edward Hyde, Lord Clarendon) conspires with Indamora. Indamora is represented in the mould of Roxolana, a consummate actress and manipulator of appearance and language to her own ends. In wresting the king's affections from Homira we are told 'she was to act a part whereto the greatest Cunning in the World was required, and which with good management should be the most advantagious to her'.[100] She is contrasted with Homira, who is driven by vengeful passion but lacks her cunning. Castlemaine received a similar treatment in *Hattige*, when the maid Razy admits that 'True it is, she hath not been admir'd for her wit, but that defect is supply'd by the obligingness of her carriage, and women's Little Arts, which she makes use of so much to the purpose of gaining the Monarchs heart, that never Prince was so deeply in love as he'.[101]

The preface to the *Amours of the Sultana of Barbary* comments that it was written in 1684 (in other words before Charles's death), 'but, for I know not what Reasons, 'twas refused the Liberty of the *Press*, and therefore under this Time of greater Freedom, it ventures into the

---

[100] *The Amours of the Sultana of Barbary. A Novel* (London, 1689).
[101] Sébastien de Brémond, *Hattige: Or the Amours of the King of Tamaran. A Novel*, trans. B.B. (Amsterdam, 1680).

World, with all its Faults' (n.p.). By 1689 the novel could serve as an allegory of a danger averted through the deposition of the Catholic James II and the peaceful 'revolution' that left Mary and her Protestant husband, William, the new rulers of England; the couple were often represented as a model of conjugal fidelity and a new moral authority after the decadent Stuart kings. Yet Charles, as elsewhere in oriental scandal fiction, is treated lightly. Unlike the lascivious sultan represented in drama and fiction (such as Ibrahim in Pix's play of a similar date), Charles is presented as an easygoing king, fond of his pleasures but not inclined to use force or pursue them if his advances are rejected; Indamora is warned that 'he cannot take pains to gain a Heart; if his Person, his Crowns, and his Heart cannot be of force enough to do it, he lets himself loose from the desire of possessing what he then sighs for . . . ' (47). A similar lack of concern about sexual fidelity and moral probity is evident in Charles's presentation in *Hattige*.

However, the presentation of a gentle easygoing king sits uneasily with the oriental analogue. Indeed, the influence of women seems less threatening than it could appear in contemporaneous accounts of Ottoman and Persian history, given the male protagonist's ultimate lack of commitment to the pursuit of any cause or course of action: political, religious, or sexual. The tolerant king is only a danger to his people in so far as he puts himself at risk by refusing to believe in the fanaticism of others; hence, it becomes possible for Indamora to poison him in order to meet her own desires, and leave the way open for the accession of his far less amiable and far from tolerant brother. Where these representations of Charles II do chime with conventional representations of the oriental despot is in their exploitation of the familiar contrast between the oriental ruler enslaved to the pleasures of the eye and the harem woman gaining access to power and influence through the subtle use of language. The king is at first fascinated by the physical charms of his mistresses, but his attention is secured by their facility with language.

Charles's brother, James, duke of York and their cousin Louis XIV—both Catholic and the former thought to harbour ambitions for the absolutism displayed by the latter—proved more productive analogues with oriental despots in the *roman à clef*. The two parts of Peter Belon's *roman à clef, The Court Secret* of 1689, produce a sophisticated analogy between Persian-Turkish relations in the sixteenth century and French-English relations in the seventeenth. Belon's fiction, like the *Amours,* is part of the flood of narrative propaganda around the deposition of James II, accompanied by accusations of the suppositious nature of the birth of his son with Mary of Modena in 1688 (the 'warming-pan scandal'). Belon presents Roman Catholicism as the minority Shi'ite sect in Sunni Turkey (Protestant England), the established Islamic sect in Persia (France), and termed in the novel 'Halists', i.e. followers of Ali. Charles I appears as the Ottoman Emperor Selim I (1512–20), his sons, Charles as Selim II (1566–74) and James as Amurat (Murat III, 1574–95). Louis XIV figures in the person of the great Safavid Persian emperor, who expelled the Ottomans and Uzbeks from Persia and presided over an efflorescence in art and culture, Abbas the Great (1588–1629), termed Cha-Abas in the novel. The two parts conclude with a promise of a third (which does not appear to have been produced) under the Title of, 'The prodigious Birth and Life, Tyrannical Government, and miserable Fall of the Christian Turk, Lewis the Fourteenth'.[102]

Both parts concern the activities of a wily and lascivious Mufti named Repset who is described in the key as 'Peters the Jesuit' (Father Edward Petre (1631–99), James II's Jesuit adviser). In the first part he persuades the infertile Sultana and her husband to fake a pregnancy; meanwhile, he pursues the Halist daughter of a leading courtier under Amurat (James II), getting his sister Zora to drug her before he comes to her chamber at night. However, Zora's lover, a Mahometan (Protestant) named Cara, visits Roxana's chamber before Repset and deflowers her, mistaking her for Zora. It is the child of this union which is presented as that of the Sultana and Amurat, but Roxana and Cara realize Repset's perfidy and expose the truth to Soliman (William of Orange) and his wife Zelinda (Mary). The second part continues the narrative opening with Amurat and the sultana (James II and Mary of Modena) living in exile in Persia (France). Cha-Abas (Louis XIV) persuades the former to go to the Halist stronghold of Leridan (Ireland) and try to regain his kingdom; this is revealed as a

---

[102] Peter Belon, *The Court Secret. A Novel,* pt. 2 (London, 1689), 237.

stratagem to gain access to the sultana in her husband's absence. She remains loyal to her husband, however, while her ladies-in-waiting, Clorineta (Lady Tyrconnel, wife to Richard Talbot, earl of Tyrconnel and James II's Lord Deputy in Ireland) and Morinetta (Madame de Maintenon), compete for the wavering affections of Cha-Abas. Repset is already engaged in a secret liaison with Clorineta, and the Persian Mufti, Chilase (Louis XIV's French Confessor), is pursuing the sultana who strings Chilase along using Clorineta as her substitute as part of her plan to expose him. It is Morinetta who engineers the two Muftis' come-uppance, inviting both to liaison with their desired mistress only for them to encounter each other in the bed and then be seized by Cha-Abas's officers and threatened with castration to become eunuchs. Cha-Abas lets them off with a warning and both spend several months recovering from fevers brought on by the shock they have endured. Meanwhile, Amurat's endeavours to regain his kingdom come to nothing and the virtuous Mahometans continue happy under the government of Soliman and Zelinda (William and Mary).

The second part of *The Court Secret* reveals a lighter and more comic touch than the first, becoming a comedy of intrigue in the style of contemporary dramatic and novelistic productions such as those of Aphra Behn. Where Repset has the status of a genuine malcontent and *agent provocateur* in the first part, he is reduced to the role of the venal priest in the latter and at no point is the Mahometan Ottoman (English) state genuinely threatened by the 'Halist' (Catholic) forces of Persia (France). In the first part, women are the victims of the hungry pursuit of power by male plotters, especially Repset and the other Halist priests. In the second, the women of the seraglio become the plotters, manipulating the vanity and lust of the priests and Cha-Abas.

The fortunes of the oriental *roman à clef* revived in the reign of George II, when the attention shifted from exposing the dangerous conspiracies of the wily prelate and the subtle courtesan to those of an unscrupulous vizier in the absence of a powerful absolutist ruler. George II, like Charles II, was commonly represented as a lazy monarch, but George was more commonly understood as spellbound by the evil magic of a minister, where Charles was seen as too willing to give himself up to voluptuous pleasures at the expense of state business. Even before the ascendancy of Robert Walpole in the 1730s, George II was subject to satirical representation as a monarch dependent on his councillors: in Eliza Haywood's *The Secret History of the Present Intrigues of the Court of Caramania* (1727) which appeared in the year of George II's accession, Theodore (George) is dependent on the assistance of his childhood friend and chief minister, Marmillio, for the management of his numerous affairs, but especially with the lovely and married Ismonda (Henrietta Howard, countess of Suffolk). Haywood's novel, like her other fictions of the 1720s, depicts women as the victims of predatory men, who pursue their desires relentlessly even to the extent of rape.[103] At one point, Theodore/George, prompted by Marmillio, adopts the disguise of an Egyptian eunuch stationed in the appropriately named Violetta's bedchamber to protect her from violation, only to rape her himself; by morning however she is reconciled to the suit of 'one of the most lovely and accomplish'd Men on earth'.[104] Despite, or perhaps because of, women's vulnerability to rape in the novel, the characters of Hyanthe (Queen Caroline) and Ismonda (Henrietta Howard) are shown learning to manage and stage-manage their responses to court scandals and the restless affections of their shared lover, Theodore (George) so as to maintain their own status, reputation, and authority. Like Roxolana, Ismonda enters an alliance with the cunning counsellor. Marmillio advises her when she fears she has lost Theodore's affections: 'By seeming not to suspect, you will keep him ever yours in show, even tho' he ceases to be so in reality; by this means your Character remains unsully'd, and our Power as great, to the World's eye, as when you first possess'd his fondest Wishes' (73). Hyanthe adopts a similar course of action, 'seeming not to suspect' her husband in order to retain the show of her authority. Theodore, meanwhile, is driven only by his lusts and desire for their immediate gratification, and never learns the power of concealment, disguise, and fictional management that his courtiers and mistresses have to acquire with rapidity if they are to survive in the dangerous world of his court.

---

[103] See ch. 5 of Ballaster, *Seductive Forms.*

[104] Eliza Haywood, *The Secret History of the Present Intrigues of the Court of Caramania* (London, 1727), 344.

George Lyttelton's *The Court Secret* of 1741 may have unwittingly invoked the parallel between Charles II and George II as 'weak' rulers by reviving the title of Belon's much earlier work; in this short but influential prose fiction, a monstrous vizier Behemoth (Robert Walpole) with the help of an agent named Ibrahim tricks the noble minister Achmet (Bolingbroke) into revealing to his mistress the sultan's secret plans to go to war against the advice of Behemoth; when Achmet is disgraced with the sultan because of his breach of confidence, he takes his life, leaving letters to the sultan and Behemoth which reveal Behemoth's perfidy and warn the latter to become honest to evade the dreadful punishment that awaits him in the afterlife. Lyttelton's and Haywood's texts, whose authors both turned to Patriot politics in the 1730s,[105] come into a form of dialogue through the production of an anonymous *Second Court Secret* (1743), a rambling, digressive, and unfocused piece of satire that deploys names from Haywood's scandal writing (a hero named Theodore, lord of Eutopia[106]) and the same broad frame from Lyttelton of the monarch prone to moments of infatuation when under the influence of courtiers who falls victim to an evil vizier.[107]

While these scandal chronicles draw on conventional prejudices about the oriental despot, they also challenge and undermine the authority and autonomy invested in the figure and especially manifested in the representation of his all-powerful gaze. These 'oriental despots' are weak figures easily led by the plots, deceptions, and superior fictional management of women and viziers. Their 'looks' are primarily desirous rather than powerful and what they see and how it is interpreted is carefully stage-managed by those around them to limit their knowledge.

The mythic 'specular' power of the oriental king is now converted into sham grandeur, like the masked ball which Cha-Abbas holds in

---

[105] The 'Patriot' party consisted of disaffected Whig Members of Parliament headed by William Pulteney and Lord Bolingbroke who from the late 1720s allied with the Tories in opposition to the Prime Minister, Robert Walpole.

[106] Haywood's other work of scandal of the 1720s was the *Memoirs of a Certain Island Adjacent to the Kingdom of Utopia*, 2 vols. (1724-5).

[107] Indeed, Lyttelton and the anonymous author of the *Second Court Secret* may have borrowed this idea from Eliza Haywood's 'Chinese' satire on Walpole; the latter appears as the evil necromancer Ochihatou who has spun a charm of infatuation over his monarch in the 1736 *Adventures of Eovaai* (see ch. 3).

the second part of *The Court Secret* by which he hopes to gain access to the sultana. Amongst the masked crowd only Morinetta has the knowledge of the major players' true identities and can orchestrate affairs so as to protect her interest with the Persian king. Cha-Abbas's vision is as occluded and limited as that of the other characters. The idea of the masked ball in which identities are concealed through adopting the dress of an 'other' invokes the idea of the *roman à clef* or scandal chronicle in which correspondences are drawn between one culture and another, one historical set of personages and another, for the purpose of satire. It also reveals the instability of this kind of analogical/allegorical technique, in that the adopted or disguised identity can also dictate the terms by which the hidden or 'true' narrative for which it supposedly stands is received and understood. The analogue or disguise of the oriental despot defuses rather than inflates the threat it is being used to signify; like an ill-fitting masquerade disguise, it shows the impotence and diminutive nature of its wearer who cannot match up to the outfit in which he is clothed. Of course, this bathetic technique is central to the success of the satire, which aims to illustrate not the power of the despot but rather the controlling influence of the women and courtiers in his western 'seraglio'; it is his weakness which makes possible their agency and authority.

'Fabulous and Romantic': the 'Embassy Letters' and 'The Sultan's Tale'

As we have seen, the Orient (and especially Persia and Turkey) provided a source of story for western Europe which, while it was enormously varied in its generic and political uses, drew on a fairly limited repertoire of character and plot. Thus, a correspondent like Pope in the letters to Mary Wortley Montagu could draw on the repertoire, confident of shared knowledge. Like Scheherazade's stories, an infinite chain of narrative could be generated from a single shared context. And that context was itself one in which the political utility of story was intimately bound to its conditions of reception; Scheherazade stages the scenario in which Schahriar can listen in on stories told by an older to a younger woman, transforming an 'innocent' scenario into one loaded with political meaning, at least for the readers outside the narrative frame who themselves listen in on such stories and their reception. I have stressed throughout that English readers and writers show through their reception and production of oriental texts an understanding of their potential as models of fiction and narrative. This understanding fed directly into the changing status and nature of the 'novel' in England. Not least in the knowing reproduction of the gendered 'frame' and the awareness of narrative itself as a form of gendered contest, in which feminized verbal agency attempts to counter masculine spatial and visual authority.

One author with a deep, first-hand, and rhetorical acquaintance with the Turkish East is Mary Wortley Montagu. Her epistolary and fictional writings indicate a complex and profound intermeshing of western and eastern traditions of storytelling which is, also, like Scheherazade's, directed towards the assertion of the political instrumentality of a temporal narrative agency for women. Mary Wortley Montagu, I suggest, 'heard' in her extensive reading in the oriental tale (her library, Isobel Grundy informs us, contained works by Galland, Pétis de la Croix, and Gueullette) a model of female narrative power which she reused repeatedly in her own rhetorical acts.[108]

This is not to claim that Mary Wortley Montagu was an admirer of all aspects of the oriental cultures she encountered. She indicts the political system in Turkey with absolute clarity. In a letter to Lady Bristol of 1 April 1717, she comments that the Grand Signor is so ruled by the army that he is 'as much a slave as any of his Subjects, and trembles at a Janizary's frown' and:

when a Minister here displeases the people, in 3 hours time he is dragg'd even from his Master's arms. They cut off his hands, head and feet, and throw them before the palace Gate with all the respect in the World, while the Sultan (to whom they all profess an unlimited Adoration) sits trembling in his Apartment, and dare neither defend nor revenge his favourite. This is the blessed Condition of the most Absolute Monarch upon Earth, who owns noe

---

[108] *Lady Mary Wortley Montagu: Romance Writings*, ed. Grundy, pp. xiv–xv.

Law but his Will. I cannot help wishing (in the loyalty of my heart) that the Parliament would send hither a Ship Load of your passive Obedient Men that they might see A[r]bitrary Government in its clearest, strongest Light, where tis hard to Judge whither the prince, people or Ministers are most miserable. (*CLMWM* i. 322–3)

Here, the Whig Lady Mary jibes at the doctrine of passive obedience to the Crown held by Tory monarchists. Rule by ministry and Parliament, she implies, is less arbitrary than rule by the army, the consequence of leaving all power in the hand of the sovereign.

However, with respect to the condition of women, the failures of absolutism bring definite advantages, Mary Wortley Montagu argues. She notes that men's absolute power over wives through their enclosure and separation from public life, like the total power of the monarch over the people through a military at his command, is not in practice what it seems in theory. Of women's wearing of the veil, she confides to Lady Mar that 'This perpetual Masquerade gives them entire Liberty of following their Inclinations without danger of Discovery' (1 April 1717, *CLMWM* i. 328). Turkish ladies make liaisons with men at Jews' shops, she claims, and since they do not let their gallants know who they are, their reputations are secure. They are in many respects, she claims, more free than European women. Married women keep all their money and take it with them on divorce, and inconstant husbands are discreet with their mistresses (329). Referring to women who are bought as slaves in the marketplace for sexual purposes, she comments sharply: 'In my opinion they are bought and sold as publickly and more infamously in all our Christian great citys' (10 April 1718, *CLMWM* i. 402).

She is scathing about the comments of other travel writers and explicit that it is the fact they are all men that has led them to make assumptions about the constraint Turkish women suffer. With reference to Aaron Hill, she mocks:

'Tis also very pleasant to observe how tenderly he and all his Brethren Voyage-writers lament on the miserable confinement of the Turkish Ladys, who are (perhaps) freer than any Ladys in the universe, and are the only Women in the world that lead a life of uninterrupted pleasure, exempt from cares, their whole time being spent in visiting, bathing or the agreeable

Amusement of spending Money and inventing new fashions. (May 1718, *CLMWM* i. 406)

Lady Mary's letters are dominated by the idea of storytelling, truth and fiction. The author works her audience, producing different personae and accounts for her different correspondents. Most striking is her silence around her encounters with Turkish women in her correspondence with men. Her letters to her husband are few and uniformly businesslike, without passion or intimacy. Those to Pope are preoccupied with poetry and culture, despite his attempts to make them flirtatious. To her sister, Lady Mar, and to Lady Rich, her intimate friend, she is most forthcoming. A letter of 1 April 1717 to Lady Rich from Adrianople gives a detailed account of a Turkish bath she visited at Sofia in Bulgaria, her first encounter with the subject nations of the Ottoman empire. She admires the beauty of the women ('They Walk'd and mov'd with the same majestic Grace which Milton describes of our General Mother' (*CLMWM* i. 314)), and describes her own interaction with them, concluding: 'Adieu, Madam. I am sure I have now entertaind you with an Account of such a sight as you never saw in your Life, and what no book of travells could inform you of. 'Tis no less than Death for a Man to be found in one of these places' (315).

Mary Wortley Montagu spends much of her time refuting other travellers' tales—Rycaut's and Hill's claims that the Sultan selects his favoured wife from the harem by dropping a handkerchief at her feet (10 March 1718, *CLMWM* i. 383), Jean Dumont's that Turkish music is unpleasant (18 April 1717, *CLMWM* i. 351), all three that the Turks do not believe women have souls (29 May 1717, *CLMWM* i. 363). She responds with severity to one female correspondent (possibly Lady Rich) whose letter, she says, 'is full of mistakes from one end to 'tother' drawn from travel-writers, adding:

'Tis a particular pleasure to me here to read the voyages to the Levant which are generally so far remov'd from the Truth and so full of Absurditys I am very well diverted with 'em. They never fail giving you an Account of the Women, which 'tis certain they never saw, and talking very wisely of the Genius of the Men, into whose Company they are never admitted, and very often describe Mosques, which they dare not peep into. (17 June 1717, *CLMWM* i. 368)

However, despite her privileged access to female communities, she confesses to Lady Mar that she has difficulty 'shaping' her own accounts in ways that convince and amuse, as well as tell the truth:

We Travellers are in very hard circumstances. If we say nothing but what has been said before us, we are dull and we have observ'd nothing. If we tell anything new, we are laugh'd at as fabulous and Romantic, not allowing for the difference of ranks, which afford difference of company, more Curiosity, or the changes of customs that happen every 20 year in every country. (10 March 1718, *CLMWM* i. 385)

Here Mary Wortley Montagu argues for a contextual, relative under-standing of travel-writing, that the position of the viewer is structural in the presentation of the 'sight'. Her position as a western woman col-ours both what she sees and how she is seen; she takes, for example, great pleasure in the curiosity that she and the French ambassadress engender, '2 young Christian Ambassadresses never yet having been in this Country at the same time, nor, I beleive ever will again' (1 April 1717, *CLMWM* i. 324).

We might then speculate that Lady Mary's letter-writing works on similar principles to the storytelling of Scheherazade with which she was so well acquainted; the tales she tells disclose her own condition and preoccupations. She tells tales to women correspond-ents of the women she encounters which can have double meanings, which reveal secrets that are not visible to her male equivalents, especially ones that illustrate female freedom in, rather than despite, the veil.[109]

One such story that opens up alternative interpretation is delivered to a female correspondent (again possibly Lady Rich) in May 1718 shortly before Lady Mary's departure from Turkey. It is paired with a short description of the discovery of the 'bleeding body of a young woman, naked, only wrapp'd in a coarse sheet, with 2 wounds with a knife, one in her side and another in her Breast' (*CLMWM* i. 407), which is assumed to be a murder in revenge by a jealous husband. The body is disposed of quietly and without enquiry, but Mary Wortley comments on the rare occurrence of 'such Tragedys' and goes on

[109] See Teresa Heffernan, 'Feminism against the East/West Divide: Lady Mary's Turkish Embassy Letters', *Eighteenth-Century Studies* 33 (2000): 201–16.

to describe another occasion which apparently demonstrates that Turks do not 'deserve the barbarous character we give them' (408).

As so often in stories of oriental lust and rape the parallel is made with Lucrece. She writes:

I am well acquainted with a Christian Woman of Quality who made it her choice to live with a Turkish Husband, and is a very agreable sensible Lady. Her story is so extraordinary I cannot forbear relateing it, but I promise you it shall be in as few words as I can possibly express it. She is a Spaniard, and was at Naples with her family when that Kingdom was part of the Spanish Dominion. Coming from thence in a Feloucca, accompany'd by her Brother, they were attack'd by the Turkish Admiral, boarded and taken; and now, how shall I modestly tell you the rest of her Adventure? The same Accident happen'd to her that happen'd to the fair Lucretia so many Years before her, but she was too good a Christian to kill her selfe as that heathenish Roman did. The Admiral was so much charm'd with the Beauty and long-suffering of the Fair Captive that as his first complement he gave immediate Liberty to her Brother and attendants, who made haste to Spain and in a few months sent the sumn of £4,000 sterling as a Ransom for his sister. The Turk took the Money, which he presented to her, and told her she was at Liberty, but the Lady very discreetly weigh'd the different treatment that she was likely to find in her native Country. Her Catholic Relations, as the kindest thing they could do for her in her present Circumstances, would certainly confine her to a Nunnery for the rest of her Days. Her Infidel Lover was very handsome, very tender, fond of her, and lavish'd at her feet all the Turkish Magnificence. She answer'd him very resolutely that her Liberty was not so precious to her as her Honnour, that he could no way restore that but by marrying her. She desir'd him to accept the Ransom as her Portion and give her the satisfaction of knowing no Man could boast of her favours without being her Husband. The Admiral was transported at this kind offer and sent back the Money to her Relations, saying he was too happy in her Possession. He marry'd her and never took any other wife, and (as she says her selfe) she never had any reason to repent the choice she made. He left her some years after one of the richest widows in Constantinople, but there is no remaining honnourably a single woman, and that consideration has oblig'd her to marry the present Captain Bassa (i.e. Admiral), his Successor. I am afraid you'l think that my Freind fell in love with her Ravisher, but I am willing to take her word for it that she acted wholly on principles of Honnour, thô I think she might be reasonably touch'd at his Generosity, which is very often found amongst the Turks of Rank. (408–9)

Here, the familiar narrative of a Christian/gentile chastity threatened by oriental lust serves as a vehicle to expound a form of rationalism and a hard-headed calculation of ways in which women may maximize their opportunities under oppression.

If Montagu expresses contempt for passive obedience in state politics, she sees domestic politics as a less clear-cut set of relations. The oriental story she delivers of the Spanish lady is emphatically not a romantic one. Lady Mary had enjoyed a youthful romance and eloped with her long-term suitor Edward Wortley Montagu in 1712, but she had already realized that her feelings for him were not passionate and was soon complaining in frequent letters to him from the country that he failed to pursue her advice about his career, left her short of cash, and neglected both her and his young son.[110] The Turkish marriage she describes in this inset tale ensures maximum freedom for the woman, a freedom the tale suggests which would not be available to her in the apparently more 'free' gender relations of the Christian West. The surface narrative is not what it seems in this story; Lady Mary discerns a mercenary motive behind the apparent rationale of honour, and sees the choice as rational. The tale affords the Protestant Lady Mary an opportunity for an attack on the oppression of women in Catholic Europe. Spanish Catholicism, unlike Turkish Islam, values women only in terms of their chastity. However, the tale's target may be closer to home than even Lady Mary recognizes. In the context of her own, all too apparent, impatience with her husband's refusal to allow her to share in his political life and his financial decisions, the story acquires a peculiarly exemplary power.

The relation here, however, is not one simply of surface meaning and 'truth', but rather of tale and interpretation. The oriental tale can carry different meanings for different readers in different contexts, as do Lady Mary's eventually published letters. Throughout her embassy letters, Mary Wortley Montagu reminds us that Orient and Occident are in relation to each other rather than in opposition. Judgement of their difference is relative rather than absolute.

Especially striking is Mary Wortley Montagu's assertion of the compulsive nature of narrativization itself: the story of the Spanish

---

[110] Grundy, *Lady Mary Wortley Montagu*, 79.

Catholic lady turned Turkish wife is 'so extraordinary' that she 'cannot forbear relateing it'. The compulsive nature of the reception and production of narrative is at the heart of the oriental tale as it was represented in western cultures.

Mary Wortley Montagu brings the compulsive, political, and hybrid nature of the oriental tale into relief in a manuscript story fragment she produced, probably long after her sojourn in Turkey, known as 'The Sultan's Tale'.[111] Lady Mary cleverly turns the tables on the *Arabian Nights Entertainments* by having the tale be one told by a sultan to a sultana queen, his tale's content involving Roman divinities whom he identifies as part of an alien tradition to his own 'oriental' knowledge. It is also a content concerned with the 'proving' of women's chastity, just as Scheherazade's tales ostensibly win forgiveness for, or prove her exemption from, generic female unchastity. Lady Mary's rendering of the tale, a marvellously ironic short narrative, demonstrates that same blend of hard-headed commonsense and passionate sexual politics which we find in her rendering of stories in the *Turkish Embassy Letters*.

In 'The Sultan's Tale', the goddess Flora decides to help her friend Diana when she complains that she cannot be sure of the chastity of her nymphs by endowing some flowers with the special property of remaining fresh for twenty-four hours if worn on the bosom of a chaste lady. Venus is enraged and Jupiter supports her complaint, instructing Diana to throw away her nosegay but Juno invests the falling flowers with the power to pass on their property to all other flowers on earth. Flora and her flowers sink in reputation as mortals, and especially women, realize the inconvenience of this capacity, and Diana is given permission to come to earth to try and rectify the situation; Venus gives her consent with the proviso that Diana can only use her powers of persuasion, and must not employ any supernatural agency. Diana passes herself off as the court favourite Bettina, who advises her mistress Emma, chaste princess of the island, to use the flowers to institute an order of unmarried women, their chastity to be proved by the 'Badge' of a nosegay of fresh flowers

---

[111] Her editor, Isobel Grundy, tentatively suggests a dating of the story to after 1749, because of a reference to 'Iphigenia' which may suggest Elizabeth Chudleigh's sensational appearance in that guise at Ranelagh on 1 May 1749 (*Romance Writings*, 25, n. 2).

(Lady Mary here pokes fun at all-male orders of chivalry, such as the Order of the Bath of which Sir Robert Walpole was so proud). The princess herself proves reluctant to wear the badge and is accorded a bunch of artificial flowers.

At first test, however, the princess finds that the company she has for supper 'were many of them so much younger than herself that she could not have much pleasure in their Conversation'.[112] She admits married women to the company to alleviate her boredom and is surprised to find that they too wear nosegays that last throughout the whole evening. 'Bettina' investigates and, despite the fact that the women of the island are remarkable for their secrecy, she discovers that the lover of a young woman has had his prayers answered by Venus who sent him the wherewithal to construct a 'gardefleur' (a small vase of tin wrapped in green silk filled with water and worn at the breast into which the flowers can be set so that they remain fresh); Iphigenia 'so celebrated for the Interpretation of Dreams that some thought her an Inchantress' (25) showed him how to construct it. 'Bettina' (Diana) instructs the princess to invite the ladies to a waterwork or firework (the sultan is not sure which) display at which the princess leads such a vigorous dance that all the ladies become soaked from the water in their gardefleurs. The princess is forgiving and they go to collect fresh flowers only to encounter Flora, who reveals that Jupiter has repealed the flowers' effects and banned the wearing of nosegays without gardefleurs altogether. He has appeased Venus by allowing both Venus and Diana the opportunity to reward a favourite and punish a foe. Bettina transforms before the company's eyes into the figure of Diana: 'The Wings of her Cap turning up form'd a Crescent; her mouchoir was changed into a deerskin Mantle and her Fan into a Bow; her hoop drop'd off and became a triumphal Carr; two of her lapdogs were transform'd into milk white Stags'(27). Before she leaves, she invests the princess Emma with 'the Gift of charming all her hearers' (27). The manuscript breaks off before we learn of Diana's and Venus's other punishments and reward.

'The Sultan's Tale' proves a recurrent claim in Mary Wortley Montagu's writing that wit is a more important quality in a woman

---

[112] Ibid. 23.

than chastity. The ability to manipulate verbal signs overrides the ability to present visual signs that 'prove' innocence. Diana must rely only on her skills in language to restore her friend Flora to public favour with the mortals. The princess is rewarded by the goddess Diana with the gift of being able to charm all those who hear her. Of course, it is a theme that was close to the heart of its author, who had been a great beauty until her looks were spoilt by the smallpox she contracted in December 1715. But it also returns to the theme of the oriental tales she loved and chimes with the account she gives of the 'freedom' of women in Turkey, who are concealed rather than confined by the veil and do not suffer the constriction of stays and western dress. At the baths in Sofia, Mary Wortley Montagu is forced to open her shirt and show her stays to explain why she cannot join the other women in their naked enjoyments. She comments 'I saw they beleiv'd I was so lock'd up in that machine, that it was not in my own power to open it, which contrivance they attributed to my Husband' (*CLMWM* i. 314). In 'The Sultan's Tale', the 'machine' of the hoop which constrains Diana converts into a carriage to take her away in a scene of magic transformation.

It is striking that 'The Sultan's Tale' is one in which it is *not* husbands who contain women in machines that inhibit their free movement or who threaten them out of suspicions regarding their chastity. With the exception of Jupiter's edicts which side consistently with Venus 'for Reasons best known to himself, tho' not hard to be ghessed at' (19) (Jupiter is notorious for his pursuit of sexual pleasure with mortal women), the tale is an all-female circuit of friendship, alliance, rivalry, and authority. It is women who suspect each other's chastity (Diana and her nymphs, Emma and her court ladies) and consider it a vital ingredient for their 'company', and it is women (Diana and Emma) who learn that chastity can be a dull and sterile virtue by comparison with the good and witty company of 'married' ladies (such as Flora and Bettina).

The reversal is complete in that here the auditor who learns from the tale is female, and the 'frame' narrator is male; the sultan tells the tale to the 'Sultana Queen'. Isobel Grundy speculates that the latter's title might suggest the 'Valide Sultan' or mother of the sultan, as the most senior female figure in the harem, which casts a different light on interpretation of the tale (16). However, given that the oriental sequences Lady Mary loved are usually sequences told to wives, courtesans, or young women in the harem, it seems more likely that the 'sultana Queen' should be taken as a wife or favourite mistress.

This identification is strengthened when we consider the reference to Iphigenia, a common sobriquet for the feminist Elizabeth Chudleigh after her appearance in this costume at Ranelagh in 1749, which suggests that the tale might have been composed very close to the publication of Diderot's *Les Bijoux Indiscrets* of 1748. The sultan who tells Mary Wortley Montagu's tale bears close affinity to Diderot's Mangogul, the king of Congo, who uses a magic ring to discover the chastity or not of court ladies. Mirzoza, Mangogul's favourite courtesan, like Emma in the tale, insists on being exempt from the test applied to the other ladies. Lady Mary may, like Diderot, be offering an elegant court satire under the guise of the oriental tale, and like him be paying a compliment to the 'common Sense' of women (Mirzoza and the sultana queen of Mary Wortley Montagu's tale who uses the phrase in her first speech) who recognize that verbal wit is more valuable to them than the simple and passive virtue of chastity.[113] The ladies in Mary Wortley Montagu's tale have more success than those in Diderot's at evading the supernatural power that makes public their sexual incontinence; where the muzzles they design fail to stifle the ladies' 'toys' from public speaking in Diderot's story, in Mary Wortley Montagu's the 'gardefleurs' prove an effective device.

The affinity between Mary Wortley Montagu's sultan and Diderot's Mangogul is also implied in that both are represented as innocent enthusiasts, less intelligent than the women who are closest to them. Mary Wortley Montagu's sultan tells his queen with delight that 'once in my Life I may have the pleasure of making you own I knew

[113] The term 'common Sense' had of course political resonance for Lady Mary who produced nine numbers of a journal entitled *The Nonsense of Common-Sense* between December 1737 and March 1738 in response to the claim in Lyttelton and Chesterfield's Tory journal *Common Sense* that the ladies and Walpole's government worshipped 'nonsense'. Montagu took exception to the appropriation of the phrase to suggest a widespread consensus against Walpole in the period. See *Lady Mary Wortley Montagu: Essays and Poems and Simplicity, A Comedy*, ed. Robert Halsband and Isobel Grundy (Oxford: Clarendon Press, 1977), 105–49. Note also that the sultan tells his story because he is 'tired of hearing the Vizir's Nonsense' (*Romance Writings*, 17).

something you did not' (17), the story which gave rise to the myth that the longevity of flowers is an indicator of chastity. His roundabout approach to delivering his story is Lady Mary's ironic and parodic response to the familiar conventions of tale-telling in the oriental sequence; he is liable to lose his thread if interrupted or broken off, his source is written rather than oral, he has a bad memory:

I have now nothing else to do and am tired of hearing the Vizir's Nonsense, and tho' I don't remember that any of my ancestors condescended to relate a Story themselves, I don't see why I should not set the example of it to my Successors, and I fancy when a Sultan will take the trouble of it, nobody will dispute his doing it better than his Vizir or anybody else; but I shall forget what I have to relate if I don't make haste, for without Vanity, I may say my Memory is very bad and it is allmost a Week since I read the curious Anecdotes I am going to entertain you with, to satisfy your Curiosity, Madam. But I would have you and the Vizir beware of interrupting me, for if once you break the thread of my Narration, I can not promise to go on again, like those who are used to make stories out of their own head: be silent therefore and attend. (17)

While Mary Wortley Montagu reverses some aspects of the tradition of the oriental sequence, she also confirms it in that the tale subtly undermines the authority of the sultan. Like other western representations of the oriental despot, this tale demonstrates his dependence on the influence of women (whether mother or courtesan) and reliance on the political skills of his vizier, as well as his failure to live up to the mythic power accorded his role in terms of intelligence and authority. Mary Wortley Montagu turns the absolute ruler into a comic figure, and the story of the violent confinement of women in order to maintain their chastity into a good-humoured story about the superior advantages of subtlety and ingenuity in women.

Central to Mary Wortley Montagu's tale is its 'reverse' hybridity. Here, an oriental storyteller imports materials from western classical myth to satisfy his auditor's curiosity, in a cultural movement that reverses the familiar move of importing fictional materials from the East into western narrative. The sultan's act provides an alienating effect in that familiar figures now appear more enigmatic or open to interpretation. Like those western scholars and translators who tried to decipher Islam, Buddhism, or 'gentile' religions of the East, he is not entirely certain about the accuracy of his knowledge; he opens with the statement 'Some Ages ago, the Goddess of Chastity, Diana I think her name is . . .' (17). He embarks on a digression about whether Flora is a terrestrial goddess or a mortal which he acknowledges is irrelevant to the story but adds 'I like to communicate what I know' (17) in the vein of the scholar of distant and other cultures. And he extrapolates a general statement about the nature of the women in a present-day culture from an example from ancient history when he comments that the attempt to keep the secret of the 'gardefleurs' 'would no doubt have proved fruitless in our Country, but the Women of that Island were remarkable . . . for their Secresy' (26) in a move that imitates that of the translators/writers of oriental tales who claim that ancient stories provide evidence of how contemporary oriental cultures operate.

Mary Wortley Montagu's use of story, oriental and western, can be illuminated by comparing it with another act of cultural hybridity, of more immediate, practical, and personal advantage. While her husband was away and with the support of a surgeon named Charles Maitland, Lady Mary had her young son inoculated against smallpox with a live vaccine following the Turkish practice. The smallpox matter was taken from a sufferer with a mild strain and administered by an old nurse in Istanbul.[114] She chose at that point not to have her recently born daughter inoculated since the child's Armenian nurse did not have immunity. After her return, however, when a smallpox epidemic swept England in April 1721, she enlisted the help of Maitland once more and had the virus 'ingrafted' into her daughter. She and Princess Caroline became the leading advocates of the practice of inoculation in their circle to great effect. Lady Mary was widely acknowledged as the importer of the practice of inoculation into English society and accordingly fêted or vilified (some claimed that inoculation caused rather than prevented deaths). Her one identified contribution to the print war, 'A Plain Account of the Innoculating of the Small Pox by a Turkey Merchant',[115] was an attack

---

[114] Grundy, *Lady Mary Wortley Montagu*, 162.
[115] *Flying Post*, 13 Sept. 1722, repr. *Romance Writings*, 95-7.

on doctors who she saw as 'protecting their income and prestige'[116] by refusing to administer the smallpox or applying it in such large quantities on gashes cut in the skin (rather than the needle pinprick observed in Turkey) as to risk the lives of their patients. Mary Wortley Montagu advocated its administration by lay operatives, even women, and for sensible domestic nursing care rather than excessive bleedings and treatments.

In the matter of inoculation, she champions folk knowledge and all-female circuits of information and action, as she does in her importation of oriental 'story' as structure and content to the West. As with inoculation, the absorption of elements of matter from the 'other' can protect and indeed strengthen, providing 'hybrid vigour', rather than undermining or weakening the self.

---

[116] Grundy, *Lady Mary Wortley Montagu*, 217.

4

'Bearing Confucius' morals to Britannia's ears': China

Tourandocte, the riddling princess

An exiled prince of the Nogais Tartars,[1] famed as 'the Hero of *Asia*, and the Phenix of the *East*' (*PT* i. 268), arrives at the city of Peking to find its people sunk into a deep collective gloom. The widow with whom he lodges has a daughter who works in the palace and keeps her informed about the source of this unhappiness, an oath extracted from her father by the lovely Princess Tourandocte that if any of her suitors should fail to answer the three riddles she poses before a company of learned men, he will be executed. The emperor made his promise in desperation when his daughter fell ill following an approach from the king of Tibet for a union with his son; King Altoun of China had thought that none would venture, but his daughter's magnetic beauty has led a succession of young men, who have fallen in love with her image in a portrait, to try their luck with her riddles.

---

[1] Located in what is now Russia.

193

Yet, the widow recounts that, 'not able to penetrate their dark Meaning, they all of them, one after the other, perished without mercy' (*PT* ii. 13). The king bitterly regrets his promise and 'seems touched with the Deaths of these unhappy Princes' but it is 'not so with his inhuman Daughter. She glories in the bloody Spectacles, which her Beauty exhibits to the People' (14). Calaf, trained to understand the mystic sense of the commentaries of the Qur'an from his youth, mocks the candidates' stupidity, but his informant assures him that 'Never were any Riddles so obscure, as the Questions of the Princess' (16). He attends the execution of Tourandocte's latest victim, the 18-year-old prince of Samarkand and picks up a picture of the princess cast to the ground by the prince's grief-stricken tutor. It is too dark for him to view the picture that night but when daylight breaks he chooses to do so, handing himself over to providence to determine his fate. He promptly falls in love.

Unconcerned by the prospect of death, Calaf introduces himself to the court of Altoun as a suitor, and holds firm to his purpose despite the attempts of the king, who is much taken with him, to change his mind. The night before his trial, the young prince suffers some doubts, but the next day he dons a handsome caftan and cloak of red silk with gold flowers, and stockings and shoes of blue silk to present himself to his beloved. Six mandarins lead him to a divan and Tourandocte enters in a robe and veil of gold tissue, flanked by two bare-breasted and bare-faced women who carry pen and paper to write down the king's bidding. The princess speaks, expressing her regret for the death of so many princes and complaining: 'why are they so obstinately bent upon having me? Why do not they let me live quiet in my Palace, without coming here to make Attempts on my Liberty?' (*PT* ii. 50).

Calaf answers the first two riddles without faltering: the creature of all countries, friend to all the world, and with no likeness in the creation he identifies as the sun, and the mother that devours all her children after she has brought them forth as the moon. Tourandocte's decision to remove her veil after her third question strikes him temporarily dumb with amazement at her beauty, but he retrieves his senses and confirms that the tree with leaves all white on one side and all black on the other is the year comprised of its days and nights. The doctors agree with him and Altoun commands his daughter 'confess thy self conquered' (ii. 52). She weeps bitterly, but her request to ask more questions the following morning is refused, the king reminding her that her own mother has died with grief at having a child who 'breath[es] nothing but Blood' (53). Calaf, however, agrees to renounce his claim to her hand if she can discover his name before the next day.

The princess confesses to her women in her apartments that she did feel some pity for her lover on first sight but her pride stepped in and 'his answering my Questions so justly as he did, made me more than ever his Enemy' (ii. 61). That night Calaf is visited by a slave-woman named Adelmule who comes to warn him that Tourandocte plans to have him assassinated before he can reach the divan for her answer. Adelmule confides that she is not herself Chinese but was enslaved when Chinese invaders retrieved her from the river in which her father, a Tartar king, had ordered her mother and her sisters to be drowned to prevent them falling into enemy hands. She urges Calaf to join her in flight to her near relation, the Khan of Berlas (under whose protection Calaf has left his elderly parents), but leaves in a fury when he refuses the offer and confesses that he cannot love her.

The next morning Calaf's progress to the divan is uneventful but Tourandocte identifies him by his name. In an unguarded moment, when filled with distress at Adelmule's disclosure of Tourandocte's treachery, Calaf had referred to himself by name in the slave-girl's presence and she has passed it on to her mistress. However, Tourandocte admits that he has won her heart if not the overall contest. Adelmule now unveils, confesses that she passed on his name in the hope of preventing their marriage, and stabs herself before the assembled company. She dies expressing her belief in the god Xaca and her conviction that she is 'returning to [her] Original Nothing' (ii. 87). A footnote explains that worshippers of this sect believe there are no rewards or punishments in the afterlife for one's mortal acts. The king of China, a believer in transmigration, expresses the hope that after passing through nine hells she will be born the daughter of another sovereign at the first transmigration and gives her a royal funeral.

After the funeral, the marriage is celebrated and Calaf's parents, the exiled King Timurtasch and his wife Elmaze, are brought to Peking with Alinguer, khan of the nomadic horde of Berlas, their protector and Calaf's patron. The latter joins forces with Altoun and Calaf to defeat the sultan of Carizme who had seized Timurtasch's kingdom from him.

They also overcome the Circassians whose disloyalty to the Nogais had resulted in Carizme's earlier victory. Timurtasch and his wife return to the enlarged kingdom of Astrakhan, which now incorporates that of Circassia, and Calaf becomes sovereign of Carizme. Tourandocte bears her husband fine princes to inherit these various kingdoms.

Given in the *Thousand and One Days: Persian Tales* of François Pétis de la Croix, the story of Tourandocte has transparent parallels with the position of the collection's frame recipient, Farruknaz, princess of Kashmir, who has expressed an unreasoning aversion to marriage which results in the lingering deaths from disappointment of her rejected suitors. The narrator of the tale, the old nurse Sutlememé, invents a character in her own likeness in the shape of the old woman who warns against Tourandocte's charms when Calaf arrives in Peking, and in the slave-girl Adelmule she provides an analogy with Farruknaz's romantic waiting-women who listen alongside their mistress with enthusiasm and sympathy to the old gossip's stories of virtuous men faithful in love.

Tourandocte shares with Farruknaz the familiar battery of characteristics associated with oriental femininity: vanity, a desire for power, exceptional beauty, and verbal authority. Like Scheherazade and many other oriental heroines, she is 'perfectly skilled in those Sciences, which are proper only to Men' (*PT* ii. 9). She can write in several languages, knows arithmetic, geography, philosophy, mathematics, law, and theology. But she also shares the characteristics of the oriental despot, taking the role of Schahriar in her pursuit of a violent and unjust edict against an entire sex. Alongside her broad correspondence with the familiar subject positions of the oriental tale, she also serves as a figure for the specificity of the oriental empire of China; she can be read as a fictionalized embodiment of China in the western imagination, a 'Chinese character' in the fullest sense of the phrase.

In particular, her identification as a 'riddler' marks her out as a Chinese 'character', that enigmatic scribal sign which is understood by western commentators as either a vestige of a pure antediluvian language or an illegible erratic mark governed by no overarching grammatical logic. The fact that Tourandocte is flanked by women who bear pen and paper is significant; China had long been known as a culture that invested authority in the written word and enjoyed technological expertise in printing superior to that in the West. Jean-Baptiste Du Halde, the Jesuit compositor of the most influential account of China in the eighteenth century, comments in his section 'Of the Chinese Language' that 'There are in *China* a prodigious Number of Books, because they have had the Art of Printing from Time immemorial, tho' in *Europe* that Art is still almost in its Infancy'. He compares Mandarin with Latin as a language of state governed by formal rules (a fitting analogy for a Catholic priest accustomed to the Latin mass) and concludes that:

The Style of the *Chinese* in their Compositions is abstruse, concise, allegorical, and sometimes obscure to those who are not well vers'd in the Characters. It requires Skill to make no Mistakes in reading an Author; they say many Things in a few Words; their Expressions are lively, animated, and intermix'd with bold Comparisons, and noble Metaphors.[2]

Tourandocte's riddles are, like fables, a form of metaphor, where the signified object must be deduced from the linguistic term which substitutes for it without naming; her speech, like the language in which it is spoken, needs to be unpacked to be understood. Verbal 'painting' takes precedence over visual acts in Tourandocte's world. Du Halde remarks that the Chinese prefer written words to painted images as a means of communication (i. 365), just as the image of Tourandocte is what charms her lovers, but her words are her means of wielding power over life and death. David Porter comments on the tendency to represent 'China' in the period as an ideograph, that is, a 'symbol expressing the idea of a thing without conveying its name':[3] the hieroglyph or the traffic light are the best-known examples.

Tourandocte's riddles might be understood as a form of ideograph and Calaf's returned challenge to her, that she find out his name, indicates his understanding of the culture he has entered and the magic power of the 'proper' name within it. Tourandocte's two first riddles refer to primary and elemental forces, the sun and the sea, suggesting her affinity to ancient and primary wisdom. China emerges, David Porter claims, as 'a uniquely privileged site not only of genealogical but also of what one might term representational legitimacy, a place,

---

[2] Du Halde, *Description of the Empire of China*, i. 365.
[3] Porter, *Ideographia*, 9.

that is, where the myriad signs and symbols that constitute culture were reliably grounded in a fixed, originary source of meaning and therefore not subject to the corrupting vicissitudes of common language and history'.[4] Jesuit informants about China claimed that, unlike the hybrid cultures contemporary with it, Chinese culture retained in every aspect an unbroken link with its ancient past. Du Halde describes its ancient and, he claims, unchanged Confucian canon; he traces every emperor back from Fo-hi, the first emperor to the twenty-second Qing dynasty 'now reigning', as well as reproducing a vast sequence of imperial edicts.

Chinese character writing achieved a special place in debates over the possibility of a universal language which pre-existed the tower of Babel in late seventeenth-century theory. Francis Bacon took an interest in the 'real' nature of Chinese characters, and John Wilkins considered adopting Chinese characters for his universal model but was put off by its 80,000 ideograms. John Webb the antiquarian published *An Historical Essay Endeavoring a Probability that the Language of the Empire is the Primitive Language*, which rehearsed the idea that the posterity of Shem had peopled China. William Whiston in his 1696 *New Theory of the Earth* equated Noah with Fohi (the Buddha). But Robert Hook in his *Some Observations and Conjectures concerning Chinese Characters* (1686) refuted the supposed affinity with an originary language.[5]

However, Tourandocte can also be read in the more negative light which emerged increasingly through the eighteenth century with regard to China and was often expressed in terms of a critique of Mandarin. Thus, another Jesuit traveller/commentator of the late seventeenth century, Louis Le Comte, comments that 'Every thing is mysterious in this Language,' and complains that

it is an heavy Cross to be forc'd all a Man's life long (for commonly it is not too long for it) to stuff his Head with this horrible multitude of Figures, and to

---

[4] Porter, *Ideographia*, 9.

[5] On Chinese language debates in the early modern period, see ch. 2, 'A Confusion of Tongues', William Worthen Appleton, *A Cycle of Cathay: The Chinese Vogue in England in the Seventeenth and Eighteenth Centuries* (New York: Columbia University Press, 1951); and ch. 1, 'Linguistic Legitimacy and the Interpretation of Chinese Writing', Porter, *Ideographia*.

be always occupied in deciphering imperfect Hieroglyphicks, that have in a manner no analogy with the things they signifie, there is not the least Charm in this, as in the Sciences of *Europe*, which, in fatiguing, do not cease to captivate the Spirit with Delight. (*Compleat History*, 180, 188)

Tourandocte's wit and learning now begin to look—as did the government of China by 'literati' with training in language and canonical texts rather than politics—like perversions rather than guarantees of good government. Indeed, Tourandocte's seizure of political authority from her paternalistic and virtuous father disturbs the ancient lineage of benevolent absolutism so admired by western commentators who saw in China the only absolutist eastern state not to decline into despotism. Interestingly, Calaf's and Tourandocte's story also inverts the traditional pattern whereby Islam is seen as the inevitable accomplice of despotism in eastern states, since here the devout Muslim Calaf wins the love of the idolatrous Tourandocte and tempers her cruel thirst for blood in so doing. It also inverts the conventional representation of a binary conflict between a civilized, sophisticated, and gentle indigenous Chinese culture repeatedly overriden by the superior military might but barbaric values of neighbouring Tartar forces. Here, Calaf is a gentle Tartar and Tourandocte a cruel and violent Chinese.

In fact, Tourandocte emerges as an incomprehensible, indeed 'illegible', figure in the *Persian Tales*. Her refusal of marriage is apparently motiveless. In his tragic opera of 1926, Giacomo Puccini was to invent a reason for Tourandocte's suspicion of men in the claim that a female ancestor was raped and subsequently died.[6] Pétis de la Croix's Tourandocte only insists on her love of 'liberty' and the tale suggests that fear of its loss is what drives her to hatred. Calaf subtly hands her back her 'liberty' by giving her the opportunity to solve his 'riddle' and then choose to marry him of her own free will. The latter choice is equally motiveless and contradictory, leaving

---

[6] Carlo Gozzi turned the story of Tourandocte into a play in 1762, the same year as he produced a play from that of Fadlallah and Zemroude (see 'Shape-Shifting', ch. 2). In his source, Pétis de la Croix's text, the elderly Fadlallah gives the fugitive prince Calaf and Calaf's parents refuge at the city of Jaic and tells them his unhappy tale. Ferrucio Busoni's *Chinesisches Fabel* were, in turn, drawn from Gozzi, and used as the basis of a comic opera staged by Max Reinhardt in 1911. In 1917 Giacomo Puccini saw Reinhardt's opera in a new translation by Karl Vollmoeller, which he transformed into his tragic version, *Turandot*,

the reader confused about whether to dismiss Tourandocte as a whimsical tyrant or a misguided woman finally softened when she encounters true love. Of course, within the logic of the frame narrative, we can interpret Tourandocte's paradoxical characterization as part of the subtlety of Sutlememé's campaign to alter her mistress's mind. Farruknaz is reminded that her own behaviour will look like that of her oriental 'sister', Tourandocte: incomprehensible, arbitrary, and despotic. The Indian princess must differentiate herself from the nonsensical precedent of the Chinese one.

The contrast with her slave, Adelmule, also complicates and obscures the reading of Tourandocte and ensures that Sutlememé leavens her criticism of her mistress with some flattery. Adelmule's passion leads her to unscrupulous and duplicitous action, whereas Tourandocte's leads her to honour and a new humility. Adelmule is revealed to have lied (inventing the story of Tourandocte's plans to have Calaf killed by assassins) in order to try and divert Calaf's attentions from her mistress. She passes on his name to Tourandocte in another attempt to introduce a breach between them. By contrast, Tourandocte is honest, open, and honourable. Oriental fictions compulsively generate such contrasts between models of oriental femininity, but the contrast does not resolve into a simple one between women who conform to and those who transgress expectations of gender until considerably later in the eighteenth century. Indeed, all oriental heroines are represented as transgressive, whether through cross-dressing, sexual aggression, a propensity to cruelty, or aspiration to influence state affairs. Puccini's early twentieth-century operatic rewriting of the tale reveals the pressures of increasingly dichotomous thinking about gender when it turns the tables, making the slave-girl Liu into the devoted attendant of the prince's father, secretly nurturing a passion for Calaf herself and proved, in her willingness to embrace death rather than part with his name, to enjoy a more refined and generous love than Tourandot.

with the help of the playwrights Renato Simoni and Giuseppe Adami who provided the libretto. It is Puccini's version (first presented in 1926 two years after Puccini's death and finished by his disciple Franco Alfana) that has secured the continuing fame of the story through the 20th c. (Antony Beaumont, 'Turandot (I)', L. Macy (ed.), *The New Grove Dictionary of Music Online* (Accessed 3 Sept. 2002), http://www.grovemusic.com.

Despite her incomprehensibility, the Chinese princess with a propensity towards despotism and a haughty resistance to the sexual advances of men is a recurrent figure in oriental fictions. This is partly owed to the popularity of the story of the Ming princess who begged her father, the Emperor Chongzhen, to stab her with his own dagger rather than let her suffer rape at the hands of the rebels, led by Li Zicheng, who entered Peking in April 1644. Elkanah Settle's play of 1676, *The Conquest of China, by the Tartars*, is a highly fictionalized version of the fall of the Ming dynasty and features two Chinese princesses in this mould. Amavanga, queen of a dependent province in China, adopts the disguise of a soldier to fight against the invading Tartars led by Theimingus and his son, Zungteus, with whom she fell secretly in love when he was being educated in China as a youth. Repressing her amorous feelings in favour of her duty to country, Amavanga enters a duel with him to decide the conflict and is, apparently, killed by his hand only to be restored to him at the end of the play, having been nursed back to health by her confidante and companion, Vangona, who has shared her cross-dressing fortunes throughout. The heroic Amavanga is contrasted with the wily Orunda, only child of the king of China, who enters the play when she is ordered by her father in a public ceremony to select two men she would be prepared to marry from the twelve royal princes before her: Quitazo, the virtuous prince she selects first, is already in love with a court lady named Alcinda. Orunda persuades Lycungus (a version of Li Zicheng), her other choice, to spy on Quitazo and when he discovers the secret pre-engagement of his rival and informs her, Orunda hires poisoners to dispense with Alcinda. The poisoners, however, come across Orunda in disguise and mistake her for their victim; when they threaten to stab her, she drinks the poison rather than 'Permit such mean hands should their Princess Kill' (Act IV, p. 47). Just as Lycungus prepares to seize power, the old king having committed suicide along with his princes and his wives, Zungteus enters with Quitazo and kills him. Zungteus is on the verge of taking his own life, his task of conquering China completed, when Vangona ushers in the recovered Amavanga.

Amidst all this gender and racial inversion, Zungteus's concluding speech relies on the familiar, if woefully inappropriate, contrast between gentle Chinese and martial Tartar to suggest the future of both regions under his joint reign with Amavanga:

> Nor shall our Loves be Fortunate alone:
> Be yours blest too, yours is the *Tartar* Crown.
> Your Milder Presence will auspicious be,
> And civilize my Rougher *Tartary*,
>   And whil'st the *Chinans* pay Allegeance here:
> I'le Teach their softer Natures Arms and War.
>
> (Act V, p. 67)

The alliance through marriage of nomadic warlike Tartar male and sophisticated urban Chinese woman becomes a familiar conclusion to eighteenth-century fictions about China, the regional and racial conflicts of the Far East resolved through the romantic conclusion of marital love. This conclusion also accords the female partner equal and public influence in the process of hybridization, in interesting comparison with other representations of oriental regions in which feminine authority is a hidden pressure apparently subsumed behind the public figure of the male. There is no suggestion at the conclusion of the story of Calaf and Tourandocte that the marriage will mean conversion of the Chinese kingdom to Islam, despite the stress on the hero's devout nature in the opening passages. Indeed, it is his son who inherits the Chinese throne and continues to govern in the tradition of his maternal grandfather. Amavanga, Tourandocte, and the other 'Chinese' heroines we meet in the following discussion retain their independence and their theological or political autonomy, ruling as queen-concubines rather than veiled if influential figures behind the scenes.

Chinese whispers

There is an English parlour game called 'Chinese whispers' in which a message is whispered from ear to ear round a circle and its final recipient has to pronounce what is usually nonsense for it to be measured against the original. The sinophobic name points to the centuries-old tradition in Europe of representing spoken Chinese as an incomprehensible and unpronounceable combination of sounds. However, it can also serve as a figure for the way in which European representations of China constantly rehash and recirculate earlier accounts, each time adjusting them to the expectations and prejudices of the new historical moment and specific culture. 'China' can carry multiple and contradictory meanings for its European consumers.

In his prologue to a play by Arthur Murphy called *The Orphan of China, a Tragedy* performed at Drury Lane in 1759, William Whitehead the poet laureate announces:

> On eagle wings the poet of to-night
> Soars for fresh virtues to the source of light,
> To China's eastern realms: and boldly bears
> Confucius' morals to Britannia's ears.

(n.p.)

Whitehead locates Enlightenment's source in the Far East rather than in western Europe, a not unusual gesture in western philosophy of the period.[7] Murphy's is a reworking of Voltaire's 1755 play *Orphelin de la Chine*, itself derived from a fourteenth-century Chinese play, *The Orphan of Zhao*, which had been translated into French by a Jesuit priest. Voltaire was one of the most vocal of China's agitators in the eighteenth century, opening his *Essai sur l'histoire générale, et sur les mœurs et l'esprit des nations, depuis Charlemagne* of 1756 on the instructive model of China for the West. However, the image of China as a source for the West of rational wisdom and abstract thought was countered equally strongly by the presentation of it as a dangerous source of insanity and spur to an obsession with bizarre material goods.[8]

---

[7] See ch. 5, 'Matters of Enlightenment', in Jonathan Spence, *The Chan's Great Continent: China in Western Minds* (London: Allen Lane Penguin Press, 1999). Spence cites Leibniz, Montesquieu, Voltaire, and Herder as enthusiasts for China's Enlightenment values.

[8] On images of China in the 18th c., see Porter, *Ideographia*; Appleton, *Cycle of Cathay*; Adolf Reichwein, *China and Europe: Intellectual and Artistic Contacts in the Eighteenth Century*, reissued from 1925 (London: Routledge & Kegan Paul, 1968); and Raymond Stanley Dawson, *The Chinese Chameleon: An Analysis of European Conceptions of Chinese Civilization* (Oxford: Oxford University Press, 1967).

Enthusiasm for China in the period is often presented as a form of madness—a madness frequently manifested in women and associated with sexual disorder. Mania for the country of China and for its most coveted and unusual product, porcelain, were often equated. For example, number 109 of *The Adventurer* (1778) describes an imaginary visit to Bedlam with Dean Swift to the cell of one Lady Harriet Brittle, filled with Chinese vases and urns. She has run mad after a waggoner inadvertently crushed her costly purchases from an auctioneer of 'a mandarin and a Jos'; the Chinese vases in her room which she believes to be 'true Nanquin' are Chelsea urns 'provided by her relations to sooth her passion'.[9]

Less extreme manifestations of the same disorder can be found at two significant points in Oliver Goldsmith's *Citizen of the World*, which first appeared as a series of 119 letters from January 1760 to August 1761 in *The Public Ledger*. The chief correspondent, Lien Chi Altangi, a Chinese philosopher who has come to live in London, is received enthusiastically by two different English ladies on two different occasions. The ladies wish to add Lien Chi to their collection of Chinese figures, but he stubbornly refuses to fit their preconceptions about his exoticism. Letter 14 (Thursday, 28 February 1760) details an encounter with a 'little shrivelled figure' who has passionately solicited Lien Chi's visit and displays her collection of porcelain figures with pride: 'sprawling dragons, squatting pagods, and clumsy mandarines, were stuck upon every shelf'. It is soon apparent that she views Lien Chi in similar terms to her collection as her persistent slips into the third person in her opening words to him indicate:

'What an unusual share of *somethingness* in his whole appearance. Lord how I am charmed with the outlandish cut of his face; how bewitching the exotic breadth of his forehead. I would give the world to see him in his own country dress. Pray turn about, Sir, and let me see you behind. There! there's a travelled air for you. You that attend there, bring up a plate of beef cut into small pieces; I have a violent passion to see him eat. Pray, Sir, have you got your chop-sticks about you? it will be so pretty to see the meat carried to the mouth with a jerk. Pray speak a little Chinese: I have learned some of the language myself. Lord, have you nothing pretty from China about you;

[9] *The Adventurer* (London, 1778), iv. 29.

something that one does not know what to do with: I have got twenty things from China that are no use in the world'.[10]

Lien Chi observes that the 'useless' decorative objects do have practical purposes in China and in fact are quite mean utensils for infusing tea.

Another hostess in Letter 33 (Friday, 25 April 1760) proves even less attentive than the first when her guest tries to correct her assumptions about the living habits of his home culture: 'I yesterday received an invitation from a lady of distinction, who it seems had collected all her knowledge of eastern manners from fictions every day propagated here, under the titles of eastern tales, and oriental his-tories: she received me very politely, but seemed to wonder that I neglected bringing opium and a tobacco box; when chairs were drawn for the rest of the company, I was assigned my place on a cushion on the floor' (142). When Lien Chi tries to differentiate China from other eastern cultures he sees as barbaric such as the 'Turk, the Persian or the native of Peru' (142) his fellow guests simply ignore him.

The China that Lien Chi's lady acquaintances understand him to represent bears no relation to the China he knows. They have derived their China from a peculiar melding together of the equally uncritical consumption of oriental tales and commodities. William Appleton comments of the collapse of the cult of chinoiserie in the second half of the eighteenth century that 'Primarily the whole movement was a superficial one. Europe was not subjected to genuine Chinese art or theories. It was subjected to an imitation of China seen through European eyes.'[11] Appleton assumes that chinoiserie was doomed because of its inauthenticity. Of course, the irony is that Lien Chi is also an inauthentic Chinese figure, a product of Oliver Goldsmith's satirical pen. His complaint that he is confused with other eastern and barbaric figures acquires a special irony when we learn from James Prior that his author's

first design according to accounts of his friends was to make his hero a native of Morocco or Fez; but, reflecting on the rude nature of the people of

---

[10] *The Citizen of the World*, in *Collected Works of Oliver Goldsmith*, ed. Arthur Friedman (Oxford: Clarendon Press, 1966), ii. 65, 63–4.
[11] Appleton, *Cycle of Cathay*, 117–18.

Barbary, this idea was dropped. A Chinese was then chosen as offering more novelty of character than a Turk or Persian; and being equally advanced in the scale of civilization, could pass an opinion on all he saw better than the native of a more barbarous country.[12]

Rather than ringing the death knell of the cult of China in eighteenth-century England, the charge of inauthenticity, or fictionality, was central to the robustness and elasticity of its dissemination. The fictional nature of China's representation was familiar and self-evident to eighteenth-century consumers.

China was a particularly distant and shadowy culture to eighteenth-century English consumers; if the importation of tea and porcelain from China was increasingly central to a European and especially English trading economy, it was carried out on the periphery of China, restricted largely to Canton by the Cohong or combined merchant companies established in 1720 with a monopoly over maritime trade with western countries. From 1760 all trade was restricted to Canton. Hence, the Chinese mainland remained a largely unfamiliar territory, especially for the Protestant English nation confined to a purely trading relation; until the late eighteenth century only the Catholics had succeeded in establishing missions in China.

Historians identify a polarity between two kinds of witness about China: Jesuit missionary accounts which are universally idealizing and merchant/trader accounts which are invariably critical. For the Jesuits, Chinese are noble, living by a natural morality and operating principles of ideal government as well as being curious about western science and religion; for merchants they are deceitful, cruel, and regressive, closed to modern principles of trade and mired in superstition and idolatry.[13] This may have been a register of very different experiences: the merchants were confined to trading in Canton, often with corrupt factors, and having to deal with those considered of

---

[12] James Prior, *The Life of Oliver Goldsmith, M.B.* (London, 1837), i. 360.

[13] See 'East Asia' in Donald E. Lach and Edwin J. Van Kley, *A Century of Advance*, vol. iii of *Asia in the Making of Europe* (Chicago: Chicago University Press, 1993). For a detailed and useful summary of Jesuit writings, see Basil Guy, 'Ad majorem Societatis gloriam: Jesuit Perspectives on Chinese Mores in the Seventeenth and Eighteenth Centuries', in G. S. Rousseau and Roy Porter (eds.), *Exoticism in the Enlightenment* (Manchester and New York: Manchester University Press, 1990), 66–85.

the lowest order in China; whereas the Jesuits enjoyed, if erratically, the indulgence of the emperors themselves in Peking. While Jesuit commentators were seeking to defend their mission to Rome and argue for the ripeness of the Chinese to conversion (to the extent that much of the eighteenth century was spent in an attempt to convince Rome that Chinese ancestor rites were civil not religious ceremonies which could be continued even after conversion), merchants were frustrated in their attempts to gain control over production and exchange of goods by the Canton Chinese licence holders.

Although there has been extensive discussion of these two dominant 'informant' accounts, the only two fictional texts about China that have been given any attention to date have received it not because they deal with China but because their authors are otherwise celebrated in eighteenth-century literary studies; Daniel Defoe's *The Farther Adventures of Robinson Crusoe* (1719) describes Crusoe's travels in China and Mongolia between 1695 and 1705, while Oliver Goldsmith's *Citizen of the World* describes the travels and experiences of a supposed Chinese philosopher in England in the mid-eighteenth century. Here too there is a polarity; Defoe's speaker is unremittingly critical of Chinese society, culture, and economy, while Goldsmith's is unremittingly critical if more gently ironic in his depiction of English society, culture, and economy. This is of course a measure of their authors' own politics: Defoe the Whig dissenter writes in praise of progress, trade, and limited forms of monarchy, while Goldsmith the Tory quietist celebrates ancient tradition, strong forms of monarchy, and rural economy.

The position articulated by Defoe gained ascendancy through the eighteenth century as David Porter and Jonathan Spence have charted.[14] Spence summarizes the transition as follows:

As the seventeenth century waned, and with it the peak of the Catholic nations' program of overseas conquest and expansion, the naval powers of the emerging Protestant states were ready to seize the opportunities this offered. Diplomats and soldiers from the Netherlands and Great Britain became the

---

[14] David Porter, 'A Peculiar but Uninteresting Nation: China and the Discourse of Commerce in Eighteenth-Century England', *Eighteenth-Century Studies* 33 (2000): 181–200; Spence, *The Chan's Great Continent*.

next group to explore China. These men saw themselves as realists, with certain tasks to perform; they viewed with a new kind of hostility China's attempts to force them to accept traditional kinds of ritualized subservience, especially the kowtow . . . (*The Chan's Great Continent*, p. xiii)

Through the course of the eighteenth century, writings on China became increasingly critical, especially of its apparent political and moral stagnation. What looked like security and ancient lineage to the Jesuits began to look like xenophobia, paranoia, and stultification to Protestant trading powers.

The fictional representations of China discussed in this book illustrate the elements of Chinese culture that gained especial imaginative currency in England: political and moral absolutism, belief in theories of transmigration, and wilful linguistic obscurity. Heroic tragedies depict loyalty to the emperor taking precedence over familial attachment, while satirical informant letters present the Chinese citizen as the prototype of Enlightenment morality, curiosity, and impartiality on the model of Confucius. By contrast, prose fictions disseminate more fanciful and contradictory versions of Chineseness, wedded to a superstitious 'nonsensical' belief in transmigration but also open to the pleasures of the imagination, the delight of intricate and multiple plotting.

Orphans and absolutism: tragedies of state

The one consistent comment on China, whether positively or negatively construed, was that its political and moral order was both unchanging and ancient. As Jonathan Spence points out, China saw between 1661 and 1799 only three different emperors, all of the same dynasty (the Qing), an extraordinary example of political stability to western minds.[15] Jean-Baptiste Du Halde's tome compiled from Jesuit missionary accounts and translations from Chinese documents, and first published in France in 1725, was translated in two different

---

[15] Jonathan Spence, *The Search for Modern China* (London: Hutchinson, 1990), 90.

editions in the mid-eighteenth century in England.[16] It served as the major source for most writers about China in England, along with the letters of the Jesuit priest, Louis Le Comte (translated into English in 1697). Du Halde asserts:

The Political Government of *China* entirely turns on the reciprocal Duty of Parents and Children. The Emperor is called the Father of the Empire; the Vice-Roy is the Father of the Province under his Command; as the *Mandarin* is of the City which he governs. This single Principle is the Foundation of that great Respect and ready Obedience which the *Chinese* pay to the Officers who assist the Emperor to sustain the Weight of Government.[17]

Du Halde provides a few examples of Chinese literature for western readers to assess: four stories which illustrate the importance of honesty and plain-dealing and a play, 'A Chinese tragedy, call'd *Chau shi ku eul*, or the little orphan of the family of Chau' (ii. 175–82). It was this translation and radical abridgement of a fourteenth-century Chinese play by a Jesuit missionary to China, Father Joseph-Henri-Marie de Prémare, that formed the basis of a succession of European dramatic representations of China. The story concerns a father's sacrifice of his own son to meet his higher loyalty to the state and a son's revenge on behalf of his dead father. It may have appealed in England especially because of similarities in plot and theme to *Hamlet* and more generally to the popular Renaissance tragedy of state.

Tu Ngan Ku, Prime Minister of War, determines to oust his rival, Chau Tun, Prime Minister of State, from favour. He trains a dog to respond aggressively to Chau Tun's presence and then claims the dog can recognize a traitor. Chau Tun flees to the mountains and three hundred of his relatives are massacred leaving only his son, Chau So, who is married to the king's daughter. Tu Ngan Ku forges an order from the emperor for Chau So to commit suicide and shortly there-after his wife gives birth to a son whom she names 'little Orphan of the

---

[16] A translation published by John Watts appeared in 4 vols. in 1736. The handsome 2-vol. folio translation published by Edward Cave in 1738 and 1741 is the version used throughout this book. On the different translations and their influence, see Cunzhong Fan, 'Dr Johnson and Chinese Culture', *China Society Occasional Papers*, NS 6 (1945): 5–20.

[17] Du Halde, *Description of the Empire of China*, i. 248.

House of Chau' as instructed by her dead husband. The princess persuades a physician and relative of Chau So who has escaped the massacre to smuggle the child out of the palace and then hangs herself to avoid torture. A noble guard, Han que, realizes that the physician Ching ing is concealing the child in his medicine chest but allows him to escape before he stabs himself to death. Tu Ngan Ku demands the death of all boy children under six months old if the orphan is not delivered up within three days. Ching ing takes the child to Kong-hun, an officer now living in retirement, who agrees to help him in substituting Ching ing's recently born boy son for the orphan. Kong-hun points out that he is older than Ching ing and might not survive into the child's adulthood to care for him. He undertakes to present himself as the sole conspirator, which will leave Ching ing free to bring up the orphan. Ching ing accuses Kong-hun and is forced to beat him to make him reveal the child's whereabouts. Tu Ngan Ku stabs the child to death in front of its father and Kong-hun commits suicide by throwing himself down some stone steps. Ching ing is rewarded by living in the palace and having his own son brought up as Tu Ngan Ku's heir. Twenty years later Tu Ngan Ku proposes to murder the emperor and take the throne himself and Ching ing intervenes by revealing his true parentage to the orphan with the help of a scroll that depicts the events around his birth. The orphan, Ching Pwey, goes to an officer of the king, Wey Song, and accuses Tu Ngan Ku who is seized and punished by public racking and dismemberment.

In the mid-eighteenth century, the Tory writer William Hatchett was the first to use the play as a foundation for an English production, turning it into a satirical attack on Robert Walpole. Hatchett's *The Chinese Orphan* (1741) follows Prémare's translation of the Chinese original closely for the first three acts, with the exception of extensive renaming. The Walpole/Tu Ngan Ku figure is renamed Siako and the virtuous physician is Kifang. Rather than a scroll, Kifang provides a christening robe for the orphan which depicts Siako's crimes and leads the king (Kiohamti) to realize the depths of his minister's perfidy. In deference to the western preference for preservation of the three unities of time, place, and action, Hatchett has his orphan remain a baby (in the 'Chinese' source he grows up twenty years between one scene and the next) and makes the emperor of Tsin the instrument of vengeance.[18]

Hatchett's dedication to the duke of Argyle illustrates the pro-ductive use of analogy in European presentations of 'the Chinese':

> As the *Chinese* are a wise discerning People, and much fam'd for their Art in Government, it is not to be wonder'd at, that the Fable is political: indeed it exhibits an amazing Series of Male-administration, which the *Chinese* Author has wrought up to the highest Pitch of Abhorrence, as if he had been acquainted with the Inflexibility of your Grace's Character in that respect. It's certain, he has exaggerated Nature, and introduced rather a Monster than a Man; but perhaps it is a Maxim with the *Chinese* Poets to represent Prime Ministers as so many Devils, to deter honest People from being deluded by them. (pp. vi–vii)

Hatchett's rhetoric clearly codes his target as Walpole (maladminis-tration, monstrosity, and devilry were key terms associated with opposition writings), while ostensibly calling attention to the *difference* between Chinese culture and English: Chinese ideals of government mean the corruption taken as commonplace among the nation's leaders in England would not be tolerated. In the concluding Act V, Siako, in the tradition of the self-aware and even self-parodying stage villain, calls attention to the analogous status of the play when he complains to the king that history is being distorted to serve political ends in Kifang's interpretation of the images on the christening robe:

> I never cherish'd, that I know, a wish
> To be the ruler of my Liege's judgment,
> Which still acts principal in all our councils:
> Nor is it new, nor yet a task so crabbed,
> To dress-up parallels, nay forge 'em too,
> And fashion history in such wrested sort,

---

[18] See Jean Baptiste de Boyer, Marquis d'Argens, *Chinese Letters* (London, 1741: first published in French in 1739) in which Choang, corresponding from Ispahan to Peking in Letter 23, discusses the play and reproduces long sections of it. He complains that, although Chinese tragedies are moral by comparison with those of other cultures, they stick to one point too much. He does not advocate the three unities but 'we should at lest preserve a little more of the Probable in our Plays' (161) and gives the instance of a child born in the middle of a play being 30 years old at the end as in 'the Little Orphan of the Family of Tchao'.

As to make truth and falshood, black or white,
Just as it serves to colour up a purpose.

(v. ii. 63)

Hatchett's *Orphan of China* becomes like so much other chinoiserie, a kind of 'false import' to which he attaches his own import or set of meanings.[19] In his dedication Hatchett comments that '*China* has furnish'd us long with the Produce of her Earth; with her Manufactures...'.[20] The tragedy from which he has derived his source is understood to be a similar kind of import, to be reproduced and 'Englished' like Lady Brittle's Chelsea urns in imitation of Chinese tableware.

François Marie Arouet de Voltaire and his English imitator, Arthur Murphy, also use the Chinese tale to address European philosophical and political ends. For Voltaire, China was a rod with which to chastise the Catholic established Church. The secular morality derived from Confucius, he points out, could structure people's lives in China without a need either for Christianity or a state religion.[21] His *L'Orphelin de la Chine*, first acted in Paris in 1755 and translated into English as *The Orphan of China* in 1756, relocates the action of the Chinese source in the fourteenth century when it was first written and China fell to the Tartars led by Genghis-Khan. Voltaire celebrates the force of civilization in that the Tartars, he claims, 'did not change the manners of the nation vanquished; they protected all the Arts established in *China*; they adopted all its Laws'.[22]

Gengis-Khan, previously raised at the court in Pekin, returns as an adult leader of the Scythian people to conquer China. He encounters the woman whom he loved as a young man, Idame, now married to the mandarin and priest Zamti. Zamti proposes to put his son by Idame in the place of the orphaned prince of the house of China who is under sentence of death from the Tartar invaders while the Korean people rally the forces of resistance around the baby prince. Idame,

---

[19] On the defining 'inauthenticity' of chinoiserie in the mid-18th c., see David Porter, 'Monstrous Beauty: Eighteenth-Century Fashion and the Aesthetics of the Chinese Taste', *Eighteenth-Century Studies* 35 (2002): 395–411.

[20] The reference is to porcelain, which is produced from fired earth.

[21] See Spence, *The Search for Modern China*, 133.

[22] Voltaire, *The Orphan of China*, Preface to Cardinal Richelieu, p. v.

however, reveals the plot to Gengis-Khan in order to save her child. Idame decides finally to die with her husband and son rather than preserve them by giving in to Gengis-Khan's romantic advances. Gengis acknowledges the superior moral virtue of the peaceful and civilized Chinese:

> Amazement! what a people have I conquer'd!
> Whence are they? whence these elevated thoughts,
> This native grandeur of the noble soul,
> Which we in our rough climes ne'er felt or knew?
> To a King dead, each sacrificing nature,
> One without murmur sees his son destroy'd,
> The other for a husband asks to die.
>
> .   .   .   .
>
> I see them an industrious, noble people;
> Their Kings on wisdom's basis built their power,
> To all the neighbour nations giving laws,
> And reigning without conquest or the sword.
>
> (iv. ii. 40–1)

In a sudden reversal, Gengis-Khan prevents Idame and Zamti from joint suicide and undertakes to raise the orphan as the future emperor, having learnt by their example that 'TO BE GOOD, IS TO BE GREAT' (v. vi. 62).

Voltaire's play exploits the familiar opposition between Tartary and China in eighteenth-century writing in which the former are viewed as a powerful, military, masculine but barbarian race by contrast with their effeminate, luxury-loving but highly civilized neighbours. Tartar martial success is contrasted with Chinese ability in crafts and arts. This opposition plays itself out in the gendered terms of eighteenth-century 'enlightened' discourse, in which China is represented as a feminine culture, a necessary example of civility but limited in its ultimate potential for advancement and development.

Voltaire's play is a hymn to the force of civilization as a counter-weight to political might, but it is also a celebration of the power of fiction over factual report. The preface pronounces that 'THE ORPHAN OF TCHAO is a precious monument, which serves better to shew us the genius of *China*, than all the relations ever made, or that ever can be made of that vast Empire' (p. xi). The play demonstrates the power of identification with the position of the 'other' as a means of crossing national boundaries and enabling the transformation of one culture by another. Gengis-Khan is 'converted' to Chinese values from his savage Tartar behaviour by his imaginative identification with Zamti and Idame; his military invasion of China is countered by China's moral and psychological victory over his brutality. So too, according to Voltaire, the French encounter and identification with Chinese values may enable progress from a state of primitive submission to the authority of Church and State to Enlightenment values of curiosity and openness.

However, Voltaire is not uncritical of China, not least because, while the Chinese 'colonize' other nations, they fail to see the value of their own identification with the distant societies that have started to take an interest in them. This myopia will ultimately, he asserts, allow western cultures to overtake the East:

THESE *Chinese*, to whom we have made voyages among so many dangers, these people of whom we have with so much difficulty obtained leave to carry them the money of *Europe*, and to come and instruct them, are yet ignorant that we are their superiors: they are not enough advanced, to dare only to try to imitate us. We have gone into their history for subjects of Tragedy, and they are ignorant that we have a history. (Preface, pp. xiii–xiv)[23]

Three years after the translation of Voltaire's play into English, Arthur Murphy rewrites it substantially and turns the theme of over-riding loyalty on the part of the virtuous citizen to a sovereign dynasty into a source for criticism rather than celebration. His preface declares his *Orphan of China* concerned with '*A Patriot zealous in a monarch's cause*' and warns the reader that if the patriot appears too zealous, '*China's tenets*' of absolutism are to blame (whereas thankfully Britain knows no divine right of kings). Murphy takes the patriarchal nature of China's system of government as proof that a divine right of kings

---

[23] See Spence, *The Search for Modern China*, who comments that: 'Even during the peak periods of eighteenth-century "evidential" *kaozheng* research, the interest of scholars in geography and linguistics was largely concentrated on Chinese territory. Chinese descriptions of foreign countries continued to contain an exotic blend of mystical tales and fantasy in which foreigners were often likened to animals or birds and were described in patronizing or belittling language' (119).

obtains, conveniently ignoring the emperor's freedom to name his successor and the overthrow of one dynasty, the Ming, by another non-Chinese dynasty, the Manchu-derived Qing, in 1644 around the time of the English civil war and deposition of Charles I.

As in Voltaire's play, female and especially maternal love is presented positively by contrast with masculine tyranny, but the loyal male Chinese subject willing to sacrifice his own child to preserve the life of the orphan heir is treated critically. Zamti plans to allow the Tartar emperor, Timurkan, to believe Zamti's natural full-grown son Hamet is the missing orphan. Hamet has been brought up in a distant cave on the principles of Confucius while the orphan, Zamphiri, has been raised as Zamti's son for twenty years at the Tartar-occupied Chinese court under the name of Etan. Mandane, Zamti's wife, attempts to prevent the death of her natural son by disclosing his identity when Timurkan, emperor of the Tartars, comes to suspect he is the orphan. Her husband is prepared to let the illusion stand and see his son die in order to protect Zamphiri/Etan, the true heir. Mandane accuses Timurkan and Zamti with her complaint:

> What are the scepter'd rulers of the world?—
> Form'd of one common clay, are they not all
> Doom'd with each subject, with the meanest slave,
> To drink the cup of human woe?—alike
> All levell'd by affliction?—Sacred kings!
> 'Tis human policy sets up their claim.—
> Mine is a mother's cause—mine is the cause
> Of husband, wife, and child;—those tend'rest ties!
> Superior to your right divine of kings!

> (p. 33)

Murphy criticizes Voltaire in a letter appended to the published text on two counts: first, that he expects theatre audiences to be engaged by the fortunes of a mere baby (Murphy propels the orphan and the substitute child into adulthood) and second, that he makes Gengis-Khan a lover whereas 'Love should reign a very tyrant in Tragedy, or not appear there at all, being unfit for the second place' (p. 92). Murphy's Timurkan is advised to approach Mandane romantically in order to deceive her into revealing the true identity of the orphan, but scorns the suggestion on the grounds that his 'passions' and 'only science' are dedicated to the art of war.

Murphy's play concludes with sacrifice rather than reconciliation. Zamti dies a slow death bound to a wheel clutching his wife's body after she has stabbed herself; rebel forces overthrow the Tartars, leaving time for Zamti to impart dying wisdom to the new and rightful emperor, Zamphiri, restored to his throne with the support of Hamet. Zamti instructs him to remember the 'moral duties of a private man' (p. 86) in order to prevent further suffering on the part of his people. Domestic virtue is now an important guarantee of public honour, rather than a necessary sacrifice for the maintenance of a persecuted dynasty.

Hatchett, Voltaire, and Murphy all provide plays that speak very explicitly to English politics in the eighteenth century. Hatchett's and Voltaire's plays function as 'Patriot' writings pursuing the popular theme among supporters of Frederick, prince of Wales, estranged son of George II, that loyalty to the country must transcend domestic and familial ties. Voltaire's play was translated into English in the same year as the Seven Years War with France broke out and hence its Francophobic preface. Gengis-Khan's assertion that 'To be good is to be great' was a refrain picked up in another Patriot text written following the death of Frederick in 1751, the libretto to George Handel's oratorio, *Jephtha* (1752), by Thomas Morrell. Jephtha vows to sacrifice the first living thing he sees on his return from conflict with the Ammonites if he is victorious; this turns out to be his daughter Iphis. When he is proclaimed leader of the Ammonites he announces, 'Goodness shall make me great'. One year into the Seven Years War, Murphy's play, like Morrell's libretto, offers a critique of 'Patriot' sentiment by presenting it as driven by the masculinist values of war and conflict; Jephtha's wife, like Idame, is alienated from her husband by his determination to put his duty to country/nation before his paternal affection.

Although these English plays serve clear political functions in relation to their own culture, they also rehearse familiar European prejudices about China. English treatments of the 'Orphan of Tchao' such as Murphy's are much preoccupied with its irregularity as a classical piece of drama, an irregularity likened to that associated with the Chinese pagodas and gardens that were becoming popular expressions of the rejection of neo-classical norms in eighteenth-century architecture.[24] Oliver Goldsmith makes the association in his review of Murphy's published version of the play:

We have seen gardens laid out in the Eastern manner; houses ornamented in front by zig-zag lines, and rooms stuck round with Chinese vases, and Indian pagods. If such whimsies prevail among those who conduct the pleasures of the times, and consequently lead the fashion, is it to be wondered, if even poetry itself should conform, and the public be presented with a piece formed upon Chinese manners? manners which, tho' the poet should happen to mistake, he has this consolation left, that few readers are able to detect the imposture. Voltaire, than whom no author better adapts his productions to the colour of the times, was sensible of this prevalence of fashion in favour of all that came from China, and resolved to indulge its extravagance. He has accordingly embroidered a Chinese plot with all the colouring of French poetry; but his advances to excellence are only in proportion to his deviating from the calm insipidity of his Eastern original. Of all nations that ever felt the influence of the inspiring goddess, perhaps the Chinese are to be placed in the lowest class; their productions are the most phlegmatic that can be imagined in those pieces of poetry, or novel, translations, some of which we have seen, and which probably may soon be made public, there is not a single attempt to address the imagination, or influence the passions; such therefore are very improper models for imitation: and Voltaire, who was perhaps sensible of this, has made very considerable deviations from the original plan. Our English poet has deviated still farther, and, in proportion as the plot has become more European, it has become more perfect. By omitting many of the circumstances of the original story, and adding several of his own, Mr. Murphy has given us a play, if not truly Chinese, at least entirely poetical.[25]

The play's progress through western pens indicates not only progressive aestheticization, but also a progressive feminization of values, to the point where Murphy seems to be presenting private domestic virtue and loyalty as displayed by women as at odds with a patriarchalism he identifies as symptomatic of Chinese culture and politics.

[24] See Appleton, 'English Chinoiserie', ch. 6 of *Cycle of Cathay*.
[25] Oliver Goldsmith, Review of Arthur Murphy's *Orphan of China* in *Critical Review* (May 1759). In *Collected Works*, i. 170–2.

The wheel has come full circle: Chinese absolutism admired by seventeenth-century French Catholic commentators is now seen as regressive and stagnant by progressive Enlightenment thinkers.

Empire of Dulness

Voltaire complains in the preface to his 'orphan' play:

The Chinese, like the other Asiatics, have stopt at the first elements of Poetry, Eloquence, Physicks, Astronomy, Painting, known by them so long before us. They begun all things so much sooner than all other people, never afterwards to make any progress in them. They have resembled the ancient Ægyptians, who having first instructed the Grecians, were afterwards incapable of being their disciples. (p. xiii)

The positive evaluation of China promoted by the Jesuits in the sixteenth and seventeenth centuries was being challenged by the end of the seventeenth century. In England, the most explicit challenge came from republican and dissenting voices that challenged the (almost universal) royalist idealization of China as an example of a long-standing absolute monarchy that had also managed to prosper in terms of trade and wealth by comparison with other oriental empires that had imploded through the pursuit of luxury.

Robert Markley has outlined John Milton's desire to maintain an image of China as a prospect of vast trading wealth for the English republic while criticizing Catholic and royalist admiration of its absolutist government.[26] Markley's evidence is gathered from a number of scattered and brief references in Milton's writings. David Porter alerts us to a more sustained and coherent critique of western idealizations of China in the third volume of Daniel Defoe's *Farther Adventures of Robinson Crusoe* (1719):

If the geography of England is increasingly defined in this period by writers like Defoe in terms of the vital flow of commerce among vibrant and

[26] Robert Markley, ' "The destin'd Walls/Of Cambalu". Milton, China, and the Ambiguities of the East', in Balachandra Rajan and Elizabeth Sauer (eds.), *Milton and the Imperial Vision* (Pittsburgh: Duquesne University Press, 1999), 191–213.

prosperous centres of trade, the Chinese cultural landscape, in contrast, emerges in these accounts as an unrelenting panorama of stagnation, boredom, and death.[27]

At the age of 60 in the mid-1690s, Robinson Crusoe embarks on what is to be his last journey and finds himself stranded in China with no means of returning home. He visits Nanquin (Nanjing) and finally leaves via a trade caravan bound for Moscow. Crusoe's encounter with China gives his author the opportunity to launch an assault on the Jesuit accounts and reveal an empire mired in idolatry, the majority of its population poor and barbarous, its buildings low and insignificant, with no navy to speak of and a vast ill-equipped army. He describes a country gentleman with whom he travels for a few miles on his way to Nanquin as an illustration of 'perfect Don *Quixotism*, being a mixture of Pomp and Poverty'.[28]

The critical perspective of a Whig Protestant on the promotion of China as a positive model of a successful absolutist trading nation is perhaps unsurprising. However, the image of China as an 'empire of Dulness' also informs the Scriblerian writings of the Catholic Alexander Pope and the Tory Anglican Jonathan Swift. Frank T. Boyle suggests that Swift's depiction of the Houyhnhyms in the fourth book of *Gulliver's Travels* sideswipes at European idealizations of Confucian rationalism, while all four books attack the modern notion of enlightened travel, revealing that the encounter with distant and very different communities only results in confusion and madness rather than systematic knowledge.[29]

Alexander Pope's *Dunciad*, the first version of which appeared in 1728, presents the 'empire of Dulness' in terms of the familiar characterization of oriental empire in eighteenth-century thought: absolutist, effeminate, trivializing, and stultifying. Set in the context of eighteenth-century sources about China, we might go further to

---

[27] Porter, 'A Peculiar but Uninteresting Nation', 181–2.

[28] Daniel Defoe, *The Farther Adventures of Robinson Crusoe,* vol. iii *Robinson* Crusoe, Shakespeare Head Edition of the Novels and Selected Writings of Daniel Defoe (Oxford: Basil Blackwell, 1927), 156.

[29] On Swift, see Frank T. Boyle, 'Chinese Utopianism and Gulliverian Narcissism in Swift's Travels', in Aileen Douglas, P. H. Kelly, and Ian Campbell Ross (eds.), *Locating Swift: Essays from Dublin on the 250th Anniversary of the Death of Jonathan Swift, 1667-1745* (Dublin: Four Courts Press, 1998), 117–28.

suggest that it is this oriental empire in particular which has a special imaginative force in the creation of Dulness's ever-expanding territory. This force gained momentum in the 1740s when Pope made the political satire of the poem more explicit and associated dulness with the figure of Robert Walpole, George II's chief minister, caricatured as a corrupt oriental minister in numerous minor satirical works of the period.[30] Satire on Walpole links Pope's 1742/3 *Dunciad in Four Books*, Eliza Haywood's 1736 *Adventures of Eovaai*, and William Hatchett's 1741 play *The Chinese Orphan*, but the latter two works and Hatchett's poem *The Chinese Tale* (1740) also suggest a consideration of the thread of 'Chinese' references in Pope's poem, which dates back to the 1728 *Dunciad*.

There is only one direct reference to China in the poem. When Settle shows Lewis Theobald/later Colley Cibber the history of dulness in the Elysian shades, he instructs him:

> Far eastward cast thine eye, from whence the Sun
> And orient Science their bright course begun:
> One god-like Monarch all that pride counfounds,
> He whose long wall the wand'ring Tartar bounds;
> Heav'ns! what a Pile! whole ages perish there,
> And one bright blaze turns Learning into air.[31]

A footnote points to the third-century BC first emperor of a united China, Shih huang-ti, as 'Chi Ho-am-ti, Emperor of China, the same who built the great wall between China and Tartary, destroyed all the books and learned men of that empire. His motive was pride: he wished all learning to date from his reign. He made an exception of agricultural and medical works' (v. 156).

More oblique references littered throughout the *Dunciad* reinforce the 'Chinese' analogy for the Empire of Dulness; Dulness uses opium to anoint her chosen laureate in book 1, Settle refers to the laureate's

---

[30] See Jerry C. Beasley, 'Portraits of a Monster: Robert Walpole and Early English Prose Fiction', *Eighteenth-Century Studies* 14 (1981): 406–31. Beasley identifies Haywood's *Adventures of Eovaai* and George Lyttelton's *The Court Secret: A Melancholy Truth* (1741) as the 'best of the orientalised political romances' directed against Walpole and his ministry' (421).

[31] Alexander Pope, *The Dunciad*, ed. James Sutherland, *The Twickenham Edition of the Poems of Alexander Pope* (London: Methuen, 1963), v, bk. 3 (1728), ll. 73–8.

posterity in his successors as a 'transmigrating soul' (bk. 3 (1728), 49), and Dulness promises her laureate 'On grinning dragons thou shalt mount the wind' (3 (1728), 278). The figure of Dulness herself recalls the representation of China as an unbroken line of government, but a feminized one prone to stagnation, and mired in redundant learning; in book 4 of the 1742/3 *Dunciad* Dulness is promised that scholars will be kept so busy with words that they will not acquire real knowledge, a charge often made against the 'literati' of China immersed in the study of language.[32]

The issues of maternity and illegitimacy in the *Dunciad* might also be related to common discourses about China in the period. Hatchett's source 'The Orphan of Zhao' concerns a mother who saves her infant son from murder by a corrupt minister until he can come of age and avenge his father to take up his rightful inheritance. Pope's is of course a fantasy of illegitimacy, in which Dulness invents a bastard maternal line of hack writers and book-trade grubs to further her empire, in a radical parodic inversion of classical values and textual order (a process that David Porter identifies as common in Augustan classicist complaints about the dangers of 'chinoiserie'[33]). Dulness emerges through the analogy with Chinese 'dulness' as a sterile circulator of inverted and perverted fictions of the 'true' and classical alternative; the oriental empire is an inverted 'figure' of the classical one it supersedes.

As early as 1728, the popular novelist Eliza Haywood was deployed in the *Dunciad* as a figure of illegitimate maternity, a shadow of the Empress Dulness herself. Haywood is the only female author whose works appear in the engraving to the 1729 *Dunciad Variorum*; the book-laden ass carries seven volumes, and two of the spines read 'Court of Caramin' and 'Haywoods Nov.'. In book 2 of the 1728 *Dunciad* Haywood is described with her two illegitimate children (a footnote implies these are two scandal chronicles, the *Secret History*

---

[32] Thus, Louis Le Comte, Jesuit missionary, complains in his *A Compleat History of the Empire of China* (1739, first published in 1697) that: 'This abundance of Letter is in my opinion the source of the *Chineses* ignorance, because they imploy all their days in this study, and have not leisure so much as to think of other Sciences, phansying themselves learned enough if they can but read' (187, Letter 6).

[33] Porter summarizes attitudes to Chinese taste on the part of classicist critics of the period as 'an emasculating feminine libido that strips art of its classical patrimony' (*Ideographia*, 184).

of the ... Court of Caramania of 1726 and *Memoirs of ... Utopia* of 1724–5)[34] clinging to her waist as the prize in a pissing competition between William Chetwood (replaced by Chapman in 1729 and by Thomas Osborne in 1741–2) and Edmund Curll, the booksellers. Curll wins and carries her off in triumph while his defeated opponent is rewarded with a 'China Jordan' (or chamber-pot) which he dons as a crown (ll. 149–82). The female body is thus part of the same circuit of exchange as the porcelain chamber-pot; we might go so far as to say that both are fabricated from a 'Chinese' source. The equation of women with china/porcelain was a familiar one by the time the *Dunciad* was written; perhaps the best-known examples are the scene in William Wycherley's *The Country Wife* (1675) when Horner and Lady Fidget copulate under the guise of viewing his collection of china; and John Gay's satirical 1725 poem 'To a Lady on her Passion for Old China'.

However, by the 1740 editions of the *Dunciad*, the image of the woman as equivalent to a piece of China—white, rounded, and losing value with every crack or flaw—gained a new resonance in association with the embodiment of female duncery in Pope's poem, Haywood. She appears to have been responding parodically to her representation in the earlier versions of Pope's poem with the 1736 publication of her own 'Chinese' fiction, *The Adventures of Eovaai*.[35] Haywood's novel concerns the near-seduction of the princess and later queen of an ancient pre-Adamitical country, Ijaveo, by the evil necromancer and minister of a neighbouring state, Ochihatou (a satirical version of

[34] See Christine Blouch, 'Eliza Haywood', in *Selected Works of Eliza Haywood I*, ed. Alexander Pettit, vol. i: *Miscellaneous Writings, 1725–43* (London: Pickering and Chatto, 2000), pp. xxi–lxxxii. Blouch suggests Richard Savage and William Hatchett as the poet and bookseller Edmund Curll identified in his *Compleat Key to the Dunciad* (1728) as the fathers of Haywood's two illegitimate children (p. xxxix). Pope's animosity towards Haywood may have been stirred by her attack on Henrietta Howard, his close friend and patron, in the *Court of Caramania*.

[35] Eliza Haywood, *The Adventures of Eovaai. A Pre-Adamitical History*, ed. Earla Wilputte (Peterborough, Ont.: Broadview Press, 1999). For a fuller discussion of this work and its relationship to Scriblerian satire, see my article, 'A Gender of Opposition: Eliza Haywood's Scandal Fiction', in Kirsten Saxton and Rebecca Bocchicchio (eds.), *The Passionate Fictions of Eliza Haywood: Essays on her Life and Work* (Lexington, Ky: University of Kentucky Press, 2000), 143–67. For a sophisticated reading of the hybridity of *Eovaai* see Srinivas Aravamudan, 'In the Wake of the Novel: The Oriental Tale as National Allegory', *Novel* 33 (1999): 5–31. Aravamudan asserts that 'Haywood playfully demonstrates that oriental anthropology and fiction are mutually constitutive even as they interrogate one another' (21).

Robert Walpole). In a parody of Pope's *Dunciad*, Haywood gives the story a complex history of translation and punctuates it throughout with learned footnotes. The tale's translator is a Chinese speaker, the 'son of a Mandarin' according to the subtitle of the 1736 edition; he resides in England and his text is a translation of a much larger work, the annals of the first ages written in a pre-Adamitical language, the language of nature. The larger text, we are told, was undertaken by seventy philosophers in the fifth century at the commission of a Chinese emperor but was cut short when the emperor died, with only three of the twenty-one histories completed. Such large-scale projects were a feature of the eighteenth-century Qing dynasty.[36] Footnotes enable the English translator to comment critically on the interpretative choices made by the Chinese Cabal and in particular on the arguments of a named commentator on the Cabal's translation, a scholar named Hahehihotu (a name possibly suggested by the 'Ho' in the name of the Chinese emperor cited by Pope and certainly implying the comic and parodic intention of the whole), who is exposed as a committed republican and misogynist (the two belief-systems are throughout conflated).

Through the use of this narrative frame and the allegorical nature of the story itself (in which Eovaai gradually acquires judgement and the virtues needed for constitutional government), Haywood successfully presents a proto-feminist challenge to the misogynist tendencies in the critique of arbitrary power, whether republican or monarchical. She also challenges the misogyny that underpins Pope's Scriblerian satire, the location of a destabilizing illegitimate cultural and political agency in the figure of female excess, exposing this as a creation of male fantasy which 'veils' the 'true' agents of cultural barbarism, male ministers, and artists.[37]

---

[36] Kangxi and his successor Yongzheng commissioned dictionaries, encyclopedias, and literary collections produced by armies of scholars, especially the 'Gujin tushu jicheng' ('Complete Collection of Illustrations and Writings from the Earliest to the Current Times') compiled by Chen Menglei. 800,000 pages of 100,000,000 Chinese characters appeared four years after Yongzheng's accession in 1723 after Chen Menglei had been banished as a traitor. Yongzheng published the work as his father's.

[37] See Elizabeth Kubek, 'The Key to Stowe: Toward a Patriot Whig Reading of Eliza Haywood's *Eovaai*', in Chris Mounsey (ed.), *Presenting Gender: Changing Sex in Eighteenth-Century England* (Lewisburg, Pa., and London: Bucknell University Press; Associated University Presses, 2001), 225–54.

Satirical reworkings of the 'Chinese' thread in Pope's satire did not necessarily entail this kind of proto-feminist challenge to misogyny, however, as the example of William Hatchett, Haywood's lover from the late 1720s until her death in 1756, demonstrates. In 1740, Hatchett produced a short semi-pornographic poem, called *A Chinese Tale*, subtitled 'Written originally by that Prior of China, the facetious Sou ma Quang, a celebrated Madarine of Letters; under the title of Chamyam Tcho Chang, or Chamyam with her Leg upon a Table. First translated by a famous Missionary; and now re-translated by a SOCIETY OF LINGUISTS. Inscribed to Thomas Dawson Esq; Cornet in Lieutenant-General Honeywood's Dragoons.' It is tempting to speculate that 'Honeywood' may be a small reverence to the author's mistress, Haywood, whose work *Eovaai* shares the conceit of translation by a society of Chinese linguists. If so, it was hardly a compliment, given that the poem returns to the traditional representation of an equivalence between the frailty of women and the fragility of china. It conformed, too, to the satirical convention of casting a transparent 'oriental' veil over western social and sexual behaviour, to suggest the secret sexual vices of women behind a surface of propriety. The work was advertised with a 'curious Frontispiece, taken from a large China Punch-Bowl, just come over, in that Gentleman's [i.e. Dawson's] Possession; Design'd and Engrav'd by Mess. Gravelot and Scotin' which could be purchased separately at a cost of one shilling (see Fig. 9). Cham-yam's besetting sin is her curiosity, a vice she shares with Eovaai, who loses a magic jewel left to her by her father (which protects her and her country from malign spirits) when she takes it out of its gold casing to investigate some mystic characters engraved on its inside and it is snatched away by a bird. Cham-yam's curiosity is of a more overtly sexual nature. A maid allows a love-lorn mandarin to conceal himself in a large jar in Cham-yam's magnificently decorated boudoir, which is filled with scenes of erotic pleasure sewn on tapestries and painted on cabinets. Cham-yam, fired by these images, lifts her leg to view her genitals in a mirror, curious to see why these treasures hold such delights for men. Inflamed with lust, the mandarin leaps from his jar and promptly deflowers her. Hatchett announces early in the poem that he has turned a series of 'Chinese' allusions into English ones to

9. Frontispiece, William Hatchett, *A Chinese Tale* (1740).

clarify (if clarity were needed) the meaning of the poem and he makes explicit reference to Pope as his model:

> A Latitude we take indeed;
> But only where the Sense has need.
> The Chinese Idiom we express,
> The rather in an English Dress:
> We clear up where we find the Text
> Is dark, and any way perplex'd:
> For what is barren, dull, and dry,
> With our Invention we supply;

225

Which is no more than what we hope
We've good Example for—viz. Pope.

Despite the reference to the 'dull', the poem owes as much to Pope's
Rape of the Lock, another poem in which the equation of women and
Chinese porcelain is deployed,[38] as it does to the *Dunciad*.

Daniel Defoe also uses porcelain to mock China as an empire of
dulness. Crusoe goes to visit a house claimed to be made of porcelain
and discovers that it is in fact constructed of lath and porcelain plaster
leading him to conclude that stories of amazing artistry in the medium
are entirely fictional. David Porter remarks that the 'porcelain' house
illustrates that 'For Crusoe, the essential vacuity of Chinese civilization runs so deep that there remains no possibility of solid ground'.[39]

Hatchett and Haywood appear to have been involved in a
concerted project to satirize English state 'dullness' through the
vehicle of oriental narrative in the troubled years of the late 1730s
and early 1740s. They collaborated on a translation of Crébillon
fils' *Le Sopha* in 1742, the same year as the novel first appeared
in France.[40] The novel must have seemed peculiarly suited to
their satirical (possibly Patriot) animus against George II and Robert
Walpole in that the frame features an exceptionally dull sultan, Schah-
Baham (grandson of the great Schahriar), obsessed with his domestic
affairs and conversant only with the tales of Scheherazade, who promotes an ambitious vizier on the sole grounds that he is 'the ablest
Pinker in the Kingdom' (p. vi).[41] The fact that the two-volume
translation of Du Halde's *Description of China* from Edward Cave's
publishing house (1738, 1741) was dedicated to Frederick, prince of
Wales—the focus of Patriot loyalty until his death in 1751—suggests

---

[38] Porter notes that the climax of the *Rape of the Lock* turns on a piece of porcelain (the
China vessels fallen from on high parallel Belinda's 'fall') and there are three appearances
of a China jar in the poem (*Ideographia*, 184–5).

[39] Porter, 'A Peculiar but Uninteresting Nation', 196.

[40] The William Andrews Clark Memorial Library holds a slip of paper which is an
invoice to the publisher T. Cooper, in Eliza Haywood's hand for two shillings received for
the translation. *The Sopha: a Moral Tale. Translated from the French original of Monsieur
Crebillon* (London, 1742). Claude-Prosper Jolyot de Crébillon was exiled from Paris for
three months after the novel, *Le Sopha: Conte Morale* (A. Gaznah (false imprint, probably
Paris), 1742) appeared.

[41] Pinking involves ornamenting cloth or leather through cutting out eyelet holes or
figures.

that the comparison between the Hanoverian court and the Chinese court (whether as twin centres of dullness, or contrasting states of dynastic longevity and order, versus contestatory relations between king and heir and misrule) was a familiar one.

Political and aesthetic uses of 'China' overlap in eighteenth-century English writing; country and product can serve as a source for allegory with the West precisely because of its character of patent fictionality as a world known largely through its manufactures, already tailored for a western market (the china vase is engraved by, presumably, French producers). Hatchett's text mimics a china bowl, a round white surface on to which the male satirist can project figures, the hybrid production of an imaginary encounter between western and eastern cultures, which turns the dull reproductive mechanics of an ancient culture into a wild accumulation of fantastic signs for the western reader. The 'empire of dulness' is transfigured into a place of imaginative richness by the western writer, who trades in the common materials of China to his imaginative 'credit' far more successfully than his merchant equivalents in the East India Company seeking financial gain through import and export.[42] This kind of figurative narrative transmigration becomes a common ploy in western fictions that take China as their setting and focus more explicitly on the idea of metempsychosis or transmigration.

Narrative transmigrations

The popularity in China of the Buddhist belief in transmigration was a source of almost equal fascination and contempt in eighteenth-century western Europe. Transmigration provides not only a narrative content but also a structure for two collections of tales with a Chinese setting

[42] On the advanced nature of Chinese manufacture, its widespread influence in the development of English industrial techniques, and the control of trade by the Chinese in the period, see Maxine Berg, 'Manufacturing the Orient: Asian Commodities and European Industry 1500–1800', in Simonetta Cavaciocchi (ed.), *Prodotti e Techniche d'Oltremare nelle Economie Europee secc. XIII–XVIII* (Prato: Istituto internazionale di storia economica F. Datini, 1998), 385–419.

'translated' into English from French at either end of the eighteenth century: Thomas Simon Gueullette's *Chinese Tales; or, the Wonderful Adventures of the Mandarin Fum-Hoam* was published in 1725 with an 'Introduction on the Doctrine of Transmigration' by Joseph Addison and *The Bonze, or Chinese anchorite, an Oriental Epic Novel*, ostensibly by a Tartar proselite named Hoamchi-Vam and translated by one Monsieur D'Alenzon, appeared in 1769 (the names of both author and translator appear to be pseudonyms). Both collections take the shape of a sequence of stories delivered by a main protagonist detailing a succession of rebirths.

Addison's essay rehearses eighteenth-century western under-standing of the origin and dissemination of transmigration theory. Pythagoras, he claims, learned the theory from Indian brahmans when he travelled to Egypt and brought it back to Italy. Addison cites the Jesuit Louis Le Comte and the jewel-trader Jean-Baptiste Tavernier as his sources for two different accounts of the historical founder of transmigration theory. Le Comte discusses the sect of Foe, a king's son born out of his mother's side who died one thousand years before Christ, and is believed by his priests (bonzes) to have transmigrated into an ape, elephant, and dragon successively so that these animals have become objects of worship for them. Tavernier derives trans-migration theory from Tonquin on the border of China, through a doctrine of Chacabout ('one of the greatest Imposters that ever was in *Asia*' (p. xiv), Addison tells us). Chacabout set ten commandments that correspond to ten distinct places of endless joy and torment after the first life in proportion to its merits: those who failed in the laws wander three thousand years in different bodies before they are happy.

Foe and Chacabout are both names derived from early encounters with histories of the life of Gautama Buddha on the part of western travellers. While 'Fo' is an early term used to refer to Gautama Buddha (along with Menipe) by Jesuit missionaries in China, the name Chacabout seems to be a variant of the Sakyamuni Burkhan described by Marco Polo as a young ascetic prince of Ceylon who experienced many reincarnations on renouncing the world.[43]

[43] See Allen, *The Buddha and the Sahibs*, 29, 33.

Transmigration doctrines were, by comparison with the moral atheism of Confucianism or the monotheism of Islam, inassimilable to western Christian thinkers, Catholic and Protestant alike, and we find no one willing to countenance their possibility.[44] However, transmigration interacted in surprising and inventive ways with the traditional structure of the oriental tale; the sequence of stories connected by a single frame was a fitting structure for the narration of the history of a single soul reincarnated in many different bodies. It also interacted with the idea of imaginative identification with the 'other' which became fundamental to eighteenth-century understandings of the role of fiction and the mediation of the Orient through fiction.

The French author of the *Chinese Tales*, Thomas-Simon Gueullette (1683–1766), was a copious and unremarkable imitator of Antoine Galland and François Pétis de la Croix. His *Mogul Tales* (discussed in Chapter 5, 'Dreams of Men Awake') and *Tartarian Tales* were also translated into English in 1736 and 1759 respectively. Martha Pike Conant dismisses his work as follows:

Extravagant in the use of magic, fantastic in its description and incident, employing European legends freely and oriental colouring very slightly, sometimes moralizing, sometimes coarse, seldom satirical, imitating the faults rather than the excellences of genuine oriental translations, these narratives are frequently entertaining, but possess little intrinsic value.[45]

Like all collections of oriental tales, the *Chinese Tales* has a frame which unifies the tales told. In this case, the mandarin Fum-Hoam gives an account of his many incarnations to the princess of Georgia, Gulchenraz,[46] who has recently married the emperor of China, Tongluk; his task is to persuade her that 'our Soul is like a Cameleon, which according to the different Bodies through which it passes, takes those different Impressions, and is subject to all the Passions of the

---

[44] See Donald F. Lach and Edwin J. Van Kley, bk. 4, *East Asia*: 'While the Jesuits tried to minimize the religious and superstitious practices of the Confucians, they, in contrast sought to maximize the image of the Buddhists as benighted idolators' (1654).

[45] Conant, *The Oriental Tale in England*, 37.

[46] Her name, like that of Gulchenrouz in William Beckford's 1786 novel *Vathek*, derives from the 'Gulshan Raz', or 'Mystic Rose Garden', composed in AD 1317 in answer to fifteen questions on the doctrines of the Sufis propounded by Amir Syan Hosaine. Sufism is the philosophical incorporation of mystical theosophy from Plato and Christianity into Muslim thought after the death of Muhammad.

Body it informs' (i. 42). Gulchenraz is a Muslim, a believer in only one God, and her new husband—who courted her in the disguise of a commoner and used Fum-Hoam's magic powers to assist her in restoring her deposed father to the throne in Georgia—has promised that China and Georgia will soon worship the same divinity, his Buddhist gods or her Allah, depending on whether the mandarin persuades her of the truth of transmigration. However, when Fum-Hoam has completed his tales, Gulchenraz asserts: 'far from per-suading me that your Religion is better than mine, they have only more and more confirmed me in the Law of *Mahomet*' (ii. 225).

Fum-Hoam's incarnations have huge geographical and physical variety: he commences as the child of a shepherd who rises to favour in Persia but is excessively cruel and luxurious; as a punishment his next short-lived incarnation is that of a flea on the body of his former favourite mistress. Later incarnations include: a dog in India who falls victim to rabies; an Indian bride who commits suttee; a young Imam; a cast-off Persian prince, the product of father–daughter incest, who narrowly avoids marriage to his own mother; a pet monkey at the Chinese court at Peking; a midwife of Astracan; and a wild man of Canada. If Gulchenraz is not persuaded by their authenticity, she is charmed by the tales' morality: 'the Morality they contain infinitely pleases me, and you cannot oblige me more than continuing of them' (i. 223). Like other auditors of oriental tales she becomes an addict, seeking the stories' continuation and frustrated by their interruption at a suitable cliffhanger each evening. Like Gueullette's other 'frames' and like Tongluk's courtship of Gulchenraz, Fum-Hoam's history is revealed to be a deceptive fiction. At the close of the novel, Fum-Hoam reveals that he is in fact Gulchenraz's long-lost brother, Alroamat, abducted at the age of 2 by 'rovers' from his father's palace in Georgia; he has been telling his tales to disprove rather than affirm the doctrine of transmigration. Tongluk obligingly announces that China will henceforth be a Muslim empire.

In 1769, the trope of the history of transmigration in a single 'Chinese' figure was reincarnated in an even more bizarre and over-written work. This overblown monster of verbal chinoiserie announces itself as a translation which 'follow[s] the eastern taste, very fond of elevated language, yet not correct in its elegance: and

10. Frontispiece, Hoamchi-Vam, *The Bonze, or Chinese Anchorite*, translated by Monsieur D'Alenzon, vol. i (1769).

indeed the nice eye of judgement, is seldom pleased in a review of ornaments'.[47] The 'ornamental style' is equated with those Chinese ornaments displayed on an English consumer's mantelpiece (see Fig. 10). And the frame imitates this idea. Two Englishmen in China, Captain Wilford and Mr Theodore Johnson 'after they had secured the rich purchase of tea, china and silk' (i. 3) turn to discussing the surprising belief of the ancient Chinese in transmigration with which Johnson, it appears, has some sympathy. Johnson leads Wilford to an

[47] Hoamchi-Vam, *The Bonze, or Chinese Anchorite* (London, 1769), 2 vols., i, pp. ii–iii.

encounter with a eunuch hermit named Confuciango, resident of the vale of Hoangti and convert to, amazingly enough, Anglicanism. Confuciango tells them the tragic story of his experiences at the fall of the Ming dynasty and the latter is paralleled with accounts of the two biblical falls, that of Lucifer and the rebel angels and that of Adam and Eve. The Chinese emperor enlists the help of the Tartars in his resistance to a rebellion led by the wicked follower of Fo, Li (a version of the rebel leader, Li Zicheng who occupied Peking in 1644 resulting in the Emperor Chongzheng's suicide by hanging). Confuciango's sister, Philasanga, who is the beloved wife of Prince Zangola, is killed by Li and after the savage murder of Li in revenge, and the seizure of China by Tartar powers, Confuciango and Zangola flee to travel through China dressed as bonzes (mendicant Buddhist priests) and sometimes Talopoins (Buddhist monks of Burma and Thailand). At one point, they join forces with Catholic missionaries (a sideswipe at Jesuit accommodationist policy with indigenous faiths) but are disgusted with Catholic heresies:

their offering up prayers to the Deity in an unknown language; their cruelly locking up the sacred laws they pretended to propagate; their silly wor-shipping pictures, and paying needless adoration to a wafer, while they made a fallible man infallible, were such bare-faced affronts to common-sense, that in giving up the priests, we were quitting their religion; but at length we were set to rights by a judicious Englishman, with whom we travelled and gained European learning. (i. 70)

If the French 'translator', d'Alenzon, is a genuine figure, he is clearly, like Voltaire, an Anglophile with an admiration for the reformed English Protestant Church. The Protestant translator of Du Halde's *Description* makes similar analogies between Chinese 'idolatrous' reli-gions and Catholic practices in a series of polemical footnotes to Du Halde's critical treatment of Taoism and Buddhism in the first volume.

His despair at the loss of his wife results in Zangola's eventual death and he then revisits Confuciango as an angelic presence and proceeds to tell him a variety of stories, some continuing the story of the fall, apocalypse, and final day of judgement, others detailing his own various reincarnations. Every narrative is designed to teach its recipient to distinguish on the ground of reason between good and evil and to choose the path of virtue, however difficult, because of the eventual reward when raised to the 'final destination' beyond the earthly body.

Zangola's reincarnations are, like Fum-Hoam's, geographically and physically varied: he is offered choices by the angel Abdiel for his reincarnations in human form but consistently chooses pleasure and luxury only to experience pain and remorse. He takes the shape of an eastern monarch who is tyrannously ambitious; a negro prince punished for haughtiness; and a model of connubial felicity as a European wife unhappily imprisoned in a Turkish seraglio. Between these mortal manifestations he experiences brief and unhappy incarnations as insects and animals which mirror or correct the sins he has indulged in human life, inhabiting a mite, a game-cock, a leopard, a turkey, and a turtle-dove. Zangola finally departs to go to his intermediate state living on Venus, the World of Love, where he has rediscovered the soul of Philasanga and which appears to be a utopian version of China as described by the Jesuit missionaries: that is, an absolute state in which the whole empire is one family governed by one king or father made up of twelve provinces, and driven by principles of eternal friendship and the pursuit of learning. Description of the language of Venus implies a reconnection with China, whose characters were a source of endless fascination for western commentators: 'we write and print for our recreation, when it suits fancy, in a manner that bears analogy to hieroglyphics, and short hand, by which with a glance of the eye, we take in and comprehend a paragraph' (ii. 275–6).

If it is theologically incoherent, the jumble of Christian, Buddhist, and Confucian theory in *The Bonze* acquires better sense if understood through the perspective of an argument for the power of narrative to produce interconnection, indeed transmigration, between Occident and Orient. The English auditors of this succession of oriental tales interspersed with dramatized images from Christian myth come to view China as a site or sight of at least fictional fusion of East and West. English readers are repeatedly reminded that this is an elaborate piece of artifice but are also encouraged to take pleasure in their imaginative immersion in a utopian space where racial, cultural, and sexual 'otherness' dissolves.

Hybridity is transformed from the ponderous to the playful in a far more satisfying and entertaining piece of fiction by Horace Walpole, who is known to have owned a copy of *The Bonze*.[48] A collection of six *Hieroglyphic Tales* written between 1766 and 1772 to entertain his friends just after the author's retirement from politics—all fanciful, comical, and sometimes grotesque reworkings of the conventions of the oriental and fairy tale—includes one entitled 'Mi Li. A Chinese Fairy Tale'. Mi Li, prince of China, is told by his oracle godmother, the fairy Hih, that he will be unhappy unless he marries a princess whose name is the same as her father's dominions.[49] In a comic play on the idea of the Chinese whisper, Mi Li's reporting of the oracle to his deaf and dumb tutor using sign language results in a confusion whereby Mi Li is thought to be searching for a woman who has the same name as that of her father. An Irish sailor at Canton promises to introduce the prince to Mr Bob Oliver of Sligo who has a daughter he has named Bob Oliver, but when they arrive in Dublin they hear she is already married. Mi Li is advised to consult a scholar named Mr Banks in Oxford, but his post-chaise breaks down on the Henley road. A beggar directs him to the Conway estate for assistance and there Mi Li meets a gardener who leads him through the garden to find its master. On the way through the estate, pursued by a crowd of small spaniels into a subterranean vault, through artificial ruins, over a mock bridge and ornamented by Chinese pheasants, the various apparently impossible predictions that Mi Li has received in a dream are fulfilled:

that he would find his destined spouse, whose father had lost the dominions which never had been his dominions, in a place where there was a bridge over no water, a tomb where nobody ever was buried nor ever would be buried, ruins that were more than they had ever been, a subterraneous passage in which there were dogs with eyes of rubies and emeralds, and a more beautiful menagerie of Chinese pheasants than any in his father's extensive gardens.[50]

[48] See the note of May 1962 by William Rees Mogg on the flyleaf of the British Library copy (Cup.403y.18).

[49] Jokes are traditionally destroyed when explained, but it is probably worth noting that if read out, the 'Chinese' names here could be made to sound like 'My lie' and 'he' (as in 'he-he').

[50] Horace Walpole, *Hieroglyphic Tales*, Augustan Reprint Society 212–13 (Los Angeles: William Andrews Clark Memorial Library, 1982), 38.

Finally, Mi Li, whom the stolid English gardener begins to suspect of lunacy because of his dancing and cries of incomprehensible excitement, encounters Lord and Lady Aylesbury and Miss Caroline Campbell, daughter of Lord William Campbell, his majesty's late governor of Carolina 'and so she became Princess of China' (43).

In this story, Walpole mocks the excesses of chinoiserie at the same time as he points to the fascinating charm of its inauthenticity. Mi Li does not recognize the mock Chineseness of the garden as bearing any relation to his own culture. In a strange reversal, it is the English who have cryptic or hieroglyphic names not the Chinese. The question of establishing authenticity is however quite beyond the point. At its opening, we are reminded that the oracle godmother Hih speaks 'with intention to perplex, not to inform' (32). The tales themselves are an exercise in hybridity; Kenneth W. Gross comments that at their best they 'distil from the Bible, the Arabian Nights, Shakespeare, French romances, English politics and anti-quarian lore a comic fantasy of an urbane, hard-edged strangeness' (Introduction, p. iii). The Chinese fairy tale also points to the often under-acknowledged attractions of an imagined China as a source of fantasy, play, and topsy-turveydom. In narrative fiction of the eighteenth century, as in no other writings of the period about China, free rein was given to this kind of vision, closer perhaps to the experiments in architectural and ceramic chinoiserie of the period.[51] As Jonathan Spence so succinctly puts it in concluding his brief discussion of Walpole's tale: 'the reality of transcultural dissonance was shrouded, for a playful moment or two, in the softer light of romantic oneness.'[52]

'Chinoiserie' in fiction may have developed in England by exploiting enthusiasm for the style in architecture and ornament, but the country came late to an encounter with translated works of genuine fiction from China, perhaps because of the difficulty of mastering the

---

[51] See Porter, 'Monstrous Beauty'. For general introductions to chinoiserie, see Hugh Honour, *Chinoiserie: The Vision of Cathay* (New York: Dutton, 1962); and Dawn Jacobson, *Chinoiserie* (London: Phaidon Press, 1993). On Walpole's shift from enthusiasm to critique of chinoiserie, see David Porter, 'From Chinese to Goth: Walpole and the Gothic Repudiation of Chinoiserie', *Eighteenth-Century Life* 23 (1999): 46–58.

[52] Spence, *The Chan's Great Continent*, 80.

Chinese language.[53] Surprisingly the most famous and classic novel of eighteenth-century China, Cao Xuequin's *Story of the Stone* or *Dream of the Red Chamber*, did not make its way into English translation until the late nineteenth century.[54] The only Chinese fiction to be translated into English in the eighteenth century appeared in 1761 in four volumes with the title *Hau Kiou Choaan or The Pleasing History* and was very far removed indeed from the fanciful, magical transmigratory worlds of European pseudo-Chinese narrative.[55]

The translation was executed in 1719 by James Wilkinson, an English East India Company man based in Canton, as an exercise in learning Chinese under instruction from a Portuguese tutor (the long-established Portuguese trading base on Macao from the 1550s even before the Jesuit missions meant that it was Portuguese orthography that was relied upon for transliteration of Chinese terms and texts). Wilkinson's family passed on the manuscript, with some sections completed in Portuguese by the tutor, to Thomas Percy, the Anglican antiquary. Percy had to learn Portuguese to complete the translation and he carefully edited the text with extensive footnotes, using Du Halde and Le Comte particularly, as well as other accounts of China which he listed for his reader's reference.

[53] Appleton notes the lack of real scholarship in Chinese until the 19th c. Shen Fo Tsung, Father Couplet's protégé, visited England in the 1680s and taught the Orientalist Thomas Hyde some Chinese. The Bodleian library had a collection of Chinese books from English nobles and merchantmen but no one to read them. No great scholars of Chinese emerged in England until the 19th c. (*Cycle of Cathay*, 35). For a survey of China in English literature, see Chung Shu Chi'en, 'China in the English Literature of the Seventeenth Century', *Quarterly Bulletin of Chinese Bibliography*, NS 1 (1940): 351–84, and 'China in the English Literature of the Eighteenth Century', *Quarterly Bulletin of Chinese Bibliography* NS 2 (1941), no. 1: 7–48 and no. 2: 41–2.

[54] Cao Xueqin, *Hung lou meng*, trans. Henry Bencraft Joly, 2 vols. (Hong Kong, 1892, 1893).

[55] A manuscript letter glued into the front cover of the Bodleian copy of the first volume of Thomas Percy's 2-vol. *Miscellaneous Pieces Relating to the Chinese* (London, 1762) from George Thomas Staunton to the earl of Macartney from Devonshire Street on December 11th (?) 1802 proves the authenticity of the *Pleasing History*. Staunton describes finding a copy of the novel in a booksellers even though the title prefixed by the English translator was insufficient 'because it is nearly impossible to give a just and precise Idea of the sounds of Chinese characters by the letters of any European Alphabet'. He encloses a copy of the title-page of the Chinese book and says that he has not compared the whole, but a look at the first volume has confirmed that the translation catches 'as much of the spirit and manner of the original' as any European translation could. In the Chinese text the chapters are prefixed by verses but these would be hard to translate, he adds.

Percy's introduction insists on the scholarly nature of the task and the morality of the text. He provides a back-handed compliment in making an explicit contrast with more fanciful versions of the East:

That there is a littleness and poverty of genius in almost all the works of taste of the Chinese, must be acknowledged by capable judges. This at least is evident in their writings; and in a narrative like the following, would make a writer creep along through a minute relation of trifling particulars, without daring to omit the most inconsiderable. The abjectness of their genius may easily be accounted for from that servile submission, and dread of novelty, which enslaves the minds of the Chinese, and while it promotes the peace and quiet of their empire, dulls their spirit and cramps their imagination.

It ought, however, be observed in favour of the Chinese, that if they do not take such bold and daring flights as some of the other Eastern nations, neither do they run into such extravagant absurdities. Whether this be owing to the cause now assigned, or to their having bestowed more attention on literature, so it is that they pay a greater regard to truth and nature in their fictitious narratives, than any other of the Asiatics. For it must be allowed to our present work, that the conduct of the story is more regular and artful than is generally seen in the compositions of the East; hath less of the marvellous and more of the probable. It contains an unity of design or fable, and the incidents all tend to one end, in a regular natural manner, with little interruption or incoherence.[56]

Percy published the novel bound in with a summary of the plot of a Chinese play (a kind of tragicomedy about a poor young man's collaboration with a series of oppressed women to resist the corrupt authority of mandarins), a collection of Chinese proverbs (mainly from Confucius and extracted largely from Du Halde), and fragments of Chinese poetry with a dissertation on its nature. The whole was clearly an attempt to provide a scholarly introduction to Chinese literary achievement as well as '*a faithful picture of Chinese manners*' (p. xv).

Percy may have thought the novel would appeal to English readers because of its similarity to popular novels of domestic courtship and embattled virginity such as Samuel Richardson's *Pamela* (1740) and *Clarissa* (1747–8). Delivered in the third person, the novel primarily concerns the fastidious but passionate love between a clever young

---

[56] Thomas Percy, *Hau Kiou Choaan: or, the Pleasing History* (London, 1761), i, pp. xii–xiv.

son of an influential Peking mandarin, Tieh-chung-u, and the wise daughter of a disgraced military commander of Tsee-nan, Shuey-ping-sin. The latter is left unprotected when her father is exiled to Tartary and her devious uncle tries to marry her off to the son of a mandarin of the privy council, one Kwo-khé-tzu. Shuey-ping-sin repeatedly avoids the marriage even though city officials conspire with Kwo-khé-tzu to trick her into compliance. She, like Pamela, is praised as a miracle of cunning. When Tieh-chung-u and Shuey-ping-sin meet, the former saves her from abduction. She returns the favour when she uncovers a plot led by Kwo-khé-tzu, aided by the corrupt bonzes who provide housing for travellers, to poison Tieh-chung-u through his tea; she engineers his removal to her own house where he is nursed back to health. However, this brief cohabitation becomes the impediment to plans later in the novel for them to marry, in that the fastidious lovers consider it may imply an illicit relation prior to marriage. Eventually, all is resolved, Shuey-ping-sin's father is restored to favour through the good offices of Tieh-chung-u and the emperor himself gives his blessing to their union, punishing the conspirators against them.

Percy's editorship of *Hau Kiou Choaan* illustrates the double, and contradictory, reception of Chinese products in English culture, providing a source both for identification and estrangement. This tension is especially evident in the lengthy footnotes which attempt to direct an English reader's interpretation of his hero and heroine. Shuey-ping-sin bears close resemblance to female figures familiar from both oriental and fairy tales. Like Galland's Scheherazade, Marie Jeanne L'Heritier de Villandon's 'Princesse Adroite', or even Samuel Richardson's Clarissa, she is the indulged daughter of an intelligent and powerful man: 'the darling of her father, who loved her with an affection, equal to that he would have had for a son of the same accomplishments, and gave her the entire management of his house: where she governed the family with . . . admirable skill' (i. 70-1).[57]

---

[57] Finessa 'danced, sang and played music to perfection. She would finish, with quite wonderful skill, all the finicky little tasks of the hand which are reputed to divert those of her sex; and when she spoke, it was with the measured caution of a chess-player making a move. She oversaw the king's household; and, once and for all, by care and vigilance, put an end to the petty pilferings of the lower officers' ('The Subtle Princess', trans. Gilbert

However, Percy fears that her cleverness may be misunderstood by English readers as artifice, and in this respect she runs the risk of appearing to fall short of the ideal of an artless female virtue, a risk Richardson's Pamela also runs. A footnote explains that

The Chinese, who are the most subtle crafty people in the world, may naturally be supposed to esteem and admire subtilty and craft. The reader must have observed that these qualities are predominant in the character of *Shuey-ping-sin*; who is yet set forth by the Chinese author, as a perfect exemplar of all virtue. The Chinese morals, notwithstanding their boasted purity, evidently fall short of the Christian, since they know not how to inspire that open and ingenuous simplicity, void of all guile, which more elevated principles of morality propose to our esteem and imitation. (i. 129)

So too, the hero's lack of gallantry might seem problematic to an audience raised on French romances and sentimental fiction. When Tieh-chung-u bluntly refuses to listen to the proposal of Shuey-ping-sin's uncle that he marry her, Percy is driven to explain in a footnote that, since:

in this, and some of the following pages, the Hero of the piece cannot but suffer in the opinion of every fair Reader, for his seeming Indelicacy and want of Gallantry: it may be proper to remark that his expressions do not possibly sound so harsh in the original as they do here: at least it appears that the lady is not offended at them. But after all it is impossible there should be any such thing as Gallantry among a people, who admit of no intercourse between the two Sexes; whose Marriages are contracted without the consent of the Parties, and even without their personal knowledge of each other: and who by being allowed a plurality of Women lessen their attention to any one. (ii. 127–8)

He concludes with an 'N.B. The Reader is desired to bear the above Remarks constantly in mind throughout this and some of the following Chapters' (129).

To be a 'pleasing history', then, Percy's translation must carefully balance the familiar and the strange. He encourages his readers to identify with the position of the hero and heroine, especially the

Adair and ed. Marina Warner, *Wonder Tales: Six Stories of Enchantment* (London: Vintage, 1996), 67–8). 'L'Adroite Princesse, ou, Les Aventures de Finette' was first published in *Œuvres meslées* (Paris, 1695).

heroine, so that the novel becomes a Chinese variant on the mid-eighteenth-century domestic fiction, but also uses the footnotes to remind readers of a different set of cultural values. Like other oriental tales, this narrative must serve the dual function of providing narrative pleasure and claiming an authority to rival the accounts of travellers and historians as a window on an 'other' culture. Percy's stress throughout is on the possibility of fiction mediating a more 'true' account of a culture than eyewitness accounts such as those of the Jesuits. His preface criticizes collections of voyages and travels, universal histories, and accounts of the present states of other countries, complaining that

Those writers may give a dead resemblance, while they are careful to trace out every feature, but the life, the spirit, the expression will be apt to escape them. To gain a true notion of those we must see the object in action. There is not a greater difference between the man who is sitting for his portrait, stiffened into a studied composure, with every feature and limb under constraint; and the same person unreserved, acting in his common sphere of life, with every passion in play, and every part of him in motion: than there is between a people methodically described in a formal account, and painted out in the lively narrative of some domestic history. A foreigner will form a truer notion of the genius and spirit of the *English*, from one page of *Fielding*, and one or two writers now alive, than from whole volumes of *Present States of England*, or *French Letters concerning the English Nation*. (pp. xvi–xvii)

Not only does Percy's comment remind us of the special power ascribed to fiction to produce hybridity and identification across cultures in its readers, but the metaphor he uses of the painting of a portrait by contrast with that of a scene or narrative returns us to that insistent slippage between China, the country, and china, the porcelain commodity so craved by consumers. Europe had little contact with Chinese high art such as calligraphy and painting in this period; the Chinese exported porcelain, lacquerware, furniture, and wallpaper (crafts of fairly low status), in abundance however. After 1709 when Johan Friedrich Böttger discovered how porcelain was made, high-temperature kilns were built at Meissen and elsewhere and vast amounts of blue and white porcelain in imitation of the Chinese were produced. 'Chinese' porcelain traditionally carried painting of delicate and platonic romance, similar to that of the hero and heroine in this tale, framed with the familiar pagodas, little bridges, and drooping willows. The fineness of the lovers' feelings in the novel is like the fineness of the paint strokes of willow-pattern, and an image of China is delivered through perceiving 'the object in action' rather than the formal state portraits provided by Jesuit accounts of the Peking court.[58] Percy's achievement can be paralleled with that of the Delft producers of blue and white China; a simulacrum of Chineseness which retains a balance of strangeness and familiarity, exoticism and domestic morality.

The frontispiece to the first volume suggests this balance, a line drawing of a wedding procession which resembles the scenes in action found on porcelain plates and vases (Fig. 11). Readers of the novel will discover, however, that the villain Kwo-khé-tzu has seized Shuey-ping-sin's sedan chair in procession to offer sacrifices at the tomb of her dead mother, but when he breaks the chair open he discovers only a red bundle of cloth filled with pebble-stones (vol. i, chapters 8 and 9). The familiar is uncovered as the strange; Chinese 'ancestor-worship', such as Shuey-ping-sin's annual pilgrimage to her mother's tomb, was a source of huge controversy in the late seventeenth and early eighteenth centuries in France, when the Jesuits were criticized for passing off idolatrous rituals as civil ceremony.[59] A fiction which seems to follow the traditional lines of the sentimental narrative of embattled virtue begins to unravel. The lines of the drawing, like the lines of the novel, indicate a hidden 'strangeness' at the heart of the novel.

The representation of China's ability to promote estrangement rather than identification came to dominate its fictional appearances in the late eighteenth century. Percy illustrates his point in his preface about fiction's particular effectiveness in conveying the spirit of a culture by making an analogy with texts which might mediate English culture to a foreign observer. The example connects Percy's work with the now best-known experiment in just such an estrangement almost exactly contemporary with the publication of *Hau Kou*

---

[58] See Lotgar Ledderose, 'Chinese Influence on European Art, Sixteenth to Eighteenth Centuries', in Thomas H. C. Lee (ed.), *China and Europe: Images and Influences in Sixteenth to Eighteenth Centuries* (Hong Kong: Chinese University Press, 1991), 221–50.
[59] See Porter, *Ideographia*, 109–22.

11. Frontispiece, Thomas Percy, *Hau Kiou Choaan. A Chinese History*, vol. i (1761).

Choaan, Oliver Goldsmith's fictional letters from a Chinese philosopher in London to correspondents in Peking.

Chinese letters of reason

Far better known than the *Hieroglyphic Tales*, which enjoyed only a vanity print run from Walpole's Strawberry Hill Press of seven copies including proofs, was Walpole's massively successful *A Letter from Xo Ho, A* Chinese *Philosopher at London, to his Friend Lien Chi at Peking* (1757), a sixpenny pamphlet which went through five editions in the year of its publication. Walpole uses the letter to satirize the factionalism of eighteenth-century English politics which, according to Xo Ho's account, led to the court-martial and execution of Admiral Byng to assuage public wrath over the loss of Minorca in the Seven Years War. Xo Ho considers the Confucian rationalism of China far superior to the unreasoning pursuit of a scapegoat in England: 'Reason in *China* is not Reason in *England*' (n.p.), he concludes.

The Chinese informant was to prove a more amenable figure than the Turkish or Persian 'Mahometan' for the dissemination of a critique of European culture. The habitual representation of Muslim cultures as warlike, libidinous, and bigoted in their religious beliefs sat uneasily with the rationalist purposes of the genre of the oriental letter. Marana's Turkish spy had to be translated into a Cartesian devotee to appear as 'a Man void of Superstition and Bigotry' (vol. i, n.p.), but he is still susceptible to a belief in transmigration derived from the Pythagorean Islamic sect in which he was reared. Montesquieu's Usbek is educated and urbane but he is nevertheless a tyrant in his domestic arrangements and the novel closes with a rebellion in the seraglio and letters which overtly criticize him for failing to extend rational principles of government to his private household. The seventeenth- and eighteenth-century versions of Chinese culture were much better suited to shape the character of oriental epistolary informant.

The association of the Chinese with advanced powers of reason is usually made through the figure of Confucius.[60] D. E. Mungello points to the paradox that the *philosophes* who drew on the idea of Confucianism as a doctrine of moral and political reason were obliged to rely for their sources on the accounts of Jesuits who, in France especially, represented the old theologically driven order that

---

[60] See William Appleton, *Cycle of Cathay*, ch. 3, 'Confucius, the good governor'; and D. E. Mungello, 'Confucianism in the Enlightenment: Antagonism and Collaboration between the Jesuits and the Philosophes', in Thomas H. C. Lee (ed.), *China and Europe*, 99–127.

'enlightened' theory sought to correct. However, thinkers of the eighteenth century, whether sinophobic (like Montesquieu) or sinophilic (like Voltaire), seem to have accepted Jesuit accounts fairly unquestioningly and especially their bias towards the political and ethical virtues of Confucianism (rather than its metaphysics or cosmology). In order to present Catholicism as a viable mission in China, the Jesuits presented Confucianism as a secular moralism, a set of doctrines for social order, rather than a spiritual system. This may have made their accounts more appropriable for the atheistical, deistic, and rationalistic tendencies of Enlightenment thought. In 1691 *The Morals of Confucius, a Chinese Philosopher* was translated from the French 1688 *La Morale de Confucius, Philosophe de la Chine* (published in Amsterdam and itself based on the Jesuits' *Confucius Sinarum philosophus* (1686)). The second volume of Du Halde's *Description* contained an account of Confucius' life and teaching and summaries of the *Five Classics* and *Five Books*. Enlightenment thinkers such as Voltaire were particularly attracted by the image of the Chinese Confucian scholar-official elite and saw China as a meritocracy where educational achievement rather than birth was the ground for political advancement.

Sir William Temple (1628–99) in his essay 'Of Heroic Virtue' singles out Confucius:

The sume of his writings seem to be a body or digestion of ethics, that is, of all moral virtues, either personal, economical, civil or political; and framed for the institution and conduct of men's lives, their families, and their governments, but chiefly of the last: the bent of his thoughts and reasonings running up and down this scale, that no people can be happy but under good governments, and no governments happy but over good men; and that for the felicity of mankind, all men in a nation, from the Prince to the meanest peasant, should endeavour to be good, and wise, and virtuous, as far as his own thoughts, the precepts of others, or the laws of his country can instruct him.[61]

Confucius' special status is also apparent in Alexander Pope's *Temple of Fame* (written 1711 and published 1715), where he is singled out as a

---

[61] Sir William Temple, *Works* (London, 1814), iii. 313.

model of proto-western moralism in a paragraph on the dazzling and fanciful excesses of eastern spiritualism:

> The Eastern Front was glorious to behold,
> With Diamond flaming, and *Barbaric* Gold.
> There *Ninus* shone, who spread th'*Assyrian* Fame,
> And the Great Founder of the *Persian* Name:
> There in long Robes the Royal *Magi* stand.
> Grave *Zoroaster* waves the circling Wand:
> The Sage *Chaldaeans* rob'd in White appear'd,
> And *Brachmans* deep in desert Woods rever'd.
> These stop'd the Moon, and call'd th'unbody'd Shades
> To Midnight Banquets in the glimmering Glades;
> Made visionary Fabricks round them rise,
> And airy Spectres skim before their Eyes;
> Of *Talismans* and *Sigils* knew the Pow'r,
> And careful watch'd the Planetary Hour.
> Superior and alone, *Confucius* stood,
> Who taught that useful Science, to be *good*.[62]

The tendency to present Confucius as singular and proto-European (the Jesuits went so far as to see him as proto-Christian and claimed him as an early prophet of Christ) is evident in the engraving of him in Father Couplet's *Confucius Sinarum philosophus* of 1686, where he stands a model of benevolent western male maturity before a very European library in which his followers/archivists tend to his works (see Fig. 12)

The genre of fictional letters by Chinese travellers drew on this idea of the singular philosopher to present figures who are both intrigued by and tolerant of the cultures they encounter. Goldsmith's *Citizen of the World* relied on a French collection for much of its source material. Jean Baptiste de Boyer, Marquis d'Argens (1704–71), a soldier who moved to Holland to gain intellectual freedom, was the author of the *Lettres Juives, Chinoises et Cabalistiques* (1736, 1738). The *Jewish Letters* and *Chinese Letters* were published as separate volumes in England in translation, the latter in 1741. Argens and

---

[62] Alexander Pope, 'The Temple of Fame', *The Rape of the Lock and Other Poems*, ed. Geoffrey Tillotson, *The Twickenham Edition of the Poems of Alexander Pope* 3rd edn. reset (London: Methuen, 1962), ii, ll. 93–198, pp. 259–61.

12. Engraving, Filippo Couplet, *Confucius Sinarum philosophus* (1686), p. cxvij.

Goldsmith in turn influenced a six-volume collection called *L'Espion Chinois* of 1763 by Ange Goudar, a disciple of Montesquieu, which was translated into English in 1765.[63] All three collections have rational, sceptical primary correspondents who find themselves the only representatives of China in the European country they visit.

[63] See Francis L. Mars, *Ange Goudar, Cet Inconnu (1708–1791): Essai Bio-bibliographique sur un Aventurier Polygraphe du 18e Siècle*, Casanova Gleanings 9 (Nice: J. Rives Childs Château des Baumettes, 1966).

D'Argens provides four Chinese travellers, all educated in French at the Jesuit missions and all *'staunch Deists'* (i, p. xi): Sioeu-Tcheou at Paris, Choang at Ispahan, Keou-Che at Nagasaki, and Tiao at Moscow. Sioeu-Tcheou and Choang provide the bulk of the correspondence, both with each other and with Yn-Che-Chan at Pekin. The latter expends his words on trying to convince them of the fallacy of deism and the rationality of belief in a single intelligent divinity ordering the universe.

Goldsmith's 119 letters sometimes reproduce whole sections from d'Argens but they are much less concerned with theological debate. Lien Chi Altangi writes to Fum-Hoam (presumably named in honour of Gueullette's transmigratory narrator), first president of the ceremonial academy at Peking, and provides him with accounts of the manners, social institutions, and domestic arrangements of the English in London. Interwoven with satirical accounts of newspapers, the graves of poets at Westminster Abbey, the theatre, gaming, horse racing, are letters that give sage pseudo-Confucian advice about accepting life's misfortunes, not falling prey to superstition, the importance of relative judgement, and a plot borrowed from oriental romances in which Lien Chi's son who has set out to follow him is enslaved in Persia, encounters and falls in love with a beautiful fellow captive, escapes to England, and rediscovers his beloved in the person of the niece of his father's dearest friend and guide, the man in black.

Ange Goudar's primary correspondent, Cham-pi-pi, arrives at Port l'Orient with two fellow travellers but at Letter 18, they part with Ni-ou-san heading to Spain and Portugal and Fin-ho-ei to Italy. Cham-pi-pi forwards their correspondence with his own to various leading figures in China including the superintendent of the religion of Confucius and the Censor, but especially a mandarin called Kie-Tou-Na at Peking. *The Chinese Spy* thus works as a kind of reverse image of the letters of the Jesuit Le Comte to appropriate figures in Paris; the matter of his letters—religious, domestic, social, etc.—alters according to the nature of his addressee.

The circumstances of these fictional Chinese informants provide an opportunity for genuine mutual 'enlightenment'. D'Argens's correspondents remind us that they know what to expect of Europe from the instruction they have received from Jesuit priests in China, but Goldsmith and Goudar present their correspondents as absolutely ignorant of Europe with only rational philosophy as a guide. Thus, Lien Chi Altangi comments 'I consider myself here as a newly created Being introduced into a new world; every object strikes with wonder and surprise' while he can only call 'the reasoning principle' to his aid (21, Letter 3). Cham-pi-pi exclaims: 'I cannot describe the state of our minds at the sight of this new world; the sky, the earth, the elements, the plants, the animals, the men, the buildings of all kinds, every thing appeared to us strange and singular.'[64] Chinese informants tend to argue for careful assessment of different standards through rational deduction, although they are rarely advocates of total moral relativism. Hence, Lien Chi acknowledges in his third letter:

When I had just quitted my native country, and crossed the Chinese wall, I fancied every deviation from the customs and manners of China was a departing from nature: I smiled at the blue lips and red foreheads of the Tonguese; and could hardly contain when I saw the Daures dress their heads with horns. The Ostiacs powdered with red earth; and the Calmuck beauties tricked out in all the finery of sheep-skin appeared highly ridiculous; but I soon perceived that the ridicule lay not in them but in me; that I falsely condemned others of absurdity, because they happened to differ from a standard originally founded in prejudice or partiality. (22)

Not only is the culture these travellers encounter new to them, but they are new to it and there are frequent mentions of the frustration of being a novelty. Cham-pi-pi complains: 'We cannot stir out but immediately we are surrounded by crouds; the silly people are as eager as ever to see us, and what is still worse, to follow us' (i. 4, Letter 1). Sieoe-Tcheou tires of people coming from all parts to stare at him and express surprise that he is like other men (i. 3, Letter 1).

Such comments of course acquire an additional irony in that the European authors are here using the fiction of Chinese identity to estrange their own culture for the purposes of satire or financial gain. The proximity of this kind of activity to the circulation of pseudo-Chinese commodities for profit in the eighteenth century is made particularly evident in Goldsmith's introduction to the *Citizen of the*

[64] Ange Goudar, *The Chinese Spy; or, Emissary from the Court of Pekin, Commissioned to Examine into the Present State of Europe*, 6 vols. (London, 1765), i. 2, Letter 1.

World. In 'The Editor's Preface', Goldsmith (always close to penury) complains that he is excluded from the status of 'a poet or a philosopher' and partakes in no club for literary lions to provide mutual support. He suggests a connection with his 'author' who is an isolated human novelty act, describing himself as 'one of those solitary animals, that has been forced from its forest to gratify human curiosity' (15). In other words, both author and fictional creation are cast adrift in a strange culture that lacks the order and hierarchy both admire.

However, the idea that the author is exploiting rather than identifying with his subject is also manifest in the dream Goldsmith recounts to the reader in the same preface. He decides to venture out on to the frozen ice of the Thames where others are successfully plying their trade at various booths in a Fashion Fair; he resolves to make 'a new adventure. The furniture, frippery and fireworks of China, have long been fashionably bought up. I'll try the fair with a small cargoe of Chinese morality. If the Chinese have contributed to vitiate our taste, I'll try how far they can help to improve our understanding' (15). The editor dresses up his activity as morally improving rather than the mere indulgence of commodity fetishism, but the association remains throughout the letters, which return insistently to the attempt to prove that the luxury trade can be morally beneficial rather than simply corrupting. As the term 'spy' implies, there may be a hidden motive in the guileless reportage of the foreign informant. What looks like innocent enquiry could serve other less worthy interests.

Closer attention to the genre of the informant letter leads us to conclude that it does not simply provide a vehicle for satire of European pre-Enlightenment culture, but also a means of satirizing rationalists themselves, either for losing their humanity when they take its logic to extremes or for consistent lapses from the ideal. For example, the aesthetic and moral relativism of the Chinese commentator is severely strained in his encounters with European women. Lien Chi Altangi begins by expressing his horror at the ugliness of English ladies:

I can hardly endure the sight of them; they no way resemble the beauties of China: the Europeans have a quite different idea of beauty from us;

when I reflect on the small footed perfections of an Eastern beauty, how is it possible I should have eyes for a woman whose feet are ten inches long. I shall never forget the beauties of my native city of Nangfew. How very broad their faces; how very short their noses; how very little their eyes; how very thin their lips; how very black their teeth; the snow on the tops of Bao is not fairer than their cheeks; and their eye-brows are small as the line by the pencil of Quamsi. Here a lady with such perfections would be frightful. Dutch and Chinese beauties have indeed some resemblance, but English women are entirely different; red cheeks, big eyes, and teeth of a most odious whiteness, are not only seen here, but wished for; and then they have such masculine feet, as actually serve *some* for walking! (24–5, Letter 3)

His attitude softens briefly when he mistakes a prostitute for a fine lady and is moved at her kindness in offering to take his watch for repair, only to harden once again as he realizes her perfidy when the watch fails to materialize (Letters 8 and 9).

Cham-pi-pi is equally unequivocal in his dislike of European standards of female beauty and he fails to apply the rigorous standards of relativism demanded of the rational observer:

The Paris women are like so many furies. The first time of my being with them in the public walks, I thought myself in the midst of a group of demons. One would think that they were perpetually distracted by some violent passion; rage and despair are painted on their faces. Their complexion is all fiery, quite inflamed, and their skin as red as scarlet. Thou canst not conceive the effect this has on a Chinese, who, after being used in his own country to converse with women formed by the hands of nature, comes to be for the first time with creatures formed entirely by art.

For my part, I am apt to think that this is providential; for considering the allowed freedom here in conversing with women, and how easily they are seduced, should they shew themselves in their natural beauty, the propensity to licentiousness would grow above controul. (i. 49–50, Letter 16)

In expressing his irrational and superstitious fear of Parisian women's make-up, Cham-pi-pi omits to mention the best-known example of art dictating standards of female beauty for eighteenth-century comparative geographers: the practice of foot-binding in China.

If Goldsmith and Goudar use the example of women to point to the frequent failures in rationalist argument on the part of their speakers, d'Argens uses it to point to the dangers of extreme rationalism when he has Sioeu-Tcheou put forward the case for foot-binding. Chinese orientals are frequently used in eighteenth-century writing not only to contrast with western European culture but also other oriental ones. The Chinese practice of having only one legal wife but allowing multiple concubinage is presented as a rational method of securing domestic harmony (one woman has priority over others in the household) and servicing men's sexual needs (one woman may not be enough), by contrast not only with European Christian monogamous marriage but also with the Ottoman seraglio. European marriage is understood to encourage infidelity and take the man away from the home in the shape of concealed mistresses, while the eastern seraglio results in internecine conflicts between the maximum of four wives allowed under Islam, not including concubines. The tri-partite structure of the *Chinese Letters* between Paris, Peking, and Ispahan is particularly productive of this contrast whereby the Chinese family is seen as an ideal rational unit.

Even foot-binding can be understood as the product of rational organization according to Sioeu-Tchcou; in the second letter he reports that French men consider it madness to cripple the female sex and make them slow walkers, to which he responds that the ancient Chinese first hobbled their women to keep them at home, adding that Chinese ladies suffer their discomfort willingly, and concluding: 'You will own, that if a Fashion ought to be approv'd and followed, 'tis when it tends to the Good of Society, and to keep Peace at Home' (i. 10–11, Letter 2). In case his readers have overlooked the grotesque logic of this argument, the Marquis D'Argens has his French inter-locutors respond that they are sure French women would walk on stumps to escape such confinement and that they prefer in any case to see their wives as little as possible. The Confucian commentator begins to look increasingly like Swift's hyper-rationalist horses in the fourth book of *Gulliver's Travels* (itself an early satire on the impossibility of objective travel), defending cruelty and dullness on the grounds of the overriding demand for order. Gulliver, as solitary traveller like these Chinese commentators, of course, finally plunges into madness when he submits himself too thoroughly to a 'rational' ideal of culture.

Madness and civilization

Two consistent, sometimes competing, features of the treatment of China in English fictions are, first, the tendency to view Chinese culture itself as rather dull and repetitive and, second, the implication that imitation of Chineseness is a kind of madness with comic potential. Oliver Goldsmith in his editor's preface comments humorously on the limitations of the source text he has been dealing with:

The metaphors and allusions are all drawn from the East. Their formality our author carefully preserves. Many of their favourite tenets in moral are illustrated. The Chinese are always concise, so is he. Simple, so is he. The Chinese are grave and sententious, so is he. But in one particular, the resemblance is peculiarly striking: the Chinese are often dull; and so is he. (*Citizen of the World*, 14)

Thomas Percy, quoted earlier, complains that '*[t]he abjectness of their genius may easily be accounted for from that servile submission, and dread of novelty, which enslaves the minds of the Chinese, and while it promotes the peace and quiet of their empire, dulls their spirit and cramps their imagination.*' Both editors imply, then, that imagination will be supplied by the European translator. And the copious, erratic nature of European imaginative redactions of China is very evident. Nowhere more so than in the coining of phonetically transcribed Chinese names that point to the comic and satiric purpose of the text and require the reader to recognize the fictionality of the Chinese context in which they are found: hence, the name of Xo Ho in Horace Walpole's 'Letter' satirizing the ministry of the 1750s, or that of 'Hahehihotu' for the Chinese commentator in Eliza Haywood's *Adventures of Eovaai* attacking the ministry of Walpole's father in the 1730s. Names can also point to the deliberate inauthenticity of the Chinese presence (the 'Cham' in 'Cham-pi-pi'). China, then, becomes a place that is decisively marked for Europe as 'close' by virtue of its very distance and inaccessibility. Goldsmith's editor summarizes it thus:

The truth is, the Chinese and we are pretty much alike. Different degrees of refinement, and not of distance, mark the distinctions among mankind.

Savages of the most opposite climates, have all but one character of improvidence and rapacity; and tutored nations, however separate, make use of the same methods to procure refined enjoyment. (Editor's Preface, *Citizen of the World*, 13–14)

China could serve as a resource for images of both an extreme rationalism and the playful unconscious bordering on insanity, because it was a manufactured product of the Western imagination, generated, however, not for imperial political ends but rather for domestic narcissism or critique.

5

'DREAMS OF MEN AWAKE': INDIA

Canzade: the illusory sati

A young Iraqi merchant is walking in the streets of Serendib (Sri Lanka) when he is so struck by the elegance of a veiled lady that he cries out in admiration. Equally taken, Canzade, the orphaned daughter of the prime vizier, entertains him with food, wine, dancers, and her own lovely singing voice; she persuades him not to leave her home that night. As the merchant Aboulfaouaris retires to his bed a prescient thought warns that these exciting new prospects 'are Snares which Chance has put in thy Way, and thou wilt without doubt soon see this tempting Scene vanish like a Dream, and the Ideas of Greatness and Pleasure with which thou are intoxicated, turn to thy Shame and Confusion' (*PT* iii. 66–7). Nevertheless, he continues to court her and within eight days they have declared their mutual passion. She, however, will only agree to marry on condition that he renounce Islam in favour of her gentile religion, espoused by the sect of the Guebres. 'I expect', she commands haughtily, 'that you adore the Fire and the Sun'.[1] Aboulfaouaris

---

[1] Herbelot glosses the term 'Ghebr' as 'Mot Persien qui signifie particulièrement un Zoroastrien, un Adorateur du feu, & celui enfin qui fait profession de l'ancienne Religion

is given eight days to make his choice and when he refuses, another eight, but he continues to stand firm in his faith. Canzade banishes him from her presence and recalls him three weeks later only to banish him from Serendib entirely in the company of a man to whom she has given him as a slave.

On the ship to Golconda, Aboulfaouaris's new master's home, the company experience a terrifying encounter with a cannibalistic man-monster taken up from the water. The crew are only saved by the intervention of the mythical bird of Arabic lore, the Rokh. Once safely boarded at Golconda, his master is so taken with Aboulfaouris that he decides to marry him to his daughter, Facrinnisa, and convert to Islam along with her: 'I am weary', he says, 'of wor-shipping Oxen and Calves, I have too much Sense not to know it is a deplorable Piece of Superstition, and am perswaded there is a Supream Being who is above all other Gods.'[2] Aboulfaouaris con-spires with his equally unwilling bride to engineer her happiness with her lover, the son of a rival merchant; a Muslim husband who regrets repudiating a wife can employ a 'hulla', another man, to marry her who will in his turn repudiate her and thus make the remarriage possible. When Aboulfaouaris uses his wife's lover as a hulla, the latter as agreed refuses to repudiate his wife and Aboulfaouaris is given his liberty by the master, now reconciled to his daughter's marriage. Of this first wife Aboulfaouaris says he looked on her 'only as a Deposite, which I was to restore, and to surrender pure and entire' (iii. 95). Like that of his narrative kin, Sindbad and Robinson Crusoe, Aboulfaouaris's language is a blend of the

des Perses; c'est pourquoy on lui donne aussie le nom de Parsi; mais en general ce mot se prend pour un Idolatre, & pour un Infidele qui ne reçoit ni l'ancien, ni le nouveau Testament, qui vit sans loi & sans discipline' (*Bibliothèque Orientale*, 385). Given that she later elects to be a sati, it is unlikely that we are expected to view Canzade as a Parsi since there is a Parsi injunction against the burning of bodies. However, the worship of fire is associated with Zoroastrianism; the special veneration of fire as the primary natural substance, from which the sovereign spirit, Ahura Mazdah, is made, led to the erroneous belief that Zoroastrians were fire worshippers.

[2] The mention of the worship of oxen and calves suggests that his owner is a con-ventional Hindu. Jean-Baptiste Tavernier observes that 'idolaters' in India believe 'God disposes them into the bodies of contempt'ble Beasts, such as Asses, Dogs, Cats, and the like; to do Penance for their crimes in those infamous Prisons. But they believe that those Souls that enter into Cows are happy; presuming that there is a kind of divinity in these creatures' ('Travels in India', *Six Voyages*, pt. 2, 167).

mercantilist and the spiritual, in which religious devotion and the pursuit of wealth and profit are not incompatible but rather mutually reinforcing.

Duped by a gentile trickster from Surat who promises him great riches if he assists him in a dangerous venture, Aboulfaouaris next finds himself abandoned on an island of wild beasts, but is saved by a passing ship bound for Basra. A storm leads them to a large steel mountain which acts as a magnet to the ship and Aboulfaouaris nobly undertakes to save the ship and its crew by sacrificing himself. He ascends to the top of the mountain and strikes a drum which allows the ship to move away but leaves him stranded. A long walk ends at a port where he is reunited with his father's factor, Habib, who first dealt with him in Serendib, and who takes him back there to seek tidings of the woman he still loves, Canzade.

The king has forced her to marry an old lord she cannot love after her recovery from a near-mortal illness caused by her separation from Aboulfaouaris. The latter's attempts to contact her through her slave go unanswered and then one day he comes across a pagod (oriental temple) being prepared for a funeral in which a wife intends to commit suttee, to be consumed in flames along with her husband's body.[3] Like so many other merchant-travellers, Aboulfaouaris cannot resist the opportunity to witness the event:

Having never seen that Ceremony, tho' I knew it was observed in many Places of *India*, I resolved to be Witness of it. I could not help deploring the Blindness of these Idolaters, whose sacriligious Piety consecrated their Fury; or rather, I condemned their Priests whom I had heard talk of at *Surat*, where this terrible Custom is also followed by the Gentiles. Those detestable Ministers of their Pagods execute this barbarous Law for their own Profits. (iii. 113)

A crowd of thirty thousand gathers and, close to the funeral pyre, stand twenty priests to assist, each holding a book:

It was almost Night when she came. She rode on a white Horse richly caparisoned. On her Head she had a Garland of Flowers. Before her was

---

[3] See Monika Fludernik, 'Suttee as Heroic Martyrdom, Liebestod and Emblem of Women's Oppression: From Orientalist to Feminist Appropriations of a Hindu Rite in Four Narrative Genres', *Ranam* 33 (2000): 145–80.

carried by six Men a stately Palaquin with her Husband's Corpse upon it. She was accompanied by twelve Women on Horse-back, adorned with Gold and Silver Rings and Bracelets. Their Hair hung down their Shoulders. They had Pearl Necklaces about their Necks, Diamond Pendants in their Ears, and on their Heads Crowns of Gold with Silver Plates, enriched with Rubies, which came down half way their Faces. They had no Vests on, but only little neat Wastcoats, the Sleeves of which reached down to the Elbow. Several Players upon instruments followed these Women, who were all Slaves to the Lady who was to be sacrificed. Her Relations and Friends came after, dancing and singing joyfully, that their Kinswoman and Friend had so much Generosity. Two Priests helpt her to alight off the Horse, and led her by the Hand to the River's Side, whither her Husband's Corpse was brought. She washed it from Head to Foot; then put it into the Hands of the Priests, who carried it to the Cabin, where it was laid on a Heap of Straw intermixed with Sulphur. She then washed her self, without undressing, and approached the Pile without changing her Cloaths. She took several Turns about it, surveying the Preparations for her Sacrifice with great Intrepidity. After which she embraced her Relations and Friends, who immediately withdrew. She was also herself embraced by her Slaves, who were all drowned in Tears. She gave them their Liberty, and distributed among them the Jewels and other Ornaments she had about her. When she lifted up the Silver Plate which hid half her Face, and hindered my knowing her, tho' I was pretty near the Pile, imagine you how I was surprised when I saw it was *Canzade*. I could not certainly have been more so, had all Nature been turned topsie-turvy.

Great God, cried I to my self, may I believe my Eyes? May I trust to their Report? is it indeed *Canzade* that is about to perish so miserably? I endeavoured for some time to deceive my self; but I could not contradict my Senses. I saw the Lady, and could not but know her. I was so troubled to think of her sacrificing her self, that I could not bear the sight of it. I left her in the Hands of the Priests, who after having exhorted her so to behave her self as to deserve the Happiness which she might expect, made her enter the Cabin, and presented her, as the Custom is, with a lighted Torch to set it on fire her self. I retired to *Habib*'s Country-House in such a Disposition of Soul, that it is impossible to paint it in lively Colours. I was so grieved, so distracted, that I knew not what I did. I looked back every now and then on the fatal Place, and saw the Flames of the Funeral-Pile rise in the Air, the sight of which rent my Heart. (iii. 125–6)

His friend the factor Habib is surprised to hear of Canzade's decision since the Muslim governor of the city, by the king's order, will have carefully questioned her and sought to dissuade her from becoming sati.[4]

Canzade's former slave now frequents the house trying to persuade a grieving Aboulfaouaris to meet with his new mistress whom he claims is equally beautiful; a mysterious letter finally prompts Aboulfaouaris to agree. The lady is, of course, Canzade herself. She reveals that she bribed a brahman to provide an underground hiding-place for her beneath the flames. Canzade explains: 'It was though I did it out of Vanity to pass for a Heroine, and to have a Statue in the Pagods: But my Reason, or perhaps my Love for you, was what induced me' (iii. 135). She has cunningly preserved enough treasure for her dowry so the pair can marry having fled to Basra and upon her conversion to Islam.

When his father dies, the family estate is divided between Aboulfaouaris and his brother, Hour, but the latter loses all their patrimony in unsuccessful trading expeditions. Aboulfaouaris departs to repair their fortunes, entrusting Canzade to his brother with the injunction: 'In a Word, so act, that at my Return I may find this precious Treasure which I now deposite with you, the same as I this Moment leave her' (ii. 142). He does not return for seven years after a series of fantastic adventures including enslavement to a barbarous horde of evil black genies; liberation by virtuous white genies; a terrifying voyage on the back of an Afrite (or Ifrit, an evil demon), cut short when he forgets to continue praying; a visit to the tomb of Solomon in which he narrowly avoids becoming instrumental in allowing Solomon's ring 'which makes its owner master of the world' fall into the hands of a rebel Afrite; a vision of the houris; and his eventual safe passage home on a cloud summoned by the prophet Elias.[5]

---

[4] François Bernier describes how the Mughal Muslim government of India attempted to prevent suttee without actually banning it for fear of revolt among the Hindu population. Women who wished to burn themselves had to seek permission of the respective Governors of their region who would remonstrate with them. Bernier describes his own attempts to persuade the wife of a clerk friend of his, Bendidas, to abandon her decision to become a sati (*Continuation*, 117–19).

[5] On different kinds of 'djinn' or 'genii', including the 'Ifrit', an especially powerful kind of 'djinn' whose name derives from 'to roll in the dust' implying 'to bring low', see Robert Irwin's ch. 8, 'The Universe of Marvels' (*Arabian Nights*, 205). The Houris (meaning 'the black-eyed') are the beautiful maidens who dwell in the Muslim paradise.

Aboulfaouaris returns to his home in Basra to find his wife has married a young man that day in order to save the family from penury. He is so changed in appearance that the young man's accusation that he is an impostor is at first believed by both Canzade and Hour. Canzade's new bridegroom describes the 'impostor' as a subtle storyteller to the Cadi (a judge) called in to assess the claim: 'he has a Fable at his Fingers End. He'll tell you wonderful Things, but you are not so credulous' (ii. 180–1). However, the Cadi determines there is enough probability in the story to send it forward to the judgement of Mahomet's son-in-law, Aly-ben-Aby Taleb in Medina, who reveals that Mahomet has prophesied the coming of this his most faithful servant. Canzade is restored to him but they cannot be happy because she has transferred her affections to the young man she married. She virtuously abstains from seeing her new love but Aboulfaouaris's feelings are too delicate for him to be truly satisfied with his reluctant wife.

The Persian king, Bedreddin Lolo, his vizier, and his favourite, who have been listening to Aboulfaouaris's account of his life as part of their long search to discover a truly happy man, now decide to return to Baghdad to try and make the best of their respective lots. The listeners of the outer frame, Farruknaz the Persian princess and her court ladies, also pass judgement, the princess again disparaging on the issue of men's fidelity and her women 'extoll[ing] very much the Constancy of the Lovers' (ii. 188). Sutlememé's stories must continue in the attempt to persuade her own haughty and reluctant princess to contemplate marriage.

Canzade's story, like that of Tourandocte in the same collection, is a tale told in the voice of a man to other romantically thwarted men by a woman to another woman to persuade her of the fidelity of the men she so distrusts. The 'framing' of Canzade parallels the 'framing' of her central act, the illusory act of suttee, which is rendered through the eyes of a curious masculine spectator, a merchant-traveller like the many European men who made suttee a centrepiece in their accounts of India. The narrative twist lies in the discovery that he is not an observer but an interested party in the fate of the sati herself.

The fantastic adventures that frame this central dramatic scenario all point to Aboulfaouaris's function as an exemplary 'Mussulman', one who not only accepts the determining providential power of his God, but also works strenuously to live a life of noble self-sacrifice and assistance to others. However, like Sindbad, on whom he is evidently modelled, Aboulfaouaris is also by analogy a model of the good Christian. This analogy between the two monotheistic religions of Christianity and Islam, otherwise so often at odds in the European West, is maintained through the contrast with polytheistic 'idolatries': Canzade's worship of the gods of fire, and Hindu belief in multiple gods and the divinity of animals (it was not until the second half of the eighteenth century that Hinduism came to be viewed as a monotheism).

A preoccupation with the scenario of 'suttee' informed representations of India from the earliest European encounters with its territories,[6] and came to form an important continuity between Mughal Muslim and British Protestant rule. Abolition of suttee in 1829 was the first major legislation of the East India Company's administration in India, serving as 'the moral pretext for intervention and the major justification for colonial rule'.[7] The British could view themselves as succeeding to, and hardening, the Mughal attempt to constrain idolatrous practices in India, the most notorious of which was suttee: the 'white' rule of both the Mughals and the British could be presented as attempts by white men to save brown women from brown men. In the course of the eighteenth century, the attitude to Mughal government on the part of British writers shifted from an earlier identification with the Mughal dynasty as a model of an advanced and civilized culture attempting to bring under control a violent and various population given to internal faction and idolatrous barbarities. As colonial rule became a real possibility for the British, Mughal government was reconceived as a predatory regime exploitative of a gentle and submissive 'native' population, the latter requiring the assistance of European powers such as Britain to liberate it from the yoke of Islamic absolutism. However, Islam in

---

[6] For a fascinating discussion of an early preoccupation with suttee, see Joan-Pau Rubiés on the 17th-c. Italian traveller Pietro della Valle (1586–1652), who describes his meeting with Giaccama at Ikkeri, and composes sonnets to her on her decision to become a sati (*Travel and Ethnology in the Renaissance*, 366–8).

[7] Rajeswari Sunder Rajan, *Real and Imagined Women: Gender, Culture, and Post-colonialism* (London: Routledge, 1993), 42.

India was also differentiated from Christianity in Europe by virtue of its treatment of women. Throughout the pre-colonial and colonial period, European writers saw affinities between Hinduism and Islam in the 'despotic' treatment of women, as fodder for the funeral pyre or luxuriously confined slaves within the zenana (harem), and claimed a measure of superiority in the freedoms afforded women in the Christian West.

Canzade embodies the ambivalent construction of a native 'India' in this earlier pre-colonial period, uncertainly placed between the oppositional roles of autocratic Muslim princess (Farruknaz) and the native 'Hindu' virtuous wife that Nandini Bhattacharya identifies as central to the discursive construction of 'India' for European writers. Bhattacharya points out that European commentators often contrasted Muslim women, enclosed in the zenana but exerting their influence on Mughal rulers, with the exotic and overt sexuality of 'public' gentile women, only to collapse the distinction in the tendency to view the female in India (whether 'Mahometan' or 'Gentile') as commanding an erotic fascination which undermines the moral fibre of empire: 'It is not claiming too much to say that ethnographers saw the public female body only to give a shape to fantasies about the unknowable but alluring private body hidden in the zenana or harem.'[8] That Canzade engineers her own 'escape' into marriage with her Muslim lover is a measure of the 'not-quite-maleness' of the Islamic government the English went on to replace, opening up a gap between the Christian masculinity of Europe and the Mughal/Muslim rule it encountered in seventeenth-century India. Canzade's ability, like that of her oriental sisters (Roxolana and Tourandocte), to manipulate spectacle and propagate a 'fabulous' version of herself as a means of pursuing her own desires, also suggests this dangerous facility to undermine the 'virtue' of the Christian and/or Mahometan male.

However, Canzade is also represented—in line with the conventional image of the Indian wife/widow always proleptically inscribed with the potential to become sati—as a victim of her own desires,

[8] Nandini Bhattacharya, *Reading the Splendid Body: Gender and Consumerism in Eighteenth-Century British Writing on India* (Newark and London: University of Delaware Press; Associated University Presses, 1998), 18.

driven by an erotic compulsion which makes her own will always subservient. She nearly dies from illness when separated from her first love, Aboulfaouaris, and cannot conquer her new passion for the second husband she takes, although she refuses him further favours. She is thus a metaphorical 'sati' in that she is consumed by internal and unquenchable fires of romantic/sexual passion. Her original designation as a 'worshipper of fire' is an accurate one on the tropological, if not the theological/ethnographical, level.

Canzade's use of illusion and spectacle to advance her own interest also aligns her with the figure more usually characterized in ethnographic descriptions of suttee by Europeans as the villainous exploiter of female weakness: the brahman. Jean-Baptiste Tavernier comments that brahmans retrieve the jewellery of the sati from the ashes after they have encouraged her to her death (*Six Voyages*, pt. 2, 170) and François Bernier complains that 'Those Demons, the *Brahmans*, that are there with their great Sticks, astonish them, and hearten them up, and even thrust them in' (*Continuation*, 126), and concludes 'For my part, I have often been so enraged against those *Brahmans*, that if I durst, I had strangled them' (127).

However, it is as a figure of 'illusion' that Canzade figures 'India' for the seventeenth- and eighteenth-century European imagination: both as wild 'dream' or 'prospect' of riches and contentment for the aspiring young merchant-traveller, and as orchestrator of a spectacular piece of fakery centred on the apparent embrace of suffering. Roxolana and Turandocte are also signifiers of immense wealth and spinners of riddling fictions for their respective geographical 'cultures', the Turkish/Persian and Chinese empires of the period. But the specificity of the representation of 'India' lies in this conjuring of the idea of a 'dream' landscape ripe for appropriation but always enigmatic, indeed incomprehensible. European writers of fictions 'from' and about India return repeatedly both to mercantile and idealist synecdoches for India—its rich resources human, philosophical, and physical—which are so characteristic of Canzade's lover-narrator, Aboulfaouaris. Canzade is 'deposit', precious jewel, illusionist, despot, and slave. The merchant-traveller-philosopher Aboulfaouaris struggles unsuccessfully fully to possess this chimerical, protean creature. And she too, unlike Tourandocte and Roxolana, is never fully self-possessed; her passionate attachments discompose and damage herself and others. Canzade/India is a shape that shifts elusively away from the desiring subject, a brittle vulnerable illusion: a 'dream of men awake' to the immense riches and power offered by the territory of India, but also to a risky alterity that may finally evade the covetous grasp.

India as illusion

The stories that make up Thomas-Simon Gueullette's collection of *Mogul Tales, or, the Dreams of Men Awake* (first translated from the French edition of 1725 into English in 1736) begin with the discovery that a lovely young man, who has swooned in the midst of a dramatic performance before the five widowed queens of the sultan of Guzurat (Gujerat) is in fact a woman, a Persian princess named Canzade. Her story of flight from the incestuous passion of her brother, Prince Cazan-Can of Ormuz (Hormuz), is introduced by her old nurse, Karabag, to the Gujerati queens (Karabag and her company have been brought drugged from a disused palace now turned into a Karavanserail for travellers). The plot thickens in that not only do the travellers consider that they are in the midst of a dream-palace, a fairyland, but the widowed queens themselves are the victims of an elaborate fiction (Fig. 13). Their husband, the Sultan Oguz, has, under the guidance of the Muslim imam Cothrob (nephew to Alroamat, king of Georgia, who, according to Gueullette's *Chinese Tales* brought Islam to China—see 'Narrative transmigrations', Ch. 4), staged his own death and he is now concealed in the secret passages expressly built in his new palace to observe unnoticed his wives' reactions to his untimely 'death' and test their continuing virtue and allegiance.

Gueullette was an inveterate plunderer of the oriental tales of François Pétis de la Croix and Antoine Galland, so it is perhaps unsurprising that the name 'Canzade' should reappear in this collection. This Canzade too is a prized 'dream' object, signifier of 'India'. Her ownership, sexual and political, is contested by her

13. Frontispiece, Thomas-Simon Gueullette, *Mogul
Tales, or, the Dreams of Men Awake*, vol. i, 2nd edn.
(1743)

brother, prince of Persia,[9] and the young heir to the independent
Muslim kingdom of Visapour, Cothbedin. The slippage between
Persian princess and Indian 'prize' is not only reinforced by the

[9] Sir John Chardin notes that many Persians were employed in the Tartary-derived
court of the Great Mogul in India: 'within this last Century, a great many *Persians*, and
even entire Families, have gone and settl'd in the *Indies*. As they are a handsomer, wiser,
and more polite People, beyond all Comparison, than the *Mahometan Indians*, who are

functional similarity between this Canzade and the Canzade conjured by the old nurse to persuade the Persian Princess Farruknaz to marry in François Pétis de la Croix's *Persian Tales*, but in the travel literature of the period which consistently singled out for attention the favourite Persian wife of the seventeenth-century Mughal ruler of India, Jahangir, named Nourmahal.[10]

Canzade experiences a dream-vision shortly after Cothbedin has declared his love for her in which he tells her that Mahomet has destined them for each other and will compel her brother to let them marry. She comments 'I awakened at that Moment, and could not for a long time persuade myself that I had slept; nor could I well distinguish whether I was to believe what I had heard, a Message really sent from Heaven, or a Dream, raised by the Thoughts floating in my Brain, since my long Conversation with the Prince'.[11] The confusion between dream and reality, or the dream and supernatural revelation, is repeated throughout the tales, both in the frame story and in the many tales told by the various visitors delivered to the Gujerati queens by one of their sons, Schirin. Again and again, tellers and listeners comment on the difficulty of differentiating between dream state and reality. Dreams often presage a truth or a future happening, while the 'real' is consistently interpreted as a dream.

Gueullette may have derived this association of the territories of India with the confusion of dream and real from another French writer whose accounts of India were enormously influential in both France and England, the physician and philosopher François Bernier. Bernier was a disciple of the sceptical philosopher Pierre Gassendi,

---

descended from the *Tartars*, in the Country of *Tamerlane*; they all advance themselves in the *Indies*' (*A New Collection of Voyages and Travels . . . Containing a most Accurate Description of Persia, and Other Eastern Nations*, trans. Edmund Lloyd (London, 1721), ii. 13).

[10] In his account of his travels in Persia and India, Jean-Baptiste Tavernier opens the second part which relates to India with a story about Nourmahal's minting of coins with her image, having persuaded her doting husband to allow her the freedom to govern for one day ('An Account of the Money of Asia', *Six Voyages*, pt. 2, 10–12). It was this same Nourmahal who provided so many impediments to Sir Thomas Roe in his attempts to broker freedom of trade for the East India Company during his 1615–18 embassy to the court of Jahangir; Dryden was to reuse her name and her reputation as a violent, lust-driven queen for his Indian play, *Aureng-Zebe* (1676).

[11] Thomas-Simon Gueullette, *Mogul Tales, or, the Dreams of Men Awake*, 2nd edn. (London, 1743), i. 94. All references are to this edition.

whose work he translated into Persian; he spent about fourteen years of his life in Asia, mainly in India. His writings, in the tradition of Michel de Montaigne and probably influencing Montesquieu, deploy oriental and distant customs as a means of criticizing French mores and highlight the relativity of 'custom' itself.[12] Bernier explained the philosophy of the 'Gentile Pendets' (pundits) he encountered in India in a letter of 1667 to his friend and fellow sceptic, Jean Chapelain, in terms of an understanding of the 'real' empirical world as dream by contrast with the materiality of the divine, a philosophy he sees as shared by Persian Sufis and English Rosicrucians. He complains that

these Indian Cabalists or *Pendets* I speak of, drive this impertinence farther than all those Philosophers, and pretend, that God, or that Soverain Being, which they call *Achar*, (immutable,) hath produced or drawn out of his own substance, not only *Souls*, but also whatever is *material* and corporeal in the Universe; and that this production was not meerly made by way of an efficient cause, but by a way resembling a Spider that produceth a webb, which it draws forth out of its own body, and takes in again when it will.

Creation, he summarizes, is spun out from the body of the divine and destruction is a return to it:

There is therefore nothing (*so they go on*) that is real or effective in all we think we see, hear, smell, taste or touch: all this World is nothing but a kind of Dream and a meer Illusion, in regard that all this multiplicity and diversity of things that appear to us, is nothing but one and the same thing, which is *God himself*.... (Bernier, *Continuation*, 169)

Alongside Bernier's account of mysticism encountered in Mughal India, we can set a further possible source of a more practical nature for Gueullette's representation of India as a dream-space. Another European physician who spent many years at the Mughal court was the Venetian Niccolo Manucci, whose manuscript memoirs of his then nearly fifty years in India—first following the fortunes of Aurangzeb's older brother, Dara, as an artilleryman and later as a doctor—were sent home in 1701 and used as the basis of the Jesuit Father Catrou's *Histoire Générale de l'Empire du Mogul*, translated

[12] See Peter Burke, 'The Philosopher as Traveller: Bernier's Orient', in Jas Elsner and Joan-Pau Rubiès (eds.), *Voyages and Visions: Towards a Cultural History of Travel* (London: Reaktion Books, 1999), 124–37.

from the French into English in 1708. Manucci described the harem at the court of Aurangzeb as a place of extreme opulence and concluded with the comment that 'The Reader will doubtless here fancy himself transported into a Fairy Land where all is Pearl and Diamonds. But the Description we have given, comes very much short of the Truth' (*General History*, 330).

A pattern emerges of a discursive construct of India in the seventeenth and eighteenth centuries in Europe and especially in England and France. Some of the first European informants were jewel merchants such as Jean Chardin and Jean-Baptiste Tavernier who presented India as a kind of physical 'fairyland' rich in minerals and precious stones, while the accounts of physicians, philosophers, and priests, such as François Bernier and the Protestant chaplain Edward Terry, understand the spiritual and mystical traditions of India as a conflation of material and dream states. The female figure has a special role embodying wealth—quite literally, in that, as numerous European travellers observed, women wear their husbands' wealth in jewellery upon their bodies[13]—and its concealment, its tantalizing dream status. India is also understood as a territory with vast but wasted potential. European intervention and agency (at first imagined in terms of trade and only later in terms of politics and government) will transform it into the valuable resource it could be. This idea extends to the representation of India as a (re)source for fiction as well as the more familiar trading commodities of spice or textiles.[14] India is thus shaped as a geographical territory ripe for conquest in ways quite different from the contemporary oriental states we have so far considered. Seventeenth-century empiricism here produces a new twist on a tradition dating back to the medieval European writings of Marco

---

[13] See Bhattacharya, *Reading the Splendid Body*, 31–4.

[14] The fictional rendering of India runs somewhat counter to the actual English trading practice in the 17th and 18th c., which did not centre on luxury goods, but mainly on bulk purchase of cotton. The company's first objective was the spices of the East Indies (Indonesia), and India was to provide cottons for sale to the spice growers. But Dutch opposition in Indonesia led to a shift of attention to India itself. The East India Company after Roe's embassy 1615–18 set up factories under Mughal grants in Surat, Bengal and Madras. When the Indians would only accept silver in exchange for their goods they developed a system of country trade with Madras and Gujarat supplying cotton goods, Gujarat indigo also; with silk, sugar, and saltpetre from Bengal. Opium was shipped to the Far East to trade in tea there.

Polo and John Mandeville in which India, along with 'Cathay' or China, figured as a space of the marvellous, a dream-scape for the Christian pilgrim and possible home of the legendary early Christian priest Prester John.[15]

The Mughal dynasty in India, informants claimed, was vastly wealthier than its Ottoman, Persian, or Chinese equivalents. Jean-Baptiste Tavernier asserts that 'The Great *Mogul* is without all question the richest and most potent Monarch of *Asia*: the Territories which he possesses, being his own Hereditary Possession; and being absolute Master of all the Territories whence he receives his Revenues' (*Six Voyages*, pt. 2, 108). In 1655, Edward Terry concludes that 'the Great *Mogol*, considering his most large *Territories*, his full and great *Treasures*, with the many rich *Commodities* his Provinces afford, is the greatest and richest known *King* of the *East*, if not of the *whole World*'.[16]

However, the Mughal empire was also understood to be enormously wasteful because premised on an insecure and absolute economic system. Bernier, writing to Jean-Baptiste Colbert (chief minister to Louis XIV from 1661), points out that India does not circulate the wealth it receives. Merchants bring in goods and take others in their place, but gold and silver, especially gold, are retained in the country, so that '*Indostan* proves . . . a kind of abyss for a great part of the gold and silver of the world, which finds many ways to enter there, and almost none to issue thence' ('A Letter to Lord Colbert', separately numbered in *History*, 13). The seraglio is extravagant, he notes, and the absolutist government that precludes the 'meum and tuum' of France, provides no incentive to its people to engage in profit-making activity, since all goods return to the Great Mogul on the owner's death (Fig. 14). Thus, both Muslim and gentile populations endeavour to conceal their wealth rather than considering

---

[15] The Andalusian traveller Pero Tafur claimed in his *Andancas e Viajes* to have received from the Venetian merchant Nicoló Conti (*c*.1385–1469) in 1437 at Mount Sinai an account of the earthly paradise of the kingdom of Prester John in India (it was more commonly located in Abyssinia) (Rubiés, *Travel and Ethnology*, ch. 3, 85–124). For a more general discussion of the imaginary nature of medieval writings about marvellous travel, see Stephen Greenblatt, *Marvelous Possessions: The Wonder of the New World* (Oxford: Clarendon Press, 1991).

[16] Edward Terry, *A Voyage to East-India* (London, 1655), 91.

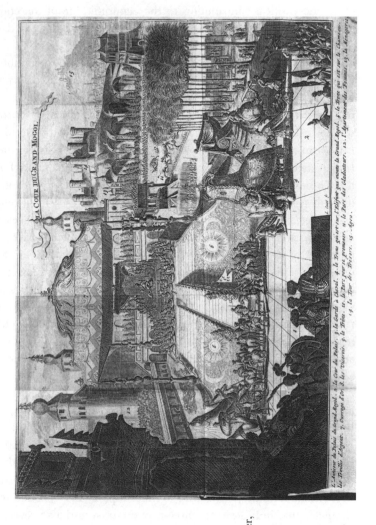

14. Engraving of 'The Court of the Grand Mogol', François Bernier, *Voyages de Fr. Bernier . . . contenant la description des états du Grand Mogol, de l'Hindoustan, du royaume de Kachemire, &c*, vol. ii (Amsterdam, 1710), p. 40.

trade and profit a contribution to the economic life of the country: 'And for this very reason it is, that we see those vast Estates in *Asia* go so wretchedly and palpably to ruine' (73).

If India was an empire in decline, it was open to intervention, but Europeans had to find ways to present themselves as the natural 'successors' to Mughal rule. As we have seen with regard to the representation of suttee, the proto-colonial ambitions of European writers, especially later in the century, fostered a tendency to identify European values with those of the Mughal and other Muslim rulers of Indian states more closely than they had done with the Grand Turk or the Chinese emperors. The role of Islamic leaders as governors of a difficult territory, combining immense wealth and great barrenness, and especially of native peoples identified as idolaters, makes them figures for analogy for the nascent or proto-colonial enterprises being pursued by European powers. By contrast, the Chinese emperors' refusal of trade relations with Europe, and the overt antagonism between Muslim and Christian represented by Ottoman incursions in western Europe, meant that these oriental empires were more often represented as impenetrable or enclosed geographical and cultural territories. European writers on India often looked for points of analogy and parallel with the Mughal government, rather than presenting a straightforward opposition between East and West.

Through the seventeenth and eighteenth centuries, 'India' was figured as a territory split between the interests of Muslims, native 'Indians' (usually referred to as gentiles or idolaters), and Christians. At points, Christian writers identify with the monotheism and civilization of the Mughal Muslim government and at others with what they represent as the gentle spirit and trading enterprise of the polytheistic Hindu population. Bernier opens his account with a summary that indicates this three-way contrast and also reveals that distinctions of colour are secondary to those of ethnicity and religion in the hierarchy of oriental cultures:

though those that are employ'd in publick Charges and Offices, and even those that are Listed in the *Militia*, be not all of the Race of the *Mogols*, but strangers, and Nations gather'd out of all Countreys, most of them *Persians*, some *Arabians*, and some *Turks*. For to be esteem'd a *Mogol*, 'tis enough to be a stranger white of Face, and a *Mahumetan*; in distinction as well to the

Indians, who are brown, and *Pagans*, as to the *Christians* of *Europe*, who are call'd *Franguis*. (*History*, 6)[17]

Histories of India present not only the territory but also the histories themselves as a rare and extraordinary treasure to be exploited by European ingenuity. Catrou describes acquiring the Portuguese manuscript of Mannucci's memoirs as a moment of discovery: *'I made some Reflexions at the sight of so valuable Materials, which determin'd me to go to Work on the Memoir that lay before me'*; he concludes that *'The Treasure* Monsieur Manouchi *has sent us from the* Indies, *is not yet wholly exhausted'* and promises a life of the present emperor Aurangzeb as a further volume if this first volume is well-received ('The Author's Preface', *General History*, n.p.).

Informants about India who were not merchants were, from the first English encounters with India in the early seventeenth century, anxious to distinguish the moral currency of their writing. Thomas Coryate, eccentric foot-soldier of Christian discovery in the early seventeenth century, writes to his mother in 1615 that he will return 'with purchase of great riches of experience, as I doubt whether any English man this hundred yeares have done the like'.[18] Edward Terry's published account in 1655 of his visit to the Mughal court with Sir Thomas Roe's embassy (1615–18) is prefaced by three poems all of which use the trope of contrasting his moral wisdom brought back from the Indies with the luxury goods of merchants. Thus Edward Creswell concludes:

> And though these leaves nothing to Merchants owe
> For Spices, Cuchineal, or Indico.
> Yet all confesse, who weigh the gains you brought,
> Your ship was laden with a richer fraught,
> While the glad world by you instructed sings,
> *Wisdom's the noblest ware that Travel brings.*

> (n.p.)

---

[17] On the primacy of religious difference in categorizing what we now construct as 'racial' difference before the late 18th c., see Roxann Wheeler, *The Complexion of Race: Categories of Difference in Eighteenth-Century British Culture*, New Cultural Studies (Philadelphia: University of Philadelphia Press, 2000).

[18] Thomas Coryate, *Greeting from the Court of the Great Mogul*, English Experience, its Record in Early Printed Books Published in Facsimile, no. 30 (Amsterdam and New York: Theatrum Orbis Terrarum; Da Capo Press, 1968), 49.

Terry himself disclaims any desire to profit materially from his account. He would not have published it, he claims, but the printer got hold of the original copy and he has enlarged it (at more expense of paper he admits) in order to stress its instructional purpose. The extra text, he argues, will:

contain matter for instruction and use, as well as for relation and novelty. So that they, who fly from a Sermon, and will not touch sound, and wholesom, and excellent treatises in Divinity, may happily (if God so please) be taken before they are aware, and overcome by some Divine truths that lie scattered up and down in manie places of this Narrative. To which end I have endeavoured so to contrive it for every one (who shall please to read it through) that it may look like a well form'd picture, that seems to look stedfastly upon everie beholder, who so looks upon it. (n.p.)

Terry presents his account as a kind of 'fable', providing moral instruction under the guise of entertainment, although he seems unaware of the rich Sanskrit tradition of fable in Indian writing that European translators were quick to exploit as we will see later. Like the fable, the 'moral' of Terry's writing will be transparent and evident, speaking directly to the reader not otherwise inclined to read didactic material. But the metaphor of the picture or portrait that captures the gaze of all beholders, convincing each that he or she is being individually addressed, disturbs this claim to transparency. Terry's metaphor of the picture reconnects with several memorable passages in his employer's, Thomas Roe's, account of his embassy in the East Indies, about the Great Mogul's fondness for pictures from Europe.

Roe writes to the East India Company on 25 January 1616 advising it that, rather than send jewellery, it should send wine and pictures to pique the avarice (apparently boundless) of the Great Mogul, Jahangir: 'I thinck 4 or 5 handsome cases of that wine will be more welcome than the richest Iewell in Cheapesyde. Pictures, lardge, on cloth, the frame in peeces; but they must be good, and for varyete some story, with many faces, for single to the life hath beene more usuall'.[19] On 2 September 1616, Roe records an uncomfortable tussle with Jahangir

---

[19] *The Embassy of Sir Thomas Roe to the Court of the Great Mogul, 1615–1619, as Narrated in his Journal and Correspondence*, ed. William Foster, Hakluyt Society, 2nd ser., nos. 1–2 (London, 1899), i. 119.

when the latter forces him to part with the image of a woman, possibly his wife, of whom Roe is particularly fond. Later, around the end of February 1617, Roe records his return from hunting to discover that Jahangir has opened a consignment of presents sent from England.

There is a controversy over a particular painting at which it is clear that Terry was present:

Of the third Picture, of Venus and a Satyre, he commanded my Interpreter not to tell me what he said, but asked his Lords what they conceived should be the interpretation or morall of that. He shewed the Satyres hornes, his skinne, which was swart, and pointed to many particulars. Every man replyed according to his fancie; but in the end hee concluded they were all deceived: and seeing they could judge no better, hee would keepe his conceit to himselfe, iterating his command to conceale this passage from me; but bade him aske me what it meant. I answered: An Invention of the Painter to shew his arte, which was Poeticall, but the interpretation was New to mee that had not seene it. Then he called Master Terry to give his judgement who replying hee knew not, the King demanded why hee brought up to him an invention wherein hee was ignorant; at which I enterposed that he was a Preacher, and medled not with such matters, nor had charge of them; onely coming in their company, hee was more noted, and so named as their conductor.

This I repeate for instruction, to warne the company and him that shall succeed to be very wary what they send may be subject to ill Interpretation; for in that point this King and people are very pregnant and scrupulous, full of jealousie and trickes. For that, notwithstanding the King conceited himselfe, yet by the passages I will deliver my opinion of this conceit, which (knowing I had never seene the Picture, and by Ignorance was guiltlesse) hee would not presse hard upon me; but I suppose he understood the Morall to be a scorne of Asiatiques, whom the naked Satyre represented, and was of the same complexion, and not unlike; who, being held by Venus, a white woman, by the Nose, it seemed that shee held him Captive. Yet he revealed no discontent, but rould them up, and told me he would accept him also as a Present. (*Embassy*, ii. 386–7)

Roe's story here challenges Terry's understanding of the picture that will speak to everybody and teach a clear and transparent morality. Jahangir, Roe concludes, interprets the image as one that disparages his government, either by suggesting that the Mughal kings are governed by their women (and Jahangir's favourite wife Nourmahal was a major impediment to Roe's mission, using her influence with her husband to promote the Portuguese interest in India) or, perhaps more subversively, that the 'white' European world is leading the 'Asiatic' one, rather than vice versa. However, this is Roe's interpretation of Jahangir's response and what he describes is in fact too enigmatic to produce any 'single' reading of what the painting may mean to the Mughal emperor. Jahangir simply refuses to disclose what he makes of the scene depicted in the painting.[20]

Terry's comment and Roe's account of this cameo can serve to illustrate the complex and multiple interpretative possibilities of the encounter with India. The attempt to reduce India to a single set of meanings for the European consumer was repeatedly undercut by the conflicting and multiple demands placed on such a representation. Just as when we try to interpret a dream, we seek to extrapolate a single moral or message, but come to recognize that it is a text put together through a variety of prompts, both consequential and inconsequential, accumulated through time and experience. That the dream expresses a desire or a wish is apparent but the means of that expression are invariably confused to the extent that the latent wish itself may become obscure(d).

Fictions claimed to derive from and about India repeatedly trope India as a dream, but not always in the positive sense of a space to be possessed by the imagination. Equally, the dream can be a kind of consoling or duplicitous fiction. India generates illusions and illusionists; the fakirs and brahmans of ethnographic report are represented as master tricksters while Islam is, as in the case of Ottoman and Persian accounts, denounced as a gross imposture. In what follows, I discuss the portrayal of India as dream in three different fictional forms: first, John Dryden's theatrical rendering; second, collections of oriental tales relating to India such as Gueullette's; and, third, 'translations' derived from a third-century Sanskrit collection of animal and human fables known to Europe in the seventeenth century as the *Fables of Pilpay*. In these narratives, the two products most coveted by European traders in India—luxury textiles and precious stones—repeatedly surface as signifiers of India's enticing prospect,

[20] See Kate Teltscher, *India Inscribed: European and British Writing on India 1600–1800* (Delhi: Oxford University Press, 1995), 109–10. Teltscher comments that 'Roe himself reads racial dominance into the painting' (109).

while the figures of the brahman, fakir, imam (and the descriptions of the supernatural elements of Indian philosophy and religion) present India not only as a source of fantasy, magic, even morality, but also of fakery and delusion.

The 'dreaming Priest': Aureng-Zebe

In his record of his embassy, Sir Thomas Roe briefly toys with the idea that the machinations at the Mughal court have all the ingredients for a fiction of intrigue. On 9 December 1616, he hears a rumour that Asaf Khan, Nourmahal's powerful brother, and Prince Khusrau, the eldest son of Jahangir, have become allies after a period of bitter enmity. Roe greets this news with enthusiasm, since he is at odds with the prince's younger brother Khurram. Roe chooses, probably wrong-headedly, to present Jahangir as above such in-fighting and comments:

> I will fynd occasion to discourse it, for that the Passages are very woorthy, and the wisdome and goodnes of the king appears above the malice of others, and Normahall fulfill[s] the observation that in all actions of Consequence in a Court, especially in faction, a woman is not always an ingredient, but commonly a Principall drugg and of most vertue; and shee showes that they are not incapable of Conducting busines, nor herselfe voyd of witt and subtiltye. It will discover a noble Prince, an excellent wife, a faythfull Counceller, a Crafty stepmother, an ambitious sonne, a Cunning favorite: all reconciled by a Patient king, whose hart was not understood by any of these. But this will requier a Place alone, and not to be mingled amonge busines . . . (*Embassy*, ii. 363–4)

Some sixty years later, John Dryden might have been responding to Roe's desire to see the internecine struggles in the Mughal court in the form of a tragic drama. Dryden's play is, however, set in the last years of the reign of Khurram, the younger son Roe so despised. Khurram took the title Shah Jahan with the throne in 1628. Dryden makes much, as did the many historians of the Mughal dynasty, of the descent from the fourteenth-century Mongol conqueror Timur, who on his death in 1405 left his conquests in India (between the rivers Ganges and Indus) to one of his sons, Miracha. Not only are Dryden's Mughal emperors the proud

successors of Timur, but the play of *Aureng-Zebe* is knowingly successor
to the most influential dramatic representation of oriental achievement
and decline, which also derived from the life of Timur, Marlowe's
Tamburlaine the Great (1587). However, Marlowe's vainglorious,
military genius, who barely has time to notice the loss of his lovely
Zenocrate, undergoes radical transformation in Dryden's play.

Like his other reworking of an oriental tragedy, Shakespeare's
Antony and Cleopatra, All for Love (1677), Dryden's play domesticates
oriental militarism and (tyrannous) government. Both *Aureng-Zebe*
and *All for Love* transform cunning military strategists, Antony and
Aurangzeb (third son of Shah Jahan who successfully engineered his
sovereignty against the competition of his three brothers in 1658), into
passionate high-minded lovers who seek domestic security rather than
military glory. Moreover, the hero of *Aureng-Zebe* is given an affinity
with the other-worldly theosophies of India. The fictional younger
son, Morat (possibly a version of Aurangzeb's younger brother,
Murad-Baksh, with whom Aurangzeb formed an alliance early in the
fraternal competition over the ailing Shah Jahan's throne), dismisses
his brother as 'a dreaming Priest'.[21] Morat has been restored to his
father's favour because the old emperor lusts after Aureng-Zebe's
beloved, the lovely captive Kashmiri queen Indamora, and hopes that
the younger brother's preferment will be Aureng-Zebe's downfall.
The brothers meet before Morat orders Aureng-Zebe to be taken
away and slowly poisoned,[22] and each characterizes the other by
imagining what animal they might transmigrate into on death. Thus:

> AUR. When thou wert form'd, Heav'n did a Man begin;
> But the brute Soul, by chance, was shuffl'd in.
> In Woods and Wilds thy Monarchy maintain:
> Where valiant Beasts, by force and rapine, reign.

---

[21] *Aureng-Zebe*, in John Dryden, *Plays*, ed. Vinton A. Dearing, *Works of John Dryden*,
xii (Berkeley, Los Angeles and London: University of California Press, 1994), III. i. 313.
Throughout, I use the spelling 'Aurangzeb' to denote the historical figure and Dryden's
spelling 'Aureng-Zebe' to denote the dramatic character.
[22] Numerous travellers and historians refer to the practice of slow poisoning by opium
used by the Mughal emperors to quietly remove rivals to their power. See e.g., Bernier
who describes how Aurangzeb has the two sons of his oldest brother, Dara, Sulaiman
Shikoh and Sipihr Shikoh, along with Murad's grandson, killed with a daily dose of poppy
seed in the isolated fortress of Gualior (*History*, 241-2).

In Life's next scene, if Transmigration be,
Some Bear or Lion is reserv'd for thee.
MOR. Take heed thou com'st not in that Lion's way:
I prophecy though wilt thy Soul convey
Into a Lamb, and be again my Prey.—
Hence with that dreaming Priest.

(III. i. 304–13)

Dryden here, as elsewhere, transfers belief-systems and practices, (in this case transmigration of the soul) common to the Hindu natives of India to the Muslim rulers of the country. He also presents a Mughal princess, Melesinda, as choosing to become a sati on her husband's death, despite the evidence in Bernier and others of Mughal/Muslim opposition to the practice. In both cases, this seems to be part of the overall tendency in the play to present the Mughal court as retreating from the world of heroic empire into domestic concerns and passions.[23] Other evidence in the play makes it clear that Dryden was well aware of the distinctions between Hinduism and Islam (his accurate portrayal of Muslim notions of paradise and the afterlife in speeches by Aureng-Zebe are just one example), so the choice to blur them must have been made on dramatic and/or ideological grounds. When Morat calls his brother a 'preaching *Brachman*' (III. i. 216), this is surely meant to invoke the association of Hindu brahmans with trickery, illusion, and deceit, but it also, for western readers familiar with travel and historical accounts, marks Aureng-Zebe's distance and difference from the Mughal dynasty, even his sympathy with the potential desire of native Indians for liberty from Mughal despotism.

---

[23] He may also have been influenced by accounts of India which noted the tendency of the Mughals to incorporate aspects of 'native' Indian culture into the court. Of all the Muslim rulers in the East, the Mughals were seen as the most prone to hybridization and accommodation with the culture of the territory they occupied. Thus, Manucci paraphrases the thinking of Sultan Akbar (1542–1605) who in 1582 sought to introduce the Din-I-Ilah (or divine faith) amalgamating elements from Islam, Christianity, Hinduism, and Zoroastrianism, as follows: 'My People, says he, are a strange Medley of Mahometans, Idolaters and Christians. I'm resolved to bring them all to one Opinion. I'll join the Baptism of the one, and the Circumcision of the other to the Worship of *Brama*. I'll retain the *Metempsychosis*, plurality of Wives, and the Worship of *Jesus Christ*. Thus compounding my Religion of those Points, which are most agreeable to the Professors of the respective Sects, I shall be able to form 'em into one intire Flock, of which I my self shall be the Leader and Head' (Catrou *General History*, 154).

Dryden chooses to represent Aureng-Zebe as a hero, if by temperament a gentle and dreaming one, driven by a passion for his country, his mistress, and filial loyalty, despite the copious evidence from contemporary historians of India that the real Aurangzeb had none of these virtues. However, Aurangzeb's religious devotion was commented on, usually with scepticism, by contemporary sources. Bernier (who seems to have been Dryden's major source for the play) presents his apparent religious devotion as a way of concealing his political ambition; comparing Aurangzeb with his older pleasure-loving brother, Sultan Sujah, Bernier tells us that he

appeared more serious and melancholy, and was indeed much more judicious, understanding the World very well, and knowing whom to chuse for his service and purpose, and where to bestow his favour and bounty most for interest. He was reserved, crafty, and exceedingly versed in dissembling, insomuch that for a long while he made profession to be *Fakire*, that is Poor, *Dervich*, or Devout, renouncing the World, and faining not to pretend at all to the Crown, but to desire to pass his Life in Prayers and other Devotions. (*History*, 18)

Mannucci's description of Aurangzeb confirms this picture of a religious hypocrite:

He appear'd Thoughtful and Reserv'd, not given to Talk except from a Zeal for the Religion of *Mahobet* [*sic*] and the Observance of the Law. He always's carry'd the *Alcoran* under his Arm. His Prayers were frequent and publick. He read over every Day certain Heads of the Praises of God, with an Attention that imposed on the most Discerning. Accordingly 'twas said he had enter'd himself into the Fraternity of *Faquirs*, and that as soon as he cou'd free himself from the cares of the World, he was resolv'd to go and spend the remainder of his Days in Prayer and Pennance near the Tombe of *Mahomet*. The better to impose on the Multitude he never appear'd Abroad but in White, very Plain, and generally without the Ornaments of Jewels, in which the *Mogol* Princes usually Sparkle. His Food was suitable to the simplicity of his Apparel. A little Rice and Pulse were the only Meats serv'd to his Table. As for Wine, he did not know the Taste of it, and his Exactness in this so essential an Article was ever unchangeable. In his very Infancy he discover'd a Disposition to Politicks and Dissimulation. Under all these Discourses of retir'd Life, *Oramgzeb* [*sic*] conceal'd a boundless Ambition; he look'd on 'em as the likelyest Means of securing himself against the Violences of a suddain Revolution. He knew his Lot after the death of *Cha-Jaham* his Father, must either be to Reign or Dye. In this Thought he resolv'd either to mount the Throne, if a way shou'd open to him, or secure his Life by seeming to renounce the World and sacrificing all his Pretentions, by devoting himself to a religious Life. In the mean time Calumny did not spare publishing that the Prince did in Private plunge himself into the most forbidden Pleasures. The *Faquirs* (say they) whose Company he affects, are the Confidents and Ministers of his Debauches. (Catrou, *General History*, 236–7).

Dryden plays fast and loose with the known historical facts in other ways. Dryden's Aureng-Zcbc is in competition primarily with his younger brother Morat. Early in the play, Darah and Sujah, his two older brothers, are reported to have fled and been killed by Morat.[24] No mention is made of Aurangzeb's violent execution of his oldest brother, Dara. The two influential sisters, Begum-Saheb (stalwart defender of Dara's claim, she lived with her father throughout her life and, some chroniclers report, enjoyed an incestuous relationship with him) and Raushan-Ara-Begum (she gave her support to Aurangzeb) are not represented in the play at all. However, their importance in historical sources may have led Dryden to invest the female characters he invents with dramatic authority and centrality. Women in this play are indeed, as Roe would put it, 'not always an ingredient, but commonly a Principall drugg'. Dryden resurrects the figure of Aurangzeb's grandfather's influential wife, Nourmahal, as the fictional empress, queen to the old emperor, and presents her as a whirlwind of passion and faction, who, because of her husband's neglect, turns her amatory attention to Aureng-Zebe, finally taking her own life with a poison when her desires, political and sexual, are frustrated. Dryden also invents two other female parts not known in the historical accounts, a captive Kashmiri queen named Indamora who is in love with Aureng-Zebe but pursued by both his father and brother, and

---

[24] The brief character sketches of these two brothers given by courtiers in the play correspond with the historical accounts. Darah, we are told, 'bears a generous mind; | But to implacable revenge inclin'd', while Sujah is brave but 'a Bigot of the Persian sect' (I. i. 90–1, 95). Bernier describes Dara as quick to anger and unwilling to listen to council and describes Shujah as a Shi'ite rather than Sunni Muslim. He also comments on the bravery of the youngest brother, Morad Bakhsh (*History*, 20), which corresponds with the description of Morat in the play as 'too insolent, too much a Brave' (I. i. 98).

Melesinda, virtuous wife to Morat, who chooses suttee on his death despite his cruel rejection of her in favour of Indamora.

Dryden's source, Bernier, as Bridget Orr has pointed out, not only provided him with plot elements but also with the suggestion that Mughal history could be understood as dramatic, especially tragic, narrative.[25] Moreover, the role of women as (secret) agents in internecine plotting was highlighted by Bernier as it had been by Roe. He implies that Mughal history is best presented in the form of a tragic drama than a romance narrative, when he defends his decision to describe the princesses' amorous dealings:

I shall not scruple to relate here some of the *Amours* of this Princess, although shut up in a *Seraglio*, and well kept, like other Women. Neither shall I apprehend, that I may be thought to prepare Matter for a Romancer; for they are not *Amours* like Ours, followed by Gallant and *Comical* Adventures, but attended with Events dreadful and *Tragical*. (*History*, 23)

And only a few pages later he returns to the importance of the women's part in the tragic action:

I esteem'd . . . that I was not to forget those two Princesses, as having been the most considerable Actors in the Tragedy; the Women in the *Indies* taking very often, as well as at *Constantinople* and in many other places, the best part in the most important Transactions, though Men take seldom notice of it, and trouble their heads of seeking for other Causes. (*History*, 31–2)

Dryden takes his cue from Bernier's characterization of the Mughal court as a scene of spectacular and dramatic action, in which women were major, if often invisible, players.

Sir Thomas Roe uses dramatic analogy also, although he is inclined to emphasize the comic or failed dramatic effects of the Mughal spectacle. Thus, on 19 January 1716 he records that the king's Durbar (Council) has 'soe much affinitye with a Theatre—the manner of the king in his gallery; The great men lifted on a stage as actors; the vulgar below gazing on—that an easy description will informe of the place and fashion' (*Embassy*, i. 108). Describing his meeting with the Prince Parwiz prior to reaching Jahangir's court in November 1615, he is scathing about the Parwiz's Durbar: 'To discribe it rightly it was like a

[25] Orr, *Empire on the English Stage*, 16.

great stage, and the Prince satt above as the Mock kings doth thear' (i. 92).

Dryden's play self-consciously stages the Mughal court, then, along the lines of these theatrical renderings by European travellers of the eastern court. But he also radically transforms and relocates plot elements and, perhaps most importantly, refuses the opposition of tragedy (Bernier) and farce or comedy (Roe) by turning his play into a tragicomedy. Although the play concludes on the deaths of two of the principal female actors, Melesinda and Nourmahal, it also offers an (equivocal) solution in the happy union of Aureng-Zebe and Indamora and the restoration, apparently, of stable government to the troubled and war-torn empire.

Why did Dryden take such liberties with recent Indian history? Numerous hypotheses have been put forward by critics. Thus, Nandini Bhattacharya concludes that Dryden's aim was to present Aurangzeb as 'a plausible, submissive object of colonial domination'.[26] Virtuous characters such as Aureng-Zebe, Melesinda, and Indamora are presented as open to control by others, nascent subaltern figures who already subscribe to the bourgeois, affective, and trade-dominated 'civil' values of western Europe which will eventually unseat the corrupt, lust-driven, and self-interested oriental despotism embodied in the old emperor, his wife, and his youngest son. She summarizes the play as a 'culturally conditioned attempt to portray a non-western culture as essentially more fragile and vulnerable, embodying certain polarized stereotypical gender identities, and therefore seeming a fair target for penetration and comparison' (78).

Balachandra Rajan is more sceptical about the proto-colonial vision inscribed in Dryden, noting that for seventeenth-century Europe, Mughal India was a sovereign state and not a potential subject territory.[27] He claims that Dryden misappropriates Mughal India for purposes of analogy with England's own succession crises of the 1670s, an appropriation which Rajan sees as 'methodically perverse' (68) rather than ignorant; he concludes that Dryden is 'not ignoring Bernier's text; he is writing a critique of it' (70). The 'historical'

---

[26] Bhattacharya, *Reading the Splendid Body*, 49.
[27] Balachandra Rajan, *Under Western Eyes. India from Milton to Macaulay* (London and Durham, NC: Duke University Press, 1999), 67.

Aurangzeb is a negative example against which Dryden can set his positive account of succession secured through moderation and the love of the people, a monitory example to Charles II's successor, James, duke of York, widely criticized for his Catholic bigotry and arrogance. Dryden can only affect his analogical aim through gross distortion of the Indian history which is the source of the analogy itself. 'The play offers itself as an endeavour to display India as exemplary, but the very comprehensiveness of its effort to do so draws attention to a historical reality that is quite the reverse of the play's apparent intention' (77). Rajan concurs with Bhattacharya that the effect of Dryden's play is to contribute to an ongoing tendency on the part of European writers to feminize India and to imagine the relationship between England and India as an amatory or spousal one, partly as a means of concealing the stark commercial interest of the East India Company, not dissimilar to the appropriative exploitation of India by the Tartar dynasty of Mughal kings evoked in the play.

Richard Braverman is even more explicit about both the analogical purposes of Dryden's play and the ambiguity that surrounds Dryden's presentation of his hero, the question mark over Aurang-Zebe's future success as a monarch. For Braverman, the play exposes the limits of romance idealism as embodied by Aureng-Zebe to resolve political division; Aureng-Zebe is a version of James, duke of York, a romance idealist who requires a strong leaven of political pragmatism if he is to unify the nation and secure his succession, a leaven that Aureng-Zebe inherits from his younger brother, Morat, on the latter's death.[28]

Mita Choudhury reminds us that *Aureng-Zebe*'s staging of Mughal history needs to be thought about in its context as performance rather than a simple rewriting or misappropriation of one text by another. It is, she claims, 'an elaborate myth framed by a nonchalant disregard for the origin of the subject matter but with a full appreciation of the contemporary dynamics of spectatorship and the English theatre'.[29] Like Braverman and Rajan, Choudhury sees the

---

[28] Richard Braverman, *Plots and Counterplots: Sexual Politics and the Body Politic in English Literature, 1660–1730*, Cambridge Studies in Eighteenth-Century English Literature and Thought 18 (Cambridge: Cambridge University Press, 1993), 125–34.
[29] Choudhury, *Interculturalism and Resistance*, 135.

text as an appropriation of India for English purposes, but one which invites spectators 'to visualize the distant in their own, familiar terms' (138). Hence, difference is established only to be denied and the Orient relocated to a familiar classical past in terms of performance (male actors adopt Roman dress for instance). Thus 'the object loses its past. And its present and future are circumscribed by a disfigured adaptation' (44).

In sum, then, critics have recognized the ideological work that the play represents in turning India into a territory for English consumption, but also the ambivalence which haunts a play that takes events from recent history in a distant part of the globe and turns them into an allegory for events in England. Laura Brown reminds us that to read heroic drama of the Restoration as Eurocentric allegory or proto-colonial ambition does not 'fully account for the genre's unique and powerful obsession with alterity'.[30] The reading I outline below suggests that the fantasy of cultural difference(s) played out in *Aureng-Zebe* is an example of the ongoing shaping of India as dream-prospect which dated back to the medieval period but acquired new resonance and complication as England began to view itself as a potential empire from the late seventeenth century onward (although colonial rule in India itself was still over a century away when Dryden wrote his play). India, like a dream, and like the act of suttee, is both other and same, analogy and ineluctable difference, comprehensible within familiar frames of reference but always liable to evade full assimilation.

Choudhury, Rajan, and Braverman all point to the play's preoccupation with temporality through the theme of succession and its tendency to undercut the sense of temporal order, the inability of the present moment fully to incorporate the past and envisage a secure future. The theme of dreaming and the visionary reinforces this sense of a disturbed and dislocated temporality and space. Indamora, like Canzade, is the embodiment of the dream of India possessed, prompting temporal confusion in her lovers and a misty prospect of future bliss. Thus Arimant, the courtier, tries unsuccessfully to woo her with a comment that 'Desire's the vast extent of humane

---

[30] Laura Brown, *Fables of Modernity: Literature and Culture in the English Eighteenth Century* (Ithaca, NY, and London: Cornell University Press, 2001), 199.

mind, | It mounts above, and leaves poor hope behind' (II. i 55–6); Morat, after listening to Indamora's arguments against fraternal conflict, comments:

> You show me somewhat I ne'r learnt before;
> But 'tis the distant prospect of a Shore,
> Doubtful in mists; which, like inchanted ground,
> Flies from my sight, before 'tis fully found.
>
> (V. i. 100–4)

However, it is Aureng-Zebe who is most consistently associated with dreaming and identified by others as a dreamer. If Aureng-Zebe is a dreaming priest, he is not one in the sense of a visionary who can imagine a paradise or order beyond the present moment. Rather he is locked in the pleasures and passions of the moment, particularly those of the amatory encounter, at the expense of his duties to the state. In this respect, he accords with the presentation of Islam as a religion of worldly pleasures, lacking a theology and securing allegiance through its promise of material satisfaction in this world and the next.[31]

In Aureng-Zebe's first reunion with Indamora in the first act of the play, Indamora chides him for falling prey to the imaginative pleasures of love in terms familiar to English playgoers from Theseus' famous speech at the conclusion of *A Midsummer Night's Dream* (V. i. 2–22):

> Love is an aery good Opinion makes;
> Which he who onely thinks he has, partakes:
> Seen by a strong Imagination's Beam;
> That tricks and dresses up the gaudy Dream.
> Presented so, with rapture 'tis enjoyed:
> Rais'd by high Fancy, and by low destroy'd.
>
> (I. i. 372–7)

Aureng-Zebe responds by casting Indamora in the role of earthly houri, once again evoking the parallel between his dreams and those of

---

[31] Edward Terry explains the attraction of Islam as lying in its promise of worldly gratification, while he condemns it as a monstrous blasphemy. He concludes that 'because it conteins much in it very *pleasing* to *flesh* and *blood*, and *soothes* up, and *complies* exceedingly with corrupt *nature*, it wanted no followers presently to embrace, and assert it' (*Voyage to East-India*, 260).

the religious aesthete:

> If Love be Vision, mine has all the fire
> Which, in first Dreams, young Prophets does inspire:
> I dream, in you, our promis'd Paradice:
> An Ages tumult of continu'd bliss
> But you have still your happiness in doubt:
> Or else 'tis past, and you have dream't it out.
>
> (I. i. 378–83)

Aureng-Zebe claims the role of breacher of temporal divisions, while he condemns his mistress as unfaithful on slender grounds. His single-minded sexual/religious love for his mistress means that he can unify the past, present, and future of India; he embodies the 'virtues' of different historical moments and different cultures: western bourgeois domestic lover, classical hero, and devout Muslim ruler. She, he complains, lacks confidence in their future or has left behind the dream of their love. However, his speech also reveals his own short-coming: that he is trapped in an eternal present of romantic love, which may limit his ability to unify a political state.

The process of simultaneously securing a parallel and marking a distance between India and England is effected by the use of classical paradigms in the play. Ancient Greece and Rome, as non-Christian cultures that provide a rich source of myth and symbol for western Europe, serve as a means of gauging ideological proximity or distance. Classical parallels are particularly important in mediating the behaviour of the women in the play to its English audience. Dryden presents the women in the plays as embodiments of a homogenized 'Indianness' distinguished only by the contrast between the lust-driven queen familiar to she-tragedy of the period (Nourmahal) and the virtuous devoted wife and/or mistress (Melesinda/Indamora). The invented names of the two virtuous heroines indicate their symbolic status in relation to the geographical territory they inhabit, in that both contain the stem 'ind'. Latin derivations suggest their names mean 'song/melody of India' (Meles-inda) and 'love of India' or 'India as love object' (Ind-amora). Dryden's comments in his dedication point to the classical analogy, first disclaiming a similarity in his comment of Indamora that he has 'made my Heroine fearful of death, which neither *Cassandra* nor *Cleopatra* would have been' (p. 198) and then suggesting a different classical analogy that might make the 'Indian wife' comprehensible to the English reader/viewer:

I have made my *Melesinda*, in opposition to *Nourmahal*, a Woman passionately loving of her Husband, patient of injuries and contempt, and constant in her kindness, to the last: and in that, perhaps, I may have err'd, because it is not a Virtue much in use. Those *Indian* Wives are loving Fools, and may do well to keep themselves in their own Countrey, or, at least, to keep company with the *Arria's* and *Portia's* of old *Rome*: some of our Ladies know better things. (p.198)

Like his source, Bernier, Dryden chastises the behaviour of the western culture he is addressing (Indian wives are more loyal than the self-interested English ladies), but he also parallels his heroine with Roman wives associated with the decline of classical empire rather than its high point, again implying the uncertain future of Aureng-Zebe's resolution of this conflict (and indeed, the decline of the Mughal empire was ushered in with Aurangzeb's accession).

The outline of a shadow over Aureng-Zebe's suitability as sovereign becomes more definite when we consider how often his own speech is shadowed by the other significant dreamer of the play, Nourmahal, a character whose name locates her as a figure of Indian history rather than classical precedent. When she enters in the second act, Nourmahal's first words concern dreaming, but in this case they refer to frightful visions rather than misty or hedonistic prospects of delight:

> EMP. What rage transports you? are you well awake?
>   Such Dreams distracted minds in Feavers make.
> NOUR. Those Feavers you have giv'n, those Dreams have bred,
>   By broken Faith, and an abandon'd Bed.
>   Such Visions hourly pass before my sight;
>   Which from my eyes their Balmy slumbers fright,
>   In the severest silence of the night:
>   Visions, which in this Cittadel are seen;
>   Bright, glorious Visions of a Rival Queen.
>   (II. i. ll.212–20)

Although Nourmahal is cast as Aureng-Zebe's opposite, apparent difference is revealed to conceal uncomfortable proximity. Both

Nourmahal and Aureng-Zebe are quick to leap to judgement as a result of their sexual frustration/insecurity and both use a language of sexual conquest and covetousness expressed in terms of the dream.

Nourmahal undertakes to act as Aureng-Zebe's guard/executioner but instead takes the opportunity to lead him to a scene of oriental luxury and lasciviousness she has prepared for his attempted seduction. A classical parallel is used to bridge the oriental/occidental divide and convey the nature of her passion, when Nourmahal narrates a dream that sees her cast as Aphrodite spurred to love by her own son (Aureng-Zebe is Nourmahal's stepson):

> I dream'd, your Love was by Love's Goddess sought;
> Officious *Cupids*, hov'ring o'r your head,
> Held Myrtle wreaths: beneath your feet were spread
> What Sweets soe'r *Sabean* Springs disclose,
> Our *Indian* Jasmine, or the *Syrian* Rose:
> The wanton Ministers around you strove
> For service, and inspir'd their Mother's Love:
> Close by your side, and languishing, she lies,
> With blushing cheeks, short breath, and wishing eyes;
> Upon your breast supinely lay her head,
> While, on your face, her famish'd sight she fed.
> (IV. i. 98 108)

When Aureng-Zebe refuses her advances, she tries to incite his suicide, but is prevented by Morat who has suspended his sentence by one day at the request of Indamora. This disclosure in turn prompts Aureng-Zebe's suspicions of his mistress's fidelity and in his next appearance he rants against Indamora and is then reconciled to her in a scene of passion which echoes the language of possession used by his stepmother:

> Love mounts, and rowls about my stormy mind,
> Like Fire, that's born by a tempestuous Wind.
> Oh, I could stifle you, with eager haste!
> Devour your kisses with my hungry taste!
> Rush on you! eat you! wander o'r each part,
> Raving with pleasure, snatch you to my heart!

Then hold you off, and gaze! then, with new rage,
Invade you, till my conscious Limbs presage
Torrents of joy, which all their banks o'rflow!
So lost, so blest, as I but then could know!

(IV. ii. 144–53)

The image of a fire stoked by a tempestuous wind is in turn reprised by Nourmahal in her final scene of poison-induced delirium; here too, the seductive dream is displaced by frightful visions and the 'fire' of the Indian woman's passion is collapsed, as it was for so many European commentators describing the scene of suttee, into association with the fires of a Christian hell:

I burn, I more than burn; I am all fire:
See how my mouth and nostrils flame expire!
I'll not come near my self—
Now I'm a burning Lake, it rowls and flows;
I'll rush, and pour it all upon my Foes.
Pull, pull, that reverend piece of Timber near:
Throw't on—'tis dry—'twill burn—
Ha, ha! how my old Husband crackles there!
Keep him down, keep him down; turn him about:
I know him; he'll but whiz, and strait go out.
Fan me, you Winds: what, not one breath of Air?
I burn 'em all, and yet have flames to spare.
Quench me: pour on whole Rivers. 'Tis in vain:
Morat stands there to drive 'em back again:
With those huge Bellows in his hands, he blows
New fire into my head: My Brain-pan glows.
See! see! there's *Aureng-Zebe* too takes his part;
But he blows all his fire into my heart.

(V. i. 641–57)

Nourmahal's ravings as she is consumed by an internal fire coincide with Melesinda's departure to join the body of her husband on his funeral pyre. Melesinda is thus the 'real' sati to Nourmahal's illusion of herself as a sati, embracing her own death by a burning poison (in her delirium she envisions her husband's body burning on a pyre and herself consumed by flames). The link is reinforced by sources on India which claimed that suttee was introduced in ancient India as a means of preventing wives from poisoning husbands who dissatisfied them.[32]

The role of Melesinda in the play has been overlooked by most critics in favour of promoting the more simple opposition between Nourmahal as exotic southern queen of fire and passion, and Indamora as rational northern idealized virtue, more often associated with the elements of water and air. Kashmir, Indamora's homeland, is frequently cited by contemporary commentators as a place of extraordinary beauty and desirability.[33] As queen of Kashmir, Indamora is the only woman in the play who might be expected to be Hindu rather than Muslim and thus a candidate for suttee on a husband's death. But it is Melesinda, Muslim wife of Morat, who claims the role of sati and it is that exemplary role which suggests we might see her as an alternative candidate to Nourmahal for identification with the figure of Aureng-Zebe. Both are characters whose sexual devotion is absolute but at the expense of their political agency.

Melesinda's speech consistently marries the elsewhere opposed imagery of fire and water (voiced by Nourmahal and Indamora). In the third act, when she agrees, at Indamora's prompting, to try and mediate on Aureng-Zebe's behalf with her intractable husband, she has a presentiment that the introduction of Indamora to Morat may be her own downfall and complains: 'Mine is a gleam of bliss, too hot to last, | Wat'ry

[32] Thus Manucci claims: '*Brama* enacted this Law for the putting a stop to a crying Iniquity. The Women grown weary of their Husbands, had frequently made 'em away by Poison. The most effectual Means that *Brama* cou'd think of to prevent a Mischief so very common, was placing the Glory of the Women in burning themselves on the Bodies of their Husbands, or living after their Decease in a perpetual State of Widowhood. Thence arises that Care, and Tenderness of Wives for those to whom Providence has once assign'd 'em. Their Lives and Liberties depend on the Lives of their Husbands' (Catrou, *General History*, 66–7).

[33] Bernier gives an evocative and moving account of his experiences accompanying Aurangzeb's court in 1664 to 'the Kingdom of Kachemire, by the Mogols called the Paradies of the Indies'. He describes the terrible suffering endured in the vast train crossing desert and mountains to reach their goal, of which he comments 'one would take this whole Kingdom for some great *Ever-green* Garden' (*Continuation*, 84). He goes on to remark that Kashmiris have a reputation for 'being a very witty people, much more intelligent and dexterous than the *Indians*, and as fit for Poesie and Science as the *Persians*' (93), and adds that they are 'also famous for their good complexion. They look as well as our *Europeans*, and have nothing of a *Tartarian* flat-nos'd and little-ey'd Face, as those of *Kachguer*, and most of the people of the great *Tibet*. The Women especially are very beautiful; and therefore all Strangers, that are new comers to the Court of *Mogol*, are furnished from thence, that so they may have Children whiter than the *Indians*, and which by this means may pass for true *Mogols*' (95–6).

it shines, and will be soon o'rcast' (III. i. 132–3). The oxymoron of the watery flame soon to be put out (by Indamora's brighter light) is later transformed by Melesinda in her closing speech into the claim for her love as an elemental fire that burns without fuel. Thus she imagines or dreams her own death for the speakers before her departure thus:

> My love was such, it needed no return;
> But could, though he suppli'd no fuel, burn:
> Rich in it self, like Elemental fire,
> Whose pureness does no Aliment require.
> In vain you would bereave me of my Lord;
> For I will die: die is too base a word;
> I'll seek his breast, and, kindling by his side,
> Adorned with flames, I'll mount a glorious Bride.
>
> (V. i. 628–35)

Melesinda here speaks as the willing, indeed ecstatic sati (Fig. 15); her name (song of India) and her speeches draw on descriptions given by

15. Engraving of suttee, François Bernier, *Voyages de Fr. Bernier ... contenant la description des états du Grand Mogol, de l'Hindoustan, du royaume de Kachemire, &c,* vol. ii (Amsterdam, 1710), p. 131

travellers to India of the sati who sings her way to death. Edward
Terry, for example, comments that

though the poor Creature who thus dies may return and live if she please,
even then when she comes to the *Pile*, which immediately after turns her into
ashes yet she who is once thus resolved, never starts back from her first firm
and setled resolution, but goes on singing to her death, having taken some
intoxicating thing to turn, or disturb her brains.[34]

In Melesinda, then, we see another alternative to the dream of India,
a more melancholy prospect than the mutinous flame of Nourmahal
which can be quashed by the domestic bourgeois virtues of the Anglo-
Indian hero, or the delightful ideal prospect of the virgin territory
of Indamora which can be wooed and possessed by him. Rather,
Melesinda's is the recalcitrant empire of the 'loving fool', addicted to
absolute authority and wedded to Mughal authoritarianism despite its
decadence, who may ultimately prove beyond possession or comprehension. This version of India was recirculated at the end of the
eighteenth century in the trial of Warren Hastings in 1788 and the
condemnation of Anglo-Indian rule as decadent, wedded to its own
pleasures, dissolute, having succumbed to the seductive song of
India.[35] If Dryden's play can be read as a proto-colonial dream, it
inscribes within it the possibility that India may finally evade the
colonial grasp, or that the cost of India's possession may involve a
counter-hybridization which will eventually, as it did Mughal rule,
undermine the enterprise. The ground for Aureng-Zebe's secure
possession of Indamora and the establishment of peaceful empire at the
close of the play is only secured by the self-immolation of the two
female characters who represent the more incendiary and destructive
aspects of his dreaming, devotional, desiring identity.

In his representation of the song of India, Melesinda, Dryden may
have been inspired by a comment in his source, Bernier, on the music he
hears at court and how he gradually learnt to appreciate its beauty, where
at first he heard only cacophony. The sound of trumpets and cymbals

in the beginning did so pierce and stun me, that it was insufferable for me; yet
I know not what strange power custome hath, for I now find it very pleasing,

---

[34] Terry, *Voyage to East-India*, 324–5.
[35] See Kate Teltscher, 'Geographical Morality', ch. 5 of her *India Inscribed*.

especially in the night, when I hear it afar off in my bed upon my Terrasse; then it seemeth to me to carry with it something that is grave, majestical and very melodious. (*History*, 38)

Dryden's *Aureng-Zebe*'s appeal to an English audience might be understood in similar terms. It is the only play of the late seventeenth century to use India as a setting for an oriental drama and it announces its own strangeness as such, an attempt to accustom English ears to a culture that otherwise might seem incoherent or incomprehensible. The use of classical analogy, the location of the play in a tradition of oriental tragedy in descent from Marlowe, and also the imagery in a chain of association from Shakespeare's *Dream*—all serve to bring a distant territory closer to home, to present strange and alien practices as comprehensible within a European frame. However, these same processes also radically distort and indeed jumble the culture(s) they relate, to the extent that the play cannot provide any access to 'India' or the Mughal court except as an elaborate and spectacular fiction for English consumption.

Like Canzade, Melesinda cannot be assimilated into the vision of an uxorious mercantile government; she is too wedded to the fire of passion. European writers repeatedly represent the sati in these contradictory terms, as both inassimilable otherness and exemplary instance of virtuous love. Rajeswari Sunder Rajan provides a powerful analysis of the problematic nature of suttee in pre-colonial and colonial discourse, as 'a negative agency, an absence of acquiescence in one's oppression'.[36] In a play which repeatedly tries and fails to imagine a political solution to contested succession which can balance romance idealism and political pragmatism, Melesinda emerges as the figure for its impossibility, an impossibility that continued to haunt and undermine the dream of English 'possession' of India.

The treasures of the East: Indian tales

Suttee is the route chosen by another female figure who also signifies resistance to appropriation by a colonizing power or imagination: the

---

[36] Sunder Rajan, *Real and Imagined Women*, 12.

Princess Padmani of Chitor, whose tale is given much attention and dramatic emphasis in Catrou's extracts from the memoirs of Manucci. The Mughal Emperor Akbar (reigned 1556–1605) invaded Chitor, capital of Mewar in Rajasthan as part of his expansionist policy in northern India. Catrou's account gives his 'Akebar' sexual as well as political motive; Akebar offers to abandon his siege if Padmani, Hindu wife to the Rana, agrees to divorce her husband and marry him. When Rana is seized, Padmani pretends to be tempted by the offer and asks to visit her husband in private in his castle prison near Agra in order to agree the divorce. She sends in her place in an enclosed palanquin her chief vizier and eight brave soldiers who liberate Rana and put him on a swift horse back to his wife in Chitor. Subsequently, Rana is killed by Akebar when the Great Mogul is taking pot-shots at those Rageput soldiers walking on the ramparts, and two days afterwards Akebar is informed that 'the generous *Padmani* according to the Custom of the *Ragepute* Princesses, had thrown herself into the Flames and mingled her Ashes with those of her Husbands'.[37] In his *Tales, Translated from the Persian of Inatulla of Delhi* (1768), Dow reprises this story with some alterations, rendering it as the story of Commladeve, a descendent of the Rajas of Chitor whose father is seized in an attack by Mohammedans. When the Muslim chief vizier makes advances to her in exchange for her father's freedom, she, like Padmani, requests one visit in an enclosed palanquin, smuggles in twenty warriors by this means, and liberates her father, although she is herself seized thereafter and carried to Delhi to be pursued further by the vizier.

Catrou's account concludes with some thoughts on the attractions of this kind of story of romantic loyalty woven into a tragedy of state for European readers, over and above stories with a more secure provenance as translations of ancient Indian narratives. Thus, he comments:

This Relation which we find, as well in *European* as in *Indian* Histories, (says M. *Manouchi*) seems to have an Air of Fable invented to Amuse; and yet it has nothing of the Stile of those Romances which are commonly written in the *Indies*, and are for the most part stuff'd with Discourses between monkies, tales of other Animals, and Miracles of the Gods of the Country, without the

---

[37] Catrou, *General History*, 128.

least Appearance of Reality. However, as this Adventure of *Akebar* and *Padmani* is not found in the Chronicle of the Empire, the Reader may give it what Credit he Pleases. As to the taking of *Chitor* and the Death of *Rana* they are incontestable Facts. (*General History*, 128)

Although the story may be a fictional invention or elaboration around an actual set of historical events, it is judged to be more 'credible' than those in the genuine and rich narrative tradition of ancient India, largely written in Sanskrit. Those discourses between monkeys, tales of other animals, and miracles of the gods of the country are presumably a reference to the *Ramayana*, in which the monkey general Hanuman, later revered as a god, is instrumental in restoring Sita to Rama; the *Pañcatantra*, in which a series of animal fables are used to debate the nature of good government and especially the role of the courtier; and the *Mahabharata, Harivamsa*, and *Puranas* as well as the Pali *Jatakas* (episodes in the Buddha's earlier lives), all of which include stories of the lives of gods. With the exception of the *Pañcatantra* (which we will turn to later), none of these tales was available in translation to European readers at the time that Catrou was preparing Manucci's memoirs for publication.

Prose narratives about or from India in seventeenth- and eighteenth-century Europe take one of two forms: either the oriental tale concerning romantic love (often questioning whether it reinforces or undermines loyalty to the state) and claimed to be 'translated' or 'transcribed' from genuine oriental sources (especially Persian); or the translated fable, often with animal protagonists, derived from ancient Indian literary tradition. However, tales with an Indian context tend to stress a distinction rarely made in their Persian, Turkish, or Chinese equivalents: between morality tales (often animal fables), told by a sage priest as wise counsel, and the tale of romantic love told with political interest by the courtier or courtesan. Yet, both these may coexist within a single publication, as in Alexander Dow's *Tales*. Scheherazade mingles tales of talking animals and tales of sexual transgression freely in the *Arabian Nights Entertainments*. The discussion that follows thus divides fictions of India into these two different areas: the oriental tale more familiar from the Turkish, Persian, and Chinese collections discussed earlier; and the 'fable', a form which is traced to specifically Indian origins. In both cases, however, the Orient continues to be associated by occidental writing with the production of fiction and the use of fiction for instrumental, educative and often political purposes.

The ambiguous status of fiction as a fabrication that can also have moral effects is made particularly apparent in the context of the representation of Indian priest-narrators. Collections of tales revolve around the opposition between the deceitful spinner of lies and fictions for self-interested ends and the virtuous user of allegory for purposes of moral instruction, whether the teller is characterized as Hindu or Muslim. Thus the Hindu brahman can appear as a trickster as well as a man of reason and mystical knowledge; the Muslim imam can teach the virtues of monotheistic loyalty and a belief in providence or promote the pleasure-seeking teachings of the 'great impostor', Mahomet. The Arabic term 'faqir', which simply means 'poor man' but came to be used to refer to a travelling mendicant 'holy' man, chimed with the English word 'fake' so that the term is always used in a derogatory way, often as a contrast to the aristocratic brahman or politically influential imam. Christian authors/translators of fictions make rich and varied use of the opposition, aligning their own religion with Hinduism and Islam variously as the occasion, their own, and their culture's ideological predilections, demand.

In the case of the sequence of oriental tales, the idea of India as a dream or vision remains central, not least because authors 'frame' their tales as parables or allegories for a western imagination. In the case of the fable, the notion of the dream is displaced in favour of a discourse that is much closer to the 'rational' satirical critique found in the epistolary fictions written in the voice of the Persian, Turkish, or Chinese informant discussed in earlier chapters. Here, the Orient appears as the voice of an enlightened, sceptical knowledge which an irrational inward-looking West is called upon to hear by disaffected and critical European writers.

Tales of India: weaving illusions

Prose fiction narratives that take India as their setting rarely concentrate on the Mughal dynasty as exclusively as does Dryden's play.

Collections of oriental tales tend to claim a setting in independent states, usually under Muslim rule but tributary to the Mughal court or so unspecific in terms of their history or geography as to be unlocatable. Thus Alexander Dow's collection of tales is told to a young prince of 'the paradisial regions of Hindostan' named Jehandar.[38] Gueullette's *Mogul Tales* are set in Gujerat and the author explicitly mentions that the native state resisted Tamerlane's Mughal descendants and converted to Islam under the leadership of a native king, Oguz. James Ridley's *Tales of the Genii* (1764) is unusual in its use of a Mughal frame; the stories repeated to a British ambassador, Sir Charles Morell at Fort St George,[39] are those originally told to Aurangzeb's son Osmir by an imam of Persian extraction, a devout Muslim educated in the mysteries of western science and an admirer of Isaac Newton.

Authors who give their tales the most geographical and historical specificity prove to have the least direct acquaintance with the territory. There is no evidence that Gueullette travelled to India, whereas Dow spent four years as a captain in the East India Company's Bengal infantry prior to his publication in 1768 of the *Tales* and a translation from the Persian of Muhammad Kâsim Hindû Shâh Firishtah's *The History of Hindostan* of the same year. James Ridley probably never visited India; he obtained a post as chaplain in the East India Company's service after his graduation from New College, Oxford, in 1760, but relinquished it to become chaplain to a marching regiment and served in the Seven Years War in France, returning to England because of ill health around 1762.

In these three collections of tales we can trace a transforming pattern of European response to India in which different aspects of Hindu, Muslim, and, later, British rule can be used as analogues of the European state, written as they were during periods of ascendancy for

[38] Inâyat Allâh Kanbû, *Tales. Translated from the Persian of the Inatulla of Delhi*, trans. Alexander Dow (London, 1768), ii. 2.

[39] The East India Company positioned their trading centre at Fort St George in Madras to be close to the weaving centres from which the company obtained goods for export to Persia and the East Indies. It became the headquarters of the company in South India in 1641, and it was the first company settlement in India to be fortified. In 1746 it was captured briefly by the French; on recovery, in 1748, it was largely rebuilt, enabling the British to defend it successfully against the French in 1758–59 (*Encyclopaedia Britannica*).

the British, and to a lesser extent (and in competition with the British) the French East India Companies in India. Gueullette's tales suggest an analogy with early eighteenth-century France struggling to come to terms with the departure of a 'golden' age signified by a powerful absolutist king, Louis XIV. Ridley's imagine the prospect of a peaceful Protestant British succession to Muslim rule hard on the heels of Britain's military success in the Seven Years War and finds parallels between the virtues required of the good Mussulman and the good Christian. In Dow's collection, Hindu philosophy and culture is rehabilitated to contrast with Muslim 'despotism' and imply that British rule in India should avoid imitating the acquisitive and corrupt behaviour of previous rulers; Dow had direct experience of Robert Clive's rapacious policy in Bengal of leasing provincial property to Indian nawabs in return for exorbitant tributes. His writings are the opening salvos in attacks on the British East India Company and especially on Robert Clive and Warren Hastings for avarice, vice, and exploitation.[40]

However, the collections make only oblique reference to the political tensions and conflicts between Christian, Muslim, and Hindu powers in India and incline rather to present to their reader 'paradisial' spaces as fresh and vivid as the scenes painted on the chintz bedspreads and hangings, and the silks, imported from India, or in the Mughal paintings so popular among collectors. We might parallel the 'imported' text of the collection of tales with imported textiles from India, both bulk imports of plain cotton and small quantities of luxury embroidered muslin and printed silks. Writers often make the contrast of their own texts with 'other' textiles, or rival

---

[40] Dow was an antagonist of Robert Clive, but was nevertheless promoted to Lieutenant-Colonel on his return to Bengal in 1769; the third volume of his translation of Firishtah's *History*, which appeared in 1772, was an open attack on Clive (Lucy S. Sutherland, *The East India Company in Eighteenth-Century Politics* (Oxford: Clarendon Press, 1952), 221). A parliamentary campaign against Clive in 1773 was the result of an increasing need to bring the East India Company and its 'nabobs' under the control of the British state to avoid the massive personal profits and despotic rule enjoyed by Company individuals in India. Criticism of Warren Hastings's despotism and luxuriousness in 1783 led by Edmund Burke resulted in the India Act of 1784 which put the Company's territories under dual government involving a new body, the Board of Control with a president answerable to Parliament (see Lawrence James, pt. 1, 'The Company Ascendant: 1740–84' in *Raj: the Making and Unmaking of British India* (London: Little Brown, 1997), 3–60).

imports. Crébillon fils' *Le Sopha* (1742)—a collection of scurrilous tales told by a young Indian brahman whose transmigrated soul is condemned to pass from sofa to sofa until the first fruits of mutual love are expended upon his covers—makes much of the analogy between embroidered textiles and embroidered tales (the pun works in both the French original and its English translation of the same year).The ignorant Sultan Schah-Baham of the Indies enjoys watching his women *'embroider* and *pink*, being Arts he had in singular Estimation' (p. v), and the only text he will read are the tales of his grandmother Scheherazade. One day, tired of these familiar tales, he commands the assembled company to tell him new stories, but his sensible queen sultaness complains that tales are 'a Work, that is built on the trivial, and the *false Marvellous*' (p. ix). The embroidered tale is fancy-work, not only because of its fantastic content, but also because of its style. Defenders of oriental tales, unlike the queen sultaness, claim that behind the florid 'oriental' diction is a simple, ancient, and basic wisdom.

Dow stages this most visibly in a rhetorical conflict between Persian (Islamic) metaphor and denotational Indian (Brahmanical) language. His collection is, he says, a translation from the Persian scholar/ translator, Inatulla:

Inatulla uses the pompous diction peculiar to the East, even in his most familiar and ludicrous tales. In some of them, the translator found it necessary to reduce his author's ideas into common language. But as the species of wit contained in them depends very much upon the idiom of the Persian, he is as little satisfied with his translation, as he is with the subject of the stories themselves.

It appears that Inatulla was not the inventor of the tales which he intro-duces as episodes, and engrafts upon a story of his own forming. They were taken from the writings of the Brahmins, and it were to be wished he had retained that simplicity of thought and language which is peculiar to the composition of those philosophers. (*Tales*, i, p. vii)

Both as source for luxury and staple textiles, East India Company imports appear to have threatened the base of English manufacture. In 1700, for instance, the sale of Asian silks and printed or dyed cottons in England was forbidden in order to protect English manufacturers, but trade continued for re-export to the Continent. Indian 'tales' are seen, however, as a contribution to the fabric of literature, adding to its moral fibre, but also providing a new set of luxurious pleasures. For example, Dow concludes that the Inatulla's 'moral tales will make up for the levity of his ludicrous stories; and that, upon the whole, Inatulla will afford some entertainment' (*Tales*, i, p. ix).

Ridley winds up his stories with the claim that the age of the genii and of Islamic belief is soon to be surmounted by the advanced morality of Christianity, but that these tales will provide the necessary moral base for the deeper spirituality of the Christian West. His is a position familiar from the writings of both Edward Terry and François Bernier who present Indian, and especially Muslim, morality as a reminder to the West of its moral failings (with a stronger and 'genuine' religious tradition, western culture is prone to more vice and hypocrisy than its 'eastern' monotheistic counterpart, Islam). Gueullette, as Terry does, presents imaginative fiction as a means of speaking to an audience who would not read more overtly didactic material: hence, *'Now to engage young People to look on Books without being forced, what were more proper Means than to indulge them in reading* Romances? *Tender Minds are greeably* [sic] *Struck with the Marvellous'*.[41] In a verse given on the title pages of both volumes of tales he asserts:

> *In pleasing Tales, the artful Sage can give*
> *Rules, how in Happiness and Ease to live:*
> *Can shew what Good can most attract the Mind,*
> *And how our Woes we from our Vices find;*
> *Delighting, yet instructing thus our Youth,*
> *Who catch at Fable—How to gather Truth.*

If readers fail to change their behaviour as a result of reading the tales, Gueullette claims they will at least have been educated about eastern culture:

The late Humour of reading Oriental Romances, such as the Arabian, Persian and Turkish Tales, tho' I will not much contend it has better'd our Morals, has however extended our Notions and made the Customs of the East much more familiar to us than they were before, or probably would ever have been, had they not been communicated to us by this indirect, and pleasant Way. (i, p. x)

---

[41] Gueullette, *Mogul Tales*, i, p. v.

European writers twin their argument about the moral effect of oriental rhetoric, however circumlocutory, with the assertion that oriental tales provide cultural, political, even scientific knowledge about the East, since morality (as in the case of Osmir, recalcitrant prince-recipient of the *Tales of the Genii*) can fall on deaf ears.

In the case of India, as with other parts of the oriental globe, the text prepared for European consumption was a deeply hybridized object, announced as new and marvellous but also tailored to the traditions, tastes, and expectations of its audience. As a result, it proves a flexible medium, incorporating different, sometimes contradictory, aesthetic impulses held together through a frame which calls attention to its own polyglossia and fabricated nature. In particular, all three collections under discussion here present the idea of the oriental 'djinn', 'genie', or 'angel' as a rhetorical device used both to convey oriental aesthetic taste and to embody a moral purpose. Gueullette's *Mogul Tales* begin with the request by the young King Oguz to four neighbouring potentates that each send a daughter to his court so that he may select one as a wife; however, his chosen bride, Gehernaz, daughter of the king of Jeselmere, reveals that she has made a pact with her rivals to persuade him to accept the other three (according to Muslim law a man may have up to four wives). He agrees subject to their fathers' approval but is fearful that the marriages may introduce faction to the peaceful court. A footnote comments on the figure of Asmong who 'according to the Oriental Theology is the Angel of Discord' and adds that 'Tho' we yield no Credit to this Notion, yet it must be own'd, the turning Strife into a Person adds Strength and Beauty to the Story, and it is one of the finest Flowers of the Oriental Rhetorick' (i. 8).

The *Tales of the Genii* reveals at its close that the 'romantick monsters' of the tales, along with their teller, Horam, are all fictional inventions to 'serve the cause of moral truth' and instructs the reader not to 'long lament' their loss since 'were the foundations of morality laid only in phantom and imagination, persuasion would be so fruitless, that every moral writer, dissatisfied with his ill success, might justly cast his work into the flames'.[42] However, the Islamic fictions of

---

[42] James Ridley, *The Tales of the Genii: or, the Delightful Lessons of Horam, the Son of Asmar, tr. from the Pers. MS. by Sir Charles Morell*, 3rd edn. (London, 1766), ii. 365–6. All references are to this edition.

genii and teller have prepared the ground for a 'true' and more 'direct' morality in the figure of Christ with the ascendancy of the western world.

Dow's tales open with a dream-vision of a beautiful Hindu maid appearing before the company he is sleeping with on the grass in a mango grove; she is an embodiment of oriental eloquence and instructs him to marry his gifts in the Persian language to 'Indian' tales. 'Of all gardens' she tells him 'that of rhetoric justly challenges the highest fame' since 'It knoweth no winter, and its flowers, like those of the jeweller, ever retain their beauty and intrinsic worth; and were the incense of the Persian tongue burnt on the Indian altar, the world would be perfumed with agla, and the lovers of sublime diction anointed as with the oil of roses' (i, pp. xiii–xiv).

All three writers, then, signal their work as a kind of hybridized rhetorical display in which oriental elements (Indian landscape and products—jewels, textiles, perfumes, brahmanical knowledge, Islamic monotheism, genii) blend with occidental morality and curiosity (Christian virtue, empirical science, trading ambition). Supernatural figures are announced as a central rhetorical device, but are not given credit or purchase as genuine. Hence, the narrators suggest, occidental genius transforms oriental matter into fictional idea with newly relevant moral purpose. Let us look in more detail at these three sequences and their interweaving of 'Indian' elements to serve didactic ends in their culture of destination. Throughout, the sequences associate eastern religions, economies, and philosophies with the collapse of a distinction between the material and the immaterial, natural and supernatural, substance and dream. If in India such categorial instability reinforces despotism and credulousness, sceptical occidental narration will, the narrators imply, simultaneously broaden the western reader's cultural experience and sharpen moral judgement.

Mogul Tales

Oguz determines to prevent his wives from competing for favours for their children by secretly marking his four sons all born at the same time, so that only he knows each child's birth mother. Gehernaz, always the wisest of his queens, persuades the others to make no distinctions between the boys. She is the only wife to bear another child, a girl. At the age of 20 the sons come into conflict when they all fall in love with the same princess, who finally makes the choice of Gehernaz's son, Assan-Allad, as her husband. In order to console his three other sons, Oguz orders his slave-merchants to assemble twelve of the most beautiful women in the land for them to choose from. He himself falls in love with a young Circassian, Goul-Saba, and is advised by an imam that he may take her as a fifth wife contrary to Muslim law because of his status as sultan. Goul-Saba bears him a son and she and her child compete for supremacy with the other queens and princes.

Oguz begins to doubt Goul-Saba's sincerity and prays for help from the prophet; he is answered by a dream in which Mohammed tells him he cannot know a woman's heart without possessing the enchanted ring of Solomon, directing him to Cothrob for assistance. The latter is living as a recluse ten miles from Cambaye, having given up the throne of China in disgust at court corruption, but he agrees to aid the sultan and instructs him to build a new palace at the city gates with a mosque and sepulchre. Oguz then feigns his own death, supposedly broken-hearted at the news of the death of two of his older sons by plague. Cothrob is left with all the ceremonial power and the wives are instructed to spend four months privately in the palace concealing Oguz's death from his people. For two months they live quietly, but Goul-Saba seeks diversion and Schirin, the one older son still living at court, undertakes to present to them travellers from the Karavanserail (the old palace) to entertain them with stories or theatrical performances. The travellers are to be brought drugged to the court and Schirin disguises himself as a fakir to ease the deceit. From secret passages in his purpose-built palace Oguz observes his wives' behaviour to see whether they do truly grieve over his death, and, over the course of eighty-nine evenings and fourteen tales, numerous princes and princesses of the oriental world are discovered among the travellers transported to the 'fairy-palace' and variously restored, through the agency of Cothrob, to their rightful beloveds.

On the sixty-seventh evening, Goul-Saba and her son, Bathal, both reveal a desire to marry, she to an actor-come-gigolo and he to a dancer-courtesan, performers in a company they have been watching. When the queens remonstrate with Goul-Saba and she with her son about such unequal matches, Goul-Saba is led to reveal that she is neither Circassian nor a princess but the illegitimate daughter of an Agra dancer who was brought to the court already pregnant with her son Bathal by a music-master hired by the Jewish merchant who owned her at the time. Cothrob persuades Oguz to rein in his anger and the pair stage a will-reading in which Oguz promises his wives their freedom if over the course of the four months of mourning they have not intended to marry another man. Goul-Saba remains determined to marry and when Oguz enters he declares Schirin his heir and sends Goul-Saba to join her player-lover along with her son and his dancer-wife with the words:

Forget then for ever, that you have had the Honour of my Bed, and follow, without Constraint, the loose kind of Life, into which you have entered yourself, thou Daughter of a common Woman, and former Mistress of a Player who art this Day become the Spouse of a Man of the same Profession; go, and exercise a Trade that suits your Genius, and for which you were born, and finish your unfortunate Days with your unworthy Son, on a Theatrical Throne, since you have not deserved to finish them on that of *Guzerat*. (ii. 230–1)

Oguz's reference to a 'theatrical throne' not only echoes the comments of observers such as Sir Thomas Roe about the theatricality of the Mughal dynasty's self-presentation and the hollowness of its power, but also to the wider play in the text on the idea of acting and performance as a way of 'tricking' the spectator into believing him or herself in a place of enchantment. Stories again and again reveal the 'hidden' motive behind performances in both low-born and aristocratic characters who repeatedly pass themselves off as someone else, from Oguz's most radical deceit that he is dead to the queens' self-presentation as pirii (fairies), to a succession of minor characters who themselves report experiences of cross-dressing, disguise, play-acting.

The tale of Zem-Alzaman, prince of Kasgar, and of Zendehroud, princess of Samarcand, is a conventional love story in the vein of the French romance in which both of the lovers adopt disguises (as young soldiers in the battle between their two states) and persuade servants to don their clothes to pass as them, resulting in a series of mistakes and near-tragedies. A story of a common character is more of a comic picaresque account of roguery and trickery; thus, Aboul-Assam, the blind man of Chitor, tells how in his sighted days he passed himself off as a skilled veterinarian, a madman, and a mountebank. Gueullette draws on reports from travellers of the hypocrisy and greed of peripatetic holy men in Indian territory to describe Aboul-Assam's most successful disguise. He joins a company of false calenders (a mendicant order of dervishes) in Golconda and travels around Persia for a year 'where we enjoyed the utmost sensual Pleasure, tho' to outward Appearance, we maintained an Air of Sanctity and Mortification; an Art, too commonly practiced by cunning Debauches, not in *Persia* only, but all the World over' (i. 170).

However, Gueullette's is not a rational allegory free of supernatural agency. The blind man of Chitor, we learn, lost his sight when he touched a book on a triangular table guarded by three mutes and buried in a mountain in Persepolis, despite a warning that only the perfectly pure man may do so. Cothrob, as we saw in the story of Zem-Alzamam and Zendehroud, can magically transport himself around the globe in a blink of an eye, like a genie of the lamp, to bring parted lovers together again in the enchanted space of the Gujerat palace.

Those who lack magical powers remain unclear whether they are dreaming or in an enchantment. Thus, when he arrives at the palace, Aboul-Assam comments to another confused traveller:

whether we are in the Western Part of *Africk*, where the *Genies* are by some Authors confidently reported to inhabit, or whether these kind and beneficent *Genies* have built them a Palace in some other Part of the World, I know not; but this I am sure of, that we are at present, either all of us in a Dream, or we have been carried by Inchantment, into such a Place as I speak of. (i. 131)

Likewise, when Canzade learns that her brother newly transported to the palace has abandoned his passion for her she is 'not able to persuade herself that what she saw was real, she fancied rather than the *Fairies* to whom she doubted not but this Palace belong'd, had, [to] flatter her, caused the *Phantom* to appear, who in a short Time would vanish again' (i. 180).

Throughout Gueullette's collection there is a tension between the 'authentic' and the 'theatrical' supernatural, the magic of the genie and

16. Engraving of Cothbedin, Prince of Visapour fighting with a genie in the air, Thomas-Simon Gueullette, *Mogul Tales, or, the Dreams of Men Awake*, vol. i, 2nd edn. (1743), p. 221.

the magic of theatre and performance which can appear genuine. Supernatural tales of genii and magical creatures—such as Cothbedin's shape-shifting combat with the giant Semandoun mounted on the legendary bird of oriental tale, the roc (see Fig. 16)—are, however, increasingly overtaken by tales of theatrical concealment and the staging of scenes of disclosure which are orchestrated to reveal a truth about protagonists. In the story of Katife and Margeon, after succeeding in fulfilling his mistress Margeon's demand that he remain a voluntary mute for a year, the hero Katife finds that Margeon has been forced to flee their country Aden, having disguised herself as a doctor able to cure Katife's muteness and on her failure faced the penalty of death by order of the vizier. Katife finds Margeon again, enslaved on the island of Brava in West Africa, and the two rehearse a performance that re-enacts the story of their courtship for their owner, the governor Almamon, himself enamoured of Margeon. Katife tries to convey a letter to Margeon in the performance which gives her instructions for their mutual flight but it is intercepted by Almamon. Tragedy is averted when their true names are revealed and it becomes clear that Almamon is Margeon's long-lost father who fled Aden when she was a child. The lovers are married with Almamon's blessing but separated again, this time by a storm, and it is Cothrob who reunites them.

This story is followed by the arrival of a troupe of dancers hired by Schirin to entertain the pirie/fairy queens; they choose to present a ribald version of the exalted story of the love of Leileh and Megnoun, in which Leileh preserves her reputation of virtue by pretending to be unchaste in a dramatic scene she is rehearsing with Megnoun, her servant. The actor playing Megnoun is Massoud, an Arab, with whom Goul-Saba becomes infatuated. Massoud spent his early years dressed as a woman in the troupe and taking female parts, as well as becoming the secret lover of a widow called Raoudah. Raoudah committed suicide when she discovered during her pregnancy that he had been conducting an affair with the daughter of her daughter's nurse.

Tales in which acting and theatrical performance serve as means of expressing sexual and romantic love are suddenly abandoned in favour of a final story, that of Abderaim of Candahar and his protection by a fairy, Banou Margeon, who gives him the gift over a year of being able to adopt whatever animal shape he chooses. He uses the gift to liberate the kingdom of the woman he loves, Zarat-Alridah, the daughter of the sultan of Carizme, from the assault of the Tartars; the ageing and despotic Tartar ruler Nemer (meaning Tiger) plans to force Zarat-Alrida to marry him. Abderain's story proves to be that of the 'good Mussulman', in the vein of that of Aboulfaouaris in Pétis de la Croix's *Persian Tales*; he is protected from harm by awaking always with the holy words 'There is only one God, and Mahomet is the Prophet' (ii. 151). Here the tale starts to interact with yet another 'oriental' genre, that of the animal fable, in that Abderain adopts successive disguises of a fly, rat, and lion to defeat the 'tiger' and bring about his own eventual marriage to Zarat-Alridah. When he omits one morning to utter the holy words, he is spirited away and can only be reunited with his wife Zarat-Alridah and the son she has borne him after she has in turn suffered a magical trial, adopting the form of an eagle and burying her beak in a rock for a year. In order to preserve the life of their son she must agree to be separated from both Abderaim and her child for a further twelve years.

It is Cothrob who also reunites this family in the fairy palace. Abderaim gives an account of his travels in search of his son and his destruction at Agra of an idolatrous temple where brahmans have been deceiving the people into sacrificing young women to the idol of a ram and using these women to serve their own sexual needs; Abderaim is seized by the spirit of the prophet and strikes the head brahman dead. The people convert to Islam when Abderaim shows them his evidence, having 'soon convinc'd themselves, that their false God was a senseless Stone, and his Priests vile debauch'd Impostors, who had impos'd upon them a ridiculous Religion, which they immediately renounced with one Consent' (ii. 196). Abderaim is transported to a fairy palace and an angel leads him to the sultana who is revealed to be his lost wife.

Abderaim's story, told by his son Mouiad, is introduced by Massoud, the handsome actor, in ambiguous terms which cast some doubt on its veracity, raising the possibility that it is another 'performance'. Thus, we are returned to the issue of the competing credibility of kinds of tales (the instability of the picaro's testimony versus the incredibility of the tale of 'marvellous' supernatural intervention in the lives of mortals). Massoud states:

I have given you a sincere Account of my Adventures, as you commanded me, from whence I hope you will believe, that it is impossible for any Body to acquit themselves in a more Simple and Natural manner than I have done.

But if you are curious to hear a History, which contains Things much more marvellous, the Person who in the Piece we played before you, acted the Part of my Slave [Mouiad], and who, by the Justice of his Performance, merited your Applause, is willing to give you a Recital of Things almost beyond Belief, yet he declares by the Faith of his Father, that there is not one Word added more than is true. (ii. 133)

The story of Massoud's cynical pursuit of his own sexual pleasure at the expense of women is contrasted with Abderaim's chivalrous protection of women.

Despite its oriental dressing, then, Gueullette's collection shares the ethics of the French salon, in which reverence for women is a measure of a culture's civility. The oriental/fairy tale is brought close to home as a fable directed towards French aristocrats and their models of *bienséance* and *vraisemblance*.[43] The metaphor of theatrical performance suggests the possibility that the oriental milieu may be a stage for the exploration of another culture under threat, one closer to home. Cothrob explains when he first meets Oguz that he has left China because, despite his best efforts, it has sunk back into the corruption common to oriental courts:

while I wore a *Crown*, it was in my Power to distinguish between the *polished Courtier*, and the *designing Sycophant*; my Behaviour was so properly adjusted in Respect to Persons of both Characters, that in the Space of a few Years I had not one of the latter about my Court. I communicated my Instruction to my Son, but in process of Time, the Respect due to them has lessened, and *China* is at present in the same Condition with other *Oriental Courts*, that is, the *Eunuchs* govern the *Sovereigns*, and by a Course of Flatteries lead them into such Acts as are prejudicial to their People. (i. 41)

Gueullette's presentation of Oguz and Cothrob as two rulers who retreat from government when they recognize a decline into faction and the potential for despotism because of the excessive power of court favourites suggests parallels with the writings of other French *philosophes*, such as Voltaire and Montesquieu.

With the death of Louis XIV, France faces the possibility of a 'theatrical throne' driven by corrupt or imitative feminized power

---

[43] See my discussion of the influence of the French romance in the English novel of the late 17th c. in ch. 2, 'Observing the Forms', in *Seductive Forms*, 31–68.

(Goul-Saba in the *Mogul Tales* or the Chinese eunuchs in the *Chinese Tales*), and lacking the central wise government of a single male ruler who is supported by but also limits the influence of his 'female' court (Oguz's four virtuous wives). As in Montesquieu's *Lettres Persanes*, published only five years before Gueullette's collection, the oriental seraglio is first posited as an alternative and negative example to French culture and then revealed to be a potent analogue.

Tales of the Genii

The satirical use of oriental models common in French literature is less characteristic of English collections of tales about India, although the deployment of Indian territory as a stage on which debates about good government can be conducted recurs in both. By contrast with the sceptical atheism of French *philosophes*, James Ridley is confident about the supremacy of Christian morality as the successor to Islam and the ideological foundation of world empire. Ridley's tales, a century after the publication of Edward Terry's Protestant account of the East Indies, echo the idea of an English authority in India premised on Christian missionary principles rather than western mercantile energies. When the ambassador Sir Charles Morell meets the sage Horam at Fort St. George, the latter complains of the hypocrisy and covetousness of the 'Christians' he has encountered in the East; Sir Charles counters that 'The *Christian* religion is professed by millions, and all are not like the merchants of *India*. If these prefer wealth to religion, there are many that have suffered for the cause of *Christ*, who have preferred an ignominious death in his faith, to all the glories of infidelity.'[44]

In Ridley's collection of tales we can trace the emergence of a Christian missionary alibi for English involvement in India in place of the early trading sallies. Horam displays the kind of hybrid Anglo-Indian education and sensibility that was to be so central to the British conception of its nation's role in India in the following century. A devout Muslim of Iranian birth inclined to spiritual rather than

[44] Ridley, *Tales of the Genii*, i, p. v.

worldly pleasures,[45] Horam takes the role of the oriental informant/ satirist familiar from Montesquieu and Goldsmith when he comes to England as the slave of an English merchant who promises him his liberty if he will continue to work as a steward. The merchant dies and asks Horam to take his goods to his brother and retain a quarter for himself, but the brother contests Horam's right to a legacy.

Horam is disgusted by the acquisitiveness and immorality of the European world, commenting:

In the countries which I passed, I saw with surprise, the magnificence of the *Popish* religion; where, however, ceremony seems to possess the seat of moral duties, and superstition is clothed in the vestments of faith. I was surprised to find such absurdities in *Europe*, where I was warned by my master to expect the most rational customs, and the purest light of virtue and religion. But the female glance will not always bear to be exposed, and the veils of the east, would well become the faces of the *European* ladies. (i, p. xiv)

Popery, superstition, and sexual, especially female, display, are, as we have seen, familiar targets for the fictional 'enlightened' oriental visitor to the West. Like the Turkish spy Mahmut and the Chinese sage Lien Chi Altangi, Horam proves an enthusiast for some aspects of the western European Enlightenment, in his case for its science and philosophy. He remains in Europe to learn 'their sciences, whose roots first grew in *Asia*, but whose fruit is with these Sons of Care' (i, p. xxiv) and concludes that 'what I could not find in the public resorts of the merchants, I discovered in the closets of the learned' (i, p. xxv).

Horam has a special fondness for Isaac Newton, whom he char-acterizes as a kind of western imam, his science a special commun-ication with the supernatural:

I adored that bright constellation of the North, the heaven-taught *Newton*, with whom I often held such converse, as the inhabitants of the East are said to hold with the *Genii* of mankind. I saw him bring down the moon from the realms of night, to influence and actuate the tides of the sea, and heard him read in his books the laws of the tumultuous ocean; he marked the courses of

---

[45] He refutes the common charge by western commentators that Islam wins so many converts because of its promise of sensual gratification in this world and the next through polygamy by employing a metaphor of love as a precious stone: 'Worldly joys are mean incitements to the love of *Alla*, and impure embraces but little signs of purest faith: had I an inestimable gem, should I honour it by placing it in the mire?' (i, p. xi).

the stars with his wand, and reduced excentric orbs to the obedience of his system. He caught the swift flying light, and divided its rays; he marshalled the emanations of the sun under their different colored banners, and gave symmetry and order to the glare of day; he explained the dark eternal laws of nature, and seemed acquainted with the dictates of heaven. (i, p. xxv)

The 'new' science in England here emerges as a variant of eastern magical and cabalistic arts, cueing the suggestion that Horam's own stories of the genii should be read as a kind of allegory or parable for English readers.

Like other writers of the oriental tale, however, Ridley blends the kind of empirical and satirical statement common to travel and missionary accounts with the fantastic and 'marvellous' parabolic discourse of prose fiction. He gives Horam a vitriolic passage of complaint about the hypocrisy and worldliness of Jesuits in India who, he claims, are only tolerated in Asia because of their useful scientific knowledge:

The monarchs of the *East* are fond of the *European* sciences; they in some measure tolerate the religion of the *Jesuits*, that they may be benefited by the ingenious labors of that insinuating society; but they are no friends to the *christian* faith, and the missionary who was to depend on his religion only, would soon fall a sacrifice to either the *Mohammedan* doctors or the *Indian* bramins. But at present religion is the pretended motive of the *Jesuits* travels into *India*, though perhaps they are as little zealous to propagate the true doctrines of *christianity* as those they serve are to believe them. They are good mathematicians, but bad saints, unless where they expect some temporal advantage from the propagation of their faith

Nothing therefore but their useful knowledge, could prevail upon the *Eastern* monarchs to caress a society whom all *Asia* despises. (i, pp. xxviii–xxix)

Ridley casts Jesuits as religious hypocrites and deceitful pretenders, occidental fakirs in fact.

The implication at the conclusion of the tales is that the 'true' and revealed religion of (English) Protestantism, free of the self-interest and hypocrisy of the Catholicism disseminated by other European nations in the East, will eventually overcome both Catholic, Islamic, and Hindu belief systems and become the dominant form of religious knowledge across the globe. Ridley's vision is no doubt prompted by the conclusion of the Seven Years War in 1763, which left Britain the dominant European power in India.

Ridley's collection of tales was published only five years before *The Bonze*, in which a Chinese prince and his learned friend convert to Anglicanism in disgust at the superstition and false doctrines of Catholicism. In this period, then, a militant Protestantism seeks to wrest Asia from its historical engagement with Christianity through Catholicism and, in the case of India, suggests new analogies between Protestant, Islamic, and Hindu spiritual belief-systems to imply a right of succession to government from Mughal rule for Britain over France and Portugal, its Catholic rivals in India and the Far East in general. The rival Protestant power, the Netherlands, is most often portrayed as interested solely in trade and hence rarely features as an ideological or political competitor.[46]

Texts like Ridley's and Dow's were instrumental in rehabilitating Arabic 'genies' and Hindu 'gods' not as symptoms of a dangerous polytheism and idolatry in eastern religion, but rather as allegorical vehicles for the exploration of spirituality and moral truth. Horam's enthusiasm for Newton suggests that Protestant, rather than Catholic, science and learning can promote English influence in India and, moreover, that fiction can be a significant factor in the advancement of 'moral' empire. Horam is a sceptic who, like his Protestant creator, has

conceived the purpose of disguising the true doctrines of morality, under the delightful allegories of romantic inchantment. Mine eye had seen the great varieties of nature, and the powers of my fancy could recal and realize the images. I was pleased with mine own inventions, and hoped to find that virtue would steal into the breast, amidst the flowers of language and description. (i, p. xxxii)

However, Horam's teachings fail to influence his young charge Osmir, heir to Aurengzebe, suggesting that for a hybrid English-Indian

---

[46] Dryden refers to the Dutch as cowardly, cynical opportunists in his dedication of *Aureng-Zebe* to his patron, the earl of Mulgrave, who had served with James, duke of York in the Dutch war of 1672. He describes Mulgrave as a sophisticated wit unlike those who 'treat wit like the common enemy, and giving no more quarter, than a Dutchman would to an English vessel in the Indies; they strike sail where they know they shall be mastered and murder where they can with safety' (190).

sensibility to flourish in Indian territory a new order of government from the Mughal dynasty will be required:

Asia received with pleasure the lessons of *Horam*, the son of *Asmar*; but yet what was *Asia*, or the whole world, while one unconquerable mind was left, for whom alone they were first intended. But although various countries were my admirers, the maxims of *Horam* had no effect on the lives of those who commanded my writings. This made me pine when the branches of honor overshadowed me, and sink under fears which none but myself might have entertained. (i, pp. xxxii–xxxiii)

Aurengzebe imprisons his vicious son Osmir, who then pretends to have been conspiring with his tutor. Although he does not believe the accusations, Aurengzebe is obliged to send Horam into exile and, perhaps unsurprisingly, the latter chooses to retreat to the British post in India at Madras, confirming the implied trajectory of the guardianship of Indian learning from Mughal to British rule. Along the way Horam seeks out copies of his 'unavailing instructions' (i, p. xxxvi) and burns them, but is persuaded by Sir Charles, who has already partially translated the stories from a copy he obtained when stationed in Bombay, to recount them orally. Hence, transcription of eastern morality passes from the Persian to the English language and Sir Charles becomes an English equivalent to Antoine Galland (who supplemented the Arabic manuscript tales he was using for the *Arabian Nights Entertainments* with stories delivered to him orally by a Syrian Maronite Christian from Aleppo).

A European editorial presence is apparent throughout the tales. Footnotes acknowledge that Morell/Ridley has intervened where the tales seem to stray from the moral purpose for which they are designed. One footnote, for example, admits that an account of how a rebel genie named Morad has instructed the simple shepherd Kauran in vice has been censored because 'bad hearts might be too far instructed by them, and good hearts could not read them without some uneasiness. I have therefore omitted them . . . though I am sensible the beauty of the tale will be lessened' (i. 162).

The 'fictional' nature of Horam himself is made visible in the frontispiece to the second volume which shows 'The author disguised in a Persian habit discovering himself' (see Fig. 17). It depicts a

17. Frontispiece, James Ridley, *The Tales of the Genii: or, the Delightful Lessons of Horam, the Son of Asmar*, vol. ii, 3rd edn. (1766)

Protestant divine, the Qur'an open at his feet and the Bible on a table behind him, welcoming two children in European dress who are led by a woman sporting a veil. This image echoes the frontispiece to the first volume in which a winged female genie leads a beturbaned girl and boy to the council of genii presided over by a silver-bearded and

18. Frontispiece, James Ridley, *The Tales of the Genii: or, the Delightful Lessons of Horam, the Son of Asmar*, vol. i, 3rd edn. (1766)

crowned figure of authority (Fig. 18). Horam's frame to the tales he tells Osmir describes how Patna and Coulor, the children of Guialar, imam of Terki, are spirited to a council of twenty-eight genii on golden thrones by a female genie in order to overhear the recounting of what 'instructive lessons' have been conveyed by the genii to mortals at the command of their chief, the silver-haired Iracagem. The frontispiece of the second volume, then, reveals the truth behind the fiction; behind the serial identities of Iracagem, Horam, and Sir Charles Morell stands James Ridley, Protestant moralist, who uses the medium of the Orient, embodied in the only partially veiled woman, to shape young European minds. In both frontispieces and footnotes, Ridley calls attention to the tricky negotiation between the invented tale as a vehicle for moral instruction and its potential for deceitful seduction, precisely because it is an invention. Can disguise be used to convey truth? The double-handed nature of the enterprise is echoed in the double nature of the address, to a British audience who will learn through an eastern allegory, and to an eastern audience who will learn British Christian morality through the reproduction of the eastern tale in English.

The Indian context is vital to the understanding of Ridley's purpose, although only one of the nine tales in Ridley's two-volume collection actually takes place in India. All the tales concern the attempts of mortals, with the help or hindrance of genii, to distinguish between dream and reality, cunning artifice and genuine moral guidance, in order to pursue the difficult path of virtue. After each story, the genie Iracagem provides a gloss that explains the message of the tale. Thus, the 'History of the merchant Abudah', in which a wealthy Baghdad merchant suffers great hardship in the pursuit of a phantom of vast wealth and political power extended to him in dreams, is used to convey the message that, since each life is a span and mortals cannot comprehend immortals, the best course is to follow the commandments of Allah and wait for reward in paradise. 'The dervise Alfouran'—in which Sanballad of Bassora, with the aid of the genius Mamlouk, exposes the devout dervish who has led the people of Eyraca into the worship of fire to the neglect of their trade as a fraud—teaches the importance of reason and revelation as a test of religious truth.

After two more tales in a similar vein, Iracagem requests that the genii provide tales which demonstrate the importance of social morality rather than simple blind obedience to Allah. Unsurprisingly, perhaps, it is female sexual continence that becomes the major theme of three of the remaining five tales. 'The Adventures of Urad; or the Fair Wanderer' describes the Pamela-like experiences of a young peasant girl in Persia who acquires the protection of an old woman, Houadir. On her deathbed Houadir provides Urad with some magic peppercorns which will guard her from danger and enable her to see through the wiles and deceits of men. After surviving numerous perils and attacks, Urad is rewarded by marriage with the sultan Almurah. This tale proves that 'female delicacy makes an unequal opposition to brutal cunning, unless the protection of the just one overshadows the footsteps of the virtuous maid' (i. 232). Part folk tale, part conduct fiction, Urad's story again indicates the generic flexibility of the oriental tale. Urad emerges as a kind of 'every woman' for both eastern and western cultures, an example of 'virtue rewarded' in an oriental landscape where the threat of rape comes from robber gangs and wicked viziers and her virtue is proved by her ability to tame a savage lion.

'Sadak and Kalasrade' is another story of embattled female virtue, in which Kalasrade is seized by the Ottoman sultan Amurat (Murat IV, who reigned 1623-40) and resists his advances even when he orders her children to be killed. Through the protection of the genius Adiram and the assistance of the virtuous chief of the eunuchs, Doubor, Kalasrade is eventually reunited with her husband and children (except for the oldest son, Codan, who has been lost at sea). Iracagem concludes that 'virtue and fidelity shall be as greatly distinguished, and as fully rewarded in the female sex, as ye see it honoured and approved among the sons of men' (ii. 232).

A third tale of embattled female virtue is an inset one: the first-person 'History of the Princess of Cassimir' (Kashmir), which forms part of by far the longest tale in the collection, 'The Inchanters of Misnar the Sultan of India'. 'Misnar' bridges the two volumes and is the only tale to take India as its location. It is, moreover, the only tale which returns to the theme of the relation between Asia and Europe and their competing claims to intellectual, moral, or military supremacy. This tale introduces another character named 'Horam', an alter ego for the exiled and disappointed narrator in that he is the successful vizier of a virtuous king who learns to defeat deceitful evil genii through cunning.

'Misnar' makes use of familiar elements in the 'Indian' oriental tale: the conflict between monotheistic and polytheistic religion (especially the worship of fire), the attraction of Kashmir embodied in a beautiful woman who is the primary love-object and symbol of ownership of the larger territory of India, the adoption of the disguise of the fakir, the insistent return of metaphors of precious stones and the tiger to stand for a native 'India' (twin signs of wealth and danger for the colonizing empire). These distinctive features of the 'Indian' oriental tale coexist with allusions and references to the model of the *Arabian Nights Entertainments* in the shape of a king and vizier who wander through the metropolis in disguise to uncover vice and virtue (like Haroun Alraschid and his visier Giafar) and in the use of the name 'Chederazade' for the virtuous and politically astute, if cold-hearted, mother of the princess of Kashmir. Finally, the tale is a fable which, despite all its supernatural dressing, teaches the importance of sceptical reading, vigilant observation of both self and others, to good government. Such sceptical reading must always, however, be guided by a larger principle of faith. Ridley succeeds in making the marvellous encounters and amorous history of a young Muslim prince of India into a Protestant parable about justification by grace through faith. Thus, Iracagem concludes:

The children of *Alla* . . . have indeed a freedom of action; but that freedom is best exercised, when it leads them to trust and depend on the Lord of all things; not that he who seeth even beyond the confines of light is pleased with idleness, or giveth encouragement to the sons of sloth; the spirit which he has infused into mankind, he expects to find active and industrious; and when prudence is joined with religion, *Alla* either gives success to its dictates, or by counteracting its motions, draws forth the brighter virtues of patience and resignation.

Learn, therefore, ye pupils of the race of immortals, not to forget your dependence on *Alla*, while ye follow the prudent maxims of wisdom and experience; for he only is truly prudent, who adds faith to his practice; and he truly religious, whose actions are the result of his faith. (ii. 83–4)

The tale of Misnar pits a virtuous young sultan of India and the woman he loves, the princess of Kashmir named Hemjunah—assisted by his wise counsellor Horam and their guardian female genius, Macoma—against seven evil genii and Misnar's ambitious younger brother, Ahubal. Misnar and Hemjunah are repeatedly tested by illusions and they often stumble. When Misnar ascends the throne of

India 'neither the splendor of his court, nor the flatteries of the east, could steal from the youthful sultan the knowledge of himself' (i. 234). He gathers the wise men of his dominions together, informing them that 'more precious are your counsels to me than the mines of *Raalconda*, or the big emerald from *Gani*' (i. 236).[47] However, when Misnar robustly rejects advice to murder his brother to prevent him challenging the throne, evil genii are exposed as lurking beneath the disguise of some of the wise men. Their true and horrible forms are exposed, mounted on the back of vast oriental creatures: a vulture, a scorpion, a tiger, a spider, a toad, a black serpent, and an alligator. They depart vowing to be revenged on Misnar, and Ahubal flees to join them. Misnar, like Gueullette's Oguz, is sent by his councillors in pursuit of magic tokens to protect him, in this case Mahomet's signet (buried with its owner in his tomb) and the girdle of Opakka worn by the evil genius and giant Kisri. He leaves his throne in the hands of Horam, his vizier, while he embarks on this fruitless quest. Both Misnar and Oguz learn that supernatural agency is not required to secure their authority, but rather vigilance and self-government; political disorder and faction result when the Indian king absents himself from his role at the heart of his empire.

Misnar first meets a group of native Indians carousing in the woods who are holding a fourteen-day festival of Tigris. They are worshippers of fire who dress him in a tiger skin and give him the choice of their women as his companion for ten days. He is reluctant to seduce the woman he selects since he cannot offer her marriage and she is revealed to be the terrible enchantress Ulin in disguise. When Misnar's faith wavers—on receiving a missive from Horam warning him that the army has rebelled and demanded to see him—it provides Ulin with a chink in the armour of his virtue and she promptly transforms him into a toad. The sweet odour of a rotting corpse

---

[47] Ridley's information probably came from the account of the jewel-merchant Tavernier, who brought precious stones back to Louis XIV. Chapters 11 and 12 of the second book of his Indian travels include a description of the diamond mines at 'Raolconda', ten miles from Golconda. But in ch. 16, Tavernier comments: 'As for Emraulds, it is a vulgar error to say they come originally from the East. . . . I confess I could never discover in what part of our Continent those Stones are found. But sure I am, that the Eastern-part of the World never produc'd any of those Stones, neither in the Continent, nor in the Islands' (*Six Voyages*, pt. 2, 144).

attracts him in his new state where he encounters three other enchanted toads who are, we discover, the princess of Kashmir, Horam (punished for his faint-heartedness when faced with the army's mutiny), and a son of a Delhi jeweller named Mahoud.

Mahoud tells the company his story of how he was tricked into befriending a young man named Bennaskar only to discover Hemjuna, princess of Kashmir, imprisoned in his cellar and preserved from rape by her good genius Macoma's edict that Bennaskar must have her consent. When Bennaskar's vice is exposed to the Kashmiri state, he deploys his own evil guardian genius to change bodies with Mahoud, and Mahoud is saved from being burned alive as a punishment for the suspected murder of the now-vanished Hemjunah by being turned into a toad. Misnar is about to obtain the story of the princess of Kashmir when a pious hermit appears and turns him back into human form telling him that he must accomplish his task against the genii by relying on his own inner resources provided by Allah rather than seeking out magical tokens:

> they shall not be able by their inchantments to foresee thy designs, nor to overpower thee by the help of their magical deceits, unless thou yield to their snares. Be prudent and vigilant, and fear them not. Only this is permitted against thee, if thou canst not overpower and destroy them unawares, they may use their art to conceal their escape, and avoid thy arm; therefore be bold and quick, and yet cautious and discerning, lest when force avail not, they employ fraud to destroy thee. (i. 299)

Misnar and Horam return to take up the reins of government. Meanwhile, Ahubal's forces have gained new strength through the aid of the genius Ollomand, who has led him to supplies of European arms.[48] Ollomand tells Ahubal that although the Europeans pretend to worship a God in the heavens, their real god is 'buried in the entrails of the earth' (i. 334–5) in the shape of the gold they pursue at any cost (like Edward Terry, an earlier Protestant churchman writing about

---

[48] Mannucci records that although there was artillery in India from ancient times, the Emperor Akbar hired Europeans to instruct his military how to use them: 'There was Artillery enough in the *Indies*. There's Reason to think that the *Chinese*, who doubtless had been formerly Masters of *Indoustan*, had left some Pieces there, of which it's impossible to discover the Antiquity. It hapned unluckily that there were but few in the *Indies* who knew how to make use of 'em, with the same Art that we do in *Europe*' (Catrou, *General History*, 136).

India, Ridley uses Islam as a means to voice criticism of failures on the part of Europeans to live up to their Christian principles). Despite these reinforcements, victory is almost with Misnar and Horam when another enchanter, Tasnar, enters the fray mounted on a bird of prey and brings new hope to Ahubal's forces. Horam employs an old woman predicted to save the sultan of India to try and poison Tasnar but the enchanter strangles the old woman and takes her shape. When Tasnar returns to Misnar in this shape, Horam realizes the trick and summarily kills the enchanter.

Horam now persuades Misnar to build himself a magnificent pavilion and the sultan begins to doubt his vizier's judgement; however, Horam is vindicated when two enchanters, Desra and Ahaback, are so attracted by the pavilion that they seize it; a vast stone erected above it at Horam's direction then falls and crushes them. Ahubal is killed by his one-time ally, the giant Kisri, who throws him against a mountain in a frustrated rage. The giant, in turn, dies when, tormented by dreams that condemn him for his act, he pulls the mountain up and it falls on his head.

Secure on his throne, the sultan now tries to seek out the princess of Kashmir and Mahoud. He and Horam roam the city in disguise as fakirs and they encounter another false fakir who reveals that he has killed a young man in a graveyard who attacked him; his victim's cryptic dying words warned that he had taken two lives rather than one. They return to the graveyard to discover the body and nearby they see the vile enchantress Hypaccusan defeated by a lovely maid who blows a flame from her mouth as a sword and kills the enchantress; the maid is later revealed to be the guardian genius Macoma. In the tomb Misnar and Horam find Hemjunah, princess of Kashmir, and her father. Hemjunah reveals that she was tricked into her imprisonment there by the turncoat Mahoud (the young man whose body is by the tomb) who had enslaved himself to Hypaccusan in return for possession of Hemjunah.

Hemjunah now delivers her own long-delayed story. We discover that Hemjunah fled from her father's court to the arms of Bennaskar when her parents instructed her to marry the prince of Georgia, who had asked for her hand. Hemjunah's tale, like that of Shuey-ping-sin in Thomas Percy's 1761 *Hau Kiou Choaan*, echoes Samuel

Richardson's *Clarissa*; to avoid being pressed into an unwanted marriage, and when the protection of her mother is not forthcoming, she relies on a stranger, a female slave, who offers to help her to 'fly from [her] father's court!' (ii. 39). The slave is revealed to be the enchantress Ulin, who has obtained her for the rich young merchant Bennaskar, but this Clarissa is saved from rape by the supernatural presence of her guardian genius, Macoma.

Bennaskar crumbles to dust when he breaks the terms of the agreement between the good and evil genius and attempts to take Hemjunah from her underground prison and flee with her from approaching retribution for his crime, leaving Hemjunah to be turned into a toad by Ulin. When Misnar kills Ulin, the spell is broken and Hemjunah finds herself returned to the seraglio at Kashmir, her mother dead and her father shut up to grieve in his wife's tomb. Mahoud then appears dressed as a prince claiming that the sultan Misnar and his vizier Horam have spurned him. Hemjunah rejects his advances and Mahoud then lures her to the tomb claiming that her father is calling for her, only to imprison both until they give in to his demand that the princess marry him and he take the throne. Hemjunah greets Misnar's arrival at the graveyard with words which recall the familiar themes of dreaming and illusion in the Indian tale: 'Helper of the afflicted, answered the princess of *Cassimir*, doubt vanishes when you are present; but wonder not at my incredulity, since my whole life has been as a false illusion before mine eyes. O *Alla*, wherefore hast thou made the weakest the most subject to deceit!' (ii. 32). This Kashmiri princess, like Canzade and Indamora before her, figures an India ripe for possession and desired by all. Like them she reveals wavering sensibilities and a vulnerability to deceit which require mature and generous government if possession is to ensure contentment. The union of Misnar and Hemjunah represents a new order of Muslim government in India, driven by their sympathies, protective of their people, monogamous in their loves.

The final story of the collection, 'Mirglip, the Persian; or Fincal, the Dervise of the Groves', marries the European tradition of pastoral to the oriental fable. This tale is told by the genius Nadan about a vainglorious sultan of Persia, Adhim, led astray by his evil vizier Lemack, who is brought to the path of virtue and monogamous love through the model of the abstemious and moral Mirglip and Mirglip's tutor, a sage hermit called Fincal, who has retired from a life of active virtue to raise his daughters in a pastoral idyll. Mirglip and Adhim marry the two sisters and banish the evil genius Falri and his henchman Lemack. Iracagem summarizes the moral as the importance of blending temperance and justice as well as teaching 'the love of virtuous friendship, and the sweet rewards which rise from generous and from noble actions' (ii. 363).

At the conclusion of the tales, the presiding genius Iracagem pronounces that 'Our mansion totters on its mouldering base! The fleeting scene rolls far away, and all the visionary dream dissolves!' (ii. 363). Like Oguz's palace, the genie's council is revealed to be an elaborate fiction for the promotion of virtue. The troubled distinction between disturbing illusion and prophetic dream, deceit or falsehood or fakery and the improving fiction, is resolved for Ridley by the transcendent and unifying vision of the global dominance of Protestant Christianity. A long passage in conclusion written in the voice of a Christian narrator, presumably Ridley in the persona of Sir Charles Morell, triumphantly imagines Christ's body on the cross as the point where the ineffable and the divine become flesh, and humankind no longer requires the mediation 'of departed soul or ministering spirits' to have contact with the divine:

In friendly guise these sheets were written to lead thee unto virtue; and the proud, gaudy trappings of the *East*, with all its wide romantick monsters, have risen far above their usual sphere, to serve the cause of moral truth. But then perchance you'll ask, what shall that truth avail, now all the beauteous wildness is no more, which was the spring and mover of this pagan virtue? The *Genii* all are fled, who watched attendant the virtuous mind, and crown'd it with success; and the reward ceasing, the incentive to noble actions ceases with it.

If then, you will yet spare me a few moments, and listen to me, I trust you shall not long lament the loss of *Horam*, and his friendly *Genii*; for were the foundations of morality laid only in phantom and imagination, persuasion would be so fruitless, that every moral writer, dissatisfied with his ill success, might justly cast his works into the flames.

Prepare then for a scene more worthy of your sight than human fancy can conceive, a scene tremendous! wonderful! and great! full of mercy and of truth, where heaven itself inclines to earth, and God becomes an offering for mankind!

Behold the moral veil rent in twain, and from thick clouds of darkness, the sun of righteousness arise! Behold death nailed on the cross, and mercy springing from the grave! Redemption brought to man by an heavenly being, far superior to angels or ministering spirits; and the voice of God declared to us by his son, whom he hath appointed heir of all things; by whom also he made the worlds; who being the brightness of his glory, and the express image of his person, and upholding all things by the word of his power when he had by himself purged our sins *on the Cross*, sat down on the right hand of the Majesty on high; being made so much better than the angels, as he hath by inheritance, obtained a more excellent name than they.

We then may make an happy exchange from pagan blindness to Christian verities, and look upon ourselves as creatures dignified with heaven's peculiar grace. (ii. 363–4)

Ridley here announces the death of the oriental tale as a vehicle for morality, ostensibly severing the analogical connection between Islam and Christianity as moral monotheisms which has served him throughout the two volumes of tales. Islam is revealed to be itself a fiction by contrast with Christianity's truth. Like Misnar, readers must see through the deceit to reach the revelation of the 'true' God, and not be tempted by worldly pleasures or retreat in fear from moral challenge.

If the *Tales of the Genii* repudiate Islam, symbolically expelling Muslim 'rule' from India, they do not challenge the notion that the Indian tale can act as a 'speculum principis' or mirror for princes in which issues of 'good government' can be addressed and debated. Ridley's tales have secular as well as religious morals. Misnar's tale returns to the theme in the *Mogul Tales* of the importance of the monarch's visibility and direct engagement in government as a means of preventing civil conflict. Misnar's relationship with Horam is similar to that of Oguz with Cothrob and the 'wise minister' is key to the king's success. Misnar's protection of the Kashmiri princess and his monogamous attachment to her also indicate his promise as a monarch who can unify the territory and promote virtue. Ridley makes clear the political parable of the work by dedicating it to the

'Dreams of Men Awake': India

2-year-old George, prince of Wales (later George IV):

As this Work is designed to promote the cause of morality, I have presumed to lay it at the feet of your Royal Highness; whose early entrance into the paths of virtue, under the conduct of an illustrious and Royal Mother, and the direction and auspices of the best of fathers and of kings, has encouraged me to hope, that these tales will hereafter meet with your Royal Highness's approbation. (i, n.p.)

Alexander Dow's collection of tales published just four years after Ridley's is also inclined to represent fantastic and supernatural elements as fictional devices for instructive purposes. And, like Ridley, Dow also suggests that the British in India need to learn from, rather than simply repudiate, previous (if waning) powers that have sought to govern the territory. British government in India will best succeed if it is understood as a reforming succession rather than a rebellion or usurpatory seizure. However, Dow's tales are also indicative of a new and direct engagement with Persian culture and sources in India, which mean that, unlike Ridley's, they are more than parables or fables of a British Protestant ethic. They are, along with Dow's other writings, directed against Clive's practices in Bengal, interventions in heated debates about the relationship between company officials in India and the administration at home, and the relationship between the East India Company and the British government. They map in fictional form the competing powers, beliefs, literatures, and cultures of India—Hindu and Muslim—for a British readership with interests financial and political in the security of newly acquired authority.

Tales from the Inatulla

By contrast with Gueullette and Ridley, Alexander Dow demonstrates an extensive and thorough knowledge of both Hindu and Muslim India. One of the earliest of those East India Company men who took an interest in the languages and theologies of India, Dow describes in his preface to his free translation from the Persian of Firishtah's *The History of Hindostan*, published in the same year as the *Tales*, how he at first pursued an interest in languages as a means of professional preferment:

The translator of the following history of the Mahommedan empire in Hindostan, having in a military capacity resided for some time in the kingdom of Bengal, dedicated the most of his leisure hours to the study of the oriental languages. The Persian tongue being the most polite and learned, as well as the most universally understood in Asia, engaged his principal attention.

The intimate connection which the British nation now have, with a part of Hindostan, renders the knowledge of the country languages of great importance to the servants of the public in that part of the world. The translator, who had extended his views in the way of his profession, thought it so capital a point for him, that he persevered for some years, in that dry and difficult study, and incurred a very considerable expence, in retaining masters, and in procuring manuscripts.

Though to qualify himself for action, and negotiation in India, was the primary object of the translator, yet in proportion as he advanced in his studies, other motives for his continuing them arose. He found, that however different the manner of the eastern writers may be from the correct taste of Europe, there are many things in their works worthy of the attention of literary men. Their poetry it is true is too turgid and florid, and the diction of the historians too diffuse and verbose. Yet in the first we meet with some passages truly elegant and sublime; and amidst the redundancy of the latter, there appears sometimes a nervousness of expression, and a manliness of sentiment, which might do honour to any historical genius in the west.[49]

The translation of Firishtah's history, he says, began as an exercise suggested by his tutors in Persian but soon transformed into a passion for the promotion of eastern learning in Europe.

Dow lays claim to be the first to provide English readers with access to the Persian sources about the history of Muslim empire, but is also critical of his source who shared the common prejudice of Muslims against the 'Brahmin religion' and, ignorant of Sanskrit, failed to recognize the ancient nature of Hindu learning and culture:

he affirmed, that there is no history among the Hindoos of better authority than the Mahabarit [*Mahabharata*]. That work is a poem not a history: It was translated into Persian by the brother of the great Abul Fazil, rather as a performance of fancy, than as an authentic account of the ancient dynasties of

[49] Muhammad Kâsim Hindû Shâh Firishtah, *The History of Hindostan*, trans. Alexander Dow (London, 1768), i, pp. i–ii.

the Kings of India. But that there are many hundred volumes in prose in the Shanscrita language, which treat of the ancient Indians, the translator can, from his own knowledge, aver, and he has good reason to believe, that the Hindoos carry their authentic history farther back into antiquity, than any other nation now existing.

The Mahommedans know nothing of the Hindoo learning: and had they even any knowledge of the history of the followers of Brimha, their prejudices in favour of the jewish fictions contained in the Koran, would make them reject accounts, which tend to subvert the system of their own faith. The Shanscrita records contain accounts of the affairs of the western Asia, very different from what any tribe of the Arabians have transmitted to posterity: and it is more than probable, that upon examination, the former will appear to bear the marks of more authenticity, and of greater antiquity than the latter. (Preface, i, pp. vi–vii)

Dow faced similar obstacles to those he describes impeding Firishtah's access to Hindu learning, obstacles he detailed in the 'Dissertation concerning the customs, manners, language, religion and philosophy of the Hindoos', which he prefixed to the first volume of his translation of the *History of Hindostan*.[50] That he gave this dissertation such prominence in the three volumes indicates the importance he attached to British engagement with the Hindu population for the maintenance and growth of their power in India.

The most stubborn impediment to an understanding of Hinduism, Dow complains, is the fact that the Hindus do not seek converts and keep their religious philosophy an impenetrable mystery. Dow relates the story of Akbar's attempt to acquire Hindu lore by representing the young brother of his secretary (Abu'l Fazl Allami), one Feizi (Fuizi, 1547–95), as a poor brahman orphan so that he could be brought up by a brahman for ten years. When Feizi disclosed his identity because his master had offered him his daughter in marriage, he saved his own

---

[50] A modern edition of this essay is available in Peter J. Marshall (ed.), *The British Discovery of Hinduism in the Eighteenth Century* (Cambridge: Cambridge University Press, 1970), 107–39. The only previous work in English that sought to explain Hinduism in the West (French Jesuits had been interested in it along with Confucianism in the 17th c.) was the second part of John Zephania Holwell's *Interesting Historical Events Relative to the Provinces of Bengal and the Empire of Indostan* (1767). Holwell was a deist deeply hostile to the Trinity. Marshall comments that 'Holwell and Dow gave the opponents of Christianity what they were looking for: a religion based on monotheism with a concept of the immortality of the soul and an acceptable moral code, which owed nothing to contact with either Jews or Christians' (Introduction, 27).

life only by vowing to the brahman never to translate the four holy books, the Bedas (Vedas), or repeat the creed of the Hindus.

Like Akbar, Dow recognizes the importance of the colonizer knowing native culture and beliefs. As in Dryden's *Aureng-Zebe*, an analogy drawn from classical culture proves a useful explanatory tool. Here, it points to the imperial advantages of learning native languages:

The learned of modern Europe have, with reason, complained that the writers of Greece and Rome did not extend their enquiries to the religion and philosophy of the Druids. Posterity will perhaps, in the same manner, find fault with the British for not investigating the learning and religious opinions, which prevail in those countries in Asia, into which either their commerce or their arms have penetrated.

Excuses, however, may be formed for our ignorance concerning the learning, religion and philosophy of the Brahmins. Literary inquiries are by no means a capital object to many of our adventurers in Asia. The few who have a turn for researches of the kind, are discouraged by the very great difficulty in acquiring that language, in which the learning of the Hindoos is contained; or by that impenetrable veil of mystery with which the Brahmins industriously cover their religious tenets and philosophy. (i, pp. xi–xii)

Dow had to discontinue his study of Sanskrit when disappointments in his military career obliged him to return to England in 1768; although he returned to Bengal in 1769, there is no indication that he resumed his study and it did not result in any published translations from Sanskrit.[51] A product of the Scottish Enlightenment (he was to become a correspondent of David Hume in 1772),[52] Dow was evidently attracted by what he could discern of Hindu philosophy and spirituality; his dissertation offers a passionate defence of the complexity, sophistication, and monotheism of Hinduism. The dissertation gives an outline of the Bedas, distinguishes between the sects of the Bedang and the Nadirsin, and gives extracts from the Brahma's explanations of the nature of divinity. Dow claims that widow-burning, or suttee, is in fact a very rare practice but he is as critical of the fakirs

[51] As well as his translation from Firishtah, and the *Tales*, Dow also published two oriental tragedies, *Zingis* (1769) and *Sethona* (1774), the latter produced on his second visit to England. He died at Bhagalpur on 31 July 1779.

[52] See Ranajit Guha, 'Alexander Dow: Philosopher and Mercantilist', in *A Rule of Property for Bengal. An Essay on the Idea of Permanent Settlement*, 2nd edn. (New Delhi: Orient Longman, 1981), 21–41.

as his European predecessors. Like Bernier, but with less scepticism, he reports the claim of his brahman interlocutors that the 'gods' of Hinduism are 'symbolical representations' of a single godhead rather than 'idols':

What has been already said has, it is hoped, thrown a new light on the opinions of the Hindoos, upon the subject of religion and philosophical inquiry. We find that the Brahmins, contrary to the ideas formed of them in the west, invariably believe in the unity, eternity, omniscience and omnipotence of God, that the polytheism of which they have been accused is no more than a symbolical worship of the divine attributes, which they divide into three principal classes. . . .

This system of worship, say the Brahmins, arises from two opinions. The first is, that as God is immaterial, and consequently invisible, it is impossible to raise a proper idea of him, by any image in the human mind. The second is, that it is necessary to strike the gross ideas of man, with some emblems of God's attributes, otherwise, that all sense of religion will naturally vanish from the mind. They, for this purpose, have made symbolical representations of the three classes of the divine attributes; but they aver, that they do not believe them to be separate intelligences. (i, pp. lxvii–lxviii)[53]

Dow suggests then that the brahmans concoct 'necessary fictions' for the explication, dissemination, and maintenance of religious belief among the Hindu castes. Like all fictions, their very nature makes it possible that, rather than promote an understanding of the abstract and the immaterial, they detract from it; the embodiment of an insubstantial idea leads to a tendency to worship the material representative rather than the abstract principle. Hence:

The Brahmins of former ages wrote many volumes of romances upon the lives and actions of those pretended Kings, inculcating, after their manner, morality by fable. This was the grand fountain from which the religion of the

---

[53] In a letter of 1667 'Concerning the Superstitions, strange Fashions, and Doctrine of the Native Indies, or Gentils of Indostan', Bernier says that the Hindu 'Pendets' told him 'That all those *Incarnations* or Apparitions, which their Books speak of, are not to be understood according to the Letter, but Mystically, forasmuch as thereby are explained the several Attributes of God. Some there were, and those of the most Learned, acknowledging to me candidly, that there was nothing more fabulous than those *Incarnations*, and that they were only the Inventions of Legislators, to retain People in some Religion' (Bernier, *Continuation*, 156–7).

vulgar in India was corrupted; if the vulgar of any country require any adventitious aid to corrupt their ideas, upon so mysterious a subject. (i, p. xlix)

It is not until the third volume of Dow's translation of the *History of Hindostan* that the political and ideological grounds for the enthusiastic defence of Hinduism become clear. Published in 1772, after Dow's return to India, the third volume has two prefixed essays by Dow: 'A Dissertation on the Origin and Nature of Despotism in Hindostan' and 'An Enquiry into the State of Bengal; with a plan for restoring that Kingdom to its former Prosperity and Splendor'.[54] Ranajit Guha argues that Dow derived his understanding of the roots of despotism in eastern climate from Montesquieu's *L'Esprit des Lois* and in the exercise of power by a sacerdotal class from Nicolas-Antoine Boulanger's *Recherches sur l'Origine Despotisme* of 1762. Dow shows his hand in the dissertation on despotism when he claims that 'The Faith of Mahommed is peculiarly calculated for despotism' (iii, p. xiii), but qualifies the admission that the Hindu caste system is also one of despotic order with the comment that it is so 'tempered by the virtuous principles inculcated by their religion, that it seems milder than the most limited monarchy in Europe' (iii, p. xxxv). The essay concludes by presenting the Hindu people as ripe for government by a less despotic form of government which values trade and industry, unlike that of the Muslim rulers before them:

Timid and submissive, from the coldness of a vegetable diet, they have a natural abhorrence to blood. Industrious and frugal, they possess wealth which they never use. Those countries, governed by native princes, which lay beyond the devastation of the Mahommedans are rich, and cultivated to the highest degree. Their governors encourage industry and commerce; and it is to the ingenuity of the Hindoos, we owe all the fine manufactures in the East. (iii, p. xxxvi)

The plans for restoring Bengal to its former prosperity in the companion essay of the third volume foreshadow the way in which

---

[54] Dow explains in his preface that he left India in some haste in 1768 and could take with him only one volume of Firishtah so that he could not provide a translation of the histories of the Deccan, Bengal, Gujerat, and Kashmir. The second (also 1768) and third (1772) volume include a continuation of Firishtah's history, and a summary of the reigns of the Mughal emperors after Akbar, compiled by Dow from a variety of Persian sources which he lists at the end of vol. iii.

British rule in India was to develop in the following century and a half: Dow advises the introduction of a British jurisprudence, the division of executive and judicial powers, the establishment of landed property to ensure loyalty among subjects, the use of paper currency rather than exchange systems, the banning of monopolies, the introduction of religious tolerance (although he says that young widows should be forbidden from throwing themselves on funeral piles, and the drowning of the sick and aged should be prohibited (iii, p. cxxviii)). He concludes with the resounding claim that all these changes will ensure increased profits for the East India Company (iii, p. cxlvii). Ranajit Guha suggests, however, that Dow's project only accorded superficially with the eventual permanent settlement (the renunciation by the British state for all time of its right to raise assessments made upon landowners in India) introduced by Lord Cornwallis in 1793. Dow's was a more mercantilist solution to the problem of Bengal property than that of Philip Francis (whose thinking informed Cornwallis). Where Francis saw security of tenure of property as the basic principle of government, Dow saw it only as secondary to his primary argument for the promotion of trade and circulation of currency.

The evidence of Dow's two essays might suggest the cynical conclusion that his interest in the acquisition of oriental languages was driven purely by the political interests of the 'ruling' class he served. However, throughout his writings in the *History of Hindostan* there runs a critical agonistic vein (largely prompted by his hostility to Robert Clive) which implies that the British can learn from the Muslim and Hindu cultures they encounter, as well as take advantage of that knowledge for the advancement of their own wealth and influence in the region. His translation of the *Bahâr-e dâneš* by the seventeenth-century Persian officer, man of letters, and later Sufi, 'Inâyat Allâh Kanbû, is organized around similar principles to those in the first two volumes of his Firishtah translation, of contrast between Hindu and Muslim cultures, and debate about the nature of good government.

Dow's collection could be paralleled with Thomas Percy's translation of the Chinese *Hau Kiou Choaan* of the same decade, in that, like Percy's work, it is presented as an exercise in translation performed in the service of acquiring a language and it is annotated with explanatory footnotes explaining obscure cultural references. However, it might also be read as a satirical exercise in which the author mocks pomposity and elaborate rhetoric in the oriental tale. The preface rehearses a number of positions familiar to readers of the oriental tale: a critique of the eastern manner of writing, the complaint of 'severity' in the author's treatment of women as a compliment to the liberty enjoyed by women in Europe, the claim for 'originality', 'novelty', and a moral purpose as a means of redeeming extravagant and 'too free' expression. Dow comments that

The grave Mohommedans of India think him [the Inatulla] too free in his expressions in some of the tales; a censure he will probably incur in this country, though great care has been taken in the translation not to offend decency. At any rate it is to be hoped his moral tales will make up for the levity of his ludicrous stories; and that, upon the whole, Inatulla will afford some entertainment. (i, p. ix)

The distinction between the 'ludicrous' and the 'moral' is maintained through the contrast between two kinds of tales in the two volumes: those told by courtiers to a young prince in order to try and dissuade him from his romantic obsession with a Chinese princess he has only heard about and seen in a portrait, and those told by a retired hermit to the same prince which provide him with a series of moral lessons about how to obtain one's desires by checking and channelling them.

A later translation of the same work, Jonathan Scott's *Bahar-Danush* of 1799, reveals the liberties Dow took with his Persian source. Scott had acted as Persian secretary to Warren Hastings and was the translator of Mubârak Allâh Irâdat Khân Wâdih's memoirs during the reign of Aurangzeb (1786), Firishtah's *History of Deccan* (1794), and an account of the Deccan from a manuscript held by Tippoo Sultan (1791), as well as being the first literary translator of the *Arabian Nights Entertainments* into English in 1811.[55] Like Dow,

[55] Inâyat Allâh Kanbû, *Bahar-Danush; or, Garden of Knowledge*, trans. Jonathan Scott (Shrewsbury, 1799); Mubârak Allâh Irâdat Khân Wâdih, *A Translation of the Memoirs of Eradut Khan . . . Containing Interesting Anecdotes of the Emperor Aulumgeer Aurungzebe, and of his Successors*, trans. Jonathan Scott (London, 1786); *Firishtah's History of Dekkan, with a Continuation from Other Native Writers and the History of Bengal*, trans. Jonathan Scott (Shrewsbury, 1794); Jonathan Scott (trans.), *An Historical and Political View of the*

Scott seems to have realized that translations of fiction enjoyed more success than those of history. In his preface to the *Bahar-Danush*, he responds bitterly to a review in the *British Critic* of his collection of tales from Persian and Arabic in William Ouseley's *Oriental Collections* (1797–1800) which recommended he should have continued with translations from Firishtah's history and the commentaries of Sultan Baber. He would have been happy to do so, he says, 'had I not experienced that oriental history meets not in this country a sale any way adequate to the labour and expense of publication' (i, p. viii). His translation of Firishtah's *History of the Deccan*, published at his own expense, was only made viable by the East India Company's purchase of forty of the five hundred handsome quarto volumes. The commentaries, he adds, are full of dull battles with harsh names of Tartar chiefs which 'occupy much of every page' (i, p. xi). His bookseller advises him that tales will sell much better.

Scott's three-volume octavo translation from Kanbû is annotated with comments that demonstrate the freedom of Dow's translation and prove instructive in a consideration of the ways in which Dow was tailoring his work to accord with European/English taste and preconceptions about 'Hindostan'. Scott opens his preface with the comment that he was prompted by a query in Ouseley's *Oriental Collections* asking whether Dow's *Tales* were genuine; the response cites the original work but encourages another translator to continue the work since 'Colonel Dow has not translated above one third part of it' (i, p. i) and yet his work has been enthusiastically received.[56]

Decan, South of the Kistnah; Including a Sketch of the Extent and Revenue of the Mysorean Dominions, as Possessed by Tippo Sultaun (London, 1791); *The Arabian Nights Entertainments. To which is Added a Selection of New Tales*, trans. Jonathan Scott (London, 1811).

[56] John Shore, a contemporary of Dow's in Bengal, confirms Jonathan Scott's judgement. In a letter to Revd Professor Ford from Calcutta on 17 September 1783 he asserts 'The Tales of Inatullah are very common: they are written in a very pleasant style, though rather inflated. Dow has not translated one-third of them: indeed I might affirm, he has not translated any; for the English version is too vague to be called a translation. I compared part of them some years ago, and endeavoured to make use of the translation for my own advantage, but without success. His character as a Persian scholar was far from being high in Bengal; and I should suppose that he took the substance of the original as read and explained to him by his Moonshee or Interpreter, and published it as a translation. His version of Ferishta is more correct, and in some parts exact' (*Memoir of the Life and Correspondence of Lord John Teignmouth* (London, 1843), i. 105–6).

Scott was prompted to compare Dow's translation with the Persian manuscript source in the British Museum and 'found it so widely distant from it, even to the insertion of whole tales, not in the original, that [he] conceived a new translation of the entire work might not be unacceptable' (i, pp. i–ii). Scott left out only six tales from the original, all of which are given in the Persian source after the death of the hero and heroine of the frame story, and these he summarizes in a short appendix at the end of volume three (one is the story of Lalla Rookh later made famous by Thomas Moore in 1817).

We can use Scott's translation to highlight the considerable and significant changes Dow made to his source. Two major shifts of emphasis are apparent. First, Dow transfers the misogyny found in the voice of the author in Scott's more literal translation to the voices of the courtiers who tell the Indian Prince Jehandar tales of women's infidelity in order to dissuade him from his amatory obsession with an unknown princess. Dow's translation takes a more favourable view of women in general and suggests that misogyny in the court at Hindostan, evidenced in its enthusiasm for tales that defame women, is one element of its inherent weakness and instability. By contrast, Scott concludes that the Persian author aimed 'to make the imper-fections of many a foil to the brilliant virtues of the heroine of his novel, who loved so truly, that she could not survive the loss of her husband' (iii. 274). Second, the narrator of four stories told to Jehandar after he leaves the court of Hindostan in disguise as a fakir, is in Dow a hermit-sage who becomes Jehandar's mentor. In Scott's translation, the same stories are delivered to the prince by a sym-pathetic miner bird (known as a Sharok), since 'As the sage was wholly occupied by his penances and devotions, he conversed but little with the prince' (ii. 156). Both these moves accord with Dow's critical position in relation to Islamic rule in India, presenting the oppression of women in the Muslim court as a symptom of its cor-ruption and decadence, and embodying a moral wisdom and doctrine of self-control in the figure of an aged Hindu brahman.

Another significant change is misinterpreted by Scott. Where Scott's translation of the 'Preface of the Author, Einaiut Oollah' describes an encounter between a beautiful young male brahman and the author and his company, in which the young man tells the collection of stories, Dow's 'The Author Inatula to the Reader' has the author and his company experience a dream-vision of a beautiful 'young maid'. In a footnote to his translation, Scott complains that

With an imitation of this Introduction Dow commences his work, in which he has retained but very little of the text. After a very sparing mixture of original metaphor with much European figure, he makes his author fall asleep, and behold in a dream a nymph of the Mussulman paradise, instead of the young bramin, whome EINAIUT OOLLA tells us, gave him the plots of his Tales, in the language of the Hindoos. (i, pp. lxxiv–lxxv)

Although the description of the maid's sparkling eyes and 'ambrosial hair' in Dow's preface might suggest a houri, the comment that she was 'of such exquisite beauty and form, that a devotee of the true faith would have worshipped the divinities which beamed in the arched temples of her eyes, and wish to wear the zinar, if woven of her ambrosial hair' (i, n.p.) implies that she is rather to be taken as a Hindu, or at least that her designation as a houri is equivocal, since the zinar is a ring of amulets worn by Hindus around the neck.[57] Dow's translation throughout, in accord with this change of the sex of the figure of rhetoric (from beautiful young man to maid), provides a more feminocentric vision of India, using the paradigm of heterosexual romance to represent the relation between governing class and native population, whereas Scott's retains the flavour of a homosocial, indeed homoerotic, encounter between Hindu India and Muslim Persia of the source text; indeed, in Scott's translation passionate and competitive relations between men (the prince and his transmigrated friend in the body of the parrot, or the author and the young tale-telling brahman) take priority over the tale of the romance between the Prince Jehandar and the princess he loves.

One explanation of Dow's decision is that he was working to transform his source text into a collection of tales that would have been more recognizable to his readers from other collections such as those of

[57] Nandini Bhattacharya points out that the public display of Hindu women's bodies was not simply represented by ethnographers in opposition to the seclusion of the Muslim woman in the zenana or behind the veil, but rather the former was taken as an alluring sign of the other, and that both were seen as forms of deceit exercised upon the male imagination to weaken its authority: 'It is not claiming too much to say that ethnographers saw the public female body only to give a shape to fantasies about the unknowable but alluring private body hidden in zenana or harem' (*Reading the Splendid Body*, 18).

François Pétis de la Croix and Antoine Galland. Hence, the use of a female figure to allegorize the seductive power of rhetoric would invoke memories of Scheherazade and Sutlememé. These female narrators associated with the Muslim harem as a space of tale-telling are contrasted with the aged brahman who springs from a different and indigenous Hindu tradition, familiar to European readers from the figure of the Hindu philosopher-sage Bidpai, in translations of the late seventeenth century from an Arabic version of a fourth-century Sanskrit collection of fables (see 'Rational Animals' below). Ageing men, older female gossips, and beautiful young women are the principal tale-tellers of the oriental tale; Kanbû's figure of a beautiful young man is an unfamiliar one to European readers of the genre.

Elsewhere in the collection, Dow seems to have been gearing his translation to what his English readers knew and expected of 'India', sometimes from his own pen. He adds stories and touches which mark the tale as more specifically 'Indian' than Scott's translation. Scott comments that the first three stories which set up the frame of the Prince Jehandar's hopeless love for the Princess Gulzara of Chanbalich are all inventions by Dow: the story of the death of Jehandar's much-loved favourite, Jewan Sadit, who is mauled by a tiger when out hunting with the prince by the contrivance of an envious courtier named Budbucht, derives from an account given in Dow's translation of Firishtah when Jahangir contrives Shere Askun's death on a tiger hunt in order to gain access to Shere Askun's wife, Mher-ul-Nissa (later Nourmahal).[58]

Dow uses his admittedly scanty knowledge of Hindu theories of transmigration to flesh out the history of the parrot, the reborn spirit of Sadit, providing him with a long speech which rehearses the argument of Brama to his son that intellect is a portion of the great soul of the universe breathed into all creatures and animating other bodies after death, an argument also given in his 'Dissertation concerning the customs . . . of the Hindoos' in the first volume of his translation of Firishta.

Finally, the story of Commladeve which the parrot recounts to Jehandar as a means of introducing him to the vision of Gulzara and

---

[58] Firishtah, *History of Hindostan*, iii. 24–30.

exposing the perfidy of Jehandar's favourite mistress, Mherpirwir, is, Scott claims, 'probably fabricated from a novel called Pudmawut, containing the adventures of a Raja and Rannee of Chitore, and founded upon facts, in which are some particulars resembling this tale. Or Dow may have taken the plot from his own epitome of Ferishta.'[59] Thus, Dow weaves familiar stories from Indian history (the reigns of Jahangir and Akbar) and his own understanding of Hindu beliefs and practices into his narrative, giving his Persian source a more recognizably 'Indian' context for an eighteenth-century British reader familiar with Mughal history from travellers' reports and histories like his own translation of Firishtah.

The framing device to the stories also indicates a preoccupation throughout Dow's tales with the seductive chimerical power of rhetoric (the Persian title of the tales means 'a new garden of the flowers of rhetoric') which can successfully invert the dominance of reality over dream. Scott complains that Dow turns the encounter in the author's preface into a dream-vision; Dow's narrator tells us 'I awoke in amaze, and mourned the absence of the daughter of paradise.'[60] Possibly under the direct influence of Gueullette's *Mogul Tales*, and more generally the tradition of the dream-vision in French and English romance, Dow liberally adds numerous instances of 'dreams of men awake' to his 'free' translation of his source.

The stories in Dow's *Tales* group into four strands. The first (frame) story concerns Jehandar's loss of his friend, reacquaintance with him in the body of a parrot, the inset story of Commladeve which introduces Jehandar to the 'dream' of Gulzara and Jehandar's commissioning of a portrait of the princess by a talented artist who travels to China disguised as a merchant and manages to obtain a glimpse behind her veil; Jehandar's story resumes at the beginning of volume two when the courtiers and king decide to try and promote his marriage rather than dissuade him, but the king's letter to the emperor of China is rudely rebuffed and Jehandar departs from court in a state of near madness disguised as a fakir and accompanied by his beloved parrot. The parrot introduces him to the wise Hindu hermit whose lessons in self-control through storytelling restore Jehandar to some

---

[59] Kanbû, *Bahar-Danush*, i. 18. [60] Kanbû, *Tales*, i, p. xv.

peace of mind. At the end of Dow's translation, Jehandar succeeds in obtaining a pair of magic slippers that transport him to the city where his beloved lives.[61]

The second group of tales consists of three stories delivered in the first volume by members of the court who plan that 'night and day should be presented to [Jehandar's] mind a fresh picture of the ingratitude and inconstancy of women, composed of such extraordinary circumstances as might engage the ear of attention, till the auditory of reason might be opened, and judgment resume her throne' (i. 108). These three tellers are treated with great contempt by Dow, who adds comments not found in his source that dismiss the first as an 'unmerciful tearer of the robes of chastity' and the second as an 'old impotent blackener of female fame' (i. 138). The first story concerns a wealthy man who loves his wife passionately but discovers she has been seduced by his friend; he pursues them when they elope and they tie him by his heels up a tree while they copulate below, only to be killed by the poison from a venomous snake which coils down over the husband's body to reach them. The second concerns a man who marries the lovely widow of a dear friend who has died from a serpent's bite when the two friends were hunting together, and then learns that the widow is having an affair with an old, fat calender (a mendicant dervish) with a reputation for religious devotion. Kerimulla, the husband, kills the lover and his wife scars his face horribly when she discovers he is the murderer; Kerimulla is arrested but the calender's servants incriminate the wife and she is condemned in his place.

The third story in this group is set in Tartary (Serendib (Sri Lanka) in Scott) and concerns a general's widow who pursues a young and

---

[61] Scott's translation continues the story beyond this point, informing us that the princess's father, after trying Jehandar's worth, consents to marriage, but on their return journey to Hindoustan, Jehandar falls prey to the transmigration trick carried out by the young dervish in the story of Fadlallah (*PT* ii) and Bennaskar in the story of Misnar (Ridley, *Tales of the Genii*, i and ii). A vizier's son, also in love with the princess, inhabits Jehandar's body, but Jehandar, with the aid of the princess, successfully reverses the trick. He then spends some time in his own country putting down rebellions caused by the tyranny of a usurper, causes his wife distress by falling in love with another woman, but dies reunited with her. She in turn dies of grief. Scott's continuation also gives two long stories told to the prince by his beloved parrot to entertain him while he waits at the princess's court for her father's change of heart.

handsome married jeweller at the instigation of her maid, posing to him as a fairy queen and appearing in apparent visions. The jeweller's cunning wife realizes the trick and plans to blackmail the lady, but when the maid posing as her mistress is taken up by the cutwal (officer of the law) for adultery, the wife takes her place in order to avert her husband's punishment and claims that they were engaged in conjugal dalliance.[62]

The third group of tales are introduced by a fourth 'companion' or member of the group of courtiers determined to dissuade Jehandar from love, but they take the form of six lessons delivered by a company of Hindu ladies to a young brahman who has been sent off by his unfaithful wife on a wild goose chase after the fifth 'bede' (or 'veda', the sacred revelations of Hindu tradition) which she calls the 'tiria' bede. On his way to Jagganat, the holy city, he meets six ladies who recognize his wife's trick and offer to 'teach' him the tiria bede by using him in a succession of their own stratagems to cuckold and humiliate their husbands. These trickster tales are often crude and comical; they recall, sometimes explicitly, Geoffrey Chaucer's *Canterbury Tales*.[63] Despite their satirical bent against the corruption of priestcraft along the lines of many of Chaucer's pilgrims' tales, this group is written with humour and considerable sympathy for the young brahman who increases in sophistication and worldly wisdom as the 'lessons' continue. The illusory pleasure of the dream is returned to, especially in the fifth lesson where the young wife pleasuring herself with the young brahman in an almond tree

---

[62] Scott includes a sixth story in this group of a soldier who marries a 7-year-old girl and brings her up in strictest virtue but she still elopes with a young lover who seduces her with passionate rhetoric delivered at her window every morning.

[63] A lesson which involves the young brahman copulating with a wife up a tree and the couple successfully persuading her elderly husband that it is all an illusion is described by Scott as bearing a resemblance to Pope's January and May (i.e. Alexander Pope's translation of Geoffrey Chaucer's *Merchant's Tale*) and he speculates that 'Einaiut Oolla acknowledges his having borrowed it from the Bramans, from whom it may have travelled through some voyager to Europe many centuries past, or probably having been translated into Arabic or Persian, been brought by some crusader, as were many Asiatic romances, which have served as the ground work of many of our old stories and poems' (ii. 68). Giovanni Boccaccio also produced a variant of the tale in his *Decameron*, in the ninth tale of the seventh day when Lidia, the wife of Nicostrato, persuades him to disbelieve the evidence of his eyes when she makes love with Pirro at the foot of a pear tree her husband has ascended.

persuades her elderly husband that it is an illusion in line with the 'Bedant' (Vedant) philosophy which 'teaches that nothing is real' (ii. 254): 'we ourselves, and all that we behold around us, are nothing but mere delusions.—No, nothing but the creatures of imagination, which amuse the mind with shadows, and stamp them with the semblance of truth' (ii. 255).

Scott informs us that the most crude of this group of tales—a story in which the six women all dress as men in order to pass the brahman off as one of their number and persuade the husband of one of them to push the swing on which the brahman sits behind his wife, thus enhancing their sexual pleasure—is not in the Persian source, although he decides to retain it, only striking out the sentences which he considered 'too free' in their description of amorous intrigue.[64] This group of tales concludes with the brahman's return to his home and violent beating of his wife's lover. When her confidante, a banker's wife, takes the wife's place in their bed that night, the Brahman cuts off the point of her nose with his knife and binds her to the bed with his turban, but the wife returns and, under cover of darkness, the two women swap places. The brahman returns with a light and thinks that a miracle has happened to prove his wife's chastity in the shape of her 'healed' nose, so women are once again proved superior in the act of deception.[65] The idea that the tales are satirical subaltern critiques of a priestly class is reinforced by Scott when he comments that the 'Tirrea Bede was probably originally written by some Hindoo of inferior cast, as a satire on the Bramins; and I was informed, that the asking one of those privileged and sacred personages if he has studied the fifth bede, is often done by wicked wits, when they find him ignorant and insolently proud of his high cast' (ii. 87).

---

[64] Kanbû, *Bahar-Danush*, ii. 88–7.

[65] This tale seems to have entered European fiction very early. In the eighth tale of the seventh day of the *Decameron*, Boccaccio tells the story of Arriguccio, the merchant, who beats and tears the hair of the woman he thinks is his wife having discovered her with a lover, but finds her unscathed, her place in the bed having been occupied by her maidservant. Walter Charleton used the same tale, citing an Italian source, in his *The Cimmerian Matron* (1668), published with the better-known *Ephesian Matron*. Neither Boccaccio nor Charleton give any indication of an 'Indian' context or setting to the tale and the abused husbands are merchants rather than priests.

The fourth group of tales is told, in Dow, by the Hindu hermit to the young Prince Jehandar after he has left the court and determined to take up the life of a mendicant fakir. He is led to the hermit by the parrot and the hermit promises to alleviate his sorrow through instruction. The hermit teaches Jehandar four 'morals' to be attended to if man is to succeed in his desires by telling him four stories: an animal fable illustrates the importance of not underestimating an apparently weak enemy (the story of the mouse and the prince of Gilan), a second tale advocates military valour (the story of Altasash, viceroy of Charizme) and two more stories warn against being misled by passion (the tale of Roshana) and avarice (the story of Fazulla).

All four groups of stories stage the conflict in the young prince between his dynastic responsibilities and his romantic passion. But they also, as we have seen with other sequences of oriental tales, form an interpretive quest, charting Jehandar's changing responses and his attempt to acquire the independent judgement required to make him fit to govern. Transmigration proves an important metaphor in this quest. Jehandar's parrot/Sadit informs him that there are three great principles in nature: intellect, life, and matter. The intellect must attach itself to matter with life but, when the body dies, if it had 'rational faculties', the intellect is accountable and must enter a creature of inferior degree until it can finally ascend back to the body of a man. The parrot's explanation of Hindu theories of transmigration can also serve to illustrate the complex and hybrid acts of narrative transmigration performed in Dow's (and later Scott's) translations. Groups of tales are sophisticated acts of transmigration in which an intellect 'ventriloquizes' the voice of an 'other' and occupies its place. Hence, the East India Company soldier/man of letters (Dow) ventriloquizes the Persian Mughal officer/man of letters (Kanbû) who in turn ventriloquizes his brahman 'source'. In each case, the absorption of an 'other' identity allows for critique of the subject-position of the ventriloquizer and the Christian, Muslim, or Hindu culture from which he habitually speaks. Hence, both the structure and the plots of the tales enable Dow to foreground the failings and strengths of the three different cultures he moves between; Jehandar's selfish passion represents the arrogance of Mughal reign, the brahman's innocence the vulnerability of the Hindu natives to exploitation, but both Muslim and Hindu cultures can still serve as sources of education for the Christian translator/reader of the tales.

Stories are not only hybrid acts of interculturalism for tellers and protagonists, but also for the consumer. Dow calls particular attention to the effect of listening to the stories on the young prince; transmigration moves both the consumer and producer of the tale. Hence, we are told that when the prince listens to the group of tales about the 'tiria bede', his mood lightens: 'The prince was observed to be very attentive to these stories, and now-and-then, a faint smile was seen to dawn on his clouded brow; this encouraged the facetious narrator to continue his humourous tale' (i. 236). Indeed, he laughs out loud at the cleverness of the sixth wife in the lesson of the swing. The effect of the hermit's tales are described in even more detail; Jehandar wipes away a stealthy sympathetic tear at the story of Roshana's madness brought on by being abandoned by her lover, and the final tale, a rather tedious account of heroic action in battles between the king of Ghizni and the prince of the Turkumans, concludes thus:

The prince, during the recital of this story, was seen agitated by various passions;—sometimes he started upon his seat, as transported to the field of action, grasping the visionary sword, and striding with swelling muscles along; sometimes with heart-breaking anxiety he hung on the words of the sage, as on the words of a judge, in the decisive moment of pronouncing the awful sentence of condemnation; sometimes a tear from his eyes insensibly fell like the dew of the morning, his colour was seen to change, and the thrill of sensibility to shake the blossoms of his whitening cheeks.

The sage observed it with uncommon pleasure, knowing that the feeling heart alone is capable of receiving and retaining strong impressions of virtue. (ii. 235–6)

Throughout the collection, Dow stresses the effect of rhetoric on the imagination and explores its ability to dupe and deceive the listener into vice or lead him or her into virtue and self-control. The *Tales* are thus, by implication, an educative medium for the English reader, and especially for a country newly acceded to government in Indian territory. Imaginative sympathy, and a careful consideration of analogical parallels between the tale told and the consumer's own situation, will provide a means of constructing an Anglo-Indian sensibility fit for government of empire. Dow's tales insist that government of the self, constant self-surveillance achieved not through looking inward but through imaginative projection into the place of the other, is the grounding principle of good government in the state. Like Ridley, Dow presents this kind of self-knowledge or self-mastery as a protective mechanism which allows the protagonist to avoid falling prey to illusion and deception by forces aimed at undermining the authority of an ascendant ruling class. The analogical burden of fiction enables one illusory medium to see through another, or rather the seductive power of rhetoric can be harnessed to a moral and just purpose (as empire is imagined by these early propagandists for British rule in India) rather than self-serving or destructive ends.

The Indian fable: rational animals

The last six chapters of Dow's collection draw on a tradition of indigenous 'Indian' writing, the *nitisastra* (treatise on government), more familiar to western readers as the *speculum principis*, or mirror for princes. The collection here introduces a shift from the courtier's politically motivated tales of misogyny, familiar from François Pétis de la Croix's *Turkish Tales*, to the use of the tale as a vehicle for the advocacy of rational and moral living on the part of a sage to a young ruler. Of especial interest is the animal fable, a form associated with the East in general. All three famous 'fabulists' of the seventeenth- and eighteenth-century West are of oriental extraction, Æsop himself, the Hindu sage 'Bidpai' or 'Pilpay', and the Muslim Lokman (mentioned in chapter 31 of the Qur'an), under whose name Antoine Galland asserts that the Arabs translated the fables of Æsop:

En effet, on trouve dans les Paraboles, Proverbes, ou Apologues de Locman en Arabe, des choses que nous lisons dans les Fables d'Æsope, en sorte qu'il seroit assez mal-aisé de décider si les Arabes les ont empruntées des Grecs, ou si les Grecs les ont prises des Arabes. Il est cependant certain que cette manière d'instruire par les fables est plus conforme au genie les Orientaux, qu'à celuy des peuples de l'Occident.[66]

[66] Herbelot, *Bibliothèque Orientale*, 517.

Joseph Harris, in a 1699 translation of a French version of the tales of Bidpai, asserts that

The Greeks were Imitators of the Eastern People; I say Imitators, since the Greeks themselves acknowledge that they gain'd this sort of Learning from Æsop who was an Oriental, and whose Life being written by the Monk Planudes, is the same with that of Lockmans; insomuch that as Mercury makes a Present to Æsop, in Philostratus, the Angels make a Present of Wisdom to Lockman, in Mirkhond.[67]

Classical and oriental worlds are thus, as so often in eighteenth-century accounts, revealed to be interwoven rather than autonomous.

Seventeenth- and eighteenth-century translators of Bidpai's fables— selected from the ancient Sanskrit cycle and brought to Europe through an Arabic version (*c*.750, Ibn al-Muqaffa's *Kalilah wa Dimnah*) of the sixth-century translation into Syriac of the Pahlavi (old Persian) translation—argued that the use of parables to instruct had its origins in India. Twentieth-century commentators on the numerous translations, adaptations, and variations of the cycle note that it may have found its origins in the tales of the lives of the Buddha (*Jatakas*) as a brahman challenge to the Buddhist tradition, but also drawing on the parallel tradition of metempsychosis, the idea of rebirth (often into the body of animals in the Jataka tales), in Hinduism; others note the use of animals to instruct men in the *Upanishads*.[68] Dow not only includes one animal fable in his collection of *Tales*, but also derives the story of removing the tip of a woman's nose as punishment for her assumed infidelity and the 'miraculous' claim of

---

[67] Bidpai, *The Fables of Pilpay*, trans. Joseph Harris (London, 1699), n.p.

[68] Joseph Jacobs, in his introduction to his 1888 edition of the 1570 'translation' of the *Pañcatantra* into English from an Italian version entitled *The Morall Philosophie of Doni* comments that of 550 birth stories, 108 involve manifestations as an animal, and concludes that because India was the home of metempsychosis it became the place where the idea of talking animals in fiction originated: 'although we cannot trace all beast-fables to India, we may, I think, give Buddhism, as represented by the book before us, the credit of those which have a moral attached, which is the case with most forms of the Aesopic fable' (Bidpai, *The Fables of Bidpai: the Earliest English Version of the Fables of Bidpai, 'the Morall Philosophie of Doni' by Sir Thomas North*, ed. Joseph Jacobs (London, 1888), p. xlix. On the sources, dating, and content of the tales, see Chaitanya Krishna, 'Story, Novel, Champu', *A New History of Sanskrit Literature* (Bombay and New York: Asia Publishing House, 1962), 361–6; and Arthur Berriedale Keith, 'The Didactic Fable', *A History of Sanskrit Literature* (Oxford: Clarendon Press, 1928), 242–65.

its restoration when the wife replaces her surrogate in her husband's bed as a proof of her chastity from a story in the same cycle.[69]

Patrick Olivelle, the modern translator and editor of the *Pañcatantra* (a Sanskrit variant of the cycle) notes that the text 'spread at an earlier time and more extensively in the world than any other piece of Indian literature' (p. x). The first translation into English, *The Morall Philosophie of Doni* by Thomas North in 1570 was announced to the reader as a 'precious Jewell . . . first founde written in the *Indian Tongue*'; it was in fact, as its nineteenth-century editor, Joseph Jacobs, summarizes, 'the English version of an Italian adaptation of a Spanish translation of a Latin version of a Hebrew translation of an Arabic adaptation of the Pehlevi version of the Indian original'.[70] North only translated the first part of the Italian text of 1552 (the second part was an unrelated collection of oriental tales largely derived from the *Decameron* under the title *Trattati diversi di Sendebar Indiano filosopho morale*) and of that part only one quarter of the Arabic from which it was translated is presented (the second and third 'parts' of North's collection).[71] Doni concentrates largely on the 'frame' story in which a cunning animal courtier (a jackal in the oriental versions but 'translated' into an ass by Doni, presumably under the classical influence of Apuleius) manages to sow dissension between a lion-king and his virtuous prime minister, an ox; the courtier brings about the death of his rival at the hands of the king and is then called upon by court and king to defend his actions. Stories— some using animal protagonists and others human, about the necessity of duplicity in statecraft and the importance of making allies—are circulated as part of the debate. Olivelle argues that the *Pañcatantra* is

[69] There are so many translations, variations, and derivatives from the cycle, and no single or 'ur' text has been found, that ascription of a single story may appear difficult. However, Patrick Olivelle's recent translation based on the extensive reconstruction work of Franklin Edgerton in the 1920s (Franklin Edgerton, *The Panchatantra Reconstructed*, American Oriental Series 2–3 (New Haven: American Oriental Society, 1924), produces a structure of five books of varying lengths with twenty-four stories and eleven 'sub-stories', which includes 'A Weaver Cuts the Nose of a Bawd' as sub-story 3.2 of story 3 in bk. 1 'On Causing Dissension among Allies' (*Pañcatantra: the Book of India's Folk Wisdom*, ed. Patrick Olivelle, World's Classics (Oxford: Oxford University Press, 1997), 23–5).
[70] Bidpai, *Fables of Bidpai*, ed. Jacobs, 13, p. xi.
[71] On early translations of the cycle, see I. G. N. Keith-Falconer's introduction to his English translation of the Syriac version, *Kalilah and Dimnah; or, The Fables of Bidpai* (Cambridge, 1885).

a text 'not about kings but about ministers' (p. xxviii) and concludes that the central message of the collection is that 'craft and deception constitute the major art of government' (p. xxxv). It is perhaps unsurprising that Renaissance England should have been considered ripe for such a lesson, especially one translated from an Italian version, given the association of the Italian states, evoked by the figure of Machiavelli, with hypocritical statecraft in the period.

Doni was not the source used for the versions of the cycle which appeared in the late seventeenth and eighteenth centuries in Europe, however. Jean de la Fontaine admitted in his 'Avertissement' to the third of the five volumes of his *Fables*, which appeared in 1678, that he had turned to the Indian philosopher Bidpai for fresh tales when his supply from Æsop had dried up:

le nombre de ces traits n'es pas infiny. Il a donc falu que j'aye cherché d'autres enrichessements, & étendu davantage les circonstances de ces recit, qui d'ailleurs me sembloient le demander de la sorte. Pour peux que le Lecteur y prenne garde, il le reconnoistra luy-mesme; ainsi je ne tiens pas qu'il soit necessaire d'en étaler icy les raisons: non plus que de dire où j'ay puissé ces derniers sujets. Seulement je diray par reconnoissance que j'en dois la plus grande partie à Pilpay sage Indien. Son Libre a esté traduit en toutes les Langues. Les gens du païs le croyent fort ancien, & original à l'égard d'Esope; si ce n'est Esope luy-mesme sous le nom du sage Locman. Quelques autres m'on fourny des sujets assez heureux. Enfin j'ay tasché de mettre en ces deux dernieres Parties toute la diversité don't j'estois capable.[72]

In 1696, Antoine Galland suggested to his publisher, Barbin, that he produce a translation of the text from a sixteenth-century translation from the Arabic into Ottoman Turkish, 'L'Homayun Nameh' (*Humayan Namah*), but problems with the library holding the copy resulted in the release instead of a translation by Gilbert Gaulmin and David Sahid from the first four chapters of a Persian translation of *Kalilah wa Dimnah*, the *Anwar-e Sohayli*, under the title *Les Fables de Pilpay* (1698).

It was this French text that formed the source for Joseph Harris's close English translation in 1699. Harris produced a corrected and enlarged version of the same text in 1747; his changes consisted of the

[72] Jean de la Fontaine, *Fables Choisies* (Paris, 1678), iii, n.p.

addition of one fable ('The Countryman and Several Rats') not found in his French source, and the addition of explanatory footnotes. Harris's footnotes confirm a tendency throughout the corrected and enlarged text to make more explicit the oriental nature of the tales and their context (for example the term 'monk' in the 1699 version is habitually changed to that of 'dervise' in the 1747 version). In 1724, Galland's translation from the Ottoman Turkish, under the title *Les Contes et Fables Indiennes*, was published posthumously, completed by Thomas-Simon Gueullette, only a year before the appearance of the latter's *Mogul Tales*. This collection contained one new fable, 'Les Singes, l'Oiseau et le voyageur' from the Ottoman source and excluded two tales from the *Fables de Pilpay*. This text does not appear to have been translated into English.

Not until the 1780s with the foundation of the Asiatic Society of Bengal headed by the Sanskrit scholar and Supreme Court Judge, William Jones, did European (and especially British) writers turn to the translation of major works of Indian literature other than those derived from this cycle of tales.[73] It may not be an exaggeration, therefore, to claim that until the 1780s, 'Indian' literature in Europe was represented exclusively by the moral, often animal, fable deployed to instruct the prince. It is therefore not surprising that, coupled with the association of the oriental tale with an act of corrective instruction by a subaltern figure of a despotic prince, the 'pseudo-oriental' and imitative tales of India discussed above should so often have taken the form of a series of stories delivered, or overseen, by an Indian 'sage', to instruct a potential ruler in the art of governing both self and people (Cothrob of the *Mogul Tales*, Horam of *Tales of the Genii*, the sage hermit in Dow's 'translation').

---

[73] Charles Wilkins published a translation of the *Bhagvad Gita* in 1785. Jones published six hymns to Hindu deities in the *Asiatick Miscellany* of 1785 and a translation of a play by Kalidasa, 'Sakuntala', in 1789. He spent a decade reading in Indian literature, law, mythology, and music. And the animal fable delivered to a prince still remained popular. Charles Wilkins published a translation from the Sanskrit of the *Hitopadesa* in 1787, followed by a translation of the same text from Sir William Jones in 1799. The *Hitopadesa* is a Sanskrit variant of the *Pañcatantra*. For a critical reappraisal of Jones's influence and ideology, see Kate Teltscher's chapter, 'Sir William and the Pandits: The Legal Research, Poetry and Translations of William Jones' (*India Inscribed*, 192-228). For a recent assessment of Jones, see Michael J. Franklin, *Sir William Jones*, Writers of Wales Series (Cardiff: University of Wales Press, 1995).

Moreover, the idea of the veiled instruction through fable could be made to accord with the representation of both Hindu and Muslim systems of government as despotic and absolute. Thus, Harris's translation rehearses a passage found also in his French source:

one of the Reasons which oblig'd the Eastern People, to make use of Fables in their Instructions and Admonitions was, because the Eastern Monarchies being for the most part Despotic, their Subjects are no less restrain'd from Freedom of Speech; however being an Ingenious People they found out this way whereby they might be able, without exposing their Lives, to inform and advise their Princes of what most nearly concerned the Welfare both of themselves and their Subjects, and instruct them, without giving Offence, in the Paths of Virtue, Honour and true Glory, who treat'em as Slaves, and will not permit'em the liberty of Speaking what they think.[74]

The idea of the tales as a covert means of instructing a prince or potential ruler continued in these French and English 'translations' and indeed gained pace in the later translations. Thomas North dedicates his 1570 version to Robert Dudley, earl of Leicester, favourite suitor of Elizabeth I; this choice of dedicatee suggests an understanding of the text as an address to ministers and an exploration of the nature of statecraft, where later European versions tend to frame it rather as an address to a potential monarch or as an instructive moral fable to the young. Often these twin aims coincided. Thus, Fontaine's fables are dedicated to the Dauphin who, he says, is at an age 'où l'amusement & les jeux sont permis aux Princes' who will find the fable a kind of instruction 'que vous apprenez sans peine, ou, pour mieux parler, avec plaisir, tout ce qu'il est necessaire qu'un Prince sçache' (*Fables Choisies*, i, n.p.).

Joseph Harris dedicated his 1699 *The Fables of Pilpay* to another young heir apparent, Princess Anne's son, the duke of Gloucester, concluding with the question: 'as this little Historical Piece, under the Cover of *Fables*, carries the Instruction and Illustration of all those *Princely Virtues*, that shine in *Courts*, and Adorn the *Throne*; where may I more properly devote these *Miniatures* of *Morals* and *Heroick*

[74] Bidpai, *Corrected, Improved and Enlarged. The Instructive and Entertaining Fables of Pilpay*, trans. Joseph Harris (London, 1747), p. xi.

Virtues, than to Your *Highness*, so shining an ORIGINAL of them?'[75] Interestingly, however, Joseph Harris did not translate the subtitle of the French source, 'la Conduite des Rois', for his title but rather subtitled his text 'Containing many useful Rules for the Conduct of Humane Life'. This accords with the general tendency in England to direct the oriental tale towards a more serious moralizing purpose than the satirical and parodic playfulness found in French uses of the form. In the summary below I refer to Harris's 1747 expanded version of the text, since this version seems to be the fullest and most influential version in eighteenth-century England.

No doubt the *Fables of Pilpay* proved so attractive a text for translation and dissemination in seventeenth- and eighteenth-century Europe because it could be presented so as to confirm and coincide with expectations about the nature of oriental culture in general and India in particular, generated by the fictional and ethnographic narratives of the region already in circulation. Pilpay's instructions to his monarch, Dabschelim, are described as a form of ancient wisdom passed down from monarch to monarch and now reaching European hands and ears at the point when European Christian powers are 'succeeding' to government in the East with the decline of Muslim authority.

Translations of the tales, although always claiming the 'Indianness' of the source, offer striking analogues and parallels with western cultures and literary traditions. Hence, Dabschelim's story is introduced in the *Fables de Pilpay* of 1698, and its 1699 and 1747 English translations, by a wise vizier out hunting with a powerful Chinese monarch who uses the example of an industrious hive of bees to indicate the importance of the well-run absolute state. Harris's 1747 'enlarged' version of his earlier text adds the line from the vizier that the bees are 'in the highest Degree remarkable for the Order of their Government', no doubt prompting in English readers' memories the analogy between the beehive and the state in Bernard Mandeville's *Fable of the Bees* (1714), which famously advocated the importance of luxury and self-interest to the health and expansion of the nation.[76]

[75] Bidpai, *The Fables of Pilpay*, trans Joseph Harris (London, 1699) n.p.
[76] Bernard Mandeville, *The Fable of the Bees*, ed. Philip Harth (Harmondsworth: Penguin, 1970).

The vizier, however, proves to be rather of the prudent camp so despised in Mandeville when he tells his king that the success of the hive depends 'upon the good Counsel and prudent Conduct of wise and able Ministers, well affected to their Prince, and Lovers of the public Peace' (4–5). He gives the influence of the Indian sage Pilpay on his king, Dabschelim, as an example and is then persuaded to relate the story to his own monarch. This story, in turn, proves to be one of one monarch serving as a model to another, in that Dabschelim is prompted by a dream of 'a Figure full of Light and Majesty' instructing him to seek out an *'inestimable Treasure, by the means of which you shall, as you deserve, exceed in Glory and Honour all other Men'* (8). The familiar tropes of India as both dream and precious jewel are thus introduced early in the text.

Like Gueullette's Oguz in search of Solomon's ring and Ridley's Misnar in search of Mahomet's signet, Dabschelim will learn that the 'jewel' he seeks is in fact moral wisdom rather than material wealth and that the dream or deceptive fiction is a disguised moral lesson. Dabschelim sets off eastward the following day and comes to a mountain where an old man sitting in a cave shows him a vast number of chests containing gold, silver, and jewels, but Dabschelim is most interested in a small barred casket which he has opened by a smith to reveal a small trunk of gold covered in precious stones holding a smaller book with some writing in Syriac on white satin. A translator is finally found who informs Dabschelim that it is an address from King 'Houschenk' who left it for the use of Dabschelim on the instruction of a divine revelation: 'I have concealed this my last Will and Testament, by way of Instruction to him, to let him know that it is not for Men of Reason and Understanding to be dazled with the Lustre of glittering Treasures' (11). There are fourteen instructions advocating the recruitment and retention of loyal servants, constant distrust of one's enemies, attentiveness to good counsel, patience, and mercy. Dabschelim is promised that if he goes to the mountain of 'Serandib' he will find 'several Fables of excellent Instruction founded on every one of these Heads' which will be explained to him and his questions answered (14).

Dabschelim consults with two ministers as to whether he should undertake the journey. This generates five fables, one ('The

Travelling Pigeon') by the grand vizier warning against travel and four by Dabschelim, three of which argue that without travelling there is no advancement ('The Falcon and the Raven', 'The Poor Man who Became a Great King', and 'The Leopard and the Lion') and one embedded story which is told by the falcon against travel for the sake of greed ('The Greedy and Ambitious Cat'). Dabschelim sets out on his quest and comes to an obscure den where he meets the hermit 'Bidpay' called 'Pilpay' by some Indian grandees, a name that means *the friendly Physician* (37).[77] Pilpay is revealed to be the 'treasure' Dabschelim seeks: 'he opened his Lips, like a Cabinet of precious Knowledge, and charmed *Dabschelim* with his admirable Discourses' (38). For each of Houschenk's fourteen admonitions, Pilpay has a fable to illustrate it for the monarch to commit to memory.

Pilpay's stories are grouped in four chapters each containing several fables, often enboxed with other fables, which demonstrate the four morals: that we ought to avoid the insinuations of flatterers and back-biters (twenty-six tales in Harris's 1747 translation and twenty-five in the 1699 translation); that the wicked come to an ill end (ten tales); how we ought to make choice of friends and what advantage may be reaped from their conversation (eight tales); and that we ought always to distrust our enemies, and be perfectly informed of what passes among them (twelve tales). The logic for this grouping is generated by a 'frame' story of the machinations of the fox Damna to gain ascendancy in the kingdom of the lion. Damna discovers that the lion-king will not leave his palace because he is frightened by the bellowing of an ox in a nearby meadow and persuades the ox to come to court and bow before the king; the ox, much to Damna's frustration, is rapidly exalted to the position of the king's favourite and Damna plots to plant doubts in the lion's mind as to the ox's loyalty resulting in a fight in which the ox is killed. A series of stories between Damna and his wife, Kalilah, between Damna and the lion, and between Damna and the ox, debate the role of deceit in government and whether it brings about good or evil ends.

[77] The introduction to Galland's translation of the Ottoman version asserts that 'Bid' and 'pai' means 'Philosophe Charitable' (p. vi) and should be preferred to the Pilpai/Pilpay derived from the Persian language which refers to elephant feet and is a designation given by the Persians at the Mughal court to native Indians whose unclad feet come to look like those of elephants.

At the beginning of the next chapter, Dabschelim asks Pilpay to reveal to him how the fox's deceit came to light and Pilpay tells him that the lion appoints a leopard minister to investigate Damna; the leopard, with the help of the lion's mother, discovers his perfidy. The leopard and the lion's mother seek to bring about disclosure from the fox's own mouth rather than accusing him outright. This results in a series of tales in which Damna proves his eloquence only to have his deceit revealed by the leopard giving witness of conversations overheard between Damna and his wife. The fox is sentenced to be starved to death between four walls. The last two chapters revert to direct narration of a series of fables by Pilpay to Dabschelim, the first proving the value of friendship and alliance between different beasts and the second the importance of distrusting one's enemies and being well informed about their doings (a frame story of war between the ravens and the owls and the victory of the ravens through the use of a spy in the owl court holds this theme together).

The Indian fable serves a similar purpose in European writing of the period to the fictional informant letter by an oriental figure—such as those of Mahmut in *The Turkish Spy*, Usbek in *The Persian Letters*, and Lien Chi Altangi in *The Citizen of the World*—in so far as it represents the oriental world as one of rational order and philosophical depth which can serve as a contrast and instructive model to a self-serving, irrational, and shallow Occident.[78] However, the frames and the tales themselves reveal conflicting impulses within this overarching purpose. As we have seen in the discussion of other collections of oriental tales, authors and translators recognize the problems that inhere in allegory which make it a difficult medium for the mediation of moral or political truth. The use of a fictional tale to convey a single moral message is always prey to the possibility that the

---

[78] The use of an 'Indian' informant in the tradition of the fictional letter did not surface in Europe until the end of the 18th c. with the publication of Elizabeth Hamilton's *Translation of the Letters of a Hindoo Rajah* in 1796 (ed. Pamela Ann Perkins and Shannon Russell (Peterborough, Ont.: Broadview Press, 1999)). Hamilton's Indian letter writers are Hindu brahmans, educated and philosophically curious in the positive vein initiated by Alexander Dow. Gulfishan Khan reveals that most genuine accounts of Europe by Indian informants were written by Muslim intellectuals in the second half of the 18th c., the most famous of them Abu Talib ibn Muhammad. See *Indian Muslim Perceptions of the West during the Eighteenth Century* (Oxford, New York, and Delhi: Oxford University Press, 1998).

audience may not recognize the message or that a duplicitous teller may deploy the tale to present an appearance of honesty. Thus, the jackal Damna tells tales of the sufferings of loyal servants at the hands of ungrateful masters to defend himself, but we, the readers, are aware of his perfidy and interpret the tales accordingly as indicators of the injustice inflicted on his rival, the ox. The lion's mother is 'afraid lest the subtle Fox should by his Eloquence put a Stop to the Course of Justice' (141), and Damna is not finally defeated by more eloquence in the shape of tales told by his accusers but by the exposure of his private conversation with his wife. Interpretive ambiguity is to some extent checked in the fable by the fact that it is always harnessed to a 'moral', where the oriental tales of the *Arabian Nights Entertainments* and others carry more oblique and multiple meanings under the guise of simple entertainment. However, the stated purpose of a tale may differ from or have a different application to the one claimed by its deliverer.

The metamorphic potential of narrative is nowhere more apparent than in the ongoing debate in the fables about whether personality can change under the influence of circumstance. The choice of animal fables and tales of different castes and professions in India suggest that readers should assume the unchanging nature of the protagonist; certain kinds of animal carry certain intrinsic characteristics and so do certain classes of person.[79] Hence, one of Damna's most interesting defences comes when a 'physiognomist' in the assembled company says he can tell from his face that he is a villain; Damna responds that if this were always true the innocent would never be accused and then says he should not be punished 'since I am not Master of my Actions, but was forced to it by the Marks which I bear' (150). Whole tales are given over to proving that animals cannot change their nature, but

---

[79] The European translators are largely consistent with the Sanskrit source(s) in this respect. Patrick Olivelle comments that brahman ascetics and animals who present ascetic practice are invariably 'hypocrites hiding their greed and lust behind their outward holiness' while merchants 'are presented by and large in a positive light' (*Pañcatantra*, p. xxx). Carpenters fare badly and low castes such as barbers and weavers are drunkards and fools with adulteresses for wives (p. xxxi). He provides a list of characteristics associated with wild and domestic animals and notes that animals with less-developed characters can play 'different and often contradictory roles' whereas animals with well-developed characters are predictable; the lion is always king, the jackal always a greedy minister, and the ass over-sexed and stupid (pp. xxii–xxv).

their telling is rarely unambiguous. Hence, Damna tells the fable of 'The Scorpion and the Tortoise' to the lion in which the tortoise carries his friend the scorpion across a river on his back only to find that the scorpion is trying to bore through his back with its sting; the tortoise sinks into the water to drown the scorpion (Fable 16, chapter 2, 1747). Damna uses the tale to demonstrate to the lion that the ox will naturally defend itself if it fears attack from the lion, since *'what is bred in the Bone, will never out of the Flesh'* (88–9). However, the tales found in chapter 4 of the 1747 *Fables* suggest that animals can behave uncharacteristically when they form an alliance. Hence, the raven, the rat, the pigeon, tortoise, and goat form an alliance despite the rat's opening assertion that 'we are of a Species so different, that we can never be either Friends or Acquaintance' (162–3). When the goat goes missing, the raven flies off to find it trapped in a net, and fetches the rat in its bill so that the rat can bite through the ropes, and the goat in turn saves the tortoise, who is too slow to escape the returning hunter's sack, by pretending to be lame until the rat can gnaw through the strings.

'The Mouse that was Changed into a Little Girl' is an especially interesting fable and the penultimate one in the French and English collections. Here, a gentleman picks up a mouse dropped from the bill of a raven and prays for it to be changed into a little girl which he raises as his own. When she is grown, he seeks the most invincible husband for her in the world, making overtures to the sun who refers him to a cloud since it can obscure the sun. The cloud sends him on to the wind since it can blow away a cloud, and the wind in turn suggests he approach the mountain because it can halt the progress of the wind. The mountain confesses the rat's superiority since it can eat out the mountain's heart. The rat and the girl are delighted to marry and the old man, determining that 'Nothing, I find, can alter Nature' (227), successfully prays for his daughter to revert to a mouse.[80]

This tale is told by a suspicious owl to argue against trusting the raven which has arrived at the owl court horribly wounded and claiming to have been rejected by his kind. The owl's judgement is

---

[80] Harris adds the father's statement to his 1747 translation to make the otherwise ambiguous meaning of this strange little tale more apparent than it was in the 1699 more literal translation from the French.

proved to be accurate in that the raven is indeed a spy who flies back to his fellows to report on the whereabouts of the owls and the means successfully to defeat them. However, the transformation of mouse into girl itself suggests the possibility of metamorphosis of the outward body, if not the inward 'character' or 'nature', which goes against the claim made elsewhere that the personality is shaped by the body it occupies (Damna claims his external markings determine his inward character).

Moreover, the claim of the fable as a form is that it can successfully bring about metamorphosis or 'shape' its auditor/consumer. The tale is told in order to change the person who listens, to correct the errant prince or bring the powerful king to realize where true value lies. European translations were quick to make the parallel with Ovid despite the distance between Ovid's notion of metamorphosis (the transformation of physical body without a change in the nature of personality) and the notion of rebirth or transmigration in Buddhism and Hinduism (where the intellect is reborn in a different body on a strict hierarchical scale as a progress towards spiritual perfection). Joseph Harris's 1747 translation of the French preface adds a long digression on the nature of fable not in his French source which identifies the fables with the mid-eighteenth-century enthusiasm for the form prompted by the work of John Gay and Joseph Addison.[81] The fable, he asserts, is 'the most ancient of all ways of instructing' (p. vii) and he makes a special claim for the coherence of Pilpay's collection. The use of frames and different narrators, he claims, rather than the simple telling of discrete stories (such as Fontaine's *Fables*), has

this particular Advantage, that thro' the whole Book one is made the Introduction to another, in such a manner, that it is not easy, when once enter'd on reading it, to leave off before the End of a Chapter.

This has been by some objected to, as a Fault in the Work, but I cannot help thinking that it is one of its greatest Beauties. This manner of making one Story introduce another, has ever been admired as one of the greatest

---

[81] On the mid-century resurgence in enthusiasm for the fable see Jayne Elizabeth Lewis, *The English Fable: Aesop and Literary Culture, 1651–1740*, Cambridge Studies in Eighteenth-Century English Literature and Thought 28 (Cambridge: Cambridge University Press, 1996).

Beauties of *Ovid's Metamorphosis*, and is plainly here of greater Use, as in the Works of this kind of other Authors, when a Person has read one Fable, which is a detached Piece, and has no Dependance on the rest, he has done, and his Mind is satisfied; whereas here when a young Person has read one Fable, the Author has so contriv'd it, that his Curiosity is excited to go thro' another, and so on to the End of that Chapter, in which also by the excellent Contrivances of the Author, the same Set of Morals are inculcated in a Variety of beautiful Relations. (p. ix)

The curiosity of the English reader should mirror that displayed by Dabschelim, who features as both consumer and narrator in the frame. No doubt Dow's brahman tale-teller, who attentively watches the response of his prince and records his satisfaction, imitates Pilpay (Fig. 19). After Pilpay has finished recounting Damna's perfidy, Dabschelim eagerly requests that he proceed to tell him how it was uncovered and the brahman comments, 'It is with Delight that I have observed your Majesty's Attention to what I have been relating' (120). Given that this comment follows an account of the dangers of a king (the lion) taking at face value the moral lessons delivered to him by an adviser (the fox), there must be a hint of irony in the brahman's pleasure at his king's positive response to his words. Sure enough, the fourth fable in this chapter (told by Damna who is publicly complaining that the favour of court is fickle even for the virtuous) concerns a retired hermit living in a wilderness who is visited by his king and persuaded to become chief minister because the king is so taken by his moral advice; at court the hermit abandons his ascetic life and becomes magnificent. Another visiting hermit upbraids him and tells him a fable of a blind man who mistook a serpent for a whip and this 'apposite Fable, and judicious Admonition awak'd the Court-Hermit from his pleasing Dream' (133). The hermit courtier's reformation only lasts one night, however, and he returns to his old ways until he executes an innocent man and is then himself executed by decree of the king.

Pilpay's fables, then, do not simply offer instructions for the behaviour of ministers and princes or, more broadly, advocate the importance of morally grounded human behaviour to the maintenance of social order and mutual interdependence; they are also fables about the nature of fable, offering instruction in how to read 'eloquence' so

Pilpay instructing King Dabschelim ^{Page 37}

19. Frontispiece, *Corrected, Improved and Enlarged. The Instructive and Entertaining Fables of Pilpay*, trans. Joseph Harris (1747)

as to improve the moral self through careful 'reading' of the narrative acts of others. This in turn would appear to be the role of the oriental fable in European culture; the encounter with an other and imaginary projection into his/her place, the simultaneous absorption in narrative and critical distance from it, will 'shape' a governing self, a reader capable of managing his own desire and recognizing that of others.

Waking from the dream

As the dream of India for English readers became a reality in the shape of the transformation of East India Company men—soldiers, merchants, and scholars—into a governing class, the narrative shapes accorded to the territory also metamorphosed. The structuring opposition between a savage, idolatrous 'native' India and a cultured, wealthy Mughal India was increasingly inverted, so that the latter could be represented as a despotic and savage colonizer of a peaceful trading people possessing an ancient wisdom with whom the British could do business. The dissemination and popularity of the fables of Pilpay/Bidpai until well into the late eighteenth century could serve as one tool in this ideological transformation. The fantastic dream-like space of the *Mogul Tales* gives way to a more pragmatic and rationalist version of India, paradoxically peopled with rational talking animals rather than fairy-tale kings and queens in a web of fanciful luxury. Dow's *Tales* looks both ways, back to a magnificent Mughal past and forward to a profitable British administration. It also moves between the two worlds of Hindu and Muslim India and weaves two different narrative traditions—the courtly oriental tale and the brahmanical fable—into a single fabric, if by no means a seamless one. In both traditions, however, the notion of the instructive and instrumental purpose of the tale, told to bring about a change in its auditor/consumer, remains paramount. In this process, fiction is not simply a medium through which a message is passed; the message is the medium. It is the process of consuming the tale that transforms the consumer, acting upon his or her sensibility to open out the consciousness and make it possible to imagine occupying the place of an 'other'. Narrative dispossession is paradoxically the route to full 'possession' of the self and of the territory it occupies and governs.

It is perhaps in the case of India—a space that over the course of the eighteenth century was transformed from a distant and independent oriental empire with which England sought favourable opportunities for trade, to a territorial possession, the cornerstone of the nascent British empire—that the appropriative nature of the European oriental tale can be seen most clearly. But India is also the site of the most intensely hybridizing activities of the European imagination, which sought analogues to itself not through flattening out cultural, racial, and religious difference but through a process of imaginative projection whereby English accession to power can be viewed as an act of 'succession' (like the European succession to a tradition of 'fable' founded in the Orient), a return to the self through departure from it.

6

EPILOGUE: ROMANTIC
REVISIONS OF THE ORIENT

Among my earliest impressions I still distinctly remember that of my first
entrance into the mansion of a neighbouring Baronet, awfully known to me
by the name of THE GREAT HOUSE, its exterior having been long connected in
my childish imagination with the feelings and fancies stirred up in me by the
perusal of the Arabian Nights' Entertainments. Beyond all other objects, I was
most struck with the magnificent stair-case, relieved at well proportioned
intervals by spacious landing-places, this adorned with grand or shewy
plants, the next looking out on an extensive prospect through the stately
window with its side panes of rich blues and saturated amber or orange tints:
while from the last and highest the eye commanded the whole spiral ascent
with the marbled pavement of the great hall from which it seemed to spring
up as if it merely *used* the ground on which it rested.[1]

So writes Samuel Taylor Coleridge in the fourth essay of *The Friend*
(1809–10). Coleridge explains in more detail in a footnote the nature of
these 'feelings and fancies':

As I had read one volume of these tales over and over again before my fifth birth-
day, it may be readily conjectured of what sort these fancies and feelings must

---

[1] *The Friend*, ed. B. E. Rooke, *The Collected Works of Samuel Taylor Coleridge*,
Bollingen Series 75 (London: Routledge & Kegan Paul, 1969), iv. 148–9.

have been. The book, I well remember, used to lie in a corner of the parlour window at my dear Father's Vicarage-house; and I can never forget with what a strange mixture of obscure dread and intense desire I used to look at the volume and *watch* it, till the morning sunshine had reached and nearly covered it, when, and not before, I felt the courage given me to seize the precious treasure and hurry off with it to some sunny corner in our playground. (148)

Coleridge's retrospective account of his relationship to the work which throughout the eighteenth century had served as a gateway to the East for the European imagination illustrates both the continuities and the changes in oriental narrative of the late eighteenth and nineteenth centuries under the aegis of the developing aesthetic of Romanticism, itself (at least partially) a response to European imperial expansion.

First, and perhaps most obviously, Coleridge identifies the *Arabian Nights Entertainments* as childhood reading, a shaping influence upon the primitive imagination. Oriental empire increasingly came to be identified as a primitive model of government superseded by new forms of European colonialism, and this may have contributed to the increasingly frequent designation of the *Arabian Nights Entertainments*' as children's reading; both William Wordsworth and Alfred Lord Tennyson recall pleasurable immersion in the stories in their youth.[2] The Orient, as Saree Makdisi identifies, came to symbolize the 'anti-modern', 'a backward, debased and degraded version of the Occident'.[3] Second, the *Nights* are equated with space and place rather than narrative time; they are a topos, a physical touchstone or metaphor for the ambitious imagination. Coleridge equates the Great House of his aristocratic neighbour with the feelings of awe and dread prompted by a small volume left by a parlour window in his father's much humbler abode slowly suffused with the light of morning sunshine. The *Nights*, like the Great House, is a space of sublimity, power, and aesthetic beauty, a 'prospect' both in terms of the young boy's future and geographical vision. But these are also magical spaces of danger and prohibition. In his letters, Coleridge records that his

[2] See Irwin, *Arabian Nights*, 269.
[3] Saree Makdisi, *Romantic Imperialism: Universal Empire and the Culture of Modernity*, Cambridge Studies in Romanticism 27 (Cambridge: Cambridge University Press, 1998), 113.

father burned the volumes of *Arabian Nights Entertainments* he owned when he discovered the effect they had on his son.[4]

Third, and perhaps most importantly, Coleridge's account places him in a position of identification with the oriental female, and especially Dinarzade. Like Dinarzade, the young Coleridge watches the approach of dawn which heralds a new immersion in story. Like Dinarzade (and Scheherazade), the young Coleridge is the educated child of an influential father who enters a space of aristocratic power which offers both the prospect of success and advancement but also danger and loss. Loss and anxiety mark Coleridge's relationship to both the visual structure (the Great House) and the verbal one (the volume of the *Arabian Nights Entertainments*). Nigel Leask has drawn our attention to 'the exotic, composite Orient of the Romantic imagination, an Orient invested with an uncanny power to disturb'.[5] The Orient is 'uncanny', both familiar and strange, an 'other' space, place, and time (Coleridge's 'distance' is both that of the adult intellectual looking back at his childhood fears and pleasures and that of the occidental reader taking pleasure in an exotic imagined world beyond his immediate experience).[6]

What factors contributed to this growing sense of the 'alterity' of the Orient? The last two decades of the eighteenth and the first two of the nineteenth centuries completed important political, social, economic, and ideological transitions across the globe. For Edward Said, this period sees the beginnings of 'Orientalism', the scientific claim to extensive and organized knowledge about the 'East'. The new formations of knowledge about the East are coextensive and dependent

[4] 'One tale . . . (the tale of a man who was compelled to seek for a pure virgin) made so deep an impression on me (I had read it in the evening while my mother was mending stockings) that I was haunted by spectres, whenever I was in the dark—and I distinctly remember the anxious and fearful eagerness, with which I used to watch the window, in which the books lay—& whenever the sun lay upon them, I would seize it, carry it by the wall & bask & read—. My Father found out the effect, which these books had produced— and burnt them' (*Collected Letters*, ed. Earl Leslie Griggs, Oxford Scholarly Classics (Oxford: Clarendon Press, 2000), i. 347).

[5] Nigel Leask, *British Romantic Writers and the East: Anxieties of Empire*, Cambridge Studies in Romanticism (Cambridge: Cambridge University Press, 1992), 4.

[6] See Sigmund Freud, 'The Uncanny' (1919), in *Art and Literature, Pelican Freud Library* 14, ed. Albert Dickson, trans. James Strachey (Harmondsworth: Penguin Books, 1985), 335–76.

upon attempts at wholesale colonization and administration of eastern states: Bonaparte's invasion of Egypt in 1798 ('the very model of a truly scientific appropriation of one culture by another, apparently stronger one', comments Said[7]), the British establishment of a civil, legislative, and intellectual state administration in India. Western European states retreat from some ventures and engagements with Far and Middle Eastern territories. The failure of the British embassy to China under Lord Macartney in 1794 sees the abandonment of a vision of trade domination in this quarter of the Far East. The Ottoman empire was recognized to be in wholesale decline and no longer a territorial threat in western Europe; Ottoman Europe, Poland, Hungary, and Russia were increasingly viewed as a composite backward territory of 'Eastern Europe'.[8] Nigel Leask cogently summarizes the position by the time Byron came to write his eastern tales in the second decade of the nineteenth century:

European orientalism, like European colonialism, had moved from being a commercial venture controlled by literature and financial freebooters or monopolizing joint-stock companies to participation in the civilizing mission of nineteenth-century European culture, or the expansionist dependence on colonial markets.[9]

The 'civilizing mission' required acquaintance with culture and language in order to administer and manage territories. Instead of an imported luxury commodity, the 'translated' literature of a colonized territory becomes the ground for building a political and moral relationship. Sir William Jones first learned Sanskrit in order to produce a digest of Indian law, but quickly came to see its discovery as a new 'classical' Renaissance for Europe, equivalent in importance to the Greek heritage.[10] Persian was the medium of official

[7] Said, *Orientalism*, 42.
[8] See Larry Wolff, *Inventing Eastern Europe. The Map of Civilization on the Mind of the Enlightenment* (Stanford, Calif.: Stanford University Press, 1994).
[9] Leask, *Curiosity*, 22.
[10] See Michael J. Franklin's 'Introduction' to *Sir William Jones: Selected Poetical and Prose Works* (Cardiff: University of Wales Press, 1995), p. xxiv. In 1950, Raymond Schwab claimed the late 18th c. saw a discovery of 'eastern' culture equivalent to the classical Renaissance in Europe of the 14th and 15th c. See Raymond Schwab, *The Oriental Renaissance: Europe's Rediscovery of India and the East, 1680–1880*, trans. Gene Patterson-Black and Victor Reinking (New York: Columbia University Press, 1984).

correspondence in British India until 1834, but the British did not confine themselves to the translation of administrative, legal, and political documents. Translated fragments from Persian poets like Firdausi, Hafiz, and Sadi appeared in England to considerable acclaim. Enthusiasm for the ancient Orient and its languages can be seen, as it is by Said, as a form of colonial power; European scholars promise to 'return' oriental cultures to a civilized classical heritage from which they have been estranged by centuries of barbaric and despotic rule: 'What the European took from the classical Oriental past was a vision (and thousands of facts and artifacts) which only he could employ to the best advantage; to the modern Oriental he gave facilitation and amelioration'.[11]

Increased knowledge about oriental cultures and increased awareness about their differences came with increased contact and consumption of oriental goods at the end of the eighteenth century. Diego Saglio argues that the period sees a significant opening out of representation from the (largely) textual confines of the early eighteenth century to an acquaintance with the Orient(s) through objects, fashions, architecture, archaeology, and philology:

As an area of consumption and production—the assemblage, demolition and reconstitution of otherness—the oriental undergoes important transformations in Romantic-period culture and, perhaps most conspicuously, in literary discourse where this shift emerges in the transition from 'pseudo-oriental' eighteenth-century textuality to the more accurate, archaeologically documented works of Romantic literature, a development parallel to the contemporaneous popularisation of the orient in the form of objects, spectacles and narratives.[12]

What begins as a search for analogy and correspondence often serves only to generate visions of alterity and difference. Enlightened pursuit of a universal humanity gives way to a sense of relativity in the late eighteenth century. Paradoxically, knowing more about the East only tends to create rather than dispel alterity. New to the representation of the East in the oriental tale of the late eighteenth and early nineteenth centuries was an awareness of racial difference, especially

---

[11] Said, *Orientalism*, 79.
[12] Diego Saglia, 'William Beckford's "Sparks of orientalism" and the Material-Discursive Orient of British Romanticism', *Textual Practice* 16 (2002): 75–92, 75.

in the representation of the seraglio woman. The narratives we have discussed so far in this book, if they deploy racial opposition at all, tend to align the seraglio woman with white European models and portray her as the victim of the lustful Turk or the black eunuch. However, late eighteenth-century depictions begin to contrast an occidental hero/anti-hero with the oriental harem female magnetically attracted by his strangeness. To 'turn Turk' is more often in this period to be drawn into miscegenation with an oriental female than to imitate the despotic behaviour of the oriental sultan.

In this epilogue, I look at how three further examples of Romantic texts—William Beckford's *Vathek* (1786), Byron's three *Eastern Tales* (1813–14) and the Ottoman seraglio scenes in cantos 5 and 6 of his *Don Juan* (1821–3)—continue the tradition of identification with the role of the oriental female inaugurated by the *Arabian Nights Entertainments*; but in so doing they register the transformation of Enlightenment systems of analogy into Romantic and neo-Gothic explorations of alterity. Coleridge prefaces his essay in *The Friend* with a quotation from Plato's *Politicus* 277d: 'TRANSLATION.—It is difficult, excellent friend! to make any comprehensive truth completely intelligible, unless we avail ourselves of an example. Otherwise we may as in a dream, seem to know all, and then as it were, awaking find that we know nothing.' Coleridge signals to his reader that the account of the encounter with both book and Great House should be read as just such an 'example', a vehicle that explains the formation of the imagination. Like the dreams of Orient that were so popular throughout the eighteenth century, however, Coleridge's example runs the risk of telling more or conveying a different set of meanings from the fable intended by its author. Indeed, the 'fabular' nature of the oriental tale starts to recede from view in this brief anecdote. 'Reading' the oriental tale now signifies a quality of experience, an aesthetic outlook on the world, rather than the acquisition of political or moral truth(s). Identification with the position of the oriental female, as we shall see, gives way in the Romantic period to impersonation—knowing, performative, and often comic.

Beckford and Byron may seem eccentric and unrepresentative examples to demonstrate the transmigration of the oriental tale in the Romantic period. However, in their combination of irony and fantasy, and in their exploitation of the topos of the Orient in order to conjure up 'feelings and fancies' while merely gesturing at the traditional didacticism of the oriental tale, they illustrate the progress of its 'fabular' elements away from moral instruction and towards the fictional and the fantastic. Beckford's and Byron's experiments in literary Orientalism combine playfulness and anxiety in equal measure to confirm the 'otherness' of the Orient and its status, precisely because of that otherness, as spur to the growth of the Romantic imagination. That preoccupation with the nature of the imagination and the 'feelings and fancies' of creativity leads also to a departure from the enthusiasm for the narrative sequence or long prose collection of tales or letters that characterized eighteenth-century oriental fiction. Romantic writers and audiences of the oriental/eastern 'tale' show a marked preference for the fragment, for the digressive (rather than dilatory) narrative: for the first- and third-person personal narrative that pays little or no attention to narrative frame.[13] These devices work to create a sense of heightened consciousness, the observation of feeling and sentiment, to which moralistic intention is always subservient and often inconsequential. Oriental landscape and scenarios are spaces into which the Romantic narrator projects (usually his) consciousness, acquiring the status of myth.

I conclude with the example of an oriental tale by Maria Edgeworth of 1802, 'Murad the Unlucky' which appeared in a collection of sketches and short stories called *Popular Tales* for young men and women. Here, a female author impersonates male narrators, taking the role of Scheherazade only to present a thoroughgoing critique of the providential, supernatural, and imperialist values of the *Arabian Nights*

---

[13] Nevertheless, continuations of the *Arabian Nights Entertainments* were still appearing well into the 19th c. as well as new translations. The Syrian priest Dom Chavis and the Jesuit-educated Frenchman Jacques Cazotte produced further translations from Arabic manuscripts in the Bibliothèque Royale as the *Suite des Mille et une Nuits* as vol. 38–41 of the fairy-tale anthology *Cabinet des Fées* (1788–90), which were translated into English by Robert Heron as *The Arabian Tales, or a Continuation of the Arabian Nights* in 1792. Jonathan Scott produced a new translation in 1811 with several new stories appended. See Robert Irwin's chapter, 'Children of the Nights', in *Arabian Nights*, 237–92. The epistolary series by an oriental informant comes to a close with Elizabeth Hamilton's *Translation of the Letters of a Hindoo Rajah* in 1796. In 1812, Henry Weber produced an anthology of oriental fiction translated from the French and by English authors, the 3-vol. *Tales of the East* which included Galland's *ANE*, Cazotte's and Chavis's *New Arabian Nights* but also texts such as Frances Sheridan's *Nourjahad*.

Entertainments and its imitations. All of these works share a critical, ironic perspective on the tradition of the 'oriental tale'. They are performative transformations of the genre that question its narrative authority and authenticity as witness of the East and didactic vehicle in the West. This ironic self-aware troping of the Orient reveals what Leask terms its 'iatrogenic' function,[14] an inoculation of otherness (rather like the smallpox inoculation Lady Mary Wortley Montagu introduced from Turkey) which may cause the 'illness' it is intended to cure.

In the works by Beckford and Byron, disruptions in narrative sequence and structure are associated with both a privileging of the 'consuming' vision of the Orient for both writer and reader and a questioning of the truth-functions of that vision. Beckford was a direct influence upon Byron and Byron acknowledges his debt to *Vathek* in the notes to all three of his *Eastern Tales: The Giaour* (1813), *The Bride of Abydos* (1813), and *The Corsair* (1814). *Don Juan*'s oriental scenes were to produce a thoroughgoing critique of the bombast and populism of these earlier poems, but also reproduce once more the story of the fascination of the harem woman with the Christian European interloper, if observed with a more jaded and cynical eye. In both Beckford's *Vathek* and Byron's poems about the Orient, narrative and/or physical agency moves from the male hero/anti-hero (whether Christian European or Muslim Asian) to the figure of the oriental woman. A flawed, sometimes childlike, masculinity is superseded by a vision of a feminine desire which, even if self-deceiving, is uncomplicated and powerful.

It is only with the introduction of Nouronihar, the daughter of the emir Fakreddin, that Beckford introduces a subject with 'feelings and fancies'. The appetite-driven antics of the despotic caliph are described with a detached and cynical irony, but Beckford adopts a third-person personal narration to introduce Nouronihar's temptation and seduction by the combined promise of adult sexuality and vast wealth. Nouronihar, having caught the caliph's eye and thrown him her jasmine in mild flirtation, follows a light about the mountains out of curiosity. In doing so, she leaves behind her childhood playmate

---

[14] Leask, *Curiosity*, 10.

and betrothed cousin, the boy Gulchenrouz—who when he 'appeared in the dress of his cousin . . . seemed to be more feminine than even herself'—with the other seraglio women and her nurse, Sutlememé.[15] 'The solitude of her situation was new; the silence of the night, awful; and every object inspired sensations, which, till then, she never had felt' (69). Nouronihar has to choose between two familiar stereotypes of the oriental male: the despotic ruler and the effeminate boy. She chooses the former, but it is apparent to the readers that Vathek is more of a child than the accomplished and sensitive Gulchenrouz. This adult male tyrant kicks and bites those who cross his desire, is given to ravenous hunger and thirst, and is entirely under the sway of his powerful mother. These mutually incompatible versions of oriental masculinity are depicted at the novel's close at complete spatial remove from each other: Gulchenrouz with his company of eternally young boys and their elderly mentor-genius living in the clouds and Vathek, with his heart consumed in eternal flames in the subterranean depths of Eblis (hell).

More important, perhaps, for our purposes is to recognize the entirely different quality to the narration of this oriental tale from the tradition that its author, Beckford, knew so well (between 1780 and 1783 he had been working spasmodically on the translation from the Arabic of manuscripts of Arabian Nights stories collected by Edward Wortley Montagu, son of Lady Mary). Beckford's Orient is a series of staged set-pieces that take place in a sublime landscape of chasms, valleys, soaring mountains, craning towers, and subterranean passages. Nouronihar is given a depth of response to this landscape and to 'sensation' never recorded in the earlier oriental tales of the eighteenth-century landscape (which are driven by plot and by allegorical, rather than subjective, meaning). In other words, the Romantic oriental tale begins to focus, as it does in other narrative genres such as the epic poem or Gothic novel, on the moment of excess or sublimity, the sudden insight or vision, rather than narrative sequence or political allegory.

Byron's three *Tales* are similarly governed by a response to oriental landscapes and scenarios, in his case the lost Greek heritage

---

[15] William Beckford, *Vathek*, ed. Roger Lonsdale (Oxford: Oxford University Press, 1983), 66.

suffocated by Ottoman expansion and failed by Christian Europe. And here too, it is the oriental woman who emerges as the figure of feeling, sensation, and action, where masculine heroism necessarily fails.

If the oriental heroines of both *The Giaour* and *The Bride of Abydos* die because of their passion for occidental heroes (the Venetian knight who seduces the Greek Leila from her Turkish husband-ruler, Hassan, and the seraglio prince turned Greek pirate, Selim, who attempts to elope with his cousin Zuleika), they also represent the prospect of resistance to despotism and the uncomplicated pursuit of desire. Their male counterparts are, by contrast, troubled and self-deceived. It is the oriental heroine of *The Corsair*, Gulnare, who emerges in the poem as the poet's 'epipsyche', or wishful projection of the poet's ego; both Nigel Leask and Jerome McGann observe that women repeatedly take this role in Byron's poetry.[16] The misanthropic corsair 'hero', Conrad, saves Gulnare from the fire started by his fellow pirates in the harem as they attack the palace of her husband the Pacha, only to be taken captive. Gulnare delays his execution by placating her husband and then frees Conrad on the night before he is to die, stabbing the Pacha to death and fleeing with the corsair despite her knowledge that his heart already belongs to the lovely western Medora, who waits for him in a tower across the bay. Gulnare receives one kiss, before the corsair disappears following his discovery that Medora has died of grief at his supposed loss. Gulnare's act of murder is also one of liberation. She tells Conrad:

> 'I felt—I feel—love dwells with—with the free.
> I am a favoured slave at best,
> To share his splendour, and seem very blest!'[17]

Like Beckford, Byron concentrates in these poems on vividly realized scenes rather than the delivery of a tale. *The Giaour* is subtitled 'A Fragment of a Turkish Tale' and is told in fits and starts by a

---

[16] See Leask, *British Romantic Writers and the East*, 6; and Jerome McGann, '"My brain is feminine": Byron and the Poetry of Deception', in James Soderholm (ed.), *Byron and Romanticism*, Cambridge Studies in Romanticism 50 (Cambridge: Cambridge University Press, 2002), 53–76, 67.

[17] *Lord Byron: The Complete Poetical Works*, ed. Jerome McGann (Oxford: Clarendon Press, 1981), iii, canto II, ll. 502–4.

Muslim fisherman and a Christian monk, who catch glimpses of the tale that the reader pieces together. *The Bride of Abydos* and *The Corsair* proceed through powerfully visualized moments rather than narrative temporality. In Byron's hands, the oriental sequence disintegrates into fragments, shards of vision, and, as in *Vathek*, it is the moment of heightened sensation, violence, or excess that is the focus of both the author's and reader's attention. The temporality of the oriental sequence, whether of tales or letters, is violently disrupted. In its place are offered the pleasures of vision; an oriental landscape of storms, troubled seas, and burning palaces represents for the reader the excess of sensation and the struggle for liberation, most often expressed by the oriental woman, of the tale told.

However, this uneven, haphazard, sometimes broken, narrative trajectory is one which enables the European male writer to represent his own desire for political agency as 'other' to himself: a role he can impersonate (but never achieve), and also ultimately repudiate. Both Nouronihar and Gulnare are figures that echo the role of Roxolana rather than Scheherazade. Their longing for freedom declines into covetousness (Nouronihar's desire for the carbuncle of Giamschid) or violence (Gulnare's murder of her husband so that she may escape with Conrad from the harem). In the harem episodes of Cantos 5 and 6 of *Don Juan*, Byron reworks the sensational and sentimental elements to which he gave free rein in his *Eastern Tales* a few years earlier. Although women in the oriental seraglio remain the vehicles for an exploration of untrammelled desire, Byron introduces an ironic critique of the claim to Romantic 'vision' which both exposes and revels in its aesthetic duplicity.

In these cantos, Byron exposes the impersonation of the oriental feminine as male wish-fulfilment when he allows the young Juan access to the enclosed harem in female disguise. Juan is forced to adopt female dress by the eunuch Baba who purchases him as a slave at the command of his mistress, Gulbeyaz, fourth wife of the Ottoman sultan. Gulbeyaz commands Juan's love and weeps when he rejects her. Her courtship is interrupted by the unexpected appearance of her husband and Juan/na is hustled off with the other maids of the seraglio. No spare bed being available, s/he is obliged to share that of the voluptuous Dudu who wakes in the night with a scream and reports a dream of being stabbed to the heart by a bee hidden inside a luscious apple. The next morning, Gulbeyaz threatens to throw the pair into the Bosphorus. The 'tale' of Juan/na's entry into the enclosed and unseen mysteries of the harem is, as all his adventures in the poem are, punctuated by the digressive interventions of the poet, which serve to complicate and confuse interpretation. The narrator pretends ignorance about the nature of Dudu's 'dream', informing us:

> I can't tell why she blushed, nor can expound
>   The mystery of this rupture of their rest;
> All that I know is that the facts I state
>   Are true as truth has ever been of late.[18]

The narrator's insouciance, as Jerome McGann observes, has the effect of exposing the dynamics of desire in reading. The narrator's readers 'see' the voyeurism of his narration where he remains ignorant of it:

the essential wit of the episode arises from the narrator's *conscious* assumption of an innocent eye, his pretence—as in the narrative of Dudu's dream—that he is himself unaware of the word-plays and double meanings of his own discourse.... Dudu does not narrate her own dream; the narrator tells it for her in indirect discourse. That indirection underscores the theatricality of his talk, the masquerade in which he is involved. The critical consequence, however, is that the narrator is himself pulled on to the stage of the poem. In that event the narrator is released from the bondage of his own imagination. We are not only able, for example, to 'see' and criticize his voyeurism, we come as well into contact with that supreme objectivity which poetic discourse, alone of our discursive forms, seems able to achieve.[19]

The two cantos develop into a full-blown critique of the deceptions of 'vision' and the claim to knowledge. When Gulbeyaz rises from her bed the narrator comments that headlong passions are the cause of inevitable woe, adding:

> And that's the moral of this composition
> If people would but see its real drift.

---

[18] *Don Juan*, eds. T. G. Steffan, E. Steffan, and W. W. Pratt (London: Penguin, 1996), canto 6, stanza 85.　　[19] McGann, ' "My brain is feminine" ', 73–4.

But *that* they will not do without suspicion,
     Because all gentle readers have the gift
Of closing 'gainst the light their orbs of vision,
     While gentle writers also love to lift
Their voices 'gainst each other, which is natural;
     The numbers are too great for them to flatter all.
                    (Canto 6, stanza 88)

Byron here notes the progress of the oriental tale from oral politically charged narrative intervention to print commodity. Scheherazade's project of correcting her husband through the intermediary role of her sister has spiralled into a vast literary competition between writers for the attention of a plurality of readers all seeking different pleasures and flatteries from their reading experience, just as Juan/na moves from the singular courtship of Gulbeyaz to the rivalry of the thousand-odd love-starved maidens of the harem. Byron's witty performance of the scenario of the oriental harem also reveals the distance such representations have travelled over the century. The western European male now knowingly performs the role of innocent abroad, acknowledging that the 'dream' of the Orient is a form of wish-fulfilment that disguises political, mercantile, or sexual interest (just as Dudu's dream both points to and conceals her sexual experience).

On the surface, Maria Edgeworth's short oriental tale is a far less sophisticated and more familiar imitation of the *Arabian Nights Entertainments*; its source lies in the brief 'Story of Cogia Hassan Alhabbal' in which two friends, the rich Saadi and the poor Saad, experiment by giving a poor rope-maker 'capital' equivalent to their means to test whether a man can become rich and happy on the basis of a small investment; the rope-maker turns a profit from the virtually worthless piece of lead donated by Saad but is unlucky with the larger investment of money given by Saadi. Edgeworth had elsewhere warned against the effect of reading oriental tales on the young; in *Practical Education*, written with her father Richard Lovell Edgeworth, she complains that the *Arabian Nights Entertainments* belongs to 'a class of books which amuse the imagination of children, without acting upon their feelings' and that the boy raised on the adventures of Sindbad will at 17 'admire the soldier of fortune, the commercial adventurer, or the nabob, who has discovered in the east the secret of Aladdin's wonderful lamp; and who has realized the treasures of Aboulcasem'.[20]

The story of Murad, who believes fate has destined him always to wreak havoc and disaster for himself and others, and Saladin, his prudent and socially responsible younger brother who does his best to improve his lot and that of others, bears out the implied critique in *Practical Education* of the application of the magical accumulation in the *Arabian Nights* as an incentive to colonial plunder on the part of nabobs and soldiers of fortune. Moreover, Edgeworth appears to associate the Romantic aesthetic of solitary growth of the imagination in communion with natural objects, landscape, and self-examination with imperial/colonial ambition, its self-regard and wilful blindness to the social fabric of the spaces it occupies. Murad's first-person account is an ironic exposure of the solipsistic mystical aesthetics of Romantic melancholy. Murad brings plague to the city of Grand Cairo when he sells on a cheaply bought chest of clothes from Smyrna purchased from a Jew. He is nursed through the plague by a generous old woman who on his recovery offers to tell him her own life-history:

As I perceived that this benevolent old woman took great pleasure in talking, I made an inclination of my head to thank her for her promised history, and she proceeded; but I must confess I did not listen with all the attention her narrative doubtless deserved. Even curiosity, the strongest passion of us Turks, was dead within me. I have no recollection of the old woman's story. It is as much as I can do to finish my own. [21]

By contrast, Saladin is sceptical about the offer of a similar chest from the same Jew and not only refuses the offer but warns his fellow merchants against it. He makes his fortune through prudential trading and is rewarded with a happy life and marriage to the woman he loves. The tale, in the tradition of Scheherazade, corrects its reader (the Caliph Haroun Al-Raschid and his vizier who have been listening to the brothers' accounts conclude that it is not fortune but prudent behaviour that governs man's success in life) and also corrects the

---

[20] Maria Edgeworth and Richard Lovell Edgeworth, *Practical Education* (London, 1798), i. 304, 302. [21] Edgeworth, 'Murad the UnLucky', 237.

tradition of the oriental tale and its imaginative attractions for the western reader. Robert Mack concludes that

There may very well be legitimate ways in which the East differs from the West, Edgeworth seems to say, but the inconsequential enchantments of the *Arabian Nights* are not among them. It is no longer possible to see the East as a convenient and mysterious repository of a world governed by genie and magic; in *Murad* we see at least one writer beginning to come to grips with the realisation that the Orientalism of the nineteenth century will have to be less fanciful and more culturally responsible.[22]

Like Lady Mary Wortley Montagu almost a century earlier, Maria Edgeworth redirects the oriental tale away from its associations with romance and magic towards an allegory about hard-headed practicality, the importance of self-government, and an openness to opportunity. But a new object of her critique is the solitary pursuit of imaginative stimulus, which she challenges through a vision of social interdependence. Once more, but differently, the oriental tale serves as modern fable for the West.

Fascination with oriental themes, settings, and narratives continued to flourish in British writing throughout the nineteenth and twentieth centuries. The figure of Scheherazade and identification with the role of the oriental woman, as purveyor and consumer of story, resurface in different forms and with different effects as the West's relationship to the East continues to shift and transform. Perhaps now, more than ever, readers need to be reminded of the dense interrelationship of traditions of storytelling across the globe and that models of female political agency have never been exclusive to western 'liberal' thought.

One last story to conclude. In A. S. Byatt's fabulous short story entitled 'The Djinn in the Nightingale's Eye' (1994) a British narratologist, Gillian Perholt, travels to Ankara to deliver a paper at an international conference about 'Stories of Women's Lives' on Chaucer's patient Griselda. Here, she experiences three mysterious 'revelations', purchases a small flask made of a Turkish glass named 'nightingale's eye' because of its spiral pattern of opaque blue and white stripes, from which in her hotel room she releases a djinn who offers her three wishes and recounts to her his previous three

---

[22] Mack, *Oriental Tales*, p. xlvi.

'liberations' into the service of women. Gillian Perholt's name recalls that of Charles Perrault, the seventeenth-century French collector of the fairy tales of Mother Goose and enthusiastic promoter of the oriental tale. At one point the djinn transforms her 'Christian' name into an oriental female equivalent, 'Djil-yarn', marrying the idea of storytelling and the activities of the 'djinn'. Perholt's surname indicates the role of the narratologist/storyteller who must deviate (the prefix 'per' from the Latin preposition meaning 'by', when attached to verbs, is used in the sense of 'away from' as in 'pervert') before she ends (halts). Her own paper on patient Griselda points to the dangers of excessive masculine narrative control. The tyrannous husband of patient Griselda, she complains, 'assumed too many positions in the narration; he is hero, villain, destiny, God and narrator'[23] and her own story, like that of Scheherezade to Schahriar, is one in which a female learns to 'forge' her own destiny through stories. Stories are woven into stories in the 'The Djinn in the Nightingale's Eye'; like modern travel, on which the story opens as Gillian takes off in her plane to Ankara, the tale effortlessly moves between different cultures (*The Canterbury Tales, The Arabian Nights,* classical mythology, Shakespeare's Hamlet, Milton's Satan, contemporary Turkish poetry). The larger narrative struggle, Gillian herself recognizes, is between the fantastic tale and the realist novel. Telling the djinn a melancholy story about the wedding of a friend in which she tries to capture the atmosphere by describing the 'three piece suite in moquette' which adorned the parents' living-room, she cries in exasperation: 'I should never have started on this. All English stories get bogged down in whether or not the furniture is socially and aesthetically acceptable' (239). As in most of Byatt's fiction, the tension is not resolved but rather the distinction collapsed. Fantasy and realism, symbolism and psychological complexity, narrative determinism and freedom of individual action—come to form a complex and hybrid wholeness in this tale, which performs the synthesis sought from the novel's inception in Europe. Ostensibly different narrative traditions of East and West appear magically to speak to each other, always multi-vocal and always hybrid.

[23] A. S. Byatt, *The Djinn in the Nightingale's Eye: Five Fairy Stories* (London: Chatto & Windus, 1994), 120.

BIBLIOGRAPHY

The Adventurer, 4 vols. (London, 1778).

ADDISON, JOSEPH, and STEELE, RICHARD, *The Spectator*, ed. Donald F. Bond, 5 vols. (Oxford: Clarendon Press, 1965).

ALLEN, CHARLES, *The Buddha and the Sahibs: The Men who Discovered India's Lost Religion* (London: John Murray, 2002).

The Amours of the Sultana of Barbary. A Novel (London, 1689).

APPLETON, WILLIAM WORTHEN, *A Cycle of Cathay: The Chinese Vogue in England in the Seventeenth and Eighteenth Centuries* (New York: Columbia University Press, 1951).

Arabian Nights Entertainments: Consisting of One Thousand and One Stories, Told by the Sultaness of the Indies . . . Translated into French from the Arabian Mss, by M. Galland . . . And Now Done into English from the Last Paris Edition, 8th edn. (London, 1736).

The Arabian Nights Entertainments. To Which is Added a Selection of New Tales, trans. Jonathan Scott (London, 1811).

Arabian Nights' Entertainments, ed. Robert L. Mack (Oxford: Oxford University Press, 1995).

ARAVAMUDAN, SRINIVAS, 'In the Wake of the Novel: The Oriental Tale as National Allegory', *Novel* 33 (1999): 5–31.

—— *Tropicopolitans: Colonialism and Agency, 1688–1804*, Post-Contemporary Interventions (Durham, NC: Duke University Press, 1999).

ARMSTRONG, NANCY, *Desire and Domestic Fiction: A Political History of the Novel* (New York and Oxford: Oxford University Press, 1987).

AUSTEN, JANE, *Sense and Sensibility*, ed. Ros Ballaster (London: Penguin, 2003).

BACKSCHEIDER, PAULA R., *Daniel Defoe: His Life* (Baltimore and London: Johns Hopkins University Press, 1989).

—— and RICHETTI, JOHN J, (eds.), *Popular Fiction by Women, 1660–1730: An Anthology* (Oxford: Clarendon Press, 1996).

BACON, FRANCIS, *Essayes or Counsels, Civill and Morall*, ed. Michael Kiernan, Oxford English Texts (Oxford: Clarendon Press, 1985).

Bibliography

BAKHTIN, M. M., 'Forms of Time and of the Chronotope in the Novel', in *The Dialogic Imagination: Four Essays*, ed. Michael Holquist, trans. Caryl Emerson and Michael Holquist, Slavic Series 1 (Austin: University of Texas Press, 1981), 84–258.

BALLASTER, ROS, *Seductive Forms: Women's Amatory Fiction from 1784 to 1740* (Oxford: Clarendon Press, 1992).

—— 'A Gender of Opposition: Eliza Haywood's Scandal Fiction', in Kirsten Saxton and Rebecca Bocchicchio (eds.), *The Passionate Fictions of Eliza Haywood. Essays on her Life and Work* (Lexington, Ky: University of Kentucky Press, 2000), 143–67.

BARTHES, ROLAND, 'Introduction to the Structural Analysis of Narrative', in *Barthes: Selected Writings*, ed. Susan Sontag ([London]: Fontana, 1983), 251–95.

BEASLEY, JERRY C., 'Portraits of a Monster: Robert Walpole and Early English Prose Fiction', *Eighteenth-Century Studies* 14 (1981): 406–31.

BEATTIE, JAMES, *Dissertations, Moral and Critical*, in *The Works of James Beattie*, ed. Roger J. Robinson (London: Routledge/Thoemmes, 1996).

BEAUMONT, ANTONY, 'Turandot (I)', L. Macy (ed.), *The New Grove Dictionary of Music Online* (Accessed 3 Sept. 2002), http://www.grovemusic.com.

BEAUMONT, DANIEL, *Slave of Desire: Sex, Love and Death in the 1001 Nights* (London: Associated University Presses, 2002).

BECKFORD, WILLIAM, *Vathek*, ed. Roger Lonsdale (Oxford: Oxford University Press, 1983).

BELON, PETER, *The Court Secret. A Novel*, 2 parts (London: R. Bentley & S. Magnes, 1689).

BERG, MAXINE, 'Manufacturing the Orient: Asian Commodities and European Industry 1500–1800', in Simonetta Cavaciocchi (ed.), *Prodotti e Techniche d'Oltremare nelle Economie Europee secc. XIII–XVIII* (Prato: Istituto internazionale di storia economica F. Datini, 1998), 385–419.

—— and CLIFFORD, HELEN (eds.), *Consumers and Luxury: Consumer Culture in Europe, 1650–1850* (Manchester: Manchester University Press, 1999).

—— and EGER, ELIZABETH (eds.), *Luxury in the Eighteenth Century: Debates, Desires and Delectable Goods* (Basingstoke: Palgrave, 2003).

BERNIER, FRANÇOIS, *The History of the Late Revolution of the Empire of the Great Mogul. To Which is Added a Letter Touching the Extent of Indostan*, trans. Henry Oldenburg (London, 1671).

—— *A Continuation of the Memoires of Monsieur Bernier, Concerning the Empire of the Great Mogol*, trans. Henry Oldenburg et al. (London, 1672).

Bibliography

BHATTACHARYA, NANDINI, *Reading the Splendid Body: Gender and Consumerism in Eighteenth-Century British Writing on India* (Newark and London: University of Delaware Press; Associated University Presses, 1998).

BIDPAI, *The Morall Philosophie of Doni [Tr. From the Fables of Bidpai and Ed. by A. f. Doni]*, trans. Thomas North (London, 1570).

—— *The Fables of Pilpay [Tr. By J. Harris from the Fr. Tr. Of G. Gaulmin and Dâwûd Sa'id]*, trans. Joseph Harris (London, 1699).

—— *Corrected, Improved and Enlarged. The Instructive and Entertaining Fables of Pilpay*, trans. Joseph Harris (London, 1747).

—— *The Fables of Bidpai: the Earliest English Version of the Fables of Bidpai, 'the Morall Philosophie of Doni' by Sir Thomas North*, ed. Joseph Jacobs (London, 1888).

BLAUT, JAMES M., *The Colonizer's Model of the World: Geographical Diffusion and Eurocentric History* (New York and London: Guilford, 1993).

BLOUCH, CHRISTINE, 'Eliza Haywood', in *Miscellaneous Writings, 1725–43*, vol. i of *Selected Works of Eliza Haywood I*, ed. Alexander Pettit (London: Pickering & Chatto, 2000), pp. xxi–lxxxxii.

BOULAINVILLIERS, HENRI COMTE DE, *The Life of Mahomet*, trans. John Gagnier (London, 1731).

BOYER, JEAN BAPTISTE DE, *Chinese Letters, Tr. [or Rather, Written] by the Marquis D'argens, and Now Done into English* (London, 1741).

BOYLE, FRANK T., 'Chinese Utopianism and Gulliverian Narcissism in Swift's Travels', in Aileen Douglas, P. H .Kelly, and Ian Campbell Ross (eds.), *Locating Swift: Essays from Dublin on the 250th Anniversary of the Death of Jonathan Swift, 1667–1745* (Dublin: Four Courts Press, 1998), 117–28.

BRAVERMAN, RICHARD LEWIS, *Plots and Counterplots: Sexual Politics and the Body Politic in English Literature 1660–1730*, Cambridge Studies in Eighteenth-Century English Literature and Thought 18 (Cambridge: Cambridge University Press, 1993).

BRÉMOND, SÉBASTIEN, *Hattige: Or the Amours of the King of Tamaran. A Novel*, trans. B.B. (Amsterdam, 1680).

BROWN, LAURA, *Fables of Modernity: Literature and Culture in the English Eighteenth Century* (Ithaca, NY, and London: Cornell University Press, 2001).

BURKE, PETER, 'The Philosopher as Traveller: Bernier's Orient', in Jas Elsner and Joan Pau Rubiés (eds.), *Voyages and Visions: Towards a Cultural History of Travel* (London: Reaktion Books, 1999), 124–37.

BYATT, A. S., *The Djinn in the Nightingale's Eye: Five Fairy Stories* (London: Chatto & Windus, 1994).

Bibliography

BYRON, LORD GEORGE GORDON, *Lord Byron: The Complete Poetical Works*, vol. iii, ed. Jerome McGann (Oxford: Clarendon Press, 1981).

—— *Don Juan*, ed. T. G. Steffan, E. Steffan and W. W. Pratt (London: Penguin, 1996).

CAO XUEQIN, *Hung lou meng; or, The Dream of the Red Chamber*, trans. Henry Bencraft, 2 vols. (Hong Kong, 1892, 1893).

CARACCIOLO, PETER L. (ed.), *The Arabian Nights in English Literature: Studies in the Reception of the Thousand and One Nights into British Culture* (Basingstoke: Macmillan, 1988).

CATROU, FRANÇOIS, *The General History of the Mogol Empire, from Its Foundation by Tamerlane, to the Late Emperor Orangzeb. Extracted from the Memoirs of M. Manouchi, a Venetian, and Chief Physitian to Orangzeb for above Forty Years* (London, 1709).

CAWTHORN, JAMES, *Poems* (London, 1771).

CAYLUS, ANNE CLAUDE-PHILIPPE DE TUBIÈRES DE GRIMOARD DE PESTELS DE LEVIS, *Oriental Tales* (London, 1745).

CAZOTTE, JACQUES, and CHAVIS, DOM, *The Arabian Tales, or a Continuation of the Arabian Nights*, trans. Robert Heron (London, 1792).

CERVANTES, XAVIER, ' "Tuneful Monsters": The Castrati and the London Operatic Public 1667–1737', *Restoration and Eighteenth-Century Theatre Research*, 2nd ser. 13, no. 1 (1998): 1–24.

CHARDIN, JOHN, *A New Collection of Voyages and Travels . . . Containing a most Accurate Description of Persia, and Other Eastern Nations*, trans. Edmund Lloyd (London, 1721).

CHARLETON, WALTER, *The Ephesian and Cimmerian Matrons* (London, 1668).

CHIEN, CHUNG SHU, 'China in the English Literature of the Seventeenth Century', *Quarterly Bulletin of Chinese Bibliography*, NS 1 (1940): 351–84.

—— 'China in the English Literature of the Eighteenth Century', *Quarterly Bulletin of Chinese Bibliography*, NS 2 (1941), no. 1: 7–48, no. 2: 41–2.

CHOUDHURY, MITA, *Interculturalism and Resistance in the London Theater, 1660–1800: Identity, Performance, Empire*, Bucknell Studies in Eighteenth-Century Literature and Culture (Lewisburg, Pa., and London: Bucknell University Press; Associated University Presses, 2000).

COLERIDGE, SAMUEL TAYLOR, *The Friend*, ed. B. E. Rooke, vol. iv of *The Collected Works of Samuel Taylor Coleridge*, Bollingen Series 75, 16 vols. (London: Routledge & Kegan Paul, 1969).

—— *Collected Letters of Samuel Taylor Coleridge*, ed. Earl Leslie Griggs, Oxford Scholarly Classics, 6 vols. (Oxford: Clarendon Press, 2000).

Bibliography

COLLEY, LINDA, *Captives: Britain, Empire and the World, 1600–1850* (London: Jonathan Cape, 2002).

CONANT, MARTHA PIKE, *The Oriental Tale in England in the Eighteenth Century*, Columbia University Studies in Comparative Literature (New York: Columbia University Press, 1908).

CORNEY, BOLTON, 'On the Authorship of the Turkish Spy', *Gentleman's Magazine*, NS 14 (1840): 465–69.

CORYATE, THOMAS, *Greeting from the Court of the Great Mogul*, English Experience, Its Record in Early Printed Books Published in Facsimile, no. 30 (Amsterdam and New York: Theatrum Orbis Terrarum; Da Capo Press, 1968).

COSTES DE LA CALPRENÈDE, GAUTIER DE, *Cassandra: The Fam'd Romance*, trans. George Digby and Charles Cotterell (London, 1676).

CRÉBILLON, CLAUDE-PROSPER JOLYOT DE, *La Sopha: Conte Morale* (Gaznah [false imprint, probably Paris], 1742).

—— *The Sopha: a Moral Tale*, trans. William Hatchett and Eliza Haywood (London, 1742).

CURLL, EDMUND, *Compleat Key to the Dunciad* (London, 1728).

DAVIS, LENNARD, *Factual Fictions: The Origins of the English Novel* (New York: Columbia University Press, 1983).

DAVYS, MARY, *The Reform'd Coquet; or, Memoirs of Amoranda; Familiar Letters Betwixt a Gentleman and a Lady ; and, the Accomplish'd Rake, or, Modern Fine Gentleman*, ed. Martha F. Bowden, Eighteenth-Century Novels by Women (Lexington, Ky: University Press of Kentucky, 1999).

DAWSON, RAYMOND STANLEY, *The Chinese Chamelon: An Analysis of European Conceptions of Chinese Civilization* (Oxford: Oxford University Press, 1967).

DEFOE, DANIEL, *A Continuation of Letters Written by a Turkish Spy at Paris* (London, 1718).

—— *The Letters of Daniel Defoe*, ed. George Harris Healey (Oxford: Clarendon Press, 1955).

—— *The Life & Strange Surprizing Adventures of Robinson Crusoe of York, Mariner*, Shakespeare Head Edition of the Novels and Selected Writings of Daniel Defoe (Oxford: Basil Blackwell, 1927).

—— *Roxana, the Fortunate Mistress*, ed. Jane Jack (London and New York: Oxford University Press, 1964).

DENNIS, JOHN, *The Critical Works of John Dennis*, ed. Edward Niles Hooker (Baltimore: Johns Hopkins University Press, 1939).

DIDEROT, DENIS, *Les Bijoux Indiscrets* =: *Or, the Indiscreet Toys* (Tobago [London], 1749).

DOW, ALEXANDER, *Zingis. A Tragedy* (London, 1769).

Dow, ALEXANDER, *Sethona. A Tragedy* (London, 1774).

DRYDEN, JOHN, *The Works of John Dryden*, 20 vols. (Berkeley, Los Angeles, and London: University of California Press, 1956–2001).

DU HALDE, JEAN-BAPTISTE, *A Description of the Empire of China and Chinese Tartary, Together with the Kingdoms of Korea, and Tibet*, trans. Emanuel Bowen, 2 vols. (London, 1738, 1741).

DUMONT, JEAN, *A New Voyage to the Levant*, 4th edn. (London, 1705).

DU RYER, ANDRÉ, *The Alcoran of Mahomet, Translated out of Arabique into French; by the Sieur Du Ryer, Lord of Malezair, and Resident for the King of France, at Alexandria. And Newly Englished, for the Satisfaction of All That Desire to Look into the Turkish Vanities* (London, 1649).

EDGERTON, FRANKLIN, *The Panchatantra Reconstructed*, American Oriental Series, vols. ii–iii. (New Haven: American Oriental Society, 1924).

EDGEWORTH, MARIA, 'Murad the Unlucky', in *Oriental Tales*, ed. Robert Mack (Oxford: Oxford University Press, 1992), 215–56.

—— and EDGEWORTH, RICHARD LOVELL, *Practical Education*, 2 vols. (London, 1798).

FAN, CUNZHONG [Fan, Tsen-Chung], 'Dr Johnson and Chinese Culture', *China Society Occasional Papers*, NS 6 (1945): 2–20.

Female Replies to Swetnam the Woman-Hater, intro. Charles Butler (Bristol: Thoemmes Press, 1995).

FIRISHTAH, MUHAMMAD KÂSIM HINDÛ SHÂH, *The History of Hindostan*, 3 vols. (London, 1768, 1772).

—— *Firishta's History of Dekkan, with a Continuation from Other Native Writers and the History of Bengal*, trans. Jonathan Scott (Shrewsbury, 1794).

FLUDERNIK, MONIKA, 'Suttee Revisited: From the Iconography of Martyrdom to the Burkean Sublime', *New Literary History* 30 (1999): 411–37.

—— 'Suttee as Heroic Martyrdom, Liebestod and Emblem of Women's Oppression: From Orientalist to Feminist Appropriations of a Hindu Rite in Four Narrative Genres', *Ranam* 33 (2000): 145–80.

FONTAINE, JEAN DE LA, *Fables Choisies*, 5 vols. (Paris, 1678).

Four Treatises Concerning the Doctrine, Discipline and Worship of the Mahometans (London, 1712).

FRANKLIN, MICHAEL J., *Sir William Jones*, Writers of Wales Series (Cardiff: University of Wales Press, 1995).

FREUD, SIGMUND, 'The Uncanny' (1919), in *Art and Literature*, Pelican Freud Library 14, ed. Albert Dickson, trans. James Strachey (Harmondsworth: Penguin Books, 1985), 335–76.

Bibliography

FRYER, JOHN, *A New Account of East India and Persia, Being Nine Years' Travels, 1672–1681*, ed. William Crooke, Works Issued by the Hakluyt Society, 2nd ser. nos. 19–20, 39 (London: Printed for the Hakluyt Society, 1909).

GILDON, CHARLES, *The Post-Boy Robb'd of His Mail: Or, the Pacquet Broke Open, Letters. Both Vols. In One*, 2nd edn. (London, 1706).

GOLDSMITH, OLIVER, *The Citizen of the World*, ed. Arthur Friedman, vol. ii of *Collected Works of Oliver Goldsmith*, 5 vols. (Oxford: Clarendon Press, 1966).

GOUDAR, ANGE, *The Chinese Spy; or, Emissary from the Court of Pekin, Commissioned to Examine into the Present State of Europe*, 6 vols. (London, 1765).

GREENBLATT, STEPHEN, *Marvelous Possessions: The Wonder of the New World* (Oxford: Clarendon Press, 1991).

GROSRICHARD, ALAIN, *The Sultan's Court: European Fantasies of the East*, trans. Liz Heron (London: Verso, 1998).

GRUNDY, ISOBEL, *Lady Mary Wortley Montagu: Comet of the Enlightenment* (Oxford: Oxford University Press, 1999).

GUEULLETTE, THOMAS-SIMON, *Chinese Tales: or, the Wonderful Adventures of the Mandarine Fum-Hoam*, 2 vols. (London, 1725).

—— *Mogul Tales, or the Dreams of Men Awake: Being Stories Told to Divert the Grief of the Sultana's of Guzerat, for the Supposed Death of the Sultan*, 2 vols., 2nd edn. (London, 1743).

GUHA, RANAJIT, 'Alexander Dow: Philosopher and Mercantilist', in *A Rule of Property for Bengal: An Essay on the Idea of Permanent Settlement*, 2nd edn. (New Delhi: Orient Longman, 1981), 21–41.

GUNNY, AHMAD, *Images of Islam in Eighteenth-Century Writings* (London: Grey Seal, 1996).

GUY, BASIL, 'Ad majorem Societatis gloriam: Jesuit Perspectives on Chinese Mores in the Seventeenth and Eighteenth Centuries', in G. S. Rousseau and Roy Porter (eds.), *Exoticism in the Enlightenment* (Manchester and New York: Manchester University Press, 1990), 66–85.

HAMILTON, ANTONY, *Memoirs of the Count de Grammont* (London, 1714).

—— *Select Tales of Count Hamilton* (London, 1760).

HAMILTON, ELIZABETH, *Translation of the Letters of a Hindoo Rajah*, ed. Pamela Ann Perkins and Shannon Russell (Peterborough, Ont.: Broadview Press, 1999).

HATCHETT, WILLIAM, *A Chinese Tale* (London, 1740).

—— *The Chinese Orphan* (London, 1741).

Bibliography

HAYS, MARY, *Memoirs of Emma Courtney*, ed. Eleanor Ty (Oxford: Oxford University Press, 1996).

HAYWOOD, ELIZA, *The Adventures of Eovaai. A Pre-Adamitical History*, ed. Earla Wilputte (Peterborough, Ont.: Broadview Press, 1999).

—— *Memoirs of a Certain Island Adjacent to the Kingdom of Utopia*, 2 vols. (London, 1724–5).

—— *The Secret History of the Present Intrigues of the Court of Caramania* (London, 1727).

HEFFERNAN, TERESA, 'Feminism against the East/West Divide: Lady Mary's Turkish Embassy Letters', *Eighteenth-Century Studies* 33 (2000): 201–16.

HERBELOT, BARTHÉLEMY D', and GALLAND, ANTOINE, *Bibliothèque Orientale, Ou Dictionaire Universel Contenant Généralement Tout Ce Qui Regarde La Connoissance Des Peuples De L'orient* (Paris, 1697).

HERIOT, ANGUS, *The Castrati in Opera* (London: Secker & Warburg, 1956).

HILL, AARON, *A Full and Just Account of the Present State of the Ottoman Empire in All Its Branches: With the Government, and Policy, Religion, Customs, and Way of Living of the Turks, in General* (London, 1709).

HOAMCHI-VAM, *The Bonze, or Chinese Anchorite*, trans. 'Monsieur D'Alenzon', 2 vols. (London, 1769).

HOLWELL, JOHN ZEPHANIAH, *Interesting Historical Events Relative to the Provinces of Bengal and the Empire of Hindostan* (London, 1767).

HONOUR, HUGH, *Chinoiserie: The Vision of Cathay* (New York: Dutton, 1962).

HOOK, ROBERT, *Some Observations and Conjectures concerning Chinese Characters* (London, 1686).

HOWE, ELIZABETH, *The First English Actresses: Women and Drama 1660–1700* (Cambridge: Cambridge University Press, 1992).

IRWIN, ROBERT, *The Arabian Nights: A Companion* (London: Allen Lane, 1994).

JACOBSON, DAWN, *Chinoiserie* (London: Phaidon Press, 1993).

JAMES, LAWRENCE, *Raj: The Making and Unmaking of British India* (London: Little Brown, 1997).

JOHNSON, SAMUEL, *A Dictionary of the English Language on Cd-Rom the First and Fourth Editions*, ed. Anne McDermott (Cambridge and New York: Cambridge University Press, 1996).

JONES, WILLIAM, *Sir William Jones. Selected Poetical and Prose Works*, ed. Michael Franklin (Cardiff: University of Wales Press, 1995).

KABBANI, RANA, *Imperial Fictions. Europe's Myths of Orient*, rev. and expanded edn. (London: Pandora, 1994).

KAMUF, PEGGY, *Fictions of Feminine Desire: Disclosures of Heloise* (Lincoln, Nebr.: University of Nebraska Press, 1982).

KANBÛ, 'INÂYAT ALLÂH, *Tales. Translated from the Persian of the Inatulla of Delhi*, trans. Alexander Dow (London, 1768).

—— *Bahar-Danush; or, Garden of Knowledge*, trans. Jonathan Scott (Shrewsbury, 1799).

KAUFMANN, LINDA S., *Discourses of Desire: Gender, Genre and Epistolary Fictions* (Ithaca, NY, and London: Cornell University Press, 1986).

KEITH, ARTHUR BERRIEDALE, *A History of Sanskrit Literature* (Oxford: Clarendon Press, 1928).

KEITH-FALCONER (trans.), *Kalilah and Dimnah: or, the Fables of Bidpai* (Cambridge, 1885).

KHAN, GULFISHAN, *Indian Muslim Perceptions of the West during the Eighteenth Century* (Oxford, New York, and Delhi: Oxford University Press, 1998).

KIRKMAN, FRANCIS, *The English Rogue: Continued in the Life of Meriton Latroon*, pt. 2 (London, 1680).

KNIPP, C., 'The Arabian Nights in England: Galland's Translation and Its Successors', *Journal of Arabic Literature* 5 (1974): 44–54.

KNOLLES, RICHARD, *The Generall Historie of the Turkes* (London, 1603).

—— and RYCAUT, PAUL, *The Turkish History. With a Continuation, Whereunto Is Added the Present State of the Ottoman Empire, by Sir P. Rycaut*, 6th edn. (London, 1687).

KRISHNA, CHAITANYA, 'Story, Novel, Champu', *A New History of Sanskrit Literature* (Bombay and New York: Asia Publishing House, 1962), 361–6.

KUBEK, ELIZABETH, 'The Key to Stowe: Toward a Patriot Whig Reading of Eliza Haywood's *Eovaai*', in Chris Mounsey (ed.), *Presenting Gender: Changing Sex in Early Modern England* (Lewisburg, Pa., and London: Bucknell University Press; Associated University Presses, 2001), 225–54.

LACH, DONALD E., and VAN KLEY, EDWIN J., *A Century of Advance*, vol. iii of *Asia in the Making of Europe*, 3 vols. (Chicago: Chicago University Press, 1993).

LAMB, JONATHAN, *Preserving the Self in the South Seas, 1680–1840* (Chicago; London: University of Chicago Press, 2001).

LAQUEUR, THOMAS, *Making Sex: Body and Gender from the Greeks to Freud* (Cambridge, Mass., and London: Harvard University Press, 1990).

LEASK, NIGEL, *Curiosity and the Aesthetics of Travel Writing, 1770–1840: 'from an Antique Land'* (Oxford: Oxford University Press, 2002).

Bibliography

—— *British Romantic Writers and the East: Anxieties of Empire*, Cambridge Studies in Romanticism (Cambridge: Cambridge University Press, 1992).

LE COMTE, LOUIS, *A Compleat History of the Empire of China* (London, 1739).

LEDDEROSE, LOTGAR, 'Chinese Influence on European Art, Sixteenth to Eighteenth Centuries', in Thomas H. C. Lee (ed.), *China and Europe: Images and Influences in Sixteenth to Eighteenth Centuries* (Hong Kong: Chinese University Press, 1991), 221–50.

LEE, THOMAS H.C. (ed.), *China and Europe: Images and Influences in Sixteenth to Eighteenth Centuries* (Hong Kong: Chinese University Press, 1991).

LE FANU, Alicia, *Memoirs of the Life and Writings of Mrs. Frances Sheridan* (London, 1824).

LENNOX, CHARLOTTE, *The Female Quixote, or, the Adventures of Arabella*, ed. Margaret Dalziel (Oxford: Oxford University Press, 1989).

LEWIS, JAYNE ELIZABETH, *The English Fable: Aesop and Literary Culture, 1651–1740*, Cambridge Studies in Eighteenth-Century English Literature and Thought 28 (Cambridge: Cambridge University Press, 1996).

LOWE, LISA, *Critical Terrains: French and British Orientalisms* (Ithaca, NY, and London: Cornell University Press, 1991).

LYNE, RAPHAEL, *Ovid's Changing Worlds: English Metamorphoses, 1567–1632* (Oxford: Oxford University Press, 2001).

LYTTELTON, GEORGE, *The Court Secret: A Melancholy Truth* (London, 1741).

—— *Letters from a Persian in England, to His Friend at Ispahan* (London, 1735).

MCBURNEY, WILLIAM HARLIN, 'The Authorship of the Turkish Spy', *PMLA* 72 (1957): 915–35.

—— (ed.), *Four before Richardson: Selected English Novels, 1720–1727* (Lincoln, Nebr.: University of Nebraska Press, 1963).

MCDONALD, DUNCAN BLACK, 'A Bibliographical and Literary Study of the First Appearance of the Arabian Nights in Europe', *Library Quarterly* 2 (1932): 387–420.

MCGANN, JEROME, ' "My brain is feminine": Byron and the Poetry of Deception', in James Soderholm (ed.), *Byron and Romanticism*, Cambridge Studies in Romanticism 50 (Cambridge: Cambridge University Press, 2002), 53–76.

MCGEARY, THOMAS, ' "Warbling Eunuchs": Opera, Gender, and Sexuality on the London Stage, 1705–1742', *Restoration and Eighteenth-Century Theatre Research*, 2nd ser. 7, no. 1 (1992): 1–22.

Bibliography

MACK, ROBERT L. (ed.), *Oriental Tales* (Oxford: Oxford University Press, 1992).

MACY, L. (ed.), *The New Grove Dictionary of Music Online* http://www.grovemusic.com

MAHDI, MUHSIN, *The Thousand and One Nights*, vol. iii (Leiden: Brill, 1994).

MAKDISI, SAREE, *Romantic Imperialism: Universal Empire and the Culture of Modernity*, Cambridge Studies in Romanticism 27 (Cambridge: Cambridge University Press, 1998).

MANDEVILLE, BERNARD, *The Fable of the Bees*, ed. Philip Harth (Harmondsworth: Penguin, 1970).

MANLEY, DELARIVIER, *Almyna: Or, the Arabian Vow. A Tragedy* (London, 1707).

—— *New Atalantis*, ed. Rosalind Ballaster (London: Penguin, 1992).

MARANA, GIOVANNI PAOLO, *The Eight Volumes of Letters Writ by a Turkish Spy at Paris*, trans. William Bradshaw, 8 vols., 6th edn. (London, 1707).

—— *Letters Writ by a Turkish Spy*, selected and ed. Arthur J. Weitzman (London: Routledge & Kegan Paul, 1970).

MARKLEY, ROBERT, ' "The destin'd Walls/ Of Cambalu". Milton, China, and the Ambiguities of the East', in Balachandra Rajan and Elizabeth Sauer (eds.), *Milton and the Imperial Vision* (Pittsburgh Duquesne University Press, 1999), 191–213.

MARS, FRANCIS L., *Ange Goudar, Cet Inconnu (1708–1791): Essai Bio-bibliographique sur un Aventurier Polygraphe du 18e Siècle*, Casanova Gleanings 9 (Nice: J. Rives Childs Château des Baumettes, 1966).

MARSHALL, PETER J. (ed.), *The British Discovery of Hinduism in the Eighteenth Century* (Cambridge: Cambridge University Press, 1970).

MATAR, NABIL I., *Islam in Britain, 1558–1685* (Cambridge: Cambridge University Press, 1998).

—— *Turks, Moors, and Englishmen in the Age of Discovery* (New York: Columbia University Press, 1999).

MAYER, ROBERT, *History and the Early English Novel: Matters of Fact from Bacon to Defoe*, Cambridge Studies in Eighteenth-Century English Literature and Thought 33 (Cambridge: Cambridge University Press, 1997).

MAYO, ROBERT DONALD, *The English Novel in the Magazines, 1740–1815: With a Catalogue of 1375 Magazine Novels and Novelettes* (Evanston, II.: Northwestern University Press, 1962).

MELMAN, BILLIE, *Women's Orients: English Women and the Middle East, 1718–1918: Sexuality, Religion and Work* (Basingstoke: Macmillan, 1992).

METLITZKI, DOROTHEE, *The Matter of Araby in Medieval England* (New Haven: Yale University Press, 1977).

MILHOUS, JUDITH, and HUME, ROBERT D, *The London Stage, 1660–1800* (Carbondale, Il.: Southern Illinois University Press, 1996).

MONTAGU, LADY MARY WORTLEY, *The Complete Letters of Lady Mary Wortley Montagu*, ed. Robert Halsband, 3 vols. (Oxford: Clarendon Press, 1965–1967).

—— *Lady Mary Wortley Montagu: Essays and Poems and Simplicity, A Comedy*, ed. Robert Halsband and Isobel Grundy (Oxford: Clarendon Press, 1977).

—— *Lady Mary Wortley Montagu: Romance Writings*, ed. Isobel Grundy (Oxford: Clarendon Press, 1996).

—— *Letters of the Right Honourable Lady M——y W——y M——e, written during her travels in Europe, Asia, and Africa*, 3 vols. (London, 1763).

MONTESQUIEU, CHARLES DE SECONDAT, *Persian Letters*, trans. John Ozell (London, 1722).

—— *Persian Letters*, trans. John Ozell, 3rd edn, corrected (London, 1736).

—— *The Spirit of Laws*, trans. T. Nugent from *De L'Esprit des Lois* (1748) (London, 1750).

MOUSSA-MAHMOUD, FATMA, 'A Manuscript Translation of the *Arabian Nights* in the Beckford Papers', *Journal of Arabic Literature* 7 (1996): 7–23.

MUNGELLO, D. E., 'Confucianism in the Enlightenment' in Thomas H. C. Lee (ed.), *China and Europe: Images and Influences in Sixteenth to Eighteenth Centuries* (Hong Kong: Chinese University Press, 1991), 99–127.

MURPHY, ARTHUR, *The Orphan of China* (1759).

NESS, ROBERT, 'The Dunciad and Italian Opera in England', *Eighteenth-Century Studies* 20 (1986–7): 173–94.

NEWTON, ADAM ZACHARY, *Narrative Ethics* (Cambridge, Mass., and London: Harvard University Press, 1995).

NUSSBAUM, FELICITY, *Torrid Zones: Maternity, Sexuality, and Empire in Eighteenth-Century English Narratives* (Baltimore and London: Johns Hopkins University Press, 1995).

—— (ed.), *The Global Eighteenth Century* (Baltimore and London: Johns Hopkins University Press, 2003).

ORR, BRIDGET, *Empire on the English Stage, 1660–1714* (Cambridge: Cambridge University Press, 2001).

OUSELEY, WILLIAM, *Oriental Collections*, 3 vols. (London, 1797–1800).

Pañcatantra: The Book of India's Folk Wisdom, ed. Patrick Olivelle (Oxford: Oxford University Press, 1997).

PARKER, KENNETH (ed.), *Early Modern Tales of Orient: A Critical Anthology* (London: Routledge, 1999).

PARKER, PATRICIA, 'Literary Fat Ladies and the Generation of the Text', in *Literary Fat Ladies: Rhetoric, Gender, Property* (London: Methuen, 1987), 8–35.

PEIRCE, LESLIE P., *The Imperial Harem: Women and Sovereignty in the Ottoman Empire* (New York and Oxford: Oxford University Press, 1993).

PERCY, THOMAS (trans.), *Hau Kiou Choaan: or, the Pleasing History*, 4 vols. (London, 1761).

—— *Miscellaneous Pieces Relating to the Chinese*, 2 vols. (London, 1762).

PERRAULT, CHARLES, *Contes de ma Mère L'Oye* (Paris, 1697).

PÉTIS DE LA CROIX, FRANÇOIS, *Turkish Tales; Consisting of Several Adventures: With the History of the Sultaness of Persia, and the Visiers*, trans. William King and others (London, 1708).

—— *The Thousand and One Days: Persian Tales*, trans. Ambrose Philips, 3 vols (London, 1714–15).

—— *The Persian and Turkish Tales, Compleat*, trans. William King, 2 vols. (London, 1714).

—— *A New Translation of the Persian Tales from the Indian Comedies of Mocles*, trans. Edward Button (London, 1754).

—— *The Persian and Turkish Tales, Compleat*, trans. William King, 2 vols. 5th ed. (London, 1767).

PIX, MARY, *Ibrahim, the Thirteenth Emperour of the Turks* (London, 1696).

POCOCK, J. G. A., *Virtue, Commerce, and History: Essays on Political Thought and History, Chiefly in the Eighteenth Century*, Ideas in Context (Cambridge: Cambridge University Press, 1985).

POISSON DE GOMEZ, MADELEINE ANGÉLIQUE, *The Persian Anecdotes: Or, Secret Memoirs of the Court of Persia*, trans. Paul Chamberlen (London, 1730).

POMERANZ, KENNETH, and TOPIK, STEVEN, *The World That Trade Created: Society, Culture, and the World Economy, 1400–the Present, Sources and Studies in World History* (Armonk, NY, and London: M. E. Sharpe, 1999).

POPE, ALEXANDER, *The Correspondence of Alexander Pope*, ed. George Wiley Sherburn, 5 vols. (Oxford: Clarendon Press, 1956).

—— *The Dunciad*, vol. 5 of *The Twickenham Edition of the Poems of Alexander Pope*, ed. James Sutherland (London: Methuen, 1963).

—— *The Rape of the Lock and Other Poems*, vol. ii of *The Twickenham Edition of the Poems of Alexander Pope*, ed. Geoffrey Tillotson, 3rd edn. reset (London: Methuen, 1962).

PORTER, DAVID, 'From Chinese to Goth: Walpole and the Gothic Repudiation of Chinoiserie', *Eighteenth-Century Life* 23 (1999): 46–58.

Bibliography

—— 'A Peculiar but Uninteresting Nation: China and the Discourse of Commerce in Eighteenth-Century England', *Eighteenth-Century Studies* 33 (2000): 181–200.

—— *Ideographia: The Chinese Cipher in Early Modern Europe* (Stanford, Calif.: Stanford University Press, 2001).

—— 'Monstrous Beauty: Eighteenth-Century Fashion and the Aesthetics of Chinese Taste', *Eighteenth-Century Studies* 35 (2002): 395–411.

PRIDEAUX, HUMPHREY, *The True Nature of Imposture Fully Displayed in the Life of Mahomet. With a Discourse Annexed, for the Vindication of Christianity from This Charge* (London, 1697).

PRIOR, JAMES, *The Life of Oliver Goldsmith, M.B.*, 2 vols. (London, 1837).

PURKISS, DIANE, 'Material Girls: The Seventeenth-Century Woman Debate', in Clare Brant and Diane Purkiss (eds.), *Women, Texts and Histories 1575–1760* (London: Routledge, 1992), 69–101.

RACINE, JEAN, *Bajazet: Tragédie*, ed. Marie-Claude Canova-Green, nouvelle édn. Classiques Larousse (Paris: Larousse, 1993).

RAJAN, BALACHANDRA, *Under Western Eyes. India from Milton to Macaulay* (Durham, NC, and London: Duke University Press, 1999).

RAVEN, JAMES, *British Fiction 1750–1770: A Chronological Check-List of Prose Fiction Printed in Britain and Ireland* (Newark and London: University of Delaware Press; Associated University Presses, 1987).

—— GARSIDE, PETER, SCHÖWERLING, RAINER, SKELTON-FOORD, CHRISTOPHER, WÜNSCHE, KARIN, BENDING, STEPHEN, and FORSTER, ANTONIA (eds.), *The English Novel 1770–1829: A Bibliographical Survey of Prose Fiction Published in the British Isles* (Oxford: Oxford University Press, 2000).

REEVE, CLARA, *The Progress of Romance: And the History of Charoba, Queen of Aegypt*, Facsimile Text Society. Series 1: Literature and Language, vol. 4 (New York: The Facsimile Text Society, 1930).

REICHWEIN, ADOLF, *China and Europe: Intellectual and Artistic Contacts in the Eighteenth Century* (London: Routledge & Kegan Paul, 1968).

RIDLEY, JAMES, *The Tales of the Genii: Or, the Delightful Lessons of Horam, the Son of Asmar. Tr. From the Pers. Ms. [Really Written] by Sir Charles Morrell*, 2 vols., 3rd edn. (London, 1766).

ROE, THOMAS, *The Embassy of Sir Thomas Roe to the Court of the Great Mogul, 1615–1619, as Narrated in his Journal and Correspondence*, ed. William Foster, Hakluyt Society, 2nd ser., nos. 1, 2 (London, 1899).

RODIN PUCCI, SUZANNE, 'The Discrete Charms of the Exotic: Fictions of the Harem in Eighteenth-Century France', in G. S. Rousseau and Roy Porter (eds.), *Exoticism in the Enlightenment* (Manchester: Manchester University Press, 1990), 145–74.

Bibliography

ROUSSEAU, G. S., and PORTER, ROY (eds.), *Exoticism in the Enlightenment* (Manchester: Manchester University Press, 1990).

RUBIÉS, JOAN PAU, *Travel and Ethnology in the Renaissance: South India through European Eyes, 1250–1625*, Past and Present Publications (Cambridge: Cambridge University Press, 2000).

RUSSELL, G. A., 'The Impact of the *Philosophus Autodidactus*: Pocockes, John Locke, and the Society of Friends', in Russell (ed.), *The 'Arabick' Interest of the Natural Philosophers in Seventeenth-Century England*, Brill's Studies in Intellectual History, vol. 47 (Leiden: Brill, 1994), 224–65.

SAGLIA, DIEGO, 'William Beckford's "Sparks of orientalism" and the Material-Discursive Orient of British Romanticism', *Textual Practice* 16 (2002): 75–92.

SAID, EDWARD W., *Orientalism* (London: Routledge & Kegan Paul, 1978).

SALLIS, EVA, *Sheherazade through the Looking Glass: The Metamorphosis of the Thousand and One Nights*, Curzon Studies in Arabic and Middle-Eastern Literatures (Richmond, Surrey: Curzon, 1999).

SCHWAB, RAYMOND, *The Oriental Renaissance: Europe's Rediscovery of India and the East, 1680–1880*, trans. Gene Patterson-Black and Victor Reinking (New York: Columbia University Press, 1984).

SCOTT, JONATHAN (trans.), *An Historical and Political View of the Decan, South of the Kistnah; Including a Sketch of the Extent and Revenue of the Mysorean Dominions, as Possessed by Tippoo Sultaun* (London, 1791).

SCUDÉRY, MADELEINE DE, *Ibrahim. Or the Illustrious Bassa*, trans. H. Cogan (London, 1652).

The Second Court Secret (London, 1743).

SETTLE, ELKANAH, *The Conquest of China, by the Tartars* (London, 1676).

SHAW, SHEILA, 'Early English Editions of the Arabian Nights; Their Value to Eighteenth-Century Literary Scholarship', *Muslim World* 49 (1959): 232–8.

SHERIDAN, FRANCES, 'The History of Nourjahad', in *Oriental Tales*, ed. Robert Mack (Oxford: Oxford University Press, 1992), 115–96.

SPENCE, JONATHAN, *The Search for Modern China* (London: Hutchinson, 1990).

—— *The Chan's Great Continent: China in Western Minds* (London: Allen Lane Penguin Press, 1999).

SUNDER RAJAN, RAJESWARI, *Real and Imagined Women: Gender, Culture, and Postcolonialism* (London: Routledge, 1993).

SUTHERLAND, LUCY S., *The East India Company in Eighteenth-Century Politics* (Oxford: Clarendon Press, 1952).

Bibliography

Tales of the East, ed. Henry Weber, 3 vols. (London, 1812).

TAVERNIER, JEAN BAPTISTE, *The Six Voyages of John Baptista Tavernier... Through Turky into Persia and the East-Indies*, trans. John Philips (London, 1677).

TEIGNMOUTH, JOHN, *Memoir of the Life and Correspondence of Lord John Teignmouth*, 2 vols. (London, 1843).

TELTSCHER, KATE, *India Inscribed: European and British Writing on India 1600–1800* (Delhi: Oxford University Press, 1995).

TEMPLE, SIR WILLIAM, *Works*, vol. 3 (London, 1814).

TERRY, EDWARD, *A Voyage to East-India* (London, 1655).

THÉVENOT, JEAN DE, *The Travels of Monsieur De Thevenot into the Levant*, trans. Archibald Lovell (London, 1687).

THORN, JENNIFER, ' "A Race of Angels": Castration and Exoticism in Three Exotic Tales by Eliza Haywood', in Kirsten T. Saxton and Rebecca P. Bocchicchio, *The Passionate Fictions of Eliza Haywood* (Lexington, Ky: University of Kentucky Press, 2000), 168–93.

—— 'The Work of Writing Race: Galland, Burton and the Arabian Nights', in Laura J. Rosentahl and Mita Choudhury (eds.), *Monstrous Dreams of Reason: Body, Self and Other in the Enlightenment* (London: Associated University Presses, 2002), 151–69.

TOOMER, G. J., *Eastern Wisedome and Learning: The Study of Arabic in Seventeenth-Century England* (Oxford: Clarendon Press, 1996).

TRUMPENER, KATIE, 'Rewriting Roxane: Orientalism and Intertextuality in Montesquieu's Lettres Persanes and Defoe's The Fortunate Mistress', *Stanford French Review* 11 (1987): 177–91.

TUCKER, JOSEPH, 'On the Authorship of the Turkish Spy: An État Présent', *Papers of the Bibliographical Society of America* 52 (1958): 34–57.

TURNER, CHERYL, *Living by the Pen: Women Writers in the Eighteenth Century* (London: Routledge, 1992).

VILLANDON, JEANNE L'HERITIER DE, 'L'Adroite Princesse, ou, Les Aventures de Finette', *Œuvres Meslées* (Paris, 1695).

VITKUS, DANIEL J. (ed.), *Piracy, Slavery, and Redemption: Barbary Captivity Narratives from Early Modern England* (New York; Chichester: Columbia University Press, 2001).

VOLTAIRE, FRANÇOIS MARIE AROUET DE, *Mahomet: Tragedie*. [s.l.]: [s.n.], 1742.

—— *Mahomet the Imposter*, trans. and adapted James Miller and James Hoadly (London, 1744).

—— *Zadig; or, the Book of Fate* (London, 1749).

—— *The Orphan of China* (London, 1756).

Bibliography

VOLTAIRE, FRANÇOIS MARIE AROUET DE, *Essay sur l'histoire générale, et sur les mœurs et l'esprit des nations, depuis Charlemagne*, Coll. complette des Œuvres de mr. de Voltaire vols. xi–xvii (Geneva, 1756).

—— *An essay on universal history: the manners, and spirit of nations, from the reign of Charlemaign to the age of Lewis XIV*, trans. J. Nugent, 4 vols. (Dublin, 1759).

WÂDIH, MUBÂRAK ALLÂH IRÂDAT KHÂN, *A Translation of the Memoirs of Eradut Khan . . . Containing Interesting Anecdotes of the Emperor Aulumgeer Aurungzebe, and of his Successors*, trans. Jonathan Scott (London, 1786).

WALPOLE, HORACE, *Hieroglyphic Tales*, Augustan Reprint Society Publication 212/13. (Los Angeles: William Andrews Clark Memorial Library, 1982).

WARNER, MARINA, *From the Beast to the Blonde: On Fairy Tales and Their Tellers* (London: Chatto & Windus, 1994).

—— *Fantastic Metamorphoses, Other Worlds: Ways of Telling the Self*, Clarendon Lectures in English Literature, 2001 (Oxford: Oxford University Press, 2002).

—— (ed.), *Wonder Tales: Six Stories of Enchantment* (London: Vintage, 1996).

WARNER, WILLIAM B, *Licensing Entertainment: The Elevation of Novel Reading in Britain, 1684–1750* (London and Berkeley, Los Angeles: University of California Press, 1998).

WEBB, JOHN, *Historical Essay Endeavoring a Probability that the Language of the Empire of China is the Primitive Language* (London, 1669).

WHEELER, ROXANN, *The Complexion of Race: Categories of Difference in Eighteenth-Century British Culture*, New Cultural Studies (Philadelphia: University of Philadelphia Press, 2000).

WHISTON, WILLIAM, *A New Theory of the Earth* (London, 1696).

WOLFF, LARRY, *Inventing Eastern Europe: The Map of Civilization on the Mind of the Enlightenment* (Stanford, Calif.: Stanford University Press, 1994).

YEAZELL, RUTH BERNARD, *Harems of the Mind: Passages of Western Art and Literature* (New Haven and London: Yale University Press, 2000).

YEGENOGLU, MEYDA, *Colonial Fantasies: Towards a Feminist Reading of Orientalism* (Cambridge: Cambridge University Press, 1998).

ŽIŽEK, SLAVOJ, 'Hegelian Llanguage', in *For They Know Not What They Do: Enjoyment as a Political Factor* (London: Verso, 2002), 99–140.

INDEX

Abbas I, shah of Persia 77, 175–6
absolutism
 in Europe 15, 43, 55, 84, 94, 297
 in Orient 17, 20, 34–5, 40, 72, 88, 142,
  171, 181, 199, 208–18, 260, 268
 see also despotism; Louis XIV
Abu Bakr, Muhammad's
  father-in-law 85 n.
Abu Talib Ibn Muhammad Isfahani 352 n.
Abu-ul-Fazi Allami 327
Abyssinia 268 n. 15, 93
actress 65, 68, 86
Adair, Gilbert 239 n.
Adami, Giuseppe 200 n.
Addison, Joseph 78, 355
 Doctrine of Transmigration 228–9, 30
 Spectator 30–1
Aden 306
Adrianople 65, 181
Adventurer, The 204
Æsop 19, 343–6, 355 n.
Africa 7, 20, 50, 75, 94, 158, 162, 304
afrite 258
Agra 293, 303, 307
Akbar, Mughal emperor 277 n. 23, 293,
  320 n., 327, 328, 330 n., 337
Alenzon, Monsieur d', *see* Hoamchi-vam
Aleppo 33 n., 114, 170, 313
Alexander the Great 63, 79, 130–1, 135
Alf Layla wa-Layla, see *Arabian Nights
  Entertainments*
Alfana, Franco 200 n.
Algeria 20, 137
Ali, son-in-law of Muhammad 175,
  259
Allah 230, 310 n., 316, 318, 320, 322
 see also Islam
allegory 223, 227, 283, 295, 304, 311, 316,
  352–3, 368, 374

oriental, as political satire 42–3, 144,
  168–9, 174, 179
 see also analogy; satire
Allen, Charles 28 n. 7, 228 n.
Almanzor, Muhammad Ibn Abu-amir
  Al-mans ur 84
al-Muqaffa, Ibn
 Kalilah wa Dimnah 344–6, 351
Amours of the Sultana of Barbary 172–4
analogy 75, 84–6, 143, 159–61,
  241, 280, 298, 343, 349
 Enlightenment preoccupation with 18,
  24, 364
 oriental and occidental politics,
  between 42, 81, 171, 175, 179, 211,
  220–1, 270, 281–5, 309, 328
 oriental and occidental religions,
  between 55, 260, 324
 sexual and state politics, between 163,
  170
Anne of Austria 146
Aphrodite 287
Appleton, William Worthen 198,
  203 n. 8, 205, 217 n. 24,
  236 n. 53, 243 n.
Arabia 33, 46, 91, 148, 156
Arabian Nights Entertainments 1–17,
  27, 81, 93, 96, 101–13, 129,
  160, 186, 299, 313, 332, 365
 as children's reading 361, 372
Aravamudan, Srinivas 63, 73–4,
  222 n. 35
Argyle, Duke of *see* Campbell, John
Armenians 65, 95, 165, 191
Armstrong, Nancy 143
Ar-Rashid, Haroun, caliph of
  Baghdad 85 n., 103–5, 318, 373
Askun, Shere 336
Astrakhan 158, 196, 230

Index

atheism 20, 51, 158, 229, 244, 309
Aubin, Penelope
*Strange Adventures of the Count de
Vinevil* 136, 139–40
Aurangzeb, Mughal emperor 276, 332
imaginative literature, in 34, 55, 57,
275–92, 296, 312
travellers' accounts, in 288–7, 271,
278, 289 n. 35
Austen, Jane
Sense and Sensibility 2
Aylesbury, Lady, *see* Conway, Caroline

Baber, Sultan 333
Backscheider, Paula R. 139 n.,
152 n. 92
Bacon, Francis 68, 198
Baghdad 25, 85 n., 104–5, 111,
123, 259, 316
bagnio, *see* bathhouse
Bajazet, brother to Murat IV 62
Bajazet, son of Suleyman I 60–1
Bakhtin, Mikhail 10
Ballaster, Ros 2 n. 3, 69 n. 13,
130 n. 74, 177 n. 103, 308 n.
Baravat 137
Barbin, Claude 346
Barthes, Roland 13 n. 19
Basra 25, 27, 256, 258, 259
Bastille 154, 157
bathhouse 124–5
Beasley, Jerry C. 220 n. 30
Beattie, James 19
Beaumont, Antony 200 n.
Beaumont, Daniel 9 n. 12, 128
Beckford, William 364 n.
Vathek 24, 74, 99, 229 n. 46,
364–70
bedouin 172
Begum-Saheb, daughter to Shah
Jahan 279
Behn, Aphra 176
Belon, Peter
Court Secret, The 175–8
Bengal 18, 267 n. 14, 297, 325,
326, 328, 330 n., 331, 333 n.
infantry 35, 296
Berg, Maxine 23 n., 227 n.
Berlas 195

Bernier, François 37, 39, 258 n. 4,
262, 265–71, 276–81, 286,
290–2, 299, 329
Betterton, Thomas 89
Bhagalpur 328
Bhagvad Gita 347 n.
Bhattacharya, Nandini 261, 267 n. 13,
281, 335 n.
Bible 235, 314
Bibliothèque du Roi 36 n. 17, 77,
113, 118, 366 n.
Bidpai 19, 24, 34, 37, 115, 274,
336, 343–58
bienséance 308
Blaut, James 7 n.
blinding 15, 74, 78, 82, 109–11,
119, 144, 153, 304
Blouch, Christine 222 n. 34
Boccaccio, Giovani
Decameron 339 n. 63,
340 n. 65, 345
Bocchicchio, Rebecca 222 n. 35
Bolingbroke, Henry St. John, first
viscount of 178
Bombay 2, 18, 313
Bonaparte, Napoleon 363
Böttger, Johan Friedrich 240
Boulainvilliers, Henri, comte de 46
Boulangers, Nicolas-Antoine 330
Bowden, Martha F. 127 n.
Bowen, Emanuel 49 n. 32
Bowen, Jemmy 90
Boyer, Jean Baptiste de, Marquis
d'Argens 43, 211 n., 245–6
Boyle, Frank 219
Bradshaw, William 41, 42 n., 145,
146 n. 87, 149 n.
brahman 15, 23, 25, 34, 37, 115,
262, 274, 275, 307, 336, 339–40,
341, 356
see also Hinduism
Brama 277 n., 289 n., 328, 336
Brant, Clare 89 n.
Braverman, Richard 282, 283
Bremond, Sébastien
Hattige 172–4
Bristol, Elizabeth Hervey, Countess of
90, 180
British Museum 334
Brown, Laura 283

Index

Index

Index

Index

Index

Index

ifrit, *see* afrite

imam
  as character 34, 230, 263, 275, 302, 310, 315
  as narrator 33, 34, 295, 296

imposture, *see* Muhammad

India
  as dream 23, 262–3, 266–8, 274, 283, 295
  as jewel 267, 274, 301, 318, 350
  and spices 267
  as tiger 318–19
  and textiles 267, 274, 297–8, 301
  see also fable, Hindu, Mughal, suttee

India Act 297 n.

Indonesia 267 n. 14

Indus river 275

interculturalism, *see* Choudhury, Mita

Iphigenia 39, 186 n., 187–8, *see also* Chudleigh

Iran 11, 133, 309

Iraq, *see* Persia

Ireland 175–6

Irwin, Robert 9, 96 n., 102, 103, 114 n. 63, 258 n. 5, 361 n. 2, 366 n.

Islam 159, 311, 325
  as accomplice of despotism 199, 297
  conversion to 202, 258, 296, 307
  as invader 79
  as monotheism 22, 260, 270, 299, 301, 324
  and polygamy 300, 302, 310 n.
  represented as imposture 49, 149
  women's souls in 71, 86, 157, 164, 182
  Shi'ite 63, 77, 78, 133, 149, 171, 175, 279 n.
  Sunni 55, 63, 78, 103, 134, 148, 149, 171, 175, 279 n.

Ismail I, shah of Persia 133

isnad 128

Isfahan 75, 77, 85 n., 114, 115, 134, 137, 169, 211 n., 251, 247

Istanbul 70, 75, 85 n., 95, 96
  ambassadors to 62 n. 5, 77
  Porte 148
  reported freedom of women in 41, 90, 184, 280

Jacobs, Joseph 344 n. 68

Jacobson, Dawn 235 n. 51

Jahangir, Mughal emperor 265, 272–4, 280, 336, 337

James II, king of England 55, 84, 92 n. 34, 172, 174–6, 282, 312

James, Lawrence 297 n.

janissaries 42, 84, 86, 87, 156, 161, 180

Jatakas, see Buddha

Jermyn, Henry, duke of St. Albans 172

Jeselmere 300

Jesuits
  as informants on China 44, 92 n. 35, 206–7, 218, 235, 241
  interest in Confucianism 40, 48, 229 n. 44, 243–4, 327 n. 50
  see also Catrou; Comte, le; Halde, Du; Petre; Prémare; Protestant, critiques of Catholicism

Joan of Arc 156, 160

John, Prester 268

Johnson, Samuel 209 n. 16
  Dictionary 19, 154
  Rasselas 78, 100

Jones, William 363
  and Asiatick Society of Bengal 18, 347

Judith 86

Kabbani, Rana 9 n. 13

Kafka, Franz
  Trial, The 15

Kanbu, Inayat Allah, 29 n. 38
  Bahar-e danes 331–7
  see also Dow; Scott

Kangxi, emperor of China 223 n. 36

Kaozheng 214 n.

Kasgar 303

Kashmir 99, 289 n. 35, 322, 330 n.
  princess of 72, 116–18, 196, 276, 279, 289, 317, 318, 320–4, 330 n. 54

Kaufmann, Linda 167 n.

Keith, Arthur Berriedale 344 n. 68

Keith-Falconer, I. G. N. 345 n. 71

Kelly, P. H. 219 n. 29

Kéroualle, Louise, duchess of Portsmouth 172–3

khabar 128

Khalifa, Hajji, *see* d'Herbelot

Khan, Asaf 275

Khan, Gulfishan 352 n.

Khurram, Prince, *see* Shah Jahan

Index

Index

Index

Index

Index

Index